The Unfree French

RICHARD VINEN

The Unfree French

Life under the Occupation

ALLEN LANE
an imprint of
PENGUIN BOOKS

ALLEN LANE

Published by the Penguin Group
Penguin Books Ltd, 80 Strand, London WC2R ORL, England
Penguin Group (USA) Inc., 375 Hudson Street, New York, New York 10014, USA
Penguin Group (Canada), 90 Eglinton Avenue East, Suite 700, Toronto, Ontario, Canada M4P 2Y3
(a division of Pearson Penguin Canada Inc.)
Penguin Ireland, 25 St Stephen's Green, Dublin 2, Ireland (a division of Penguin Books Ltd)
Penguin Group (Australia), 250 Camberwell Road,
Camberwell, Victoria 3124, Australia (a division of Pearson Australia Group Pty Ltd)
Penguin Books India Pvt Ltd, 11 Community Centre,
Panchsheel Park, New Delhi – 110 017, India
Penguin Group (NZ), cnr Airborne and Rosedale Roads, Albany,
Auckland 1310, New Zealand (a division of Pearson New Zealand Ltd)
Penguin Books (South Africa) (Pty) Ltd, 24 Sturdee Avenue,
Rosebank, Johannesburg 2196, South Africa

Penguin Books Ltd, Registered Offices: 80 Strand, London WC2R ORL, England

www.penguin.com

First published 2006
1

Copyright © Richard Vinen, 2006

Set in 10.5/14 pt Linotype Sabon
Typeset by Rowland Phototypesetting Ltd, Bury St Edmunds, Suffolk
Printed in Great Britain by Clays Ltd, St Ives plc

A CIP catalogue record for this book is available from the British Library

ISBN-13: 978-0-713-99496-4
ISBN-10: 0-713-99496-7

For Katie

Contents

List of Illustrations

Photographic acknowledgements are given in parentheses.

1. The railway carriage in which the armistice of June 1940 was signed (*Imperial War Museum*).
2. Pétain and Laval (*AKG-Images, London*).
3. French volunteers leaving to fight with the Germans on the Eastern Front (*Imperial War Museum*).
4. Playground with sign excluding Jews (*Roger Viollet, Topfoto*).
5. A French girl insists on being taken prisoner along with defeated German soldiers (*Imperial War Museum*).
6. French prisoners of war (*Imperial War Museum*).
7. Inscription on wall (*Imperial War Museum*).
8. Young men forced to work in Germany leave from the station at Nice (*AKG-Images, London*).
9. German office for recruiting French people to work in Germany (*Imperial War Museum*).
10. Hair in a courtyard in Chartres after women have been punished for 'collaboration' (*Imperial War Museum*).

Acknowledgements

Simon Winder suggested that I write this book and has been a very supportive and helpful editor during the disgracefully long time that I have taken to do so. I am also grateful to Simon's colleagues at Penguin and especially to Chloe Campbell. Elizabeth Stratford copy-edited the script with great care and patience. She saved me from many errors and frequently helped me to express myself more clearly.

Research on modern French history has become much easier in recent years. This is partly because of decisions, by central government, to open archives. More importantly, it is because a new generation of archivists and librarians have brought such energy and dedication to their job. I am particularly grateful to Jean Astruc and Anne-Marie Pathé at the Institut d'Histoire du Temps Présent, Rosine Hallavant and Michel Thibault at the archives of the Eure-et-Loir in Chartres and Cécile Simon at the Archives Nationales. In London, the staff of the photograph archives at the Imperial War Museum made great efforts to help me locate illustrations. Éditions de Minuit kindly gave me permission to quote from *En Attendant Godot*.

I have enjoyed, and learned from, my discussions with students at King's College, London, especially those who have taken my course on twentieth-century French history. The benevolent despotism of Arthur Burns and Laura Clayton ensures that the history department remains an easy place to work. Julian Jackson, Olivier de Maret, Kevin Passmore and Tristan van der Stegen read drafts of the book and made many helpful remarks.

My father and mother were, as ever, both my sharpest critics and my staunchest supporters. I am grateful to Alison Henwood for everything and particularly for our children, Emma and Alexander.

Maps

Map 1 French departments in 1940

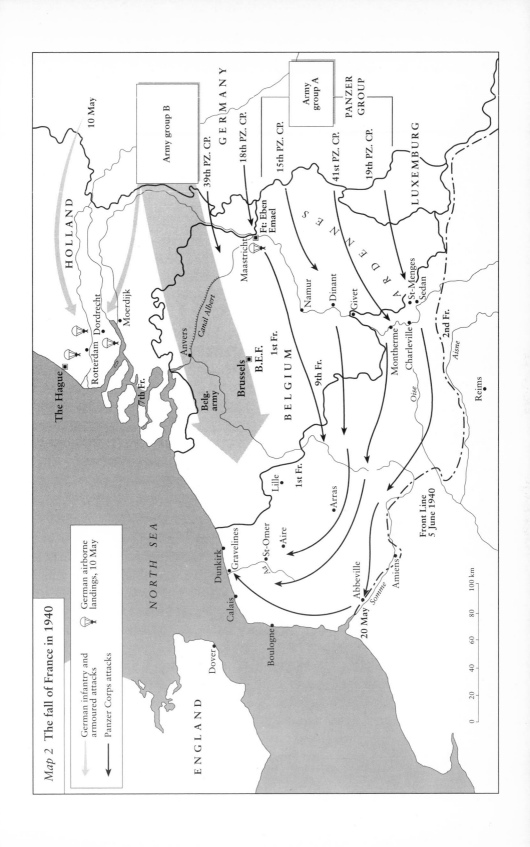

Map 2 The fall of France in 1940

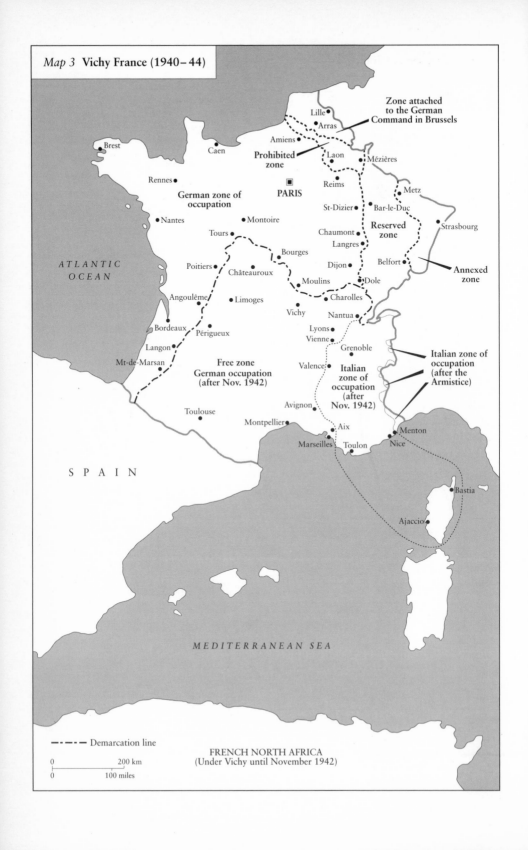

Map 3 **Vichy France (1940–44)**

Zone attached
to the German
Command in Brussels

Lille

Arras

Amiens

**Prohibited
zone**

Laon

Mézières

Brest

Caen

Rennes

Reims

Metz

**German zone of
occupation**

■
PARIS

St-Dizier

Bar-le-Duc

Strasbourg

Nantes

Montoire

Chaumont

**Reserved
zone**

Tours

Langres

Bourges

*ATLANTIC
OCEAN*

Poitiers

Châteauroux

Dijon

Belfort

**Annexed
zone**

Angoulême

Moulins

Dole

Limoges

Charolles

Bordeaux

Périgueux

Vichy

Nantua

Langon

Lyons

Vienne

**Italian zone of
occupation
(after the
Armistice)**

Mt-de-Marsan

**Free zone
German occupation
(after Nov. 1942)**

Grenoble

Valence

**Italian
zone of
occupation
(after
Nov. 1942)**

Toulouse

Avignon

SPAIN

Montpellier

Aix

Menton

Marseilles

Toulon

Nice

Bastia

Ajaccio

MEDITERRANEAN SEA

—·—·— Demarcation line

FRENCH NORTH AFRICA
(Under Vichy until November 1942)

0   200 km

0   100 miles

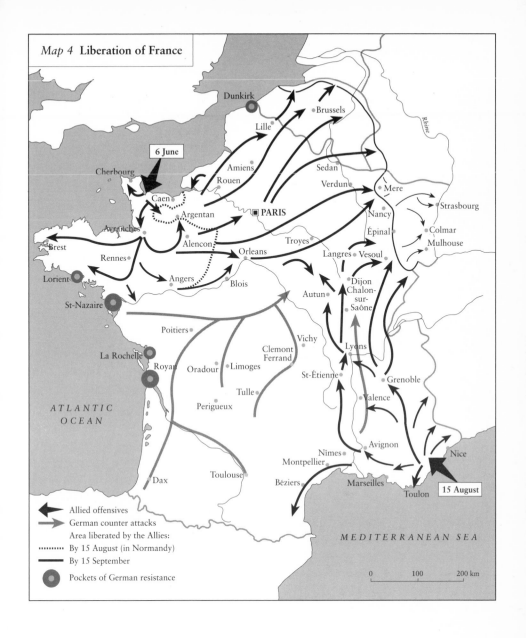

Map 4 **Liberation of France**

Dunkirk

Brussels

Lille

Rhine

6 June

Cherbourg

Amiens

Sedan

Rouen

Verdun

Mere

Strasbourg

Caen

Argentan

■ PARIS

Nancy

Épinal

Colmar

Avranches

Alencon

Troyes

Mulhouse

Brest

Orleans

Langres

Vesoul

Rennes

Angers

Blois

Autun

Dijon

Chalon-

sur-

Saône

Lorient

St-Nazaire

Poitiers

Vichy

Lyons

La Rochelle

Royan

Oradour

Limoges

Clemont

Ferrand

St-Étienne

Grenoble

Tulle

Valence

Perigueux

ATLANTIC

OCEAN

Avignon

Nice

Nimes

Montpellier

Dax

Toulouse

Béziers

Marseilles

Toulon

15 August

Allied offensives

German counter attacks

Area liberated by the Allies:

•••••••• By 15 August (in Normandy)

——— By 15 September

Pockets of German resistance

MEDITERRANEAN SEA

0   100   200 km

The Unfree French: Introduction

All of my life, I have had a certain idea of France . . . It is inspired by emotion as much as by reason. My spirit naturally imagines France, like the princess in the fairy tale or the Madonna in the frescos, destined for fantastic things. I instinctively feel that providence has created her for ultimate success or exemplary misfortune. If mediocrity happens to mark her, I feel that this is an absurd anomaly that can be attributed to the faults of the French, not to the spirit of the country. (Charles de Gaulle, opening page of *Mémoires de guerre* (1954))

Unlike de Gaulle, I am interested in the French rather than in France. This book is about how the French lived rather than abstract ideals of what France ought to have been. De Gaulle, of course, had no monopoly on abstract ideals. For all its talk of realism, the Vichy government, too, had very idealized notions of France and was often contemptuous of those French people who failed to live up to them. Many leaders of the Resistance and many of those associated with radical collaborationism also had their ideas of France and sometimes took pride in the fact that those ideas seemed unrealistic to most of their compatriots.

By 'the French', I mean, in this context, people who were normally resident in France. I do not mean people who held French citizenship, because quite large numbers of people who normally lived in France did not have French citizenship and because, in any case, Vichy and the Germans changed definitions of citizenship in ways that excluded certain groups.

The emphasis on the French rather than France has two implications. First, I want to understand this period in terms of people's individual lives and in terms of the constraints and problems that faced particular individuals. This is not to deny the influence of social and economic contexts – indeed, if anything, I want to stress the importance of those contexts by showing how they affected particular people. Secondly, I want, so far as is possible, to look at the lower end of the social scale.

By 'unfree', I mean, on the simplest level, those French people who did not join de Gaulle in London. More generally, I wish to stress that I am looking at those people whose lives were governed by circumstances beyond their control. This means looking at people who were prisoners or who were deported to work in Germany. However, constraint was not just a matter of barbed wire and guards (even French prisoners of war were rarely kept behind barbed wire). People's freedom was restricted by a complicated range of considerations, to do, for example, with fears about sanctions that might be taken against their families. Some people – foreigners, criminals and others who lived in the margins of respectability – found that the severe constraints that already existed on their freedom were intensified by the circumstances of the occupation.

I should perhaps stress that, though my interpretation is un-Gaullist, it is not anti-Gaullist. Some historians, particularly those from Britain and America, have specifically defined their work in opposition to the 'Gaullist myth', a myth which, apparently, suggests that the French were united in their opposition to the German occupation and in their support for de Gaulle himself. I am reluctant to present myself as a destroyer of myths. This is partly because a dragon can only be slain so many times, and there is no reason for me to jab my lance into the corpse of an animal that has been attacked by so many of my colleagues. More importantly, de Gaulle's own reference to his understanding of France as being like a 'fairy tale' suggests that he himself understood that myths can be useful even if one does not believe them. Indeed, one might suggest that the most important Gaullist myth, enunciated in his speech in Paris on 25 August 1944, that France had 'liberated itself' drew its power precisely from the fact that everyone knew it to be untrue (see Chapter 10). Besides, a sharp dichotomy between the 'myths' that the French believe about themselves and the 'realities' that historians dig out of the 'archival bedrock'[1] may work for those who study the high politics of the Vichy regime. Robert Paxton has demonstrated, for example, that the Jewish Statute of October 1940 was devised by the Vichy government for its own reasons[2] and was not, as well-informed Frenchmen believed it to be, a 'plagiarism' of a German model.[3] However, when we turn to the history of French society, there is not one reality and not one myth. There were numerous sorts of experience and numerous ways in which people interpreted and remembered that experience.

If there is a 'myth' of wartime France as a united nation of Resistance supporters then it might be argued that it is the English who have done much to create that myth. The French Resistance plays an important part in English literature. It pops up as a symbol of moral good in novels as diverse as Graham Swift's *Shuttlecock*, Sebastian Faulks' *Charlotte Gray*, Piers Paul Read's *The Free Frenchman* and Mary Wesley's *Not that Sort of Girl*. A heavily decorated veteran of the Special Operations Executive who had been parachuted into occupied France was even called as a witness for the defence in the *Lady Chatterley's Lover* trial. The Resistance leader Jean Moulin, a quintessentially French figure rooted in the political culture of the Third Republic, is often presented as a kind of honorary Englishman, free from the vices that the English ordinarily attribute to the French. Perhaps it is not entirely flippant to suggest that English denunciation of French behaviour during the occupation sometimes has the bitter tone of the disappointed romantic.

Popular presentations of the occupation in France itself, at least in the two decades that followed the war, were remarkably unheroic. The novels of Marcel Aymé and Jean Dutourd described lives that were dominated by petty calculations about food and the black market. Films, too, were often notable for their focus on the struggles of daily life. *La Traversée de Paris* (made in 1956, and taken from an Aymé story) describes two men transporting the meat from an illegally slaughtered pig across Paris in a suitcase. *Léon Morin, prêtre* (1961) describes life in a small town that is occupied first by the Italians and then by the Germans. It is mainly a film about love and religion but its depiction of the occupation itself revolves around the constraints of everyday life rather than the clash between the Resistance and Vichy. *La Vie de château* (1966) describes a Norman aristocrat, played by Philippe Noiret, who spends the later part of the occupation trying to retain the affections of his pretty young wife, who is simultaneously being pursued by a German officer and by an agent of the Free French. The Norman aristocrat only becomes a hero of the Resistance by accident.

Curiously, however, academic historians often neglected the very issues that the bulk of the population talked about most. Some seemed to feel that too much attention to society risked downplaying the moral and political choices that people made during the occupation. In his last book, written when he was an underground Resistance activist, Marc Bloch (the founder of the *Annales* journal) suggested that social history's emphasis on long-term shifts risks giving insufficient attention to the element of human choice. Historians of the *Annales* school turned away from contemporary history after 1945, perhaps precisely because the Second World War did not fit into their increasing interest in the *longue durée*, and when Marc Ferro, an editor of the *Annales*, returned to the period in 1987 he did so with the most conventional political history imaginable: a biography of Pétain. Those scholars who talked most about the occupation were often political scientists who had an understandable focus on the purely political history of the process. But some historians seem to have been influenced by a conscious reaction against the popular preoccupation with the social history of the occupation. Annie Kriegel, who survived in France as a Jew and Resistance activist, recalled that she felt uncomfortable during the 1950s with discussion of issues such as food supply because they seemed to suggest that the real issues of occupied France were not political.[4]

It is notable that books dealing with the social history of the occupation often came from non-professional historians[5] and that they also often came from people who were seen to have been, in some way, sympathetic to the Vichy regime. Henri Amouroux, a journalist who had worked under Vichy and who was sometimes accused of being an apologist for it, wrote a collection of books on the social history of the period.[6] An emphasis on social history can sometimes seem to run close to apologia for the government because Vichy ministers laid such emphasis on the way in which their actions were merely a 'response' to social and economic circumstances. Speaking at a conference of historians discussing the political history of Vichy in 1970, François Lehideux, who had been Vichy's Minister of Industrial Production, argued that historians gave insufficient attention to 'refugees, food shortages and prisoners of war'.[7]

My own approach aims to stress social history rather than political history. I do not, however, see this as part of any attempt to justify or apologize for the Vichy government. I have little new to say about Vichy itself. More generally, I do not see my approach as a particular reaction against any other group of historians. Indeed, this book is primarily based on the work of other historians and its use of archival research is a question of providing illustrative detail rather than suggesting completely new interpretations.

I differ from other historians mainly in terms of emphasis. I have chosen the particular issues on which I focus partly by looking at the flip sides of standard academic accounts. For example, historians of the summer of 1940 generally look at events on the battlefield or at the high politics of Vichy. The huge numbers of refugees on the road and the huge number of soldiers captured by the Germans are generally presented as backdrops to these dramas. I have chosen to make refugees and prisoners the centre of my narrative and to try to understand how events looked from their point of view. Similarly, the drafting of young men to work in Germany is generally seen as a prelude to the development of large-scale resistance. I have chosen instead to concentrate on the young men themselves, to try to explain why some of them went to Germany and some of them did not.

To some extent, my approach is justified by the concerns that French people themselves expressed during the occupation. Certain words crop up repeatedly in documents of the time. Those words are 'refugees' (used particularly in 1940 to describe the six or eight million people who fled their homes to escape the German advance), 'prisoners' (used to describe the almost two million men captured by the Germans in 1940) and 'deportation', or Service du Travail Obligatoire (used mainly to describe the 600,000 or so young men who were compelled to go to work in Germany from 1942 onwards). Throughout the occupation French people referred to food supplies (*ravitaillement*) and to the means by which food might be procured (the black market), though these references were probably particularly insistent during the harsh winter of 1941–2 (partly because the initial shock of defeat had passed and the new horrors of labour deportation and civil war had yet to be felt).

Attention to particular words, however, illustrates the potential complexities of a study such as this. Such words do not have a fixed and uncontested sense. Everyone agreed that the black market was central to survival in occupied France but almost no one used it with reference to their own informal economic dealings. Some words that people used to describe their circumstances have simply disappeared from the language. The term J3 (meaning the ration category assigned to those between the ages of three and eighteen) was quite widely used to describe a particular generation in the immediate post-war period but it has now been almost forgotten. When one author republished his autobiographical account of life as a 'J3' he changed the title as he thought it would no longer mean anything to contemporary readers.[8] Service du Travail Obligatoire, or STO, was a phrase widely used during and immediately after the war but it was often inaccurately applied to anyone who had gone to Germany, regardless of whether they had been compelled to go under the specific legislation establishing compulsory labour service. Sometimes French people talked of deportation meaning the drafting of labour to Germany. Here again words have changed their meaning. 'Deportation' is now mainly used to refer to people who were sent to concentration camps. After a court case in 1979, victims of STO were forbidden to refer to themselves as 'deportees', a term henceforth reserved for those who had been sent to Germany for 'political or racial reasons'.

In the last twenty years, the study of memories of wartime France has itself become an academic industry. Sometimes this has gone with an increasingly sharp divide between the study of memory and the study of history. One group of historians studies how views of experience have been constructed after 1944; another attempts to explain how things were at the time. Several historians have specifically renounced the use of retrospective testimony and based their studies exclusively on contemporary documents. The most spectacular example of this process is Daniel Cordier. Cordier had a distinguished career in the French Resistance and, in particular, acted as secretary to Jean Moulin. He is not an academic historian, but he might have expected a certain deference from those whose study of occupied France has been undertaken from the safety of libraries, and particularly from those historians who were born after the Second World War. He might also have expected his personal memories and those of his Resistance comrades to be accepted as important historical sources. In fact, however, when Cordier wrote his massive biography, and defence, of Jean Moulin, he explicitly eschewed the use of his own and other people's memories and insisted that he would say nothing that could not be supported by contemporary documents.[9]

I have not been as scrupulous as Cordier. I have leaned quite heavily on retrospective published accounts. The distinction between contemporary and retrospective accounts seems artificial to me: all sources are, to some extent, retrospective. This is especially true of documents concerning the occupation. Very few people wrote much down during, say, June 1940 or July 1944. Even documents that purport to be contemporary pose problems. For example, diaries that have influenced historians so much were often written up a long time after the events they describe. Published diaries pose particular problems because the reader rarely knows what has been suppressed. We know that the diary that Micheline Bood kept as a schoolgirl in wartime Paris is missing some pages that her mother tore out in fury. Bood does not tell us what was in those pages. When she published her diary in the early 1970s, she seems to have conceived it primarily as a record of her anti-German and pro-Resistance sentiments and may have thought that the missing pages had no relevance to this, but historians of the last few years have mainly read Bood's diary as evidence of the relations that French girls had with German soldiers.

Published memoirs by people who are prominent in public life are often explicitly works of apologia designed to defend a certain course of action. Pétain is said to have declared that he would publish no memoirs 'because he had nothing to hide'. A politician's desire to present his own action in the best possible light is not, however, the only thing that can make an autobiography deceptive. A whole group of brilliant, non-conformist figures in post-war France cared very little what people thought of their actions (or, at least, cared very little whether people approved of their actions). Such people often presented the war in deliberately anti-heroic terms or revelled in their own associations with Pétainism or collaboration. The fact that an account is shocking, however, does not mean that it is frank. Men (such figures were usually men) who did not care if people thought they were cowards or collaborators certainly would have cared if people regarded them as dull writers. Jacques Laurent, for example, recognizes that he himself is not always able to say whether the striking stories that he tells about the occupation are true or not.[10]

Away from both political and intellectual elites, there is a very different category of memoir associated with wartime France. Many people who were not prominent in public life and who would not normally have written anything for publication felt that they needed to record their wartime experiences in print. Particular things encouraged this burst of publication. Many people who had been young during the 1940s retired in the 1980s and consequently had time to write. Some wanted to record their experiences before they died. Many wanted to leave a record for their own families, particularly their grandchildren. Technological changes made small-scale publishing easier in the 1980s. Some people published books themselves. Others entrusted their work to small enterprises: La Pensée Universelle specialized in publishing authors who were willing to pay to see their names in print, and it produced a particularly large number of memoirs relating to the Second World War.

Memoirs such as this are rarely explicit works of apologia in the way that, say, the memoirs of Paul Reynaud are. Autobiographies by 'ordinary' people can of course be deceptive. For one thing, autobiographers are, almost by definition, not ordinary and a peasant who keeps a diary or writes his memoirs is, in fact, less typical of his milieu than, say, a lycée *professeur*. Some autobiographies were written by *instituteurs*, primary school teachers. In economic terms, *instituteurs* may have been similar to the great mass of the French people, but in cultural terms men who spent their lives surrounded by books and paper felt very different from the peasants amongst whom they lived. Many working-class autodidacts also wrote their autobiographies, but these people's sense of themselves was often dominated by the idea of separation from those amongst whom they lived.

Two of the most famous peasant autobiographies concerned with

wartime France are those of Ephraïm Grenadou, who farmed in the
Beauce, and Gustave Folcher, a man from the Var who was taken
prisoner in 1940 and who subsequently worked on farms in Germany.
Historians, including me, have made heavy use of these two accounts
because they describe aspects of French life that are otherwise unreported and because both authors describe their lives in such striking
terms. However, neither Grenadou nor Folcher was 'ordinary'. Grenadou was a left-winger who despised the Vichy government, and a
humane man who seems to have treated his employees with consideration. It is hard to tell how common these characteristics were amongst
French peasants during the occupation. Certainly some of Grenadou's
neighbours did not express their contempt for Pétain as openly as he
did. Grenadou was also an exceptionally enterprising man who seized
opportunities that most peasants neglected. He had been a prisoner
during the First World War and, unlike the vast majority of French
people during the occupation, he was able to speak to the Germans
in their own language. Folcher, too, was unusual. Though he had
good relations with his comrades, he seems to have been something
of a solitary man. He did not play cards in the evening, which is one
of the reasons he had time to keep a diary. He was also unusually
determined. When the Germans tried to persuade members of his
work Kommando to accept 'transformation' into civilian workers,
Folcher refused and encouraged his comrades to do so too. There is,
so far as I know, no first-hand account by any of the 250,000 men
who accepted transformation, though there are several by men who
refused it. Perhaps the determination and self-confidence that made
some men write their autobiographies are also qualities that made
them stand up for themselves in prisoner of war camps.

For all their problems, autobiographies are a useful source. They
provide a sense of how the occupation felt to French people – how
they experienced the various pressures that bore down on them. In
this realm of subjectivity, all interpretation is difficult and it is perhaps
naive to imagine that one can distinguish clearly between the 'real'
experience, how it is described and how it is remembered. Is the
account that a woman of seventy wrote of her youth more or less real
than the letters she wrote to her mother at the time? Are the Gaullist
sentiments that the economist Charles Rist recorded in his diary more

or less real than the conversations he had with German officers over dinner in expensive Paris restaurants at the same time?

My book is in no way complete or definitive. The people in whom I am most interested are those whose relations with official agencies were most awkward. The peculiar circumstances of the Second World War in France often meant that such people's lives were recorded in some detail, precisely because Vichy – and, for that matter, the post-war French state – intruded into the lives of those of whom it disapproved in a particularly aggressive manner. However, such intrusions usually only provide us with a limited picture of some-one's life at a particular moment. One aspect of my own research illustrates how misleading such pictures can be. In the summer of 2003 I went to Mont-de-Marsan in the south-west of France to read archives relating to young men returning from Germany in 1945 with foreign women. Flicking through cartons of documents I came across the Gheldman family on several occasions. Berthe Gheldman was a Jew of Hungarian origin. In 1940 she was divorcing her husband (also Jewish). She had not seen him since he had joined the Foreign Legion in 1939 and she had last heard of him in Syria. However, it turned out that he had returned to France and been placed in an internment camp (the decision to return almost certainly cost him his life). The authorities discussed Berthe Gheldman's divorce and also took measures to 'aryanize' her perfume shop in Dax. Local officials had nothing against Gheldman personally – they stressed that she seemed moral and patriotic, though they added that the motives for her divorce were unclear. In July 1942 she was arrested. The last trace of the family that I encountered came in a letter from Monsieur Cougouille, who had apparently been entrusted with the care of Berthe Gheldman's ten-year-old son Georges. Cougouille said he knew nothing of the boy's whereabouts and assumed that he had followed 'one of his parents'. I drew three conclusions from these documents. First, it seemed obvious that Georges Gheldman must have died – how could a ten-year-old Jew have survived in an area that was crawling with Germans? Secondly, Cougouille seemed to illustrate French indifference to the persecution of the Jews: he seemed concerned only to avoid trouble with the authorities. Thirdly, the separation of Berthe Gheldman from her husband seemed to illustrate how the war pulled families apart; I assumed that they never saw each other again after their parting in 1939.

As I sent this book to press, I discovered I was wrong on all three points. Georges Gheldman survived. He was a witness in the trial of Maurice Papon in 1997–8 and published a book about his experiences in April 2005. Monsieur Cougouille was not a callous bystander. He was a man in his fifties who had got to know Berthe Gheldman when she took drawing classes with him (she was in her early forties). Cougouille made desperate attempts to extract Berthe Gheldman from the clutches of the Germans, and hid her son, thus saving his life. Finally, it is possible that Berthe Gheldman and her ex-husband did see each other again – though they would have done so in terrible circumstances (see Chapter 4).

I would also like to stress that my book is not intended to pass judgement on the French. When I was working on the French social elite during the Second World War, survivors of that period (usually Pétainists) would sometimes ask me what I would have done if I had found myself in their position. This is an understandable but futile question. If I had been alive in France in 1940 I would have been a different person, and how I would have reacted would have depended on the social and political circumstances of my upbringing. An Englishman born in 1963 cannot put himself in the place of someone who grew up in the 1920s watching his father die from the consequences of wounds inflicted at Verdun, or of a farmhand enduring the bitter conditions of the Breton countryside. This book is an attempt to understand and evoke the circumstances that governed how people behaved. But real sympathy in these circumstances must begin with a recognition that our circumstances are different.

I

Summer 1940

In June 1940 Raymond Aron was in a British army barracks in Aldershot. Aron, a Jewish philosopher, had been a sergeant in the French army. During the German invasion of 1940 he had retreated south with his unit and then managed to get to England on a ship taking Polish soldiers from Toulouse. When the French government, now under Marshal Pétain, signed an armistice with the Germans, Aron joined the small group of French soldiers who chose to stay on British soil in the hope that they might continue the fight. Late one night another Frenchman, a junior officer, arrived in his room. Aron knew nothing about his new companion except that he had come to England via North Africa. The following morning, the new arrival asked him the time in a sleepy voice and, on being told, said, 'Twenty to seven already.' Aron went to shave and when he returned his compatriot had shot himself: Aron never found out why.[1]

It is hard to know how common suicide was amongst French people in the summer of 1940. Many deaths of all sorts during the period must have gone unexplained or perhaps unreported. There were at least sixteen suicides in Paris on 14 June 1940, and as late as 20 December there were seven.[2] Certain suicides, or attempted suicides, became famous gestures. Thierry de Martel, an eminent brain surgeon and descendant of Mirabeau, injected himself with strychnine in his smart apartment as the Germans entered Paris on 14 June.[3] Jean Moulin, prefect of the Eure-et-Loir, cut his throat with a piece of glass

1. (previous pages) *The Germans insisted that their armistice with France in June 1940 be signed in the same railway carriage that had been used to sign the armistice of November 1918.*

in an unsuccessful suicide attempt on the night of 17 June, after German soldiers had beaten him up for refusing to sign a document blaming black soldiers in the French army for a massacre.

Suicide had particular meanings in France. It went with a certain kind of nineteenth-century romanticism – General Boulanger had killed himself on the grave of his mistress – and also perhaps with a certain kind of republican culture; French republicans often looked to ancient Rome for models of behaviour. Martel's suicide has entered into French patriotic mythology, and there is now a street named after him in the 16th arrondissement of Paris. Equally, Moulin's attempted suicide is often presented as a first step along the path that would take him to London in 1941, and then to a hero's death at the hands of the Germans in 1943. However, it is not clear that Moulin planned to resist the Germans in 1940: after recovering from his suicide attempt he returned to his post for some months and worked well with the German authorities, who seemed to regret his treatment at the hands of their soldiers. Martel's act is also hard to read. He was a right-wing anti-Semite, and he had been a fierce anti-Dreyfusard. Had he survived, it is hard to imagine that he would have disapproved of the Vichy government that came to terms with the Germans. Perhaps the suicide of a sixty-five-year-old man who had lost his son in the First World War had personal as much as political implications, and this seems to be true of many similar acts in the summer of 1940. An old man shot himself in his apartment in Reims after almost all the rest of the town's population had moved out to escape the German advance; in a Burgundy village the only family not to flee the Germans killed themselves in their home.

Regardless of political or patriotic concerns, most French people experienced this period as a time of uncertainty and loneliness. War and defeat separated lovers and relatives. Call-up for the army had already taken many husbands and fathers from their families. Almost two million men were then taken prisoner in 1940, and over a million did not return home until the summer of 1945. Some families had no news of captured soldiers for more than a year.

Historians of France generally describe the summer of 1940 in one of two ways. Some emphasize the military defeat. Their story concerns two armies and particularly the strategic decisions made by commanders. Other historians focus on the internal politics of France. Their story concerns the machinations of those politicians who overthrew the Third Republic and established an authoritarian regime at Vichy. Both schools make relatively brief, though confident, references to the great mass of the population. Military historians are concerned by the collapse of army morale; political historians refer to the French national mood that, apparently, made public opinion 'welcome' the Vichy regime. In fact, almost any generalization about the mood of the French population in the summer of 1940 is open to question. Many French people seem to have difficulty in evoking or explaining their own feelings, let alone those of their compatriots. Many recall the few weeks or months after the German entry into France as a period that was somehow separate from the rest of their lives. Simone de Beauvoir talked about the 'no man's land' in time that existed between the departure of French troops and the arrival of the Germans in the village of La Pouèze, to which she fled in June 1940.[4] 'No man's land' would be a good description of the whole summer of 1940 for many French people.

We can, perhaps, be sure of only two things in the summer of 1940. First, most French people had limited and often inaccurate information. They simply did not know what was going on, and many decisions they made were based on false assumptions. Thus, for example, French soldiers surrendered to Germans because they believed that a permanent peace settlement would soon free them from captivity. French civilians ran away from their homes because they believed that the German advance might still be halted somewhere to the south or the west. Secondly, the institutions that bound French people into some wider network of loyalties – regiments, political parties or even daily newspapers – all collapsed for a time. French people recalled this period in terms of what happened to them and to those around them: the idea that these multiple individual dramas were part of a broader national drama only developed later.

FRENCH SOLDIERS

The first point to be made about French experiences in the summer of 1940 is that the nature of the defeat was unexpected. The French had anticipated a long and gruelling war of attrition. Most of them believed that the Germans would be held off by the Maginot line. French strategists believed that the German economy was weak and that it would be ground down by the need to sustain a long war; eventually the Germans would collapse. In early 1940 a long war still seemed likely. After six months neither side had made any significant advance. The Germans had taken only about 1,000 French soldiers prisoner and the French had captured around 500 Germans. In Montpellier, bourgeois young men stayed on at the local lycée to spend a year preparing for the exams that would give them entry into the officer training academy at Saint-Cyr. One of them recalled their thinking thus: 'A war is four years of fighting, we had the time to take the exams, do a year at Saint-Cyr and then join the front and take part in the offensive that we would undoubtedly launch.' As it turned out, the boys from Montpellier were still taking their exams when the Germans invaded. Those of them who fought did so with the Maquis or the Free French or, in a few cases, with German forces on the Eastern Front.[5]

In the spring of 1940, Douglas Cooper, a wealthy and middle-aged English dilettante, returned to Paris from a skiing holiday in Saint-Moritz and worked with the French Red Cross organizing deliveries of books to soldiers in the Maginot line. French soldiers had plenty of time to read. Jean-Paul Sartre wrote to Simone de Beauvoir describing his daily routine: he rose at six, wrote his 'war journal' from seven to seven-thirty, and worked on his novel until eleven when he had lunch and attended roll-call. He then wrote again until the mail arrived at four, spent up to three hours replying to letters and then worked a little more in the evening – except when distracted by guard duty. Raymond Aron spent most of his time in the army before the invasion reading Machiavelli and preparing an edition of Élie Halévy's *History of Socialism*.

Everything changed on 10 May when the Germans attacked the

Low Countries and then when they swept past the Maginot line by going through the Ardennes forest and entering northern France. Douglas Cooper entrusted his Picasso sketches to the doorman at the Ritz (he got them back in 1944), joined the French army as an ambulance driver (he had previously been considered too old), and was posted to the front within days. Aron applied for a transfer into a combat unit as the Germans entered France; even a man as prescient as he still believed that the war was just beginning for France at the moment when it was in fact ending.

Because the French had not expected the German attack to come in the north, they had posted their least-well-trained troops there. A large part of the French armed forces were in places that the Germans did not initially attack, some of them in North Africa. Many units retreated from the Germans. Some went to Brittany, and some went south. About 140,000 French soldiers were evacuated by the British at Dunkirk, and other French units fought to protect the British retreat; 40,000 French were taken prisoner at Dunkirk.

Most French soldiers who reached Britain were sent back almost immediately to continue fighting. Even amongst those still in Britain after it became clear that France was defeated, most chose to be repatriated. Gradually, and rather grudgingly, the British, who never treated Vichy as an enemy state, shipped French soldiers back to France. Some soldiers and sailors saw the decision to stay in Britain or return to France as a political choice between Pétain and de Gaulle, but not everybody thought in these terms. Some people who stayed in Britain did not join the Free French forces but simply continued their civilian lives there. Groups of Breton fishermen, for example, operated out of Cornish ports. Equally, some people who chose to be repatriated from Britain were not Pétainists. Decisions at this stage seem mainly to have been made on the basis of personal circumstances, and were particularly rooted in the desire of French men to return to their families. Julien Cain, the Jewish director of the Bibliothèque Nationale, was on board a British ship moored off Bordeaux and ready to sail for England on 18 June, when he and his wife decided that they could not face leaving their homeland and insisted on being taken back to shore, to face several years of anti-Semitic persecution.[6] The novelist Paul Morand was in London, attached to the French embassy, when France was defeated. If he had stayed in London, he might have returned to France as a conquering hero in 1944. As it was, he went back in July, against the wishes of his Vichy superiors, and became a supporter of Pierre Laval – he was sent into exile in 1945, and his candidacy for the Académie Française was blocked until after de Gaulle lost power. His desire to return to France seems to have had as much to do with desire to keep in touch with the son that a woman married to another man had recently borne him as it did with his right-wing political sympathies.[7] For other people, decisions made in the summer of 1940 had even more dramatic consequences. Simon Sabiani, a Communist-turned-fascist politician in Marseilles, had a son, François. In early July 1940, François, a member of a tank unit, was on the verge of crossing the Spanish frontier in order to make his way to England. Simon Sabiani drove to the frontier and managed to turn his son back. In June 1942, François was killed fighting with German forces near Smolensk.[8]

As German soldiers advanced into France, France's political leadership changed. Marshal Pétain was brought back from Madrid, where he had been France's first ambassador to Franco's government, to become deputy Prime Minister on 18 May. On 16 June Paul Reynaud resigned as Prime Minister and was replaced by Pétain. On 17 June Pétain formed his first government and broadcast a message calling on Frenchmen 'to cease fighting'. The printed version of his speech talked about the need 'to try to cease fighting'. The speech was addressed to demoralized soldiers and fleeing civilians, people who were in no position for calm reflection. Raymond Aron was convinced that he had heard the words 'we must try to stop fighting' (that is, the version that subsequently appeared in print), rather than 'we must stop fighting'. Douglas Cooper heard Pétain's speech in a restaurant crowded with refugees in Bourges. He later described the reaction of the audience:

The crowd started to eat, then to talk. What had the Maréchal said? Did it mean that a state of armistice already existed? Were the English also suing for peace? Were hostilities to cease against Italy too? These were the questions on everyone's lips. We had all heard the same speech, yet no one had rightly understood. It was a masterpiece of ambiguous phraseology. Like others we collated our version of what had been said. Some maintained that hostilities had already ceased, others that no armistice had even been asked for, while still others professed no interest whatsoever.[9]

Pétain's speech was followed by a period of great uncertainty. French government negotiators did not even set out to meet their German counterparts until 20 June. The armistice with Germany was signed on 22 June and that with Italy on 25 June. In theory, France remained at war throughout this period; in practice there was little point in dying for a government that had decided to sue for peace. Many French soldiers were already separated from their units, on the run or captured, but over half of all French prisoners of war fell into German hands after 17 June.

The circumstances of their capture varied. Some gave in after desperate fights in which they had run out of ammunition or been wounded. Some went looking for Germans to surrender to.[10] Some were ordered to surrender by their own officers. The fact that the Germans swept around behind the Maginot line meant that large numbers of French soldiers never had a chance to engage the enemy. Some did not make contact with the Germans until after the armistice had been signed and, understandably, they were perplexed to discover that they were considered to have been defeated, let alone captured. Commandant Elie Charnal, who had served on the Maginot line, wrote: 'The gestures of courtesy that the German authorities lavished on the garrisons of the Maginot line from 26 June to 2 July, explain [the fact] that these troops were sadly surprised, first to be taken into captivity and then to be kept there.' Charnal himself first met German units, much more lightly armed than his own, on 26 June, the day after the armistice was signed with Italy and consequently a moment when all fighting was supposed to have ceased. The Germans welcomed his help in making sure that there were no misunderstandings and that German soldiers did not step on landmines. He was allowed to keep a car and driver and given a pass. At the German headquarters in the Château de Bettange, he was served tea. On 2 July a German colonel gave him a bottle of wine, an invitation to shoot on his property in Bavaria and a photograph inscribed with the words: 'In memory of a time of war spent together and au revoir for a time of peace.' The next day Charnal and his men were taken prisoner. A year later he was still writing bewildered and indignant letters about his capture from Oflag VIA.[11]

A few men who ended up in German prisoner of war camps had never really been combatant soldiers at all. A group of soldiers guarding political prisoners on the Île d'Yeu were allowed to operate, and to fly the French flag, until 15 August. After this, they were taken to the mainland by their German interlocutors who wished them luck before they were dispatched to Saumur and, much to their surprise, declared to be prisoners.[12] Léo Malet, a writer who subsequently did something to create the popular image of prisoners of war, was arrested for draft evasion in Rennes in 1940. As the city fell in June 1940 he, along with many other prisoners, was released, but then the Germans, assuming that he was a deserter from the French army, declared him a prisoner of war.[13]

Prisoners were herded into temporary places of detention and their lives during this period were often chaotic. Sometimes they were not fed, and sometimes they were organized into looting parties by their captors. Gustave Folcher recalled being kept with 30,000 other prisoners in a factory, and described fights over bread and the belief of some prisoners that they had been served human flesh.[14] Some prisoners remained in France for months.

During their five years of captivity French soldiers often recalled their last glimpses of France with particular poignancy. French civilians usually went out of their way to be generous with food and drink and kind words, but sometimes this generosity merely served to underline the prisoners' humiliation. Some prisoners felt that natural roles had been reversed as Frenchwomen, the very people they had been meant to protect, now became their protectors. Francis Ambrière recalled a peasant woman in Alsace who intervened to prevent one of his comrades from being beaten by a sentry. The woman, seized with rage, then pursued the column, haranguing the sentry in Alsatian dialect.[15]

Escape during this early period would have been relatively easy for many prisoners. They were kept in makeshift structures, and once outside these there was very little to prevent them, in their own

country, from getting home. Some of them were able to bribe guards
in order to get out and see their wives. The demarcation line between
the occupied northern and unoccupied southern zones, once it existed,
was not hard for a fit Frenchman to cross, and the Vichy authorities
never made much effort to compel prisoners who reached the free
zone to return to Germany. Only about 225,000 men (less than a fifth
of the total) took the chance to escape while still in France.[16] Prisoners
who subsequently endured five years of harsh captivity reproached
themselves for not having seized the opportunity. What stopped them
was almost invariably lack of information. Defeated soldiers were
confused. They were usually separated from their officers, whom they
had often in any case ceased to trust. Many assumed that the armistice
between France and Germany would bring their release, or that the
imminent defeat of Britain would bring the whole war to an end: no
one expected that five years of captivity lay ahead. If French soldiers
assumed that the price of not escaping would be relatively low, many
also believed that the price of trying to escape would be high. They
knew that German soldiers were capable of great brutality – in one
camp, Germans responded to a minor act of indiscipline by firing a
machine gun at random into a crowded courtyard, leaving three men
dead and eighteen wounded[17] – and they feared that reprisals would
be taken against the comrades or the family of any prisoner who tried
to escape.

An idea of how prisoners saw escape can be gleaned from the story
of Albert Husson from the Saône-et-Loire. After his unit surrendered,
he was ordered by German soldiers to make his own way to an
assembly point. Instead of obeying the order, he simply went home,
but then, fearful at rumours that escaped prisoners would be shot, he
turned himself in. The Germans released him on parole and gave him
a pass that allowed him to cross the demarcation line between the
occupied and 'free' zones of France every day in order to go to work.
On 28 August his period of relative freedom was ended and he was
sent with a convoy of other prisoners to Dijon, a staging post on the
way to Germany. At this point Husson finally escaped for good.[18]

Slowly prisoners were marched eastwards, usually making the last
part of their journey by train or, more rarely, by barge. Once again
uncertainty reigned. Very few French prisoners spoke German or

knew anything about the geography of Germany; many of them were not even sure that they were going to Germany. One prisoner reported that the colonel of his regiment made a brief speech to his soldiers before officers and other ranks were separated. The colonel, who had been a prisoner in the First World War, gave them a grim view of what was ahead of them. His most important advice was that they should always keep hold of their spoon and mess tin and never miss their turn to eat.[19]

GERMAN SOLDIERS AND FRENCH CIVILIANS

How did German troops behave? After the defeat, some French people argued that the German army was marked by its 'correct' behaviour. The Germans took pains to present their soldiers in the best possible light: the first units of the Wehrmacht to reach Paris paused to wash themselves in the Canal de l'Ourcq before entering the capital.[20] Sometimes the emphasis on 'correct' behaviour by the Germans reached absurd proportions. A schoolboy wrote approvingly in August 1940 that a group of Germans he had seen in a cake shop 'ate their millefeuilles very properly'.[21]

Two comparisons made the German behaviour appear relatively restrained. First, French people had some idea how badly the Germans had behaved during their invasion of Poland in 1939, and were thus relieved that brutality in France was not worse. Bernard Pierquin, a bourgeois Parisian who celebrated his twentieth birthday in June 1940, wrote: 'The boche is well disciplined; in Poland, he is ordered to murder and rape: he murders and rapes. In France, he must smile and excuse himself.'[22] The French also tended, in retrospect, to contrast German behaviour of 1940 with their behaviour later in the war, particularly after 1942, when the SS took over the policing of France from the army, and in 1944, when populations of villages suspected of being linked to the Resistance were sometimes massacred.

These images went with broader stereotypes. They suggested a contrast between the Wehrmacht of 1940 – a regular army commanded by aristocratic Prussian officers who were veterans of the 'honourable' war fought between France and Germany between 1914 and 1918 – and the SS of 1944, brutalized by combat on the Eastern Front and led by committed Nazis, often from outside the frontiers of the 1933 Reich. Léon Werth explicitly contrasted German behaviour of 1940 with that later during the occupation: 'This was the time when they were correct, which preceded the time when they gave us lessons in courtesy.'

It is true that the Germans were less brutal in 1940 than they were in 1944 and that their invasion of France was less brutal than their invasion of Poland or the Soviet Union. However, the Germans were not gentle in 1940. Sometimes they enforced rules ruthlessly. A French policeman was arrested for failing to salute a German officer. In Lille, a girl was rebuked by a German sentry for smiling at a French officer in a column of prisoners. The girl stuck out her tongue at the sentry and was rewarded with a month in prison.[23] German brutality was applied in uneven ways, which partly explains why it was comparatively under-reported. The Germans behaved worst when they first arrived, when they still did not know that the war against France would be so quick and, from their point of view, easy. There were sharp changes over quite a short period of time. Jean Moulin received a fulsome letter of thanks from a senior German officer only a couple of months after being beaten up by German NCOs.

The Germans behaved differently to different sections of the population. Upper-class French officers who resisted the Germans with particular determination were buried with full military honours or accorded punctilious respect when they finally surrendered. Black soldiers in the French army who displayed similar courage were often murdered. Class also influenced German behaviour. Generally, and sometimes after a tense first encounter, German officers treated notables and civil servants well; they knew they needed the co-operation of such people. Workers and peasants were handled more roughly.

German treatment of Frenchwomen played a particularly important part in their image in French eyes. The French feared rape, which they believed to have been common during the First World War. A group of young women refugees in the region around Chartres smeared themselves with Dijon mustard, 'to sting the Germans when they rape'.[24] Generally, however, the French (or at least bourgeois Frenchmen) were relieved by what seemed to be the restrained behaviour of German soldiers. Micheline Bood, a teenage girl, recorded in her diary the following exchange between her relatives just before the family fled from their home in June 1940: 'Cousin Jules said that the Germans do not rape women "because they are correct". Uncle Fritz, who spends his days sucking his false teeth, never intervenes in conversations. But at this point he adjusted his dentures and said: "Not at all, not at all! It is because they do not have the temperament." '[25]

The Germans may not have carried out the mass rapes that some Frenchmen feared, but it is not true that the Germans raped no women in the summer of 1940. French police recorded at least three assaults on women in the Seine region on a single day (21 June). German soldiers entered apartments in Saint-Denis, Saint-Ouen and Stains.[26] Several points are clear from these reports. First, some women had experiences that were remote from bourgeois Frenchmen's perception of German soldiers as being 'correct'. Secondly, even when the French authorities knew what had happened, they were in no position to do anything about it. French policemen could hardly act against a victorious army, and they were not likely to complain to the German authorities at a time when German behaviour still seemed unpredictable. Thirdly, women's experience of the Germans was defined by class. The reports of rape in Paris came from working-class districts. Generally speaking, both the French and German authorities seem to have taken rape most seriously when bourgeois women were involved in some way.[27] Finally, definitions of rape were sometimes ambiguous. The views of German soldiers were heavily influenced by national stereotypes about the sexual availability of Frenchwomen and very few ordinary soldiers understood French. Many Germans clearly believed that incidents which Frenchwomen perceived as rape were in fact consensual, perhaps even amicable: in one case, German soldiers asked their victim to make them coffee before they left.[28]

FRENCH SOLDIERS AND
FRENCH CIVILIANS

Sharp distinctions between soldiers and civilians had been important for Third Republic France. Soldiers were drawn from a particular part of the population: they were all adult, all relatively young and, most importantly, all male. Male military service had been almost universal since the 1880s and had come to be recognized as a rite of passage into manhood. The First World War had seen fighting confined to a clearly defined and immobile front line. Casualties had been terrible amongst soldiers but mortality rates amongst the civilian population had hardly been affected. During the 1930s bombing had seemed to take death to civilians, away from the front line, but, after an initial scare, French civilians had suffered little until May 1940. The distinction between soldiers in their concrete bunkers on the Maginot line and women and children behind the lines had seemed more clear-cut than ever before.

The chaos that came with the German invasion changed all this. Soldiers who wished to avoid falling into German hands took off their uniforms, hid their weapons and destroyed their military papers. Marc Bloch wrote that in 1940 many French soldiers had proved unable to fight while many French civilians had shown themselves to be born warriors. Bloch's own military career illustrated the blurred lines between soldiers and civilians. When he was repatriated to Cherbourg after having crossed into England from Dunkirk, Bloch changed into civilian clothes and checked into a hotel. Four years later, whilst his brother officers who had kept their uniforms in 1940 were enduring the tedious but relatively safe life of German Oflags, Bloch was shot as a Resistance leader.

The experience of other soldiers illustrates the peculiar situation of the army in the summer of 1940. Men could not be certain whether they were part of a fighting army, part of a defeated army, prisoners or civilians. Guy de Rothschild was evacuated with his unit from Dunkirk and then, after having noted the apparent British indifference to the military crisis, returned with his unit to Brest. On board the ship taking them back to France, some of his men had nightmares, believing that they had fallen into German hands. Back in France, Rothschild was captured but, realizing that the Germans were in no position to guard all their prisoners, he ordered his men to escape. Some of his troops disobeyed this order because they believed that the war was over and that they would therefore soon be released. Rothschild himself rejoined the French army and was demobilized several weeks later.[29]

Jacques Benoist-Méchin was in the west of France in June 1940. He and a few comrades had no weapons and were separated from the rest of their unit. They had not eaten for some time, their uniforms were torn and they had spent some days 'playing hide and seek' with German tanks. On 22 June a German armoured column entered the village of Mazières-en-Gâtine in which Benoist-Méchin and his comrades had taken refuge. Encouraged by the mayor, who was keen to avoid any fighting around his village, Benoist-Méchin negotiated with the young German commander. Neither side knew whether an armistice had been signed yet, and both French and German soldiers realized that they did not know what they should do. Benoist-Méchin was told that he was free to go. On 24 June he left with a friend on a motorbike, hoping to return home to Paris. The two men kept their uniforms though they had clearly ceased to be soldiers. They were then taken prisoner by German soldiers near Saumur, released the following morning, on the grounds that the armistice with Italy had been signed and the war was thus over, and then recaptured a little later in the same day. Apparently, new orders had been given. Benoist-Méchin remained a prisoner for three months; some of his comrades were prisoners for the next five years.[30]

Benoist-Méchin, Bloch and Rothschild were all unusually well-informed men, but life for ordinary soldiers, or for those who might find themselves defined as soldiers, was even more confusing. Frenchmen from the class of 1912 (that is, men born in the late nineteenth century who had already served in the First World War) were demobilized just before the German invasion, but many of them were still wearing uniform and were thus likely to be taken prisoner by the Germans. Many young men who had not yet been called up were ordered to report to military authorities in the south of France as the Germans invaded. *Affectés spéciaux*, men who had been granted exemption from military service because of their work in reserved occupations, did not know what they were supposed to do. Notices in Paris on 10 June told all *affectés spéciaux* except firemen and policemen to rejoin the army (easier said than done under the circumstances), but a notice pinned up two days later told all men working for the public services to remain at their post.[31] Boys who were too young to have been called up believed that the Germans were likely to treat them as being of fighting age and fled to avoid the oncoming army. In Belgium, 300,000 men of military age (that is, between sixteen and thirty-five) were ordered to head for Belgian army recruitment centres in the south of France: 100,000 men reached such centres.[32] Belgian soldiers in uniform also congregated in the south of France, though their status as combatants seemed dubious after the Belgian king surrendered.

Most importantly, the roles of men and women were challenged by the nature of the French defeat. The French army was keen to maintain a sharp distinction between male soldiers and female civilians. One of General Weygand's first acts on becoming commander-in-chief was to order women away from the front line. In practice, such an order was impossible to enforce at a time when the front line was moving so fast and when so many civilians were being moved out of their houses. The pilot Antoine de Saint-Exupéry, who watched the defeat unfold from his plane, pointed out that French soldiers in the summer of 1940 were no longer the protectors of Frenchwomen and children. Sometimes they seemed to play the opposite role, forcing civilians to remain in towns that were going to be bombarded or provoking bombardment by attempting to halt the German advance in a particular place. There were arguments between mayors and senior officers as the former sought assurances that there would be no fighting in their towns.

The mingling of women refugees and retreating, often deserting, French soldiers also undermined the French army's image as the protector of female honour. Two reports by French soldiers describing their own behaviour are revealing. Corporal Bordet and his comrade Mourges met three girls from Alsace during the debacle of 1940. The soldiers swapped their uniforms for workmen's overalls and hid their military papers in the girls' purses. The five of them headed south until they stopped at an inn for two days:

time enough to make the girls pay in kind. Two let it happen . . . even though one of them was a virgin, the third did not want it, but she ended up submitting like the others after Mourges threatened that he would cut off food for the whole group.

Another group of soldiers in the Cher gave a lift to fourteen women:

Six seemed to know the score, but the eight others were as prudish as possible. None of them was exactly raped, in spite of the discomfort of the woods or the trucks. The oldest must have been twenty-two and she explained to Maupetit that she had decided, like her friends, to give herself to Frenchmen because it was all they could do for the soldiers and because like that the Germans, if they caught them, would only have the left-overs.[33]

EXODE

The dominant French civilian memories of 1940 did not come directly from contact with either French or German troops but from the large-scale flight of civilians away from the advancing German army. Population movement began in France before the German invasion, as civilians were evacuated from threatened areas on the eastern frontier and as factories were moved with their workforces to parts of France that were seen as safe from attack. Private individuals, especially those wealthy enough to afford hotels or lucky enough to have relations in the country, sometimes moved away from cities because they feared air attack, though many of these people had moved back by May 1940.

The French government had plans for further evacuation in the event of German invasion. These plans involved moving the populations of affected areas into reception centres in the south and west. The plans depended on efficient train services and on precise calculations about the accommodation available in receiving areas. They also depended on the assumption that people who were not seen to be at risk could be prevented from moving.

These carefully laid plans were thrown into confusion by the unexpected speed and nature of the German advance. What the French came to call the *exode* started in the Low Countries. People from

Holland, Luxembourg and, most of all, Belgium flooded across France's north-eastern border. There were probably about two million of these people in all. Refugees from the Low Countries crossed France, heading south and west. In the process, they helped to sow panic amongst the population of northern France who, like the Belgians, had memories of the previous German occupation between 1914 and 1918.

Towns that had not been scheduled for evacuation at all emptied in days. The population of Lille, Roubaix and Tourcoing dropped from 400,000 to 40,000, that of Reims from 250,000 to 5,000. Parisians were initially spectators to the *exode* as refugees passed through the Gare du Nord, but on 10 June Paris itself was declared an open city and a large part of its population left. A police report of 13 June stated: 'Paris has been declared an open city, but it is already almost a desert.'[34] The population of Paris had dropped from its normal three million to something between 700,000 and one million by 13 June; the population of its surrounding banlieue had dropped from two million to something between 600,000 and 800,000.[35] The 'emptiness' of Paris in June 1940 was, like so many things at that time, partly a matter of bourgeois perception. Emptiness was most visible in the *beaux quartiers* in the west of the city. The prefect of the Paris police described dining with his wife and a couple of friends at the Ritz on 12 June: 'There was absolutely no one in this great restaurant in an already deserted Paris.'[36] Since, however, one assumes that the guests at the Ritz did not wait on their own tables or wash their own dishes, at least a certain proportion of the working-class population of the city must have stayed.

Eventually around eight million people were on the roads; six million of these were French, about a sixth of the entire population of the country. Experiences of the *exode* could be deeply unpleasant. Columns of refugees were sometimes strafed by German or Italian planes. People piled into chaotic and overcrowded towns on their way south and west. For some people, such as women due to give birth or very young children – the baby brother of the future historian Pierre Vidal-Naquet died during the *exode* – conditions were unbearable. Given the heat, the crowds and the chaos, France was lucky to escape a major epidemic.

In retrospect, it seems that the dangers and discomforts of staying to face the Germans were less than the perils of facing the open road. This was particularly striking for France's rural population. The countryside, especially away from main roads, was less threatened by German bombing than the towns. Furthermore, peasants had much to lose. Leaving their farms in June 1940 meant leaving their fields at an important point in the agricultural year, leaving their livestock (France lost more horses than men that summer) and leaving their property to be pillaged by the Germans or by fleeing refugees. In spite of this, many peasants defied advice given to them by soldiers and fled.[37] Yves Durand recalled that a family from Normandy arrived at his father's farm in the Auvergne with their car and horse-drawn plough – though not, presumably, with their horses.[38] Ephraïm Grenadou was a wily farmer from the Beauce who had grown rich by defying conventional wisdom (he bought land during the Depression), but even he packed forty members of his family and staff into two cars and four horse-drawn wagons and headed to the Loire. Grenadou returned relatively quickly to eject the refugees who had installed themselves in his farm, prevent the village from distributing the mutton from his sheep, establish working relations with the Germans and prepare for the harvest. All the same, he had lost a hundred sheep, a hundred sacks of oats, a pig and a cow during his ten-day absence.[39]

Why then did people leave their homes at all in the summer of 1940? One important answer to this question is that the French did not know in the summer of 1940 what was going to happen. It was possible that the war would drag on for years, in which case those who found themselves on the wrong side of the German lines might be cut off from their own government. This was what had happened in Belgium and parts of northern France during the First World War, and memories of that war seem to have played an important part in persuading the inhabitants of these regions to leave their homes. No one knew how brutal the Germans would turn out to be. Fears that notables might be taken hostage for the good behaviour of their regions, or that young men of military age might be seized, played an important part in the decision to leave: the chaotic movement of huge numbers of people provided propitious circumstances for rumours to spread.

Douglas Cooper was in Provins on 23 June. The *exode* had already begun in many other parts of France and refugees were streaming through Provins, but the citizens of that town itself seemed relatively calm. Attitudes began to change when a British pilot baled out of his aircraft: a large part of the town's population believed that this single airman was in fact part of a large contingent of German paratroops. Cooper watched as a group of women decided that it was time to leave:

We learned for the first time that no official orders had been given and that the local exodus was quite impromptu on the part of the farmers and townsfolk. It was appalling; a whole country-side moving without orders – this was something that we had not visualised. Unorganised, undisciplined hordes flooding and cluttering up the roads!

As we listened to the women we realised how this dreadful thing had come to pass. At first their talk had been of trivial nothings with no hint of scare. Casually and only occasionally, even a little disdainfully, they had watched the mob below, but they had given no sign of taking any part in it. Now, only half-an-hour or so later, the air raid, the excitement of the parachute and finally the news, brought by an excited new-comer, of their townspeople fleeing, had changed their whole attitude. They agreed that the air-raids had been getting worse and worse; at first they had been an excitement, then a nuisance – now it was serious. They click-clacked on; each one looked pre-occupied. The woman with the embroidery jabbed her needle in more firmly and pulled her cotton more tightly; the little boy got fewer caresses and was cuffed more rapidly and frequently. Their chatter was more staccato.

An old, dried-up, wise-looking woman was the first to say *it* – 'I shall take my bottles of liqueurs; I have a fine *marc* and nothing will persuade me to leave that behind . . .' At first the others looked at her in surprise – surprise at her daring to be the first to express their unspoken thought . . . We realised then that each woman had come to a premeditated, not to a hasty decision.

. . . Here was a group of women who had woken sane and calm on the morning of June the 13th and who by nightfall would in all probability have joined the lost legions . . . on the long roads to the South.[40]

The *exode* snowballed. Evacuation of some regions provoked the evacuation of others. Sometimes people waited until the inhabitants of a nearby area arrived and then concluded that the war was too close for comfort. Some people moved for mundane reasons. People who needed to cash cheques or to claim money from the state wanted to make sure that they were in an area where the writ of the French government would run. Shops often closed (shopkeepers were prudent people and they were more likely than the rest of the population to have cars), and this meant that it sometimes became impossible to get food in towns that lay on the route of the German advance.

Edmond Dubois, a correspondent for a Lausanne newspaper, had difficulty in providing a complete explanation for his departure from Paris in June: 'It would be a clever man who could explain it. My Swiss nationality put me in a privileged situation, nothing and nobody obliged me to join the millions of city-dwellers who suddenly left.' At first he carried on with his work. When he went to the Hôtel Continental to get an article on the flight from Paris passed by the French censors, he found that the civil servants themselves had fled. The very emptiness of the city began to disconcert: 'The day that the street sweepers do not appear and the newspaper kiosk stays closed is the day that the street begins to panic.'[41] It should be added that Dubois seems to have found the *exode* a more benign experience than most Parisians. He had a car and good maps that allowed him to escape from the traffic jams on main roads and to 'drive almost alone ... among fields in which the peasants continued to work'.[42] Most importantly, Dubois knew that he had the money to pay for a hotel in the Pyrenees and that his ultimate destination was his house in Cassis.

Local authorities sometimes left towns and invited the inhabitants to do the same. Schools, hospitals and prisons were evacuated – some inmates in the latter took advantage of the confusion to escape, and the presence of escaped prisoners amongst the fleeing crowds further increased the sense of confusion and fear.

Decisions about what to do in the face of the German advance divided local notables. Mayors sometimes tried to negotiate with the invaders, and with their own army, in order to prevent fighting in their towns. However, mayors were frightened because they knew that the Germans were likely to take them hostage in order to secure the good conduct of the town. Many were, briefly, taken hostage and some in the north, who had already been hostages during the First World War, fled rather than risk repeating the experience. Whole municipalities moved south. That of Reims established itself at Nevers and then at Garnac in the Tarn, which happened to be the birthplace of the mayor. Local populations were often bitter about the flight of their politicians, especially when refugees were prevented from going to the very places where their town councils had taken refuge. Sometimes people considered that the departure of local politicians marked the moment when they themselves should leave.

Prefects, who were paid civil servants, seem to have held their nerve better than elected politicians in the summer of 1940. Men who stayed at their post were admired. Jean Moulin remained in Chartres to greet the Germans and worked with the local bishop to protect the town – not the only occasion on which a member of the anti-clerical Radical Party found himself knitted into a new *union sacrée* with the Church during the summer of 1940. Moulin's actions earned him the gratitude of the local population, the Vichy government and, after a brief moment of tension, the Germans. However, his pre-war record was sufficiently left-wing to make Vichy dismiss him and he later joined the Resistance. Those who stayed at their post too long, on the other hand, could eventually become regarded as collaborators. Fernand Carles remained in place as prefect of the north in 1940, but then also stayed on during the conflicts between the Germans and the Resistance in 1943 and 1944. In 1945 he committed suicide, shortly before being tried for collaboration.

Sometimes the behaviour of officials in the face of the *exode* was farcical. In Reims, the concierge of the Palais de Justice left taking the only set of keys with him. In a Paris juvenile court, the clerk solemnly noted with regard to every single one of the eleven cases due to be heard on 24 June that proceedings were suspended 'in view of the absence of the concerned parties'.[43] At the Quai des Orfèvres, Paris police inspectors spent two days in June loading the archives of the Renseignements Généraux onto a barge for transport out of Paris – the barge was also loaded with dynamite so that it could be scuttled rather than be captured by the Germans.

Initially, the evacuation was largely conducted by train. Railways, however, quickly became overstrained and trains made easy targets for enemy planes. The singer Barbara recalled being on a train on the plain of Châtillon-sur-Indre which was abandoned by its locomotive and remained motionless for seventeen days, strafed by German planes.[44] In Chinon, a train arrived in the station on 18 June and was still there two days later when the authorities asked the refugees to leave it and seek refuge in neighbouring farms because the Germans were expected to arrive.[45]

Increasingly, refugees took to the roads, seizing whatever transport they could get. Some peasants left northern and eastern France on horse-drawn carts. Some people walked, often using pushcarts or prams to transport their belongings. Observers made much of the division between the wealthy travelling in expensive cars and the peasants who tried to transport their possessions in pushcarts. Cars could, however, have disadvantages in 1940. They needed petrol, which was not always easy to obtain (some travellers were said to have tried to swap expensive cars with a high fuel consumption for more economical models), tyres burst and engines broke down. Most of all, cars got trapped in huge traffic jams that developed on main roads and, particularly, around bridges.

Probably the best off were young men who travelled by bicycle. They were relatively independent, they could change their route quickly and get past traffic jams with relative ease. Arthur Griffon left his home in Franche-Comté with fifteen or twenty of his friends on bicycles and eventually got to his aunt Cécile in the Saône-et-Loire.[46] One thousand Belgian boys of military age cycled from Rouen to the Gers (a distance of more than 800 kilometres) under the leadership of a young lieutenant.[47] Bernard Pierquin cycled from Paris to the Côtes du Nord before joining his family who continued to Nantes by car.[48] François Cavanna recalled his exit from Paris. He and other young employees of the Paris post office, all technically under military discipline, were required to report for transport to Bordeaux by coach. The coach did not arrive and Cavanna then set off by bicycle with eight of his colleagues. They planned to cycle through southern Paris and leave through the Porte d'Orléans but found their progress blocked by traffic on the Boulevard Voltaire (in north-eastern Paris). Eventually they left by cycling on pavements until they reached the Porte de Bercy (in the east of Paris) and then cut around the outskirts of the city to get onto the road south. Cavanna's progress was slowed by the propensity of the tyres on his expensive racing bicycle to burst. Eventually he abandoned his colleagues and walked pushing his bicycle until, in defiance of regulations, he hitched lifts from military lorries. Finally, he managed to salvage a less elegant but more practical bicycle from the side of the road, and he rode on this until overtaken by the Germans and turned back to Paris.

It is hard to overstate the importance that bicycles had during the *exode*. Zoltán Szabó, a Hungarian living in Paris, bought one of the last three bicycles on sale at the Grand Magasin du Louvre on 11 June and cycled south (unlike Cavanna he managed to get through the Porte d'Orléans, though it took him three and a half hours to cover a distance of a few hundred metres). He wrote: 'We cyclists were by far the luckiest . . . We could cling on to lorries. We picked up the skill of a thin trout who, in a mountain stream, slides amongst the pebbles and the rocks.'[49] Just before the French parliament was evacuated from Paris, Pierre Cot, a left-wing ex-minister, claimed to have bought a bicycle from his parliamentary colleague, and bicycle manufacturer, Chichery.[50] Cot did not ultimately have to escape from the Germans on two wheels, but thousands of people did. The Women's Volunteer Service, which managed the refugees who reached Britain, reported on 25 May: 'Practically everyone is bringing over a bicycle . . . on a train carrying 642 men, women and children there were 175 bicycles.'[51] The French police reported on people returning to Paris on 26 June that 10,300 came by rail, 4,060 on foot, 832 by car and 1,500 on bicycles.[52]

The *exode* did not, as far as most of its participants were concerned, have a clear destination. The most fortunate refugees had friends or relatives in the south or west of the country with whom they could stay. A few prescient and wealthy people (including some Jews from Belgium and Luxembourg) had bought properties in the south-west specifically in order to provide themselves with places of safety. In political and military terms, Bordeaux was the last stop in the flight from the Germans. It was in Bordeaux that the French government decided to cease fighting, and it was at Bordeaux airport that General Louis Spears, Churchill's envoy, bundled Charles de Gaulle aboard an aircraft bound for London. Bordeaux was the last mustering post for British citizens in France. Ian Fleming, an officer in naval intelligence, drank grand vintages at the Chapon Fin before presiding over the launches that took bad-tempered old ladies in fur coats and jewels out to the last ships bound for England – this was the nearest that James Bond's creator ever got to seeing real action.[53] Most refugees, however, had little idea about where they were going. Many of them had hoped that the German advance would be halted on the Loire. They carried on until the Germans overtook them, or until they reached a place that seemed safe, or until they were too exhausted to go any further.

Families were often broken up in the *exode*. One writer recalls seeing a desperate woman standing by a roadside asking the hordes who passed by whether they had seen 'a girl of twelve with a red apron'.[54] Local papers in the south carried heartbreaking advertisements as parents tried to locate lost children. A family from Le Mans placed an advertisement in *Le Courrier du Centre* on 4 July in which they asked for news of 'Madeleine Dorée, aged six months, Jean Dorée, aged nine years and Francine Dorée, aged ten years', all of whom had last been seen getting on board a tanker lorry heading from Poitiers to Limoges.[55] Letters to officials carried similar messages. On 12 August Madame Goirot wrote to the mayor of Brive asking him if he had news of her son, aged ten and a half, whom she had last seen on the bridge of Saint-Salut on 16 June (a bridge on a river blocking the route south would have been a particularly crowded and chaotic place).

Parents lost their children in tragic accidents, but families often made more ruthless decisions to separate from old relatives who would not be able to stand the rigours of a long journey. Jackie, a seventeen-year-old half-Jewish Parisian, left Paris on foot with her thirty-eight-year-old mother and her sixty-eight-year-old grandmother (her father and uncle stayed behind in the unrealized hope that they might help defend Paris). When it became obvious that the old woman could walk no further, Jackie's mother persuaded a passing motorist to take her. The family arranged to meet up at Chartres, where the grandmother was to take a hotel room. There were, in fact, no hotel rooms in Chartres; the grandmother was taken much further on and was not reunited with her family for some time.[56] Stanley Hoffmann's mother (an Austrian Jew who had good reason to fear the Germans) took her son from his sickbed and left Paris in a friend's car on 12 June; she was obliged to leave her paralysed brother in the care of a loyal maid.[57]

DÉSUNION SACRÉE

The *exode* was not a time of national unity. In the army, officers and other ranks, regulars and reservists blamed each other for the defeat. A generational struggle began during this period as the middle-aged victors of the First World War blamed the young soldiers who had been defeated in the Second. The veterans of the First World War were to become an important part of Marshal Pétain's support, whilst young men were to provide the support for both resistance and radical collaborationism.

Political divisions were sharp during this period. Some Communists attempted to resume publication of *L'Humanité* in Paris. Rumours, often highly fanciful, of fifth columnists and German infiltrators swept France. The British had to ask that the French refrain from shooting at lone parachutists (most of whom were downed French or British pilots). A number of men from French or Belgian prisons who were believed to have German sympathies were shot by their French jailers.

Regional divisions were also sharp. Most refugees came from the north and east and moved to the south and west. The accommodation of refugees had already caused problems in 1939. Prefects in receiving areas complained that they were being sent excessively large numbers of people, and after May 1940 this problem increased. Seven departments in the south-west received more than 100,000 refugees. In the Hérault, refugees came to make up more than a quarter of the population. For all the talk of national unity that marked both the last days of the Third Republic and the first days of the Vichy regime, local considerations were highly important during this period. Communications had broken down. Prefects and mayors in the south-west had no contact with their colleagues in the north-east except through the floods of refugees from those areas. The national government was itself on the run (from Paris to Tours to Bordeaux to Vichy) and in no position to impose a co-ordinated response.

There was often hostility between refugees and the population of the areas that received them. France contained vast social and economic variations within its frontiers, and life in Lille was very different from life in rural Corrèze. Southerners who were used to drought nicknamed the northerners who were careless with water 'canards'. Northerners were contemptuous of the low, dark, dirty houses they found in the south-west. Differences of diet struck both sides. A woman from the Ardennes wrote a recipe book based on her experience of the *exode* in the Vendée.[58] More commonly, such differences caused hostility.[59] In Georges Simenon's novel *Le Clan des Ostendais* (1947), a group of Flemish refugees offend their hosts in the Charente-Inférieure by refusing to eat *moules à la crème au curry*.

More obviously political differences emerged. Alsace-Lorraine and Belgium were Catholic whilst the south-west of France was anti-clerical. Alsatians and Flamands spoke languages that sounded like German, which aroused suspicion in the paranoid climate of 1940. As early as April many claimed that people from Alsace-Lorraine were celebrating Hitler's birthday or that refugee trains from the east of France had been decorated with swastikas. The de facto annexation of Alsace-Lorraine by Germany in July made the status of people even more uncertain (though, in the long run, people from Alsace-Lorraine who chose not to return home came to be seen as French patriots). The Belgian king's surrender made the French suspicious of those of his subjects who had fled to France – though many of those subjects were now violently hostile to their own government.

Looting was widespread. Refugees stole things as they moved through deserted towns. Sections of the French army looted on a grand scale in the abandoned areas of eastern France where they were stationed. In the north of France, 56 out of 109 cases of 'pillage' reported during the whole period from 1940 to 1944 occurred in the summer of 1940.[60] Looting contributed to the terrifying chaos of the *exode*: on one occasion a dead looter was found with a bottle of stolen rum still in his mouth.[61] Sometimes theft involved real violence, and certain units of the French army seem to have been feared even by other soldiers. The release of prisoners during the *exode* also swelled the criminal population. However, degrees of confusion varied from area to area. Things were worst in the north where the flight from the Germans was most precipitate and where there still seemed to be a risk of real fighting. In Paris, looting was less common,[62] perhaps because 25,000 French police remained in the city[63] and continued to patrol, and because large numbers of German soldiers arrived quickly, or perhaps just because an apartment is harder to loot than an isolated *maison de notable*.

Sometimes looting was recognized as necessary for survival when there were no conventional means of obtaining supplies. In Reims, the municipality summoned a locksmith to open abandoned shops.[64] Sometimes shopkeepers left their properties with the doors open and invited refugees to help themselves.[65] Sometimes the privileged took advantage of their positions: the mayor of the village of Épehy in northern France was found to have hundreds of thousands of francs' worth of 'requisitioned property' in his house.[66] On other occasions crimes were committed by people who had no other means of obtaining food. A large proportion of crimes during this period were committed by housewives and also by adolescents, perhaps those who had lost contact with their families. Courts, both those operated under Vichy and those operated after the liberation, seem to have recognized that crimes committed during the *exode* often involved otherwise 'respectable' people.

THE END OF THE *EXODE*

On 19 June, Charles Pomaret, the Minister of the Interior, declared that the *exode* was damaging the reputation of France and called on refugees to go home. The armistice ended the fighting and established working relations between France and Germany. German troops pulled back behind a newly agreed demarcation line that cut France in half. Trains to convey refugees back to the north and east of France, and to Belgium, began running on a large scale in August.

The collection of the harvest in September provided a certain return to normality (particularly important for those who accepted Vichy's ruralist rhetoric). The start of the academic year, also in September, brought many bourgeois families back to the cities and especially back to Paris. The *exode* had disrupted the baccalauréat examinations – one student from Dijon sat her written papers in Montauban and her oral in Toulouse a month later.[67] For teachers and academics, who so often wrote the diaries and memoirs that have influenced our view of wartime France, the resumption of the academic year was experienced with relief. The Belgian office for refugees in Toulouse closed on 15 October and, most significantly, from 4 November 1940 the Germans began to enforce the demarcation line between the two zones of France, thus making movement between the north and south more difficult.

The truth was, however, that large sections of the French population did not return to normal in 1940. Most French prisoners of war were now in Germany and most of them would not return for five years. Many people from the north and from Alsace-Lorraine were not able to return to their homes, which were in areas that the Germans ruled under special regulations. Most of all, individual lives had been disrupted. For many French people, especially the young and the poor, the *exode* marked a sharp break in their lives. Routines they had taken for granted up to then had been broken and 'normality' never entirely returned.

The horrors of war were not equally shared amongst the French. Things were worse for the inhabitants of the north than for those of the south-west. The *exode* sometimes went with a superficial social levelling as rich and poor were thrown together. The conservative politician and future Vichy minister Jacques Le Roy Ladurie sent his wife and mother-in-law to take refuge with a left-wing farmer in the Vendée who had, only a few days previously, given shelter to the Russian revolutionary Victor Serge. Meanwhile Le Roy Ladurie himself took in a snobbish aristocratic cousin, who talked incessantly about the family lineage. Le Roy Ladurie's brother received the Comte de Paris, who had been ejected from his normal place of exile in Belgium; the French government turned a blind eye to the illegal presence on French soil of the pretender to the throne. Other associates of royalty were caught up in the confusion. The children of the Belgian king were sent to the village of Bussy-en-Bessin in Normandy, accompanied by a retinue of servants and tutors, including their gymnastics teacher, and by Belgian policemen on motorcycles who cleared the roads for their cortège.[68] Alice Keppel, the former mistress of Edward VII, caught the last British boat out of Bordeaux on 25 June.

However, the 'losses' of the wealthy were not the same as those of the poor. When the head chemist of the Mumm champagne firm finally reached safety in the south-west, his employer sent him all the way back to Reims in order to collect an ivory cigarette holder that had been a gift from Emperor Hirohito. The rich had powerful contacts, country houses and the money to buy themselves out of trouble. Some advantages were less obvious. Several writers have suggested that the most important class privilege of 1940 was the possession of Michelin maps. Those who had these were able to navigate along comparatively empty minor roads; those who did not were obliged to stick to the crowded main roads.

Some French people seem to recall the *exode* with a kind of nostalgia. This nostalgia was probably increased by the events that came later in the war. Albert Castères was one of the French forced labourers in Germany who experienced a second *exode* when he joined terrified Germans fleeing from the Red Army during the winter of 1945. As he marched through the snow hunting for food, he looked back on his bicycle ride south from Versailles under the blue skies of June 1940 as having been a happy time.[69] Young men especially, perhaps the group who had most reason to feel relieved they were not living through a repeat performance of 1914, often had happy memories of the *exode*. François Cavanna lost his virginity in a barn on the way to Bordeaux (sexual opportunity was a theme that many male writers stressed when talking about the *exode*). Vladimir Lossky, a young man of Russian origins and mystical inclinations, had different, though apparently agreeable, memories. He took the opportunity to visit medieval cathedrals on his way to Vierzon, where he was told to abandon the attempt to join the army and return to his family.[70] Children, too, sometimes welcomed the suspension of normal routines and constraints.

The worst consequences that might have ensued from a chaotic defeat – large-scale massacres, plague, starvation – were generally avoided. Robert Paxton points out that the most important feature of the French defeat was that it left much of the population with a sense that it still had something to lose. It also left many people with a curious sense of their own absurdity.[71] Simone de Beauvoir recalled that she received a lift from a bourgeois Parisian in July 1940. Her driver said that he did not now understand why he had left Paris so precipitately the previous month and driven hundreds of kilometres in a rickety car: 'I can tell you, Madame, my private parts really suffered.'[72]

Many French people lived through the summer of 1940 in a kind of haze and found it difficult to remember exactly how they had felt. Some found it difficult to understand or explain their feelings even at the time. Micheline Bood wrote in her diary on the evening of 12 June: 'I forgot to say for my first bombardment, I had a terrible desire to laugh. I could not stop myself. So I hid my head in my hands. It was ridiculous and I do not know what came over me.'[73] Françoise Giroud, a journalist who drove from Paris to Clermont-Ferrand in June 1940, recalled the *exode* in interesting terms: 'It had a comic side. The number of people who dreamed of freedom, of rupture with a wife, husband, family, office and who had there a unique chance to take the plunge, to disappear, suddenly set about frantically searching for those they claimed had made them slaves.'[74]

People derived their information in the summer of 1940 mainly from rumour, and many of them sincerely believed things that we know in retrospect to be false. Simone de Beauvoir heard on 9 June that English and Russian troops had landed in Hamburg.[75] Charles Rist was told that a division of German soldiers might have arrived in Haute-Savoie by seaplane.[76] Jacques Benoist-Méchin, a prisoner of the Germans in the Beauce during the summer of 1940, reported repeated rumours, some promising imminent release of all prisoners and some suggesting that massacres were common. One of his comrades said that he would rather block his ears than be tormented by such extremes of hope and fear.

The *exode* is probably recalled now more often in works of fiction than of fact. René Clément's film *Jeux interdits* appeared in 1952. Nevil Shute's novel *The Pied Piper* was published in England in 1941. Régine Deforges's *La Bicyclette bleue* was published in 1983. Georges Simenon, who served briefly as Belgian Commissioner for Refugees in the Charente-Inférieure, wrote two novels about the *exode*. *Le Clan des Ostendais* has already been mentioned; *Le Train* was published in 1961. It concerns a man in northern France who leaves his house in 1940 and is separated from his daughter and pregnant wife. On the train, he meets a half-Jewish refugee from Czechoslovakia who has come to France via Belgium. He helps the woman to conceal her lack of proper papers from French officials, and the two become lovers. Finally, the hero is reunited with his wife and child and returns home. His lover is later shot by the Germans.

Le Train is uncharacteristic of Simenon's work in that it is rooted in a particular time and contains a number of dates relating to the First World War and to the early stages of the Second. The last date cited in the book, however, is 10 May 1940, the date on which the Germans entered Belgium and the *exode* began. The dates in June and July 1940 that historians might consider memorable – 17 June, when Pétain called for the cessation of fighting; 18 June, when de Gaulle made his broadcast calling on the French to resist; 22 June, when the armistice with Germany was signed; 25 June, when the armistice with Italy was signed; and 10 July, when parliament voted full powers to Pétain – are all ignored. Historians tend to see France in the summer of 1940 as part of a bigger story, one that involves the battle between the Germans and the Allies or one that involves the collapse of French democracy. The majority of French people, however, thought of this period in terms of much more personal dramas of displacement and separation. The hero and narrator of the novel explains:

There are official landmarks, dates, that one must be able to find in books. I suppose that everyone, according to where they found themselves at that time, their family situation, their personal concerns, has their own landmarks. Mine are all associated with the reception centre, simply, the centre, as we said, marked by the arrival of such and such a train, by the preparation of a new barracks or by incidents that appeared banal.

2

Vichy

Vichy was a strange place for a capital city. It was a small town, with a permanent population of 30,000. It is in the Auvergne, on the right bank of the Allier river; the train journey from Paris took around four and a half hours in peacetime (it took longer during the occupation). Vichy was not even a departmental capital. It was not an old town, and it had not, unlike its neighbour Riom, been a centre of judicial authority under the *ancien régime*. The nomenclature of Vichy's streets said something about its comparatively recent creation: it contained an Avenue President Wilson and a Rue Jean Jaurès, named after the Socialist leader who had been assassinated in 1914; the latter was to be renamed the Rue Nationale in 1941.

Vichy owed its prosperity to its spa waters; the railways had made it accessible to wealthy invalids and hypochondriacs in the late nineteenth century. By the outbreak of the Second World War, 140,000 *curistes* visited the town every year. Vichy prospered between the wars partly because political turbulence and inflation damaged its rivals in Germany, partly because France was seen as an elegant destination for foreign tourists (especially Americans) and partly because it was a convenient base for motoring tours. It was a smart, cosmopolitan town, which had played host to Lord Rosebery and Count Witte before 1914, and which had more in common with Marienbad than Cheltenham. An English guide published just after the First World War insisted that 'there is none of the dullness of an English watering place'.[1] The town had a lake, a casino, a golf course, a park, a suburban sprawl of villas and over three hundred hotels.

2. (overleaf) *Pétain and Laval.*

45

Once it became the capital of France, the permanent population of Vichy expanded to 130,000. Pétain's headquarters were in the Hôtel du Parc; the Foreign Ministry was eventually installed next door at the Hôtel Majestic; the Ministry of Colonies was in the Hôtel de l'Angleterre. The wealthy clients of these hotels were gradually, and acrimoniously, squeezed out: the decision of 26 August to ban dogs from the Hôtel du Parc aroused particular indignation.[2] Power and prestige could be measured by hotels. Proximity to Pétain's rooms was a sign of power.[3] The pilot Antoine de Saint-Exupéry, admired by Pétain, was granted the favour of a room in the Hôtel du Parc, though only in the servants' quarters. As Paul Morand clawed his way back into favour after abandoning his post as a diplomat in London in 1940, he moved from the Hôtel de la Paix to the Hôtel des Ambassadeurs.[4]

Almost everyone whose duties took them to Vichy disliked it. Henri Du Moulin de Labarthète, who spent two years there as head of Pétain's *cabinet civil*, wrote that it was 'a derisory, cramped and tawdry provisional capital'.[5] Lucien Rebatet spent two weeks in Vichy as an employee of state radio and wrote: 'Everyone knows that Vichy is an absurd hotchpotch of hammams crowned with vaguely Turkish domes that sum up more or less all the architectural incongruities of the last century.'[6] Alfred Fabre-Luce, who spent a few days there in order to get a book past the censor, described it as 'a cardboard façade'.[7]

Vichy suffered particularly from the comparison with Paris and from the perception that real power still lay in France's pre-1940 capital. On 13 August 1940 Pétain said that Paris, 'the heart and brain of the nation, the forge in which the destinies of the nation are always elaborated, remains for all French people the natural seat of governmental authority'. When Pierre Laval was dismissed from the Vichy government in December 1940, he went to Paris and joined politicians such as Marcel Déat and Jacques Doriot who wanted more explicit collaboration with Nazi Germany. The German authorities subsidized these men and their political groups partly in order to create rivals with whom they could threaten Vichy (though the Paris collaborationists were never overtly hostile to Pétain). Vichy had an official representation in Paris in the form of the Délégation Générale du Gouvernement dans les Territoires Occupés, which was based in the Rue de Grenelle. From December 1940, the delegation was headed by Fernand de Brinon, closely associated with Laval. All French ministries, except that of war, kept some formal presence in Paris and some ministers (particularly those concerned with economic administration) spent much of their time there.

It was the Gaullists in London who gleefully labelled Pétain's government as the 'Vichy regime'. The derogatory connotations of the name became so strong that an English cook book renamed vichyssoise as 'crème gauloise'. The town became France's capital partly by a process of elimination. Many of the most important cities, including Paris, Bordeaux and Tours, which had served successively as the French capital during the *exode* of June, were in the part of France now occupied by the Germans. Lyons and Toulouse were said to be too closely associated with the Radical Party (though Maurice Sarraut, the most powerful Radical in Toulouse, became a prominent Pétainist). Marseilles was considered too dangerous.

Vichy had advantages. It was near the demarcation line that divided the occupied and unoccupied zones of France and it could accommodate the ministers, civil servants and political camp followers who clustered around the new government. It was an orderly town. The spa was neatly divided into three classes (the most luxurious of which offered the 'Zander system' and 'electropathic therapy'). The spa and casino were regulated by the government.

Most of all, the location of the capital city was not supposed to matter, because it was intended to be temporary. Vichy was a summer town (the bathing season lasted from May to September), and in July 1940 no one thought that they would still be there at Christmas. The regime established by the armistice was meant to be ephemeral. Laval told another minister in July that the 'situation' would last six months: 'That is the time needed for Anglo-Saxon belligerence to be ended, either by the defeat of Great Britain or by a compromise peace.'[8] Peace would bring a return of the government to Paris (this was explicitly foreseen in the armistice), the withdrawal of German forces from most of France (though it was obvious that they were not going to leave Alsace-Lorraine and possible that they would not leave parts of northern France), and the drawing up of a new constitution. Pétain was eighty-four when he became head of state. For all the talk of him as a symbol of permanence and solidity, most of his entourage assumed that he was a prestigious expedient designed to conclude the peace, extract France from her present crisis and then retire. The fact that Pétain became the recognized symbol (perhaps the only recognized symbol) of the new regime, and the fact that Vichy remained its capital until 1944, were both signs that the expedient had failed.

THE ESTABLISHMENT OF THE REGIME

Vichy began as the last government of the Third Republic. Pétain had been appointed as Prime Minister by Albert Lebrun, the President of the Republic, and led a cabinet composed largely of politicians who had made their careers before 1940. Most importantly, Pétain's power was underwritten by the Third Republic parliament. The French parliament (or National Assembly) consisted of two chambers: the Chamber of Deputies and the Senate. The Senate, which was slanted to give disproportionate representation to rural constituencies, was considered to be the more conservative of the two. The Chamber of Deputies of 1940 had been elected in 1936 and was dominated by the left, though most of the 72 Communist deputies had been disqualified after the Hitler–Stalin pact. The National Assembly was convoked to Vichy, where it met in the casino. The cabinet agreed on 4 July on a proposition to be put to parliament granting Marshal Pétain full powers to govern and to draft a new constitution. Pierre Laval, deputy for Aubervilliers, who had become deputy Prime Minister on 23 June, put Pétain's case in parliament. On 9 July parliament voted by 625 votes to 4 that the constitution should be revised; the following day parliament voted by 569 to 80, with 17 abstentions, to grant Pétain full powers to revise the constitution. Pétain then issued a series of acts that ended the Republic, made himself head of state, adjourned parliament and appointed Laval as his successor.

The parliamentary votes of July 1940 assumed enormous importance in retrospect. The eighty men who had voted against granting full powers to Pétain were celebrated after the liberation; those who had voted in favour were, in theory, excluded from holding public office, though very large numbers were excused on the grounds of their services to the Resistance. Did the vote really matter so much? From the moment that Pétain called for an armistice, it was clear that a French government would come to terms with the Germans, and coming to terms with the Germans would always have meant the suspension of democracy in France. July 1940 was not the first time that powerful Frenchmen had discussed reforming the Third Republic constitution. André Tardieu and Georges Mandel (the latter an impeccably anti-German and republican figure) had both called for executive powers to be strengthened.

Most importantly, the implications of supporting Pétain in July 1940 were not clear. This was not, for all its subsequent mythology, a vote that divided Pétainists and/or collaborators from resisters. A number of those who voted in favour went on to serve the Resistance in some way – one of them, Joseph Laniel, was a member of the Conseil National de la Résistance. On the other hand, Isidore Thrivier, who had voted against the grant of full powers, later joined Vichy's Conseil National.[9] Certain tendencies can be seen in the votes of French parliamentarians in July 1940. The left was generally more anti-Pétainist than the right. The Socialist Section Française de l'Internationale Ouvrière provided more opponents of voting full powers to Pétain than any other party, though the majority of its members still voted in favour. Parliamentarians from the south and west, whose constituencies were not directly threatened by the Germans, were more willing to vote 'no' than those who came from the north, though the four deputies from Algeria who were present in Vichy all voted 'yes'. Attitudes to the new regime often cut across divisions of party or region. The eleven members of the Independent Republican grouping in parliament included Georges Scapini and Jean Chiappe, both to be dedicated servants of the regime, along with Henri de Kérillis, who went into exile in order to oppose Vichy, and Georges Mandel, who would be put on trial by Vichy and then murdered by its supporters in 1944.[10] One Breton deputy said that he had voted 'yes' on 10 July in order to show the Germans that Bretons were loyal to France; another said that he had voted 'no' for the same reason.[11]

The truth was that parliamentarians in 1940 acted from a wide variety of sometimes contradictory motives. Laval proposed a reform of the constitution in order to fit in with German aims, but Pierre-Étienne Flandin, who was to succeed Laval as Prime Minister in December 1940 and was to pursue an almost equally pro-German policy, argued that giving powers to Pétain would make it easier for him to stand up to the Germans. Charles Spinasse, a Socialist deputy, spoke of parliament's guilt and the need for it to 'crucify itself', but other deputies seem to have had no sense of the gravity of their situation; on 10 July Auguste Chambonnet, senator for the Creuse, asked the president of the Senate if he could borrow his office in order to send postcards to his constituents. This epitome of Third Republic petty mindedness subsequently had a distinguished career in the Resistance.[12]

Vichy was, in the eyes of international opinion, a legal government. It was a neutral state, not a German puppet. More than forty governments (including the Soviet Union) had diplomatic relations with Vichy, and six, the most significant of which was the United States, had embassies there.[13] Vichy broke off diplomatic relations with Britain after British ships sank a large part of the French fleet in the harbour at Mers-el-Kebir in Algeria on 3 July 1940. However, the British did not regard Vichy as illegal, and they did not recognize dé Gaulle as the head of a government until 1944. The British government decided not to stop a Canadian life assurance company from paying Marshal Pétain a pension. Vichy consuls operated in Britain alongside others who regarded themselves as loyal to the Free French. The relationship between the two was sometimes confused. Elizabeth Wiskemann travelled from Spain to Switzerland across southern France in 1941 with a visa stamped in her passport by the Gaullist consul in London: 'Se rend à son poste à la Légation britannique à Berne.'[14] Jean Giraudoux was at first a loyal Pétainist who wrote a book to justify the signing of the armistice, but he continued to correspond, via the diplomatic bag, with his son, who had joined the Free French.[15]

There was no one Vichy government. Not a single minister remained in office for the whole period from 1940 to 1944: the Ministry of Education was headed by six different men during this time. Some of those who had served Vichy most loyally in 1940 were either in the Resistance or in German prisons by the time the regime ended.

The first Vichy government was that in which Pierre Laval served as Pétain's deputy and designated successor: it lasted until Laval's dismissal (of which more below) in December 1940. After Laval's departure, Flandin was appointed as Minister of Foreign Affairs and became the most important figure in the government. Flandin, born in 1889, was a deputy for the Yonne in Burgundy and leader of the Alliance Démocratique, a centre-right party. He did not change Vichy's policy of collaboration with the Germans, though the Germans were suspicious of him and insisted on his dismissal in February 1941.

When Flandin left office, Admiral Jean-François Darlan (born in 1881) was appointed as Pétain's heir and as vice-president of the Council of Ministers. Darlan drew prestige from being the head of the only branch of the French armed forces untouched by the defeat of 1940.[16] The French navy was famous for being right-wing. It recruited mainly from Catholic areas of the west of France and its officers were proud of their service's origins in the *ancien régime*. Darlan was an unusual kind of naval officer, however. He had been born to the purple of Third Republic politics. His father had been a member of the Radical Party, and had served as Minister of Justice. The admiral's own rise owed much to political patronage. He had been careful to maintain good relations with the political left when it was in power and had even urged military intervention on the side of the Republicans during the Spanish Civil War. In 1940, many observers, including some English ones, had believed that Darlan was anglophile and anti-German.[17] In practice, Darlan too continued Vichy's policy of collaboration with the Germans until he himself was displaced as Foreign Minister by Laval's return. Darlan remained Pétain's nominal heir until December.[18]

In April 1942 Pétain was forced to accept Laval's return as 'head of government'. The new title suggested that Laval would be the effective ruler of France. Though Pétain insisted that Laval would work 'under my authority', the wording of his speech was changed in an interesting way between draft to delivery: 'my government' became 'the government'.[19]

PÉTAIN

Pétain was at the centre of the Vichy system. In a speech of 10 November 1940 he said: 'This policy is mine. Ministers are only responsible to me. History will judge me alone.' The regime had no ideological text, no party and no constitution. Loyalty to the regime could only mean loyalty to Pétain, though loyalty to Pétain did not always mean loyalty to the regime. Pétain's rank and age meant that he had no equals and no friends: Weygand shrewdly observed that his heart was 'very open to collective affections ... but closed to individuals'.[20] Weygand himself had suffered from Pétain's fondness for reminding those around him of their subordinate status when Pétain refused to make him a marshal: he pointedly reminded his associates that this was a distinction reserved for victorious generals. Even Pétain's closest confidants were not secure in their positions. Henry Lémery, the senator from Martinique who had done much to construct Pétain's reputation during the 1930s, lasted only a few weeks as Minister for Colonies – though the appointment of a black man to the government, even for so short a period, revealed some of the ways in which Vichy differed from Nazi Germany. General Laure, who served as Pétain's secretary and published an adulatory biography of him in November 1940, was dismissed in 1942 and subsequently arrested by the Germans.

It is significant that Pétain's personal physician, Bernard Ménétrel, came to exercise great influence at Vichy. Ménétrel was in his early forties. An amiable and conventional man, he had followed his father into medicine and established a fashionable practice. He had vague youthful associations with the right, and his father had been a senator, but Ménétrel's influence at Vichy did not depend on knowledge, experience or ideology. His power sprang from the personal affection that Pétain had for him and from his control over physical access to the Marshal.[21]

Members of Pétain's entourage knew that there was something absurd about the old man's image and self-image. He liked to present visitors with a volume of his 'collected thoughts' – 'comme Pascal et les autres'. Even loyal associates laughed at his vanity and philistinism.

Joseph Barthélemy, who served as Minister of Justice from January 1941 to March 1943, recalled a conversation in cabinet. Barthélemy, a devout Catholic, countered a characteristically materialistic argument of Laval's by saying, 'Man does not live by bread alone'; Pétain interrupted: 'Oh, that's a beautiful phrase. Who said it?'[22]

Realism about Pétain's limitations did not prevent his associates from cultivating his public reputation. The Marshal went on brief trips (eight in 1940 and fifteen in 1941) that took him to the most important towns of the southern zone. Newsreels and newspaper reports described the enthusiasm that the Marshal evoked. This is not surprising since journalists were given strict instructions about how Pétain's visits should be described. The reality of his encounters with the French people were more complicated. He himself recognized that the 'mass demonstrations' that greeted him on his first journey (to Toulouse and Montauban, in November 1940) were orchestrated. Often there was an element of farce: the trip to Toulouse revolved around a floral competition in the Hôtel Assezat. It involved Pétain being greeted by an honour guard of horticulturalists with artificial tulips and being declared the patron of flower shows. Soldiers, sailors, veterans, Boy Scouts and priests all played a large part in his public appearances. In Lyons, *anciens combattants* filled the Place des Terreaux whilst the pigeons, which normally occupied the square, circled overhead. Henry Bordeaux, looking down on the thousands of bald heads, said that the scene reminded him of a 'living ossuary'. Churches, public squares in town centres and, most of all, monuments to the dead of the First World War were the most important sites on Pétain's itinerary. Left-wing towns or working-class quarters were not always welcoming. The mood in Toulouse was cooler than that in Montauban. In Lyons, Pétain barely bothered to be polite to municipal officials, mostly men who owed their appointment to the recently dismissed Radical mayor Édouard Herriot. Most striking was his visit to Marseilles in December 1940.[23] This was a city known for crime and for having a large immigrant population. In the previous few months it had also become a place of refuge for Jews and left-wingers, who had fled from the invading Germans and who hoped to get a passage on a ship across the Mediterranean or the Atlantic. The police warned refugees to make no trouble, and closed cafés frequented by Communists. The city's prisons could not hold the twenty thousand people who were taken into preventative detention so the police requisitioned four ships to accommodate their new prisoners.[24]

Pétain's visits varied with time as well as place. In 1940, they had a strongly martial character. As Vichy's subordination to Germany became more blatant, Pétain's visits became more pacific and more likely to stress local folklore rather than military patriotism; young girls in traditional costumes replaced soldiers in uniform.

Pétainism made much of tradition: the Marshal's admirers liked to suggest that his appeal was rooted in a 'real France' that antedated the political institutions of the Third Republic. Oak trees – symbols of age, strength and naturalness – featured large in Pétainist iconography and an oak tree in the Tronçais forest was named the 'Pétain oak'; it was later 'executed' by the Resistance.

In reality, the 'traditions' associated with Pétainism were often dreamed up in a few months. A medal, the Francisque, was designed by Robert Ehret, of the jewellers Van Cleef et Arpels, and given to those who showed special attachment to the Marshal's person and sympathy for the ideas that he represented. Some 2,500 of these were awarded during the life of the regime. René Benjamin, a royalist who had already written admiring books on Mussolini and Maurice Barrès, accompanied the Marshal on some of his travels and wrote three absurdly hagiographic books about him in as many years. Two songwriters, whose previous compositions had included 'Youp par ci et youp par là', wrote 'Maréchal nous voilà' and this, often sung by schoolchildren, became a semi-official anthem of the regime.

Most of all, Pétain communicated with the French through speeches that were broadcast from an improvised studio in two rooms at the Hôtel du Parc. Pétain did not write his own speeches. Sometimes they were composed, at least in part, by men he had never met. Some of his advisers came to feel that they understood the 'Pétain' style better than the Marshal understood it himself. When Pétain wished to deliver a speech that had been composed by Gaston Bergery (a politician from the Radical Party), Du Moulin de Labarthète insisted that it be rewritten on the grounds that 'the word "fallacieux" is not an adjective in your vocabulary'.[25]

The fact that Pétain's image was cultivated by other people did not, however, mean that Pétain himself was not in ultimate control, at least during the early period of his rule. During the first few months of the Vichy regime, those people who might have thought that they would be able to manipulate the Marshal were put in their place. Pétain particularly disliked the notion that anyone might succeed him – which partly accounted for both his hostility to Laval, his officially designated successor, and for his coolness towards the pretender to the French throne, who was tactless enough to discuss the issue of succession during a meeting with Pétain in August 1942.[26]

Pétain's prestige did not remain the same throughout the life of his regime. In 1941 his star began to shine less brightly. It was obvious that he had failed to achieve any of the significant concessions that French people might have hoped from the Germans. Most French prisoners of war were not released, German troops remained on French soil, the division between occupied France and the 'free zone' remained in place and the government continued to be excluded from Paris. On 17 June 1941 Pétain played a recording of the speech that he had made a year previously, and accused the French of having 'short memories'. On 12 August 1941 he recognized that an 'ill wind' was blowing over French public opinion. Revealingly, he also recognized that people who claimed to be loyal to him were not loyal to his government: 'My patronage is invoked too often, even against the government, to justify supposed enterprises of salvation that are, in fact, calls to indiscipline.'

Pétain's image by 1944 was very different from what it had been in 1940. He was more likely to be seen as an expiatory martyr, an image that came easily to devout Catholics,[27] than as a heroic saviour. The word 'chef', leader, appeared less often in his speeches. Just before the liberation, however, large crowds turned out to greet the Marshal in towns that he visited, including Paris. The increasingly blatant way in which the Germans exercised power in France made the French turn against Vichy. Curiously, however, Pétain's apparent weakness often protected him from public disapproval. Increasing German power over Vichy meant that it could be plausibly argued that Pétain was not free to express his real opinions. Laval's return to power made Pétain seem 'above' conventional politics. Jean Guitton was a

Catholic philosopher in a German prisoner of war camp for French officers (a place where the Pétain myth had particular potency); in December 1942 he devised a metahistorical context for the relationship between Pétain and Laval:

> The political leader is a technician of internal and external affairs, he is asked to succeed [it is interesting to note that Pétain was, apparently, not asked to succeed]; if necessary, this role can be undertaken by a foreigner. Example: Mazarin or Disraeli. The national leader incarnates the tradition of the nation. In extreme necessity, he can be a woman or a young girl (Joan of Arc for us). Pétain is above all the national leader. Even supposing that the 'political' function were reduced to a purely administrative function, the national function would remain.[28]

Pétain's forced withdrawal to Germany in August 1944 did not necessarily damage this image. In November 1944 the mayor of the village of Bourgneuf-en-Mauges in the Vendée, a right-wing and Catholic area, refused to take down Pétain's portrait in the town hall. He insisted that Pétain was the 'doyen of prisoners and deportees in Germany'. The government dismissed the mayor, who was then re-elected by 244 of the village's 272 voters.[29]

Where did Pétain's appeal come from? He was born in 1856. His father, already forty years old, was a farmer in Picardy. Pétainist hagiography was later to make much of the way in which his origins rooted Pétain in rural France, but he was unsentimental about his origins, as about almost everything else. His family was relatively poor and life in the countryside was harsh; Charles de Gaulle was later to remark that the Marshal had grown up in the kind of family that cared more about animals than human beings, and that called the vet out more frequently than the doctor.[30] Pétain's mother died young, and he was raised by his father's second wife. Modest circumstances, or lack of enthusiasm for family life, deterred Pétain from marrying until late in life and from having any acknowledged children. Having led the peripatetic life of a professional soldier, he had no particular attachments to his native region, or to anywhere else. He owned a house at Villeneuve-Loubet in the south of France, but had rarely lived there. Life in a suite of hotel rooms between 1940 and 1944 suited him.

As an officer, Pétain rose through the ranks at a steady but unspectacular pace; his career was hampered by his stubbornness, refusal to defer to his superiors and insistence on the importance of defensive warfare at a time when French military orthodoxy stressed the offensive. If it had not been for the First World War, Pétain would have retired with the rank of lieutenant colonel. As it was, he prospered. Trench warfare fitted in with his strategic conceptions. His command during the battle of Verdun became particularly important to his image because troops were rotated there (seventy out of ninety divisions in the French army served at Verdun) so that a large proportion of French veterans had served under him.[31]

After the 1918 armistice, his reputation grew. As other commanders from the First World War died, he came to seem more and more special. The funerals of his former comrades provided him with occasions for the ceremonial public appearances that he enjoyed. George Orwell described Foch's funeral in 1929 being marked by the arrival of 'a tall, lean, very erect figure, though he must have been seventy years old or thereabouts [he was seventy-two], with great spreading moustaches like the wings of a gull', who evoked the murmur of 'voilà Pétain' from the crowd.[32]

Pétain's entourage worked hard to build his reputation. Pétainist mythology made much of the Marshal's reluctance to talk to journalists,[33] but his aides and supporters nurtured contacts with both these groups. Ghostwriters, notably Charles de Gaulle, wrote books to be published under Pétain's name until the Marshal, who read little and wrote almost nothing, was elected to the Académie Française in 1929. Verdun became a symbol of French endurance during the First World War (a gigantic ossuary and memorial was inaugurated there in 1927), which further enhanced the importance of the commander most associated with the battle. People not directly associated with the Marshal helped to build his reputation. Gustave Hervé, a journalist who had originated on the left, launched a campaign in 1935 to draft Pétain as President of the Republic – Pétain ultimately asked for the campaign to be stopped but not before it had collected 35,000 signatures. Hervé stressed Pétain's supposedly republican credentials, and this too became an important part of his image. In 1939 the Socialist leader Léon Blum complained that Pétain, 'our most humane and most republican general', had been sent as ambassador to Franco.

Being France's most republican general was not hard. The French officer corps had been a refuge for those who did not wish to serve the civilian, and more obviously political, branches of the republican state. It drew an important part of its recruits from Jesuit schools. Well-informed observers would have assumed that Charles de Gaulle (a member of a monarchist family and son of a man who had gone into exile rather than accept a job as a history teacher in a secular school) was a long way to the right of Pétain. They might have noted too that the devout Madame de Gaulle refused to call on the divorced Madame Pétain.

SERVANTS OF THE REGIME

In the summer of 1940, Vichy was a huge job market. Political purges created vacancies; the establishment of new institutions created others. The disbanding of parliament, of most of the army, and of part of the diplomatic corps meant that all sorts of people were looking for jobs. Du Moulin de Labarthète claimed later that there were more than a thousand candidates for forty vacancies in the prefectoral corps.[34] The boundary between politics and administration, which had been so important to the Third Republic, blurred. Civil servants took ministerial offices that had formerly been reserved for elected politicians: Yves Bouthillier, for example, moved from being an official in the Finance Ministry to heading it. Elected politicians sought embassies or prefectures to compensate themselves for the loss of their parliamentary salary. The whole nature of office-holding could be strange because a regular place at the Marshal's dinner table could confer more real influence than the highest formal position.[35] Some Pétainists advertised their disdain for ordinary categories of appointment: when Lucien Romier became *ministre d'état*, he referred to himself as *ministre hors d'état* (minister outside the state).

Preferment did not always go to those who expected it. Large numbers of those who had had the highest hopes of the new regime were disappointed. Lucien Rebatet, a right-wing anti-Semite who denounced the Third Republic in savage terms and supported collaboration with Nazi Germany, was sacked from his post in the Vichy radio service after a few weeks.[36] On the other hand, René Belin, who had led France's main trade union confederation during the strikes of 1936, reckoned that he would be lucky to get a job as a village postmaster from the new regime: he was made Minister of Labour.

At least three men who held high office at Vichy had, at first, seriously considered joining de Gaulle in London. In 1940 Jacques Le Roy Ladurie, a right-wing Norman aristocrat and bitter opponent of collaboration with the Germans, got as far as obtaining a pass that would have got him onto a ship bound for England before deciding to stay in France. A friend drove him to Vichy where he bumped into Jacques Guérard, a civil servant and a friend of his brother's, on 5 July. Guérard told him: 'I work with Laval and I am staying at the Hôtel du Parc. There is a room free next to mine . . . There is no bed – you will have to sleep on the floor. If you want it run quickly. Number 62. On the third floor. Same as the Marshal. You will have a ringside seat.'[37] Le Roy Ladurie stayed in touch with Vichy and in 1942 Pétain appointed him as Minister of Agriculture, a job he did for six months before leaving Vichy and joining the Maquis.

François Valentin was a right-wing member of parliament who had joined the army in 1939. On 23 June 1940 he wrote to his wife:

I consider the attitude of the Pétain government to be mad. We are beaten. That, alas, is true. But we must not give in and accept as definitive something that, with a will, may just be temporary. To negotiate is to submit! It is to reinforce Germany against England, our last hope; it is to dishonour ourselves in giving arms to our enemy against our ally. We must hope and thus hold out. First, I will intervene in parliament, an outdated method, but one that I do not want to neglect. If there is still a parliament, there will be a voice to protest. Secondly, if there is a chance to escape to London, I will not let it slip . . . In human and political terms (with open eyes and judging by appearance) I place my faith in two men: Darlan in internal matters, de Gaulle outside France.[38]

Valentin did not go to England and join de Gaulle. He voted full powers to Pétain, and subsequently served the Vichy government faithfully, notably as an official of the Légion Française des Combattants, before he publicly denounced Laval in 1943 and joined the Free French in Algeria.

Hesitation about which side to join in 1940 was epitomized in the person of Jean Borotra, a well-known tennis player. In 1940 he was, at first, convinced that his duty required him to continue the fight against the Germans. He did not, however, want to leave for London without having obtained appropriate authorization from his military superiors. Since he had been taken prisoner by the Germans, Borotra first asked his colonel's permission to escape. He then cycled to the Gironde in order to ask for his demobilization papers from the Ministry of Defence. On 27 June, he obtained the personal authorization of General Weygand to leave the French army and, having been demobilized on 1 July, he finally obtained the approval of Paul Baudouin, the Minister of Foreign Affairs, in Clermont-Ferrand on 2 July. However, shortly after this, the British sank the French fleet at Mers-el-Kebir and Borotra changed his mind about going to London. He subsequently became Vichy Minister for Sport before joining the Maquis in 1943.[39]

All sorts of incongruous people got jobs lower down in the Vichy regime. Georges Pelorson had spent his early life preparing for the horrifically competitive examinations that governed entry to the École Normale Supérieure. In pre-war Paris, he had befriended James Joyce and Samuel Beckett. For two years he taught at Trinity College Dublin, where he came to despise the clericalism and intolerance of the Irish Free State.[40] This bespectacled intellectual was given a job in Vichy's youth organization, responsible for promoting the virtues of fresh air and vigorous physical exercise. The novelist Paul Morand, a famous libertine, wangled himself a job as president of the Commission for Film Censorship – this meant that he was obliged to ban a film for which he had written the script.[41]

Veterans of the Third Republic never entirely disappeared from Vichy. Xavier Vallat, the former conservative deputy who became secretary general for *anciens combattants* and later commissioner for Jewish questions, maliciously pointed out that numerous Vichy ministers and officials had tried and failed to be elected to parliament.[42] The most eminent of these electoral rejects was Raphaël Alibert, the Minister of Justice.

Some of the most loyal Pétainists were former deputies. Jean-Louis Tixier-Vignancour, a conservative deputy, was in charge of propaganda at Vichy. Georges Scapini, who had been blinded in the First World War before entering parliament, became the government's representative to prisoners of war in Germany. There were some absurdities. When Vichy ordered members of those quintessential Third Republic institutions, masonic lodges, to declare themselves, one of the men caught in the net was Marcel Peyrouton, the Minister of the Interior. General Weygand illustrated the contradictions of Vichy's anti-parliamentarianism when he commended Xavier Vallat to Pétain by saying that he was only 'half a parliamentarian (because he had lost an arm and a leg in the [First World] War)'.[43]

The two most important figures in the foundation of the Vichy regime were Pierre Laval and Maxime Weygand. Laval was born in 1883 of humble origins. He rose through academic ability (he studied biology), qualified as a lawyer and became a member of parliament. He opposed the First World War and attended the Zimmerwald peace conference in Switzerland in 1915. He voted against the Versailles Treaty because he considered it too harsh on Germany and, though he moved to the right between the wars, opposition to war remained the most important motif of his career. In the 1930s Laval had worked to prevent conflict between France and her neighbours, particularly Italy. He blamed Britain for his failure. More than anything else, Laval was a talker. He disliked communicating in writing and during the occupation he sometimes forbade people who heard him speak from making notes of what he said. He had huge faith in his ability to persuade men through face-to-face discussion.

Laval urged the National Assembly to sweep away the institutions of the Third Republic and insisted that, if France did not reform itself along the lines of the German or Italian regime, Hitler would do it for them. Laval was at his most aggressive during this period: he exalted power and disdained discussion. It was a position that seemed strange for one who had made his whole career in the French parliament, even stranger when we consider that Laval did not bother with such rhetoric when he returned to power in April 1942, by which time he was more closely associated with support of German interests.

Many believed that Pétain had been manipulated in 1940; that

Laval had tricked the Marshal into a policy that aligned France with Germany. Emmanuel Berl has suggested that it was the other way round. Pétain had manipulated Laval by using him to persuade parliament to vote for its own effective extinction in July 1940. It may well be that Laval manipulated neither Pétain nor parliament; both would probably have acted in the same way without him.[44] Whether there was any conscious manipulation one way or the other, Laval certainly suited Pétain's purposes, not least because his image as a grubby parliamentary politician highlighted Pétain's prestige as a man who stood above such things, and because Laval could be blamed for the most unpopular policies of Vichy.

Initially, Laval mattered to Pétain because he provided a link with parliament. Increasingly, he came to matter because he seemed to provide a link to the Germans. Laval was a friend of Otto Abetz (German representative and eventually ambassador in Paris). Laval was supremely confident in his abilities to reach a deal with Hitler. It is not, however, true, as sometimes suggested, that Laval dealt with Hitler behind Pétain's back. On the contrary, Pétain's initial attempts to arrange a meeting with Hitler took place in August 1940 without Laval's knowledge. Laval himself was due to meet a senior German, the Foreign Minister Ribbentrop, he assumed, on 22 October. Two days before the meeting, Laval learned that he was actually to meet Hitler – he greeted the news with the words 'merde alors'. Hitler was passing through France on his way to his encounter with Franco in Spain. He and Laval met at Montoire, a railway station in south-western France, where Laval suggested that Hitler should meet Pétain. Two days later Pétain and Laval went to Montoire where they met Hitler as he returned from Spain. The meeting produced few concrete results. The French said that they could not declare war on Britain (Laval pointed out that only the dissolved parliament had the power to declare war), but suggested that they might be allowed more freedom in military matters to resist assaults on the French Empire (a combined British and Gaullist force had tried to take Dakar in West Africa the previous month). It was agreed that Laval would have further meetings with the Germans in order to hammer out the details of the agreement, but the Germans repeatedly delayed the proposed meeting, which had still not taken place when Pétain dismissed Laval in December 1940.

Pétain seems to have considered dismissing Laval as early as July. Laval's style – his scruffiness and his habit of blowing smoke in his face – annoyed Pétain, as did his lack of deference. Most importantly, perhaps, Pétain simply disliked the idea that anyone's power might rival his own; he said that Laval had 'done him too many favours'. The dismissal of former parliamentarians from the government in September 1940 weakened Laval's position. His associate Adrien Marquet was removed from the Ministry of the Interior, and a group of conservatives who particularly disliked Laval acquired new influence. Pétain's visit to Toulon and Marseilles in early December strengthened his desire to deal with Laval. He was now more than ever persuaded of his rapport with the French people, and hence of his ability to dispense with a political intermediary. He also saw the remains of the French fleet, and was thus reminded of the independent military power that France still possessed. However, he still hesitated. Laval was keen that Pétain should go to Paris in order to attend the ceremony marking the return of the ashes of Napoleon's son, which had previously been in Vienna. Pétain seemed tempted by the prospect of another triumphal visit during which he would be acclaimed by his loyal subjects. At the last minute members of his entourage persuaded him that the visit was a trap designed to deliver him into German hands. Laval was tricked into resigning at a cabinet meeting on 13 December and then briefly arrested before being rescued by German forces who stormed into the 'free zone' and took him back to Paris. Immediately after Laval's dismissal, Pétain broadcast a speech to the French people stressing that the move was a purely internal matter and had no implications for Franco-German relations.

Weygand's origins could hardly have been more different from Laval's. He was born in 1867 of mysterious, though apparently patrician, origins. He had Belgian nationality until he was twenty-one years old, when a French accountant recognized him as his son. This declaration of paternity seems to have been an expedient to obtain for Weygand the French nationality that he needed to be commissioned into the French army. Neither Weygand nor his biographers ever established who his real father was. It was rumoured that he was a royal bastard[45] and Hitler, who came to hate Weygand, referred to him as a 'renegade Habsburg'. Weygand was a Catholic right-winger.

He had been Foch's aide de camp during the First World War and returned as commander-in-chief of French forces in May 1940, just before France's defeat.

Weygand urged an armistice on France, but he was strongly anti-German. He interpreted the armistice not as a definitive solution of disagreement between France and Germany but rather as a truce designed to make France better equipped to fight Germany in the future – men such as Weygand liked to compare France's position in 1940 to that of Prussia after its defeat at Jena in 1808. Weygand's notoriously anti-German sentiments encouraged the government to appoint him, in September 1940, as delegate to Algeria, where he was able to train an army without much German interference. A year later, unwilling to support Vichy concessions to Germany, he returned to France. In November 1942, when the Americans invaded Algeria, Weygand asked Pétain to call on French troops to support the Americans. Pétain refused and, on his way back from the meeting, Weygand was kidnapped and imprisoned by the Gestapo.

Beneath their soldierly exteriors, Pétain and Weygand were very different. Weygand, who said that reading Corneille's *Le Cid* for the first time was one of the most moving experiences of his life, had emotional depths that would have been alien to Pétain. Weygand's political sympathies were stronger and more openly displayed than Pétain's. In the aftermath of the Dreyfus case, Weygand had been punished for giving money to support Dreyfus's accuser; Pétain, who probably believed Dreyfus to be innocent, had made no public statement on the matter. Weygand had rarely exercised command: de Gaulle gibed that he was a 'brilliant number two', while Pétain was completely at home with the loneliness of power. In spite of all this, Weygand was a loyal Pétainist; he was to preside over the Association pour Défendre la Mémoire du Maréchal Pétain after the war. Pétain's position with regard to Weygand was, as ever, ambiguous. He seems to have been happy for the general to be removed from mainland France in 1940, and did not protest very energetically about his later arrest.

Weygand was a soldier who despised parliament, Laval a parliamentarian who spent much of his life in conflict with the army (he had himself been excused military service on account of varicose veins).

The two men disliked each other, but they had important things in common. Both were anti-Communist. Weygand had led the French military mission to Poland during that country's war with the Soviet Union in 1920, and fear of Communism seems to have played a part in his desire to seek an armistice in 1940. Laval had also turned against Communism during the inter-war years. In June 1942 he said that he hoped for German victory because 'without her, Bolshevism would soon be established everywhere in Europe'. Interestingly, the two men drew opposite conclusions from their anti-Communism. In his last conversation with Laval, just before his own arrest by the Germans, Weygand argued that Laval's policy of collaboration would leave the way open for Communism in France.

Though Weygand and Laval disagreed about both internal and external policy, they shared a belief that external policy should take precedence over internal. Laval liked the Third Republic but was willing to see it suspended in 1940, if that eased a reconciliation with Germany. Weygand disliked the Third Republic but had been willing to serve it when, as during the First World War, it had been the most effective means of uniting Frenchmen against Germany. Similarly, although the two men disagreed about Franco-German relations, they saw those relations in similar terms. Both were obsessed with the consequences of the peace that had been imposed on Germany by the victorious allies after the First World War. Weygand had announced the terms of the armistice to the German generals at Rethondes, and continued to use the battered briefcase that had once contained this document for the rest of his life. Subsequently, Weygand supported Foch's campaign to make the terms of the peace treaty harsher. Laval, by contrast, had voted against the Treaty of Versailles because he believed that it was too harsh. What both men shared was a belief that Franco-German relations in 1940 could still be understood in the terms that had been used to explain Franco-German relations immediately before and after the First World War. Neither man had much sense of the novelty of Nazism.

All who held office at Vichy were Pétainists in the sense that they drew their authority from the Marshal. They could, however, deploy that authority in very different ways. In his most notoriously collaborationist speech (that of June 1942 in which he expressed hope for German victory), Pierre Laval insisted: 'I speak in his [Pétain's] name.' Six months later Darlan insisted that he was acting in the Marshal's name, and fulfilling the Marshal's secret wishes, when he made a deal with American forces in North Africa and urged Frenchmen to take up arms against Germany.

There was probably a degree of conscious duplicity in the words of Laval and Darlan, though their credentials as representatives of Pétain mattered to those whose support they were trying to enlist. Some servants of the regime, however, seem to have been perfectly sincere. The conflict between sincere but different, and mutually hostile, forms of Pétainism can be seen in the history of the Légion Française des Combattants. The Légion was the most important movement established by Vichy. It was founded in 1940 to group war veterans, and to replace the divided and overtly politicized veterans' leagues of the inter-war period. The Légion was, in theory, open to veterans of both wars. In practice it appealed more strongly to veterans of the First. Its membership was relatively old and its leaders were often drawn from amongst established local notables. The ideology was conservative and patriotic. Its leaders were intensely loyal to Pétain but also often anti-German. As Vichy became increasingly implicated in collaboration with Germany, and especially after the return of Laval to power in April 1942, légionnaires became uneasy. Many resigned from the movement or simply ceased to carry out their functions. François Valentin, the man who had come so close to joining de Gaulle in 1940 and a leader of the Légion, was particularly hostile to Laval. His response to this was to lay ever heavier emphasis on loyalty to Pétain: 'The arrival of Pierre Laval in the government need pose no problem to the légionnaires ... there is only one watchword ... preserve at all costs our unity against the ambitions, hastiness and immoderate initiatives' (these last three phrases were coded references to Lavalist policies). 'On the general level, the watchword remains, confidence in the Marshal.' In June 1942 Valentin left the leadership of the Légion (it is hard to know how far his departure had been brought about by Laval). Once again, he stressed his Pétainism: 'At the moment when I leave the post in which I have had the honour of serving since September 1940, my first duty is to express my unchanging gratitude to the Marshal for the confidence that he has always shown in me ... More than ever unite around the Marshal and the leaders that he chooses for you.' Finally, Valentin turned against the Vichy government and issued a call, broadcast by the BBC in August 1943, for *légionnaires* to support the Resistance. Valentin's call contained no direct reference to either Pétain or de Gaulle. The only politician mentioned by name was Pierre Laval, who was violently attacked.[46]

Valentin's disenchantment with the Légion, and with Vichy in general, ran parallel to the rise of Joseph Darnand. Darnand, born in 1897, led the Légion Française des Combattants in the Alpes-Maritimes. At the end of 1941 he founded a Service d'Ordre Légionnaire that drew younger recruits and adopted more muscular policies than its parent organization. In January 1943 the SOL was transformed into the Milice which quickly became a paramilitary force designed to fight against the Resistance. Darnand epitomized much of what conservatives such as Valentin disliked. He joined the SS in the summer of 1943 and consequently took an oath of personal loyalty to Hitler. Members of the Légion came increasingly to define their ideology in explicit opposition to that of Darnand and his associates. In December 1943 a senior member of the Légion issued a circular in which he emphasized how different his own movement was from both the Milice and the Légion des Volontaires Français contre le Bolchevisme (a unit of Frenchmen fighting with the Germans on the Eastern Front): 'At a moment when some leaders of the Milice sign on to serve under the authority of foreign leaders, we must, more than ever, establish as clear a distinction as possible between ourselves and the *miliciens*, whose conceptions differ from ours as much as those of the Gaullists and the Giraudists.' The circular concluded that 'in matters of foreign policy we set ourselves the task of following the Marshal blindly'.[47] However, though conservatives defined their Pétainism in terms of an opposition to Darnand, Darnand never ceased to think of himself as a Pétainist. His German allegiances did not prevent him from holding office at Vichy (where he became responsible for maintaining order). Furthermore, Darnand's collaboration was, in some ways, rooted in similar beliefs to those that impelled Valentin to resistance. Darnand was a royalist from an intensely Catholic background (one of his sisters had become a Trappist nun);[48] he had little in common with Laval's opportunism or Déat's secularism. Most importantly, Darnand had wept when Pétain in person had pinned the *médaille militaire* onto his chest on 20 July 1918, and his personal loyalty to the Marshal was as intense as that of conservatives who left the government in 1942 and 1943. On 6 August 1944 Pétain finally wrote a letter of complaint to Laval about the conduct of the Milice in which he commented on the 'tortures often inflicted on innocent people in places that, even in Vichy, seem less like prisons of the French state than those of Bolshevik Chekas'. Darnand felt betrayed by this letter. He wrote to Pétain: 'For four years, I have received your congratulations and your compliments; you encouraged me. And today, because the Americans are at the gates of Paris, you start to tell me that I am going to be a stain on history.'[49]

VICHY IN INTERNATIONAL CONTEXT

Where did Vichy fit into international political alignments? There were some at Vichy (especially during the summer of 1940 and then again after the end of 1942) who regarded the German or Italian regimes with admiration. However, there were at least an equal number who regarded Germany, the traditional enemy of French nationalism, with distaste. Even amongst French people who admired Germany, some found its regime to be inappropriate to France or regarded Hitler as absurd. Others looked west rather than east. Antonio Salazar's Portugal, an authoritarian but not totalitarian or even completely undemocratic state, was probably the single regime that was most often cited as a model by Pétainists, particularly because Salazar himself had drawn inspiration from French royalists. But different kinds of lessons could be drawn from Salazar. Portugal was, along with Germany and Italy, a model for those who wanted to create a single-party state. But Salazar could also be a different kind of model for those who wanted to resist political violence and avoid alignment with Nazi Germany. Supporters of Vichy found other possible models all over Europe. A number of men who held office at Vichy had been associated with the *Nouveaux Cahiers* group of the late 1930s. The *Nouveaux Cahiers* had hailed Sweden as an example of a country that had learnt to live within its modest means and renounced the painful striving to be a great power. Pétain himself said in 1940 that he regarded the Swiss constitution as an ideal,[50] and Switzerland was to be important to Pétainists, if only because so many of them sought refuge there after 1945. Some Pétainists looked to Ireland as an example of a corporatist, Catholic state[51] – though, as has been pointed out, Georges Pelorson, the Pétainist who knew the Irish Free State best, despised it.

The single most important country in Pétainist imagination was the United States. The Rue des États-Unis ran past the Hôtel du Parc and, unlike some Vichy streets, it kept its name throughout the period from 1940 to 1944. France's self-image in the inter-war years had often been defined in contrast to America. Pétainists had often seen Americanization as a threat to French traditions. Pétain's adviser, Lucien Romier, had published a book in 1927 entitled *Who Will Be Master, Europe or America?* Yet after 1940 Pétainists knew that America mattered hugely to their country. It was the most important of their diplomatic partners. It mattered, first, as a source of food and then as a potential broker of a compromise peace (a few at Vichy continued to believe in the possibility of such a peace until the summer of 1944).

The American embassy in Vichy was a strange place and became all the more so after Hitler declared war on the United States in December 1941. Men such as 'Woody' Wallner, and 'Doug' Mac-Arthur II, the nephew of the general, spent their time swimming, playing tennis or drinking cocktails. Wartime Vichy was excruciatingly dull for east coast patricians who had spent most of their career in European capitals. After April 1942, the embassy was run by Pinkney Tuck, the chargé d'affaires. Tuck, a career diplomat, was a conservative and seems to have been anti-Jewish (he opposed American recognition of Israel). However, like many French anti-Semites, Tuck was appalled by evidence of Nazi atrocities against the Jews in the autumn of 1942 and tried to get American visas for Jewish children in France. His efforts were thwarted by the German invasion of the southern zone. By the time the Germans arrived at Vichy, the American embassy contained only a couple of junior officials who had been left behind to shut up shop before being interned in Baden-Baden.[52]

It is probably wrong to look for much ideological coherence in

American attitudes to Vichy. The general tone of American policy can be deduced from the code names that Americans used for French affairs: Pétain was 'Popeye', Laval was 'black Peter' and France in general was 'the Frog pond'.[53] American policy was mainly directed towards the practical matter of ensuring that French resources were not deployed against the Allies, and bolstering what the Americans took to be anti-German elements at Vichy. To this end, they sent William Leahy, a sixty-four-year-old admiral, to be their ambassador to Vichy. Leahy was a brisk conservative who spoke almost no French and judged men mainly on whether or not they looked their interlocutors in the eye. Leahy's particular concern was to prevent the remainder of the French fleet from falling into German hands. The Americans also wished to persuade some eminent French figure to establish an anti-German government in French North Africa and, initially, they hoped that Weygand might undertake this task.

Pétain was believed to have had good relations with American soldiers during the First World War and had been well received during an official visit that he made to the United States in 1931.[54] The only interview that Pétain accorded to a foreign newspaper during his time as head of state, scripted by Du Moulin de Labarthète, was given to the *New York Times*. His admirers believed that his opinions would still be taken seriously in Washington. An important part of Pétainist thinking revolved around the idea that there was a gap between the British and the Americans and that Pétain would be able to exploit this gap. This belief persisted even after the Americans invaded French North Africa. In his 1943 biography of Pétain, René Benjamin recognized that the Marshal faced many problems, but implied that good relations with America might provide him with an escape from some of these: 'The Marshal thinks of Admiral Leahy.'[55]

NATIONAL REVOLUTION

Men at Vichy talked of conducting a 'Révolution Nationale'. It was a phrase that had been circulating in French political discussion since at least 1933.[56] It implied a radical reform of French institutions that would be different from the international revolution proposed by the

Socialists and Communists. Beyond this, however, the words were open to an almost infinite variety of interpretations. Almost all Vichy projects were subject to considerable disagreement and almost none came to fruition.

The first attempt at reform in Vichy France concerned political parties. A committee of seventy-two politicians drew up a proposal for the creation of a single party. Half the committee's members came from the pre-war right and half from the pre-war left, though it was three members of the latter group – Marcel Déat, a former Socialist, Jacques Doriot, a former Communist, and Gaston Bergery, a former Radical – who were most prominent. The single party failed. This was partly because its promoters could not agree amongst themselves, and also because Pétain was not willing to support it. The battle over the creation of a single party can be seen partly as a battle between 'fascists', who were sympathetic to Nazi Germany and fascist Italy, and traditional conservatives, who wanted a specifically French way. It could also be seen as a battle between men whose pre-war careers had been in party politics, and who assumed that the future must involve a party of some kind, and those authoritarians drawn from outside parliament who wanted to do away with parties altogether.

During Flandin's reign another sort of political reform was launched. A law of 22 January 1941 established a Conseil National to represent the 'living forces of the nation'. The Conseil National contained notables ranging from Pastor Boegner, France's most senior Protestant, to Claude Gignoux, pre-war leader of the main French industrial association; 78 of its 188 members had been members of parliament. Pétain disliked the Conseil, perhaps because of its parliamentarianism. The Conseil never met in full session but its various commissions did meet. The most important of these prepared a constitution that revolved around two councils of notables operating under the head of state. The constitution was finished at the end of 1941 but never put into effect.

Vichy also wanted to reform the economy. National unions and national employers' associations were dissolved. Complicated corporate structures were forbidden. Pétainists aimed to replace an impersonal capitalism of class conflict and exploitation with something that bound workers and employers together. Conservative Catholics and fascists had both used the word 'corporatist' in the 1930s and many at Vichy now wanted to implement a corporatist system. They did not, however, agree on what corporatism meant in practice. Belin, the Minister of Labour, wanted to preserve separate unions for employers and workers at local level, whilst creating corporations to bring the two together at national level. Conservatives wanted to impose corporations at all levels. The dispute became so heated that one of Belin's drafts was snatched from the printing press and destroyed by his opponents. A Labour Charter was eventually promulgated in October 1941. In practice, however, neither employers nor workers showed much interest in corporatism: of the twenty 'professional families' foreseen by the Labour Charter, only three had been established by 1944.

In part, the problem with the National Revolution lay in the diversity of Vichy's ideological origins. Most, though not all, who held office at Vichy came from the political right. However, the right in the Third Republic had been a kaleidoscope of parties that sometimes both overlapped with each other and denounced each other. New political parties had sprung up in the late 1930s. Sometimes a single individual had more than one affiliation. Pierre Pucheu, Vichy Minister of Industrial Production and, later, of the Interior, moved from the Parti Social Français (a conservative grouping that made much of war veterans) to the Parti Populaire Français (a more radical grouping led by an ex-Communist that came to define itself as fascist).

The most cited political thinker at Vichy was probably Charles Maurras. Maurras, born in Provence in 1868, had come to political prominence after the Dreyfus case, when he urged his compatriots to restore the monarchy, to give greater power to the regions and to increase the influence of the Catholic Church. The movement that he led, Action Française, had a considerable influence in the 1930s, particularly through the newspaper of the same name; a number of those who held office at Vichy, notably Raphaël Alibert, the Minister of Justice, had been members of Action Française.

However, Vichy was not a Maurrassian regime and it is not clear that anyone, including Maurras, would have been able to say what exactly a Maurrassian regime would be. Pétain respected Maurras, but, according to his own *chef du cabinet*, had probably not read more than twenty pages of his work. Pétain was not a monarchist, a fact his monarchist admirers were careful to stress. Maurras's interests in practical politics had always been surprisingly limited. He had never made great efforts to place his followers in positions of power or to influence their actions if they got there, and he visited Vichy only four times. Maurras's ability to communicate with his own followers was hampered by the fact that he had been deaf since the age of fourteen. Furthermore, in some ways, the defeat and the advent of the Vichy government made Action Française less influential rather than more. Maurras himself moved to Lyons, and this deprived him of the éclat that he had possessed in Paris: Philippe Ariès complained that the Action Française newspaper now seemed 'old and provincial'.[57]

In any case, the very ubiquity of Maurrassian influence meant that it was difficult to associate it with any one course of action. In the inter-war period, almost every conservative bourgeois Frenchman had read *Action Française*. Yet few of them supposed that the movement was associated with a precise and realizable programme. There were obvious absurdities in Maurrassianism. A movement that purported to revolve around the restoration of the French monarchy was led by men who were on bad terms with the pretender to the French throne. A movement that purported to wish to restore Catholicism to power in France was led by a man who had lost his religious faith as a teenager, and who published a newspaper that had been on the Vatican's index of forbidden reading between 1926 and 1939.

What most people took from Maurrassianism was a general tone of disdain for the parliamentarianism of the Third Republic rather than a precise project. This tone of disdain could merge with support for Vichy but it could equally well lead in other directions. Some Maurrassians were influenced by the anti-Semitism and verbal violence of the movement in ways that took them into outright support for the Germans. Lucien Rebatet and Robert Brasillach both belonged to this group, and both men ended up in Paris during the occupation, pouring out vitriol against their former comrades from Action Française. Other Maurrassians were influenced by the strong current of anti-German nationalism in Action Française. A number of early Resistance leaders had been Maurrassians, as had, to some extent, Charles de Gaulle. Maurras himself supported Vichy, but anti-Germanism remained important in his thinking.

Maurrassianism was not the only set of ideas to influence Vichy. Many conservative republicans also supported the regime. These people did not regard the revolution of 1789, or even the foundation of the Third Republic in 1875, as bad things in themselves, but they had often been alarmed by the rise of the left during the 1930s, and particularly by the strikes and disorder that accompanied the election of a Popular Front government in 1936. Such people were often graduates of the École Libre des Sciences Politiques (designed to train French diplomats) or professors of law. Some of their positions were, in theory, diametrically opposed to those of Maurras. They believed in the rule of law where Maurras had denounced the artificiality of the *pays légal*; some of them had worked for Franco-German reconciliation during the inter-war years.[58]

A third group of men at Vichy might be described as the 'modernizers'. They were marked by training at France's elite *grandes écoles* (particularly the École Polytechnique engineering school) and had often worked for large-scale industrial enterprises before 1940. Some of them had been involved in the discussion circles that flourished during the 1930s: the *Centre des Jeunes Patrons*, *Nouveaux Cahiers* or *X Crise*. The divisions between the three groups at Vichy – traditionalists, liberals and modernizers – were never clear-cut. Many people belonged to more than one group or did not fit neatly into any. In the end, the one thing that all at Vichy had in common was failure. None of the projects put forward by any of the groups described above was implemented. In part, this failure was linked to the very disparity of Vichy's politics. Grand projects for reform ended up being buried under acrimonious squabbles in committees.

Failure was also rooted in the circumstances of the war. Long-term projects for the rebuilding of France only made sense when the regime itself seemed likely to have a long life. As German defeat loomed, this prospect receded. Furthermore, Vichy was discussing long-term construction at a time when most French people were concerned with short-term survival. Germany exercised ever greater influence whilst Pétainists sought authentically French solutions. Sometimes pragmatic schemes, devised in haste and without explicit ideological associations, proved to have more real effect than the reforms by which Vichy set such store. Thus, for example, the organization committees, established in August 1940, and the supply mechanisms for raw materials, established the following month, had more impact on the French economy than the Labour Charter. Similarly, the 'regional prefects', civil servants appointed by central government to coordinate administration across several departments, mattered more than Vichy's attempts to create regional identities that would be rooted in folklore and customs.

Pétain himself disliked the phrase 'national revolution',[59] and only used it four times in public. At his trial in 1945, Laval dismissed the ideological ambitions of the regime that he had served thus: 'I never knew what the national revolution was, it was never defined and it was an expression that personally I never used ... Everyone put his own desire, ideal and the regime that he saw into these words, but the national revolution was never defined in any form at any time.'[60] 'National revolution' was a phrase used by intellectuals. It appealed to men brought up on the grand abstractions that floated in the higher reaches of the French education system. Pétain was surrounded by men who thought in terms of principles and theories, but Pétain's own thinking was rooted in the pragmatism of an infantry officer – his most celebrated pre-1940 maxim was 'le feu tue' (gunfire kills).

Proponents of the 'national revolution' covered huge amounts of paper. They drew up explicit and detailed schemes for the reconstruction of France. Pétain, by contrast, was notable for saying nothing (or nothing of significance). Pétainism was a matter of style rather than clearly worked out schemes. Pétain's appeal revolved around apparently small matters of personal appearance and bearing (he was proud of his blue eyes and careful to keep his kepi on to hide his bald head). Pétain's admirers made much of his taciturnity, which they contrasted with the chattering of the leaders of the Third Republic: 'What is most moving about him is his silence';[61] 'he has never ceased to govern his feelings in silence';[62] 'this taciturnity which shows energy and firmness';[63] 'governed for centuries by lawyers, France expects much of this man of few words'.[64] Pétain himself lauded silence, and said on 9 October 1940: 'If it [the government] says nothing, it is because it is working.' As time went on, he said less and less. His speeches after the end of 1942 were notably shorter than those of his first two years in power. His silence went with ambiguity. By not identifying himself too precisely with particular projects he avoided being discredited when those projects failed.

Maurice Martin du Gard observed the gulf between Pétain and those who claimed to promote the 'national revolution' in his name:

It is curious to observe the delegates of the Marshal in the provinces; there are young Catholics who employ a revolutionary vocabulary and whose violence, one feels, will remain purely verbal; others also denounce the big economic interests [trusts], but if they attack the freemasons, they [also] enthusiastically attack priests. They are impatient to act, while the art of Philippe Pétain is precisely that of not acting.[65]

POPULAR PÉTAINISM?

In the summer of 1940 Pétain seemed enormously popular. Letters of support, gifts and proposals to help poured into the Hôtel du Parc. Towns all over France (122 in the department of the Meuse alone) named streets after the Marshal.[66] Knowing how to interpret such expressions of loyalty is, however, more difficult than it might seem at first glance. They involved many people but these did not come near to being a majority of the French population. Much of what we know about 'public opinion' under Vichy comes from an unrepresentative sample of people who made public statements – parliamentarians, journalists, priests – or from those who kept diaries. Even within this privileged circle, assessing opinion is difficult. People did not think of their own conduct in the terms – resistance, collaboration, Pétainism – that have been used by historians.

Jean Guéhenno wrote in February 1941: 'What genius historians of the future will need to recognize the real causes and motives . . . in these texts, these communiqués, in which not a word is exact or sincere.'[67] Historians have become ever more aware of the complexities of opinion under Vichy. They have devised new words to describe the positions that people adopted. They have distinguished collaborationism (ideological commitment to the German cause) from *collaboration d'état* (a belief that helping the Germans in certain ways might further French interests). They have devised the term *maréchalo-résistant* to describe those who combined hostility to the Germans with loyalty to the head of state. They have divided the evolution of public opinion into short phases (one writer suggests six or seven of them[68]) rather than depicting a simple move from Pétainism to resistance.

Much of what people said and did under Vichy, however, remains inscrutable. This is true even of the elite, whose words and deeds were often recorded. Consider, for example, one of the most public ways in which people expressed 'support' for Vichy: swearing an oath of loyalty to Pétain. Oaths of loyalty were required of most public servants. Very few refused to take them. In the French judiciary, only one man, Paul Didier, said 'I refuse to swear' when judges were asked to take the oath in 1941. Didier was dismissed, briefly interned and subsequently kept under house arrest, though, unlike some magistrates who had taken the oath, he did not join the Resistance. The very fact that oaths were required of public servants meant that many people took them while expressing vigorous private hostility to the regime; this was true of schoolteachers such as Simone de Beauvoir or Jean Guéhenno. Far from marking an acceptance of the regime, swearing the oath could provide people with a chance to define, if only to themselves, the limits of their loyalty. Bernard Lecornu, a prefect, recalls travelling to Angers in the spring of 1942 to take the oath of loyalty, along with other prefectural officials from the area, in front of the regional prefect (who had himself taken the oath in front of Pétain).[69] On the way, Lecornu met Ivan Labry, an official from Nantes. The two men dined together and discussed the significance of the ceremony in which they were about to participate. Neither was an unconditional supporter of the regime. Lecornu explained his own position thus: 'In my opinion . . . the prefectural corps need feel all the less obliged to obey because Marshal Pétain, in his speech of 1 January, has talked of the "semi-liberty" in which he finds himself . . . Does not that phrase authorize us in advance to sabotage all instructions that the government gives under the pressure of the circumstances?'[70]

Increasingly, the swearing of oaths to Pétain became an object of struggle amongst different kind of Pétainists.[71] Consider, for example, the difference between the Légion Française des Combattants, which represented mainly a conservative and patriotic form of Pétainism, and its offshoot the Service d'Ordre Légionnaire (SOL), which had a younger membership and more radical politics. The oath taken by men who joined the Légion was relatively vague and, as the Légion became increasingly alienated from Vichy, its leaders stressed that their oath bound them 'only to the head of state, who represents the nation'.[72] The oath taken by members of the SOL, by contrast, was extremely detailed, and bound its members on twenty-one specific points, including a commitment to be against 'Gaullist dissidence' and 'Jewish leprosy'.[73]

Officials from the Scapini Mission, which watched over the interests of prisoners of war, attempted to administer an oath to those prisoners who were repatriated to France: 'Marshal, you have shown us an example by making a gift of your person to France. We, the prisoners of war who owe you our liberty, swear to obey you and to follow you come what may.' Personal loyalty to Pétain seems, in this case, to have been a means of distancing prisoners of war from other elements in the Vichy government. The officials of the Scapini Mission resisted attempts to insert references to Laval, or Laval's protégé, André Masson, into the oath.[74]

People judged the regime in the light of what they knew, or thought they knew, about the wider circumstances that governed its action, and their information was often false. Even well-informed people were buffeted by rumours about the war. Charles Rist was an economist and banker who had regular contact with German authorities and good relations with some at Vichy; he was almost made ambassador to Washington. He believed that Jacques Doriot was dead (in November 1942), that the Tehran conference had failed (in December 1943), that Hitler had joined a Japanese suicide cult (in July 1944) and that the Germans would round up all French males over ten years old (in August 1944).[75] Edmond Duméril, an academic who served as an official interpreter linking the prefecture of Nantes with the German authorities, believed in 1940 that the Montoire meeting had been imposed on Pétain after he refused Laval's policy of closer co-operation with Hitler.[76] The writer Louis Guilloux wrote that a friend had told him, apparently in all seriousness, that Adolf Hitler had been seen buying fish in the market at Saint-Brieuc.[77]

Paris police compiled reports on political rumours. On 1 May 1941 it was said that various parliamentarians in Paris believed that a separate peace was to be signed (presumably one between France and Germany), and that if this did not happen a Pétain government would be established in Paris. On 8 May *agents de change* were said to believe that Bouthillier's departure as Minister of Finances was inevitable. On 9 May the mayor of Boulogne-Billancourt was said to believe that all Socialist mayors were to be dismissed. On 12 May it was said that Laval was to establish a government in Paris with Pétain being based at Versailles. On 13 May it was said that Darlan was to re-establish the Radical Party in the southern zone. On 14 May it was said that Hitler was about to visit Paris and that he would meet Pétain and agree to release 300,000 prisoners. None of the events anticipated in these rumours happened.[78]

How people judged the Vichy regime depended particularly on how they understood the relation between Pétain and Laval. This relation involved a high degree of uncertainty. The rumour of April 1941 that Pétain's view of Laval 'changed day by day according to whom he had spoken to most recently'[79] probably contained a large element of truth. Shifting relations between Pétain and Laval did not necessarily mean changes in government policy. Pétain shared Laval's view about the need to co-operate with the Germans and this remained the key to Vichy policy. However, French conservatives often believed that there was a wide gulf between Pétain and Laval, that Laval had imposed collaboration on Pétain,[80] and that Laval's dismissal meant a renunciation of it.

Liliane Schroeder, an anglophile bourgeois Parisian girl, wrote in her diary on 10 January 1941:

Marshal Pétain, in spite of his great age, would have the right to a chapter all by himself. He fights his corner [*se défend*] calmly ... with a diplomatic skill that many younger brains have never had and will never have. About a month ago, a plot having been discovered, he sacked Pierre Laval, the man of the Germans. A high-ranking enemy personality went to Vichy with an armed escort to threaten, shout, order. Faced with the threat of a total occupation of France, the Marshal replied: 'If it takes you five days to invade France, it would take me five minutes to deliver my colonies and my fleet to Great Britain'; a striking argument that makes one think.[81]

Henri Drouot's diary reflects attitudes to Pétain in a particularly interesting way. Drouot was a university professor in Dijon. Bourgeois, Catholic, patriotic, anti-Semitic and anti-German, he had the characteristics that would normally be associated with a certain variety of Pétainism. In fact, however, he was almost unfailingly hostile to Pétain. In October 1940 he wrote: 'The Marshal continues to "give himself to France, and France to Hitler".'[82] A week later he was willing to concede that Pétain had an equivocal attitude to the Germans and that 'a morsel of French dignity remains in him'.[83] After Laval's dismissal, Drouot experienced a brief moment of enthusiasm for the head of state: 'The cunning Laval has been dismissed by the brave and unfortunate Marshal who has asked the great Flandin to replace him.'[84] Six weeks later Drouot had lost faith again and wrote that France proceeded 'with Pétain for the complete realization of Laval's policy'.[85]

Laval's return to power in April 1942 disgusted many Pétainists. Some now supported de Gaulle or the Resistance. However, some managed to square this with continued personal loyalty to Pétain. In May 1943 the leader of the highly Pétainist Légion Française des Combattants in Switzerland wrote:

It is a fact that the foreign policy of Laval displeases the whole nation; it is also a fact that people believe that the Légion supports this policy, hence the disaffection with regard to the Légion. This is why I constantly recall to the Swiss Union that the Légion is only a civic organization and not a political one ... that the *légionnaire* has the right to think what he likes, that he consequently has the right to judge the French dissidence favourable to France ... Two policies are necessary for France: one, that which the Marshal, faced with the occupier, follows and that lays the basis for a rebirth; the other, that which the dissidence employs to deliver us.[86]

People fitted their views of Vichy into a variety of international perspectives. Curiously, the key division here did not concern Germany since most French people, including most Pétainists, were anti-German in the sense that they would have preferred Germany to lose the war. The most important foreign policy division of the 1930s had concerned Italy. Italy had been France's ally during the First World War and the fascist regime in Italy seemed to pose no threat to French interests. A large part of the French right resented the imposition of sanctions by the League of Nations on Italy after her invasion of Abyssinia in 1935. They believed that this had driven Mussolini into the arms of Hitler. In 1940 the British journalist Alexander Werth wrote:

After 1934 France could roughly be divided into a pro-British half and a pro-Italian half. Though the British alliance was nominally accepted by everybody, a large body of opinion, especially on the Right, disliked England. The wildest anti-British outburst during these years was Henri Béraud's article in *Gringoire* in October 1935, 'England must be reduced to slavery'.[87]

If we accept Werth's division, then, in terms of high politics, the summer of 1940 saw the triumph of the 'Italian party' in the person of Pierre Laval. In terms of public opinion, however, things were different. The French were bitterly anti-Italian in the summer of 1940. They resented Italy's belated declaration of war and the 'unearned' gains that she had made at French expense. Many believed that Italian planes had strafed columns of French refugees during the *exode*. Italian military reverses of 1941 were the occasion for many cruel jokes in France.[88] Anglophobia was less common than either Vichy or German propagandists liked to think – many French conservatives had, after all, spent the previous two decades celebrating the virtues of every English institution from public schools to the House of Lords. The commissions set up by Gaston Bergery to investigate the state of opinion in 27 French departments reported that 80 per cent of the population wanted a British victory.[89]

One incident above all affected French views of the British. The British were determined that French ships should not fall into German hands. Those in British harbours were boarded and seized, their sailors being mainly repatriated to France. The largest concentration of French ships, however, was in the Algerian port of Mers-el-Kebir. On 3 July Admiral Somerville approached the French fleet and insisted that it should either join the British and let the British take control of its ships or leave its ships disarmed in a French port in the West Indies (perhaps under American control). When the French admiral Marcel-Bruno Gensoul rejected these demands, the British opened fire. They sank the battleship *Bretagne* and badly damaged the *Provence* and the *Dunkerque* (the latter's name was an awkward reminder of the fact that French troops had recently covered the retreat of their British comrades). The British had fired on the ships of a country with which they were not at war, one with which they had been allied only a fortnight previously. They had refused to trust French officers, though in fact no French ship was ever handed over to the Germans, and the *Strasbourg*, which had managed to escape from Mers-el-Kebir, was scuttled along with most of the rest of the French fleet in Toulon in November 1942. Most importantly, the British killed over 1,200 French sailors.

Mers-el-Kebir had important but complicated effects on French public opinion. Some people found reports of the incident hard to believe. Some turned, for a time at least, against the British. Jules Roy, who had previously been very anti-Pétainist, wrote in his diary on 5 July: 'Between Churchill and Pétain my choice is made.'[90] Antoine de Saint-Exupéry was also shocked by Mers-el-Kebir. Though it did not lead him to support Vichy, it does seem to have contributed to his decision to go to the United States rather than joining the English in their fight for 'their Ceylon tea and their weekend'. Even when Mers-el-Kebir made the British unpopular, however, it did not necessarily make Vichy popular. It may have shown many French people that Britain was ruthless and contemptuous of French interests, but it also showed them that Britain was determined to fight on against Germany, and thus that Vichy would not be able to benefit from a general peace settlement in the near future. In any case, it was possible to want the British to win the war without liking them, and it was possible to like Britain without approving of everything that she did. In Douai, in the anglophile north of France, Germans were horrified to find that schoolchildren were being set the following passage in a dictation: 'England I love you, because, for all your faults, you are my country.'[91]

Thinking about England and her fate was an area where rumour and myth played a particularly large part in forming French opinion. During the summer of 1940, French people repeatedly recorded their belief that German soldiers attempting to invade England had suffered some reverse. Rumours that the English had caused appalling German casualties by setting fire to oil on the water or that German troops had rebelled were particularly common. Drouot reported that 'The boches have tried to cross the Channel and failed, with troops wounded and drowned.'[92] Liliane Schroeder believed that many German troops had been executed after a mutiny by those ordered to cross the Channel.[93] The psychologist Marie Bonaparte wrote a book about 'myths' in wartime France. In it, she told a particularly striking story. A woman was woken late at night by the German officer billeted on her. He said that his chauffeur was not available and that he needed to make an urgent journey. At gunpoint he ordered her to take him in her car. They drove hundreds of kilometres. When they arrived at their destination, the officer went into a building for a short time and emerged devastated. He told the woman that his son had refused an order to depart with an invasion force for England and was consequently to be executed the following morning. Bonaparte reported seventeen occasions on which she had been told of German losses suffered whilst attempting to cross the Channel. The reports all reached her between July and September 1940. She received them in Paris and Saint-Tropez, though her informants also came from Brittany, Toulon and Marseilles. Her son in Constantinople heard the story of German reverses in September.[94]

German invasion of the Soviet Union in June 1941 increased active support for the Resistance, because Communists were committed to Allied victory, but it also made some support collaboration with Germany. Philippe Henriot was a conservative but anti-German Pétainist until June 1941. After Hitler's invasion of the Soviet Union, he became a radical supporter of collaboration, and was assassinated by the Resistance in the summer of 1944. Anti-Soviet feelings became the most important reason for supporting collaboration with Germany, though many convinced anti-Communists did not do so.[95] Events on the Eastern Front in the summer of 1941 may also have made some more sure of German victory. In a report of 8 November 1941, a little more than a year before he threw in his lot with the Allies, Admiral Darlan expressed the certainty that Germany would win.

Hitler's declaration of war on America in December 1941 had more complicated effects. Many Pétainists were favourable to the United States and Vichy maintained diplomatic relations with Washington for most of 1942. By the end of 1942 the combination of Soviet and American participation in the war made Allied victory seem almost certain, and this certainty may have been stronger amongst the edu-cated in France, who tended to focus on the broad strategic picture dominated by economics and demography, than it was amongst the educated population of Britain or America, engaged in the day-to-day events of war. On 27 October 1942 Flandin sent a postcard to Pétain, the man who had appointed him as Prime Minister less than two years previously, in which he openly mocked Pétainist, or Lavalist, bets on German victory:

The few workers who refuse to go [to work in Germany] are bad Frenchmen who understand nothing of the situation and still think Germany will lose the war. You did well to shoot some, it is the only way to convince them . . . It only remains for Germany to crush Russia, England and America and to share with France the remains of these three countries.[96]

How much did members of the Vichy government know about the opinions of those over whom they ruled? Vichy was, especially in the early months of its existence, remarkably isolated from the bulk of the French population. In July 1940 it was hard even to get a telephone connection. Adrien Marquet, then the Minister of the Interior, said that he felt like a pianist who produced no sound when he struck the keys. Later on it was often difficult for Vichy ministers or officials to reach the occupied zone, where most of those who were nominally subject to their rule lived, and, for a time, it was impossible for them to reach the 'forbidden zone' in northern France. Everyone recognized that the regime needed some mechanism to connect it with the popu-lation. Xavier Vallat wrote that the disappearance of party politics had created 'a gap that could become an abyss of incomprehension'.[97] Pétain himself remarked that he sometimes felt as though he were floating in a hot air balloon.

Some at Vichy made great efforts to find out about 'public opinion'.

Dr Ménétrel employed 'experts' (a retired officer, a journalist and a policeman) to provide him with information about public opinion, but eventually he realized that all his informants relayed little other than their own opinions. The police collected information about people's political views, and prefects wrote monthly reports on opinion in the areas they administered.

Most dramatically, the *contrôle technique* listened to telephone conversations and opened between 320,000 and 370,000 letters in an average week. Even this source, however, did not make public opinion easy to read. Interception of letters and telephone calls gave disproportionate weight to the most privileged sections of society (only a small proportion of the population had telephones and letter-writing was more common amongst the educated than amongst the population at large). In any case, people often knew that their letters would be opened.

Official reports could be reductive and schematic. The *contrôle technique* reports were compiled by ticking boxes that represented various kinds of opinion. Often the categories used indicated the ideological assumptions of the person compiling the report. The Renseignements Généraux of Carcassonne prepared a report in March 1943 on the attitude taken by 1,200 primary school teachers to 'the policy of the government and the main events of 1942'. It concluded that half of them were 'honest and conscientious employees who concerned themselves purely with their professional task'; a quarter 'wholly approved of the policy of the government'. A further quarter (made up of Communists, Socialists and advanced Radicals) was 'almost completely hostile' to the policy of the government, though 'at the moment they did not show their feelings; on the contrary they carry out orders, sometimes with a rather ostentatious zeal'.[98] When the prefect of the Ille-et-Vilaine recommended people to serve on the department's administrative council, he divided them into four categories, ranging from those marked by 'devotion to the head of state or the government' (twenty-four people were thus described) to those with a 'correct attitude' (two people were described like this and both were, as it turned out, Resistance activists).[99] The Centre Départemental d'Information de la Loire suggested that 10 per cent of the population were 'eternal malcontents'; 15 per cent were partisans of the 'Old Regime' (that is, the Third Republic); 50 per cent were 'indifferent' and only 25 per cent were 'convinced patriots loyal to the regime'.[100]

Those who compiled reports on public opinion were not just neutral recorders of fact. This was especially true of the prefectural corps. French prefects were closely linked to the political culture of the Third Republic. Some were dismissed by Vichy, especially in the purge of July 1940, and people from other, more straightforwardly conservative, parts of the state apparatus, the army or the *inspection des finances*, were brought in to replace dismissed men. However, many firmly republican members of the prefectural corps survived and some of them – René Bousquet and Maurice Papon – became energetic servants of the regime. The opinions of prefects themselves were sometimes hard to categorize. In the Maine-et-Loire, all prefects were investigated and disciplined after the liberation. Jean Roussillon was described as 'a Vichy prefect in the full sense of the word. From the racial point of view as well as the political one, he gave, or tried to give, his services with energy to satisfy his masters whom he served with passion, that is to say Marshal Pétain, de Brinon and Laval.' However, Roussillon had in fact been relieved of his functions by Vichy after he made his hostility to the deportation of French workers to Germany clear. Even post-war investigations recognized that he had 'sometimes shown courage and firmness' in his dealings with the Germans. Charles Donati, a prefect appointed from the *inspection des finances* by Vichy, was described as dictatorial and repressive. He was responsible for numerous arrests but again post-war authorities recognized that his 'intimate opinions were no doubt anti-German'. Most complicated of all was the case of Pierre Daguerre. Daguerre had served in Maine-et-Loire as prefect delegate from July 1941 until July 1943. He was described there in relatively favourable terms as having never made a secret of his pro-Allied opinions. However, in Mayenne, where he had served before, post-war opinion of the prefect was less favourable and he was blamed for 'Pétainisme aigu'; whilst in the Charente, where Daguerre served after leaving the Maine-et-Loire, he was remembered with outright hostility. No doubt Daguerre's own attitude changed over time: it is easy to see why he might have been keener to associate himself with Vichy in 1940 than after July 1941, though it is harder to see why he was considered more Pétainist again after July 1943. Verdicts on Daguerre may also have owed something to the different contexts in which he operated. It was easier to seem left-wing in a Catholic conservative area, such as Maine-et-Loire, than it was in an area such as the Charente. Besides, how prefects acted and how they were judged by the population depended largely on what they were asked to do. All three prefects in the Maine-et-Loire tended to be pro-Vichy when asked to repress Communist activity, but less enthusiastic when asked to help with the deportation of French labour to Germany. All three were very hostile to the action of the Milice, which was, nominally at least, a Vichy agency.[101]

Sometimes reports on opinion had an almost paranoid feel as Vichy officials tried to pin down particular political positions. A Vichy official described a ceremony organized by Marcel Déat's Rassemblement National Populaire (a collaborationist movement of left-wing origin) to welcome home repatriated prisoners of war in 1941: 'The speeches, without containing a single subversive word, were, however, found by some [prisoners] to be a little brief with regard to the Marshal, whose name was never mentioned, and the policy of national union, which was discreetly pushed aside.'[102] The Service d'Ordre Légionnaire asked potential recruits a series of detailed questions that said much about the fears of the movement's leaders: 'What do you think of de Gaulle and his movement?'; 'do you make a distinction between the Marshal and his government?'; 'if you received orders from your leaders in the SOL that were in complete opposition to the policy practised by your old political party or by the official authorities or even of the Légion, what would you do?'[103]

Often French opinion was hard to fit into any category at all. People saw Vichy through a prism of personal and local considerations. The prefect of the Nièvre wrote gnomically: 'The population follows events with interest, comments on them and draws conclusions, often linked to their own sentiments.'[104] Sometimes Clochemerlesque local squabbles underlay the way in which a particular village orientated itself with regard to Vichy. In 1941 'a group of national revolutionaries' (that is, supporters of Vichy's 'National Revolution') wrote to both de Brinon (the French ambassador to the occupied zone) and the sub-prefect, about the state of the village of Meilhan.[105] Their letters denounced fourteen people for a variety of offences, most connected with support for the Communist Party or involvement in the black market. The authorities investigating these complaints concluded that they all sprang from an argument between rival sporting clubs established by the priest and the *instituteur* (the latter was regarded as vaguely left-wing) in 1937. A total of three boys were members of the 'clerical' sporting club, whose supporters seem to have caused so much trouble.[106]

The circumstances of war and occupation increased localism. Electoral politics and compulsory military service (the things that had bound men into a national political culture) were both suppressed under Vichy. Travel was difficult and material conditions (particularly relating to food) differed hugely from one area to another. These new divisions tied in with old ones. Simple matters of language were important. In Brittany, 7 per cent of the population spoke no French; elsewhere many people would have discussed politics in a patois that bore only a tangential relation to the language spoken by Vichy propagandists and their London-based enemies. The Hungarian historian François Fejto was one of the few people in France to hear Charles de Gaulle's 'call to honour' of 18 June 1940, but he had to translate it for the benefit of the peasants from the Vendée with whom he had taken refuge.

Three generalizations can be made about opinion in Vichy France. First, people distinguished between Pétain and his government. As early as October 1940, Colonel de la Rocque (leader of the Parti Social Français) said to his followers: 'I ask you to be behind the Marshal, I do not ask you to be behind his government.'[107] The prefect of the Ain wrote: 'The French venerate their head of state, give him their respect, their confidence, their devotion, but they do not give their unconditional attachment to the policy of the government.'[108] The prefect of Rodez reported: 'The majority of the population continue to venerate the Marshal, but it follows him less as a leader than as a personality of legend, a magnificent old man of astonishing gifts and virtues.'[109]

Secondly, loyalty to the regime, and to its head, varied from area to area in inverse proportion to the German presence. Vichy meant least to the inhabitants of the 'forbidden zone': that part of northern France ruled by the German command in Brussels. This area was almost completely cut off from the rest of France for the first year of the occupation. Vichy officials had difficulty in getting access to the zone. Many people in the area believed that it was likely to be annexed into greater Germany and perhaps even that Vichy had traded it for sovereignty in the rest of France. Here, even members of the *grande bourgeoisie* were often hostile to the government. Vichy counted for more in the 'free zone', which was spared occupation by the Germans, though this was also an area with left-wing traditions that made some people hostile to Vichy.

Vichy was most popular amongst those people whose attachment to Marshal Pétain was not sullied by any direct experience of what was happening in France. French people in the overseas empire were often very Pétainist. An English report suggested that Léon Cayla, governor of Madagascar, was 'more pro-Vichy than Pétain'.[110] Madagascar was the only part of the world in which people actually fought for Vichy for any length of time – indeed, Vichy forces defended the island against an Allied invasion for six months, longer than the French army had defended metropolitan France against the Germans in 1940. Pétainists in overseas colonies sometimes sought to blend their beliefs into local cultures: the governor of Indochina wrote that Pétainism 'fits unexpectedly well into Confucian philosophy'.[111]

Probably the most Pétainist area in all of the French Empire was North Africa, especially Algeria. Algeria never saw German soldiers and the European population there found it easy to believe that Vichy would combine conservative reform with preparation for a military revenge against Germany. Algeria had a large population of indigenous Jews, who had been given French citizenship by the Crémieux decree of 1875. Both the European settlers in Algeria, about a million people, and the Muslim majority, about nine million, resented the Jews, and Vichy's revocation of the Crémieux decree was popular amongst both Europeans and Muslims. Some Muslim notables were sympathetic to Pétain, either because they found his emphasis on authority and patriotism to be appealing, or because they believed that Vichy might grant them political concessions; they were mainly disappointed in this expectation, though some Muslims were appointed to Vichy's Conseil National. The European population of Algeria, the most significant in terms of French politics, was largely made up of people with origins outside France (Spaniards, Italians, Maltese), who had been granted French citizenship by a law of 1889. Most European settlers were comparatively poor and settled in the major cities of the coast (Algiers, Constantine, Oran and Bone). This was not a naturally right-wing population but it was one that had sometimes moved to the right under the influence of anti-Semitism, opposition to Algerian nationalism and sympathy, on the part of Spaniards, for Franco's cause during the Spanish Civil War. French people in Algeria were initially confused by the armistice; they had not seen the French defeat at close quarters. However, Pétain's prestige counted for much as, perhaps even more importantly, did the prestige of General Weygand, who became delegate of the French government in Algeria in September 1940. Weygand's particular brand of Pétainism – patriotic, military and, at least implicitly, anti-German – was particularly suited to Algeria. The armistice signed with Italy on 25 June 1940 had anticipated that only 30,000 French soldiers would be permitted in North Africa. However, after the English attack at Mers-el-Kebir, this limit was increased to 120,000 men, which meant that the French army in North Africa was now larger than the French army on the mainland. Whatever Weygand's true intentions, many in Algeria believed that he was secretly planning a military revenge against Germany. Weygand's dismissal in 1941 marked a decline in Vichy's fortunes in Algeria.

However, in spite of, or because of, the arrival of American troops there in November 1942, Pétainism never ceased to exist in Algeria. In some ways, the American arrival and the apparent deal with Pétain's dauphin Admiral Darlan (see Chapter 10) confirmed the view in Algeria that there was no sharp divide between being pro-Vichy and anti-German. Furthermore, the leader installed in Algeria by the Americans for the first six months of 1943, General Henri Giraud, shared many of Pétain's projects for internal reform in France.[112]

Finally, and most unexpectedly, there was a pocket of Pétainism in the middle of the British Empire. Three million French speakers lived in Quebec in Canada. This was an area with anti-republican traditions – some monarchist *émigrés* had sought refuge there after the French

Revolution. It was also an intensely Catholic area, whose Catholicism had been made more aggressively political by the arrival of priests expelled from France during the separation of Church and State in 1905. Maurrassianism gained an influence in Quebec, one that was particularly exercised through Lionel Groulx, a priest at Montreal University. French-speaking Canada was also often anti-Semitic, partly in response to Jewish immigration during the 1930s. Many French speakers espoused ruralist, anti-big-business ideology, because large-scale industrialization was mainly in the hands of their English-speaking compatriots. All these conservative currents influenced the right-wing Quebec government under Maurice Duplessis from 1936 to 1939. They also encouraged some *Québécois* to regard the Vichy regime with favour. Such favour was most vigorously expressed in the pages of *Le Devoir*, a Montreal newspaper founded in 1910. Though its circulation was fairly limited (just over 20,000 in 1940), it seems to have had an important influence on elite opinion in Quebec. *Le Devoir* greeted Pétain's accession thus: 'There is perhaps in all the recent history of France no more noble figure than that of the old Marshal.'[113]

The third, and simplest, generalization that can be made about Vichy is that, though its popularity ebbed and flowed in complicated ways, the overall trend was downwards and disenchantment with the regime set in relatively early, certainly by the middle of 1941. Vichy's own ministers were painfully conscious that their support was declining over time. Official reports about public opinion were full of terms such as 'lassitude' and 'attentisme' (that is, waiting to see what would happen). In mid-August 1941 Henri Drouot wrote: 'The truth is that Pétainism is dissolving by itself from lack of faith and ardour.'[114]

The political significance of disenchantment with the regime could, of course, be as complicated as the political significance of support for it. People could dislike the government without liking its most active opponents. Many who opposed Vichy also disapproved of organized Resistance attacks when they began in August 1941, partly because such attacks brought reprisals. If any single institution united the French by 1942, it was probably the BBC. Listening to French-language broadcasts from London became so common that one journalist said the corridors in the hotels of Vichy itself went silent when the nine o'clock news came on.[115]

MANAGING PUBLIC OPINION

Perhaps it is more instructive to look not at how 'public opinion' viewed Vichy but at how Vichy viewed public opinion. Here, as in so many things, Laval was unusual. As a man who had spent his life cultivating an electoral clientele, he wanted to find out what the public thought. Most at Vichy did not want to measure public opinion. When Laval was out of office, the interception of letters and telephone calls was mainly used to repress specific activities rather than to judge the public mood. Vichy was never as repressive as Hitler's Germany or Stalin's Russia but it was certainly not a regime that encouraged its opponents to speak freely: in 1942 a man in Rennes got several months in prison for making rude remarks about Pétain in a bar.[116]

Suppressing anti-Vichy opinion produced an absurd situation, because all sorts of acts could be interpreted as the expression of such opinion. In cinemas, people were warned not to boo newsreels. Lights were kept on, so that culprits could be identified, and cinema doors were closed, to prevent people from showing their disapproval by missing newsreels altogether. However, the authorities became ever more paranoid about what might constitute an expression of disapproval. In February 1941 Liliane Schroeder's mother was threatened with arrest for powdering her nose during the newsreel in a Paris cinema.[117] People could even be arrested for coughing in cinemas, and two men, aged fifty-five and eighty-six, had to produce doctor's certificates to prove that their throat conditions were real before the police released them.[118] In the end, cinema audiences expressed themselves most eloquently through silence. In 1943 a policeman sent to report on the Pathé in Belleville admitted that the only reaction to a speech by Laval shown on a newsreel was his own applause.[119]

Benoist-Méchin, who was to become Secretary of State for the Council of Ministers under Vichy, wrote of his contempt for public opinion:

The crowd possesses no organ for thought. Victim of its mental hallucinations and its nervous reactions, it is without defence against rumours and delirious dreams . . . It would be easy to take these lightly if there was not the risk that they would have serious consequences, because the sum of these phantasmagorias makes up what is solemnly called 'public opinion', and that will soon poison relations between the French and the occupying authorities.[120]

For men such as him, public opinion was not a given that constrained government policy but rather something to be manipulated and mastered. René Benjamin, one of Pétain's hagiographers, recorded that Maurras told Pétain that opinion was 'une grande folle'. Benjamin wrote in 1943, when Pétainists began to feel that the regime was becoming unpopular, 'the Marshal is firm and virile, public opinion is nervous and feminine'. Around the same time, Abel Bonnard, Minister of Education, told *miliciens*: 'Opinion is just an enormous female. I count on you, the male part of the population.'[121]

The remarks of Benjamin and Bonnard reflect Vichy's anti-democratic instincts, but they also draw attention to something more interesting. Politics in the Third Republic had been the business of adult men. They alone had the vote. Electoral politics went with the rough camaraderie of the *café de commerce* and agricultural fair. Vichy's suspension of parliamentary democracy meant that this kind of politics was swept away. To a small extent, Vichy's politics opened opportunities for women. They were allowed to sit on Vichy's appointed town councils, while they had never had a presence on the Third Republic's elected councils. More importantly, Pétainist rhetoric made much of women and children: it illustrated its concern for both by celebrating 'mother's day' in France.

A large proportion of Pétainist rhetoric was directed at children. Pétain appealed to them directly in his speeches, asking them not to cheat at school. The children's comics that survived in Vichy France were intensely Pétainist. *Le Journal de Mickey* continued to be published in Marseilles, with the authorization of Walt Disney. In September 1940 its editorial, signed by 'Your old uncle Léon', told its readers: 'The Marshal, in granting you the support of his prestige and a confidence that you must all merit, has traced the route ahead: great things remain to be accomplished to make a better France and it is up to you to undertake this duty.'[122] In October 1940 *Robinson* told its readers: 'Every word that comes from him [Pétain] is a counsel from the heart and an order dictated by the highest reason.'[123] In 1943 René Benjamin conceded that the French were beginning to turn away from Pétain and added, revealingly, that 'hardly anyone except children and prisoners [of war] still show him their love'.[124]

Vichy's definition of the 'public' as mad, infantile or female went with a belief that public opinion could be moulded and constrained. This belief could be seen in schools. The apparently enthusiastic crowds that greeted Pétain in towns he visited were largely made up of schoolchildren, whose presence was more or less required by the authorities. Jacques le Goff was a schoolboy in Toulon who joined a demonstration of loyalty to the Marshal in 1941, but in fact he hated Pétain (even more than he hated the Vichy government), and his father's career as a teacher had been impeded by his anti-Pétainism. Jacques le Goff only agreed to join the demonstration in order to spare his family from further reprisals.[125]

A similar degree of coerced enthusiasm could be seen in the higher reaches of the education system. At the beginning of each academic year, the senior professor of each university gave an address. In October 1940 such addresses were usually full of Pétainist rhetoric. However, reading the private diaries of academics shows that such Pétainism was not spontaneous. University professors, like other notables, worked hard to strike a balance between the requirements of the authorities, the expectations of their community and their own private beliefs. In Dijon, Drouot noted:

Chabot made the required speech, eulogy of Pétain, commentary on the programmes published by the Vichy government: work, moral rule, the fatherland (!). He had to seem warm enough to satisfy the ministry and skilful enough not to contradict the ideas of the majority of the professors, who are very hostile to the government of the Marshal. He got through it quite well, with a grave tone and all sorts of fine words, and the applause of the young men and women was quite warm. In the details, there were expressions of reserve . . . that the young no doubt did not completely understand – while the faithful republicans, for their part, seemed to appreciate this manner of discharging the duty [corvée].[126]

Drouot's diary entry reflects the fear of authority (many believed that lecture halls at the university were bugged[127]), and also the uncertainty about opinion outside his own immediate milieu. Edmond Duméril had to give the start-of-year speech at the University of Nantes at the beginning of the academic year in 1940. He too seems to have struck a balance by reading Marshal Pétain's declarations but then 'forgetting' to read one that struck him as particularly anti-English.[128]

Deciphering any kind of political symbolism under Vichy was difficult because the same act could have many different meanings. Vichy inherited a political culture that had woven military patriotism and republicanism together. This made life awkward because some reactionaries at Vichy wanted the military patriotism without the republicanism whilst the Germans were often willing to tolerate the republicanism, which mattered to their collaborators drawn from the French left, but disliked the military patriotism. Vichy kept the tricolour flag and members of the Légion des Volontaires Français contre le Bolchevisme (LVF) fought with the Germans under this flag (indeed French collaborationists tried to recast the LVF as the 'Légion Tricolore' in 1942), but members of the LVF also attacked women in cafés wearing red, white and blue clothes, because they believed that such clothes were being used as emblems of support for de Gaulle.

Vichy devised its own ceremonial around particular dates and institutions. Remembering the war dead, particularly those of 1914–18, was important to the regime and consequently 11 November (armistice day) was a crucial anniversary. However, from the moment when students staged anti-German demonstrations on 11 November 1940, armistice day was also increasingly associated with 'Gaullism' and hence opposition to Vichy. Bastille Day (14 July) was an equally awkward date. Vichy encouraged the French to mark this day in a quiet and dignified manner (implicitly, the regime wanted to distance itself from the noisy popular left-wing festivities that had accompanied the Popular Front during the 1930s), but it could not simply abolish an anniversary that was so closely tied up with French military patriotism, and it could not prevent people from imbuing this date with a pro-Resistance meaning (this was particularly awkward, because Bastille Day fell so close to the anniversary of Pétain's accession to power). Most awkward for Vichy was 1 May. This was the day of

Saint Philippe and, in the naive optimism of early 1941, it seemed a good idea to associate the personal cult of the Marshal (also Philippe) with an appeal to the French working class. Quickly, however, older traditions of working-class radicalism re-emerged: 1 May was a favourite day for strikes.[129]

The most striking illustration of ambiguous symbolism is provided by the contexts in which French people sang the 'Marseillaise'. Anglo-Saxon observers assumed that singing the French national anthem was a sign of patriotism (perhaps also a sign of left-wing sentiments since it was a song that originated with the French Revolution), and that it would be associated with opposition to both the Germans and Vichy. In the film *Casablanca* (1942), Rick tells a café orchestra to 'play the Marseillaise' when a group of German soldiers comes in. However, it was possible to sing the 'Marseillaise' and to be a Pétainist. It was often sung at official Vichy ceremonies, though often only the first and sixth verses, thus omitting those that are most revolutionary and most martial.[130] Pétain himself preferred the fourth verse: 'C'est le plus beau. On n'y égorge personne.'[131] The two peasant brothers interviewed in Michel Ophuls' 1971 film *The Sorrow and the Pity* (both of whom were non-doctrinaire Socialists) recall that they sang the 'Internationale' when they inaugurated their Resistance cell – 'because Pétain sang the Marseillaise'. Singing the 'Marseillaise' could be an anti-German act. The Germans forbade the national anthem in the occupied part of France, though they sometimes granted special permission for it to be sung at Pétainist meetings. Paul Seguin in the Jura became a local hero by singing the 'Marseillaise' outside the headquarters of the Wehrmacht on 14 July 1943 (though doing so does not seem to have brought very severe reprisals down on his head).[132] However, it was not just resisters who sang it in defiance of the Germans. In Paris in 1944, members of the LVF (men who had chosen to fight with the Germans) entered a café and demanded that the orchestra play the 'Marseillaise' (that is, do something that was forbidden by the Germans).[133]

Young men departing from France in order to perform compulsory labour service in Germany illustrate the different interpretations that could be given to the same act. All observers agreed that the young men sang the 'Marseillaise' as they left. The men themselves, usually recalling events years afterwards, interpreted this act as anti-German and anti-Vichy; many also recalled having sung the 'Internationale' and shouting 'Laval for the firing squad' (though no one seems to have shouted 'Pétain for the firing squad'). However, Vichy's own reports did not interpret the singing of the 'Marseillaise' as an anti-regime act. On the contrary, they commented favourably on it as a sign of patriotism.[134] Most peculiar of all was an incident in Grenoble in 1943. A group of Frenchmen called up under the labour service programme were being taken to the station in a coach when they were attacked by Italian soldiers. The Italians believed that the Frenchmen had been singing an anti-Italian song about macaroni. A German officer then intervened and, according to a Vichy report, 'put the Italians firmly in their place by saying that the young men were singing the "Marseillaise" and that this was their right and their duty'. The coach driver was also interviewed. He said that the Italians had beaten up the Frenchmen for no good reason, but he did admit that they had been singing a song about macaroni – food was the main preoccupation of young men in Vichy France.[135]

3

Living with the Enemy

Everything was thus put back in order, but with the Germans. They had occupied Saint-Loup for several days . . . They came to buy eggs. I talked to them all the same because I had been in Germany [as a prisoner during the First World War]. (Ephraïm Grenadou describing Germans in the Beauce in June/July 1940)[1]

Month by month it seemed that the troops posted near our building got older in front of our eyes. No doubt the Eastern Front needed personnel, as one says in military language.

'My word,' said my mother, 'they must be getting them from a retirement home.' She felt no real hatred. Just some bad memories of the German occupation around Warsaw in the First World War . . . When I accompanied my mother shopping and we passed in front of the hotel [in which the German soldiers were housed] . . . she squeezed my hand as if to tell me there was no danger in facing such an enemy. (Maurice Rajsfus describing Germans in Paris in 1942)[2]

Incident with Elie . . . We had just turned into the Rue Victor-Hugo which runs alongside the girls' school, which had become Prinz Eugen Kaserne. On the other side of the road, a German sentry appeared . . . And straightaway, the German turned round, insulted us and threatened us. Elie opened his mouth wide, spreading out his arms as if to say 'And so what, we were not thinking!' The German shouted and seized his machine gun. I shouted in turn and raised my hands. I shouted in German that we were unarmed. We walked

3. (overleaf) *Young Frenchmen on their way to fight with the Germans on the Eastern Front.*

away backwards. Instinctively, I thought that he would not shoot as long as I kept looking him in the eyes. (Louis Guilloux describing a German in Saint-Brieuc in March 1943)[3]

These three encounters between French people and Germans all happened in the part of France occupied by the Germans from June 1940 rather than in the zone that was left 'free' until November 1942. All involved French people who were hostile to the German occupation and all involved ordinary German soldiers rather than SS men or committed Nazis.

Beyond this, the encounters were differentiated by time and place. Grenadou met Germans in 1940, at a time when their victory seemed assured and when there was no longer any point in fighting. He lived on the flat and fertile plain around Chartres. The Germans never had much reason to be scared in this area, because there was nowhere for enemy soldiers to hide, and the availability of food made the occupation bearable for both sides. Guilloux met his German soldier later in the war, at a time when the Germans were in increasingly sharp conflict with the French (a conflict mainly produced by the introduction of compulsory labour service) and in an area, Brittany, where they were beginning to prepare to face Allied invasion. Rajsfus and his mother encountered Germans when the war was turning against Germany. If Maurice's mother believed that the occupation in general, rather than particular German soldiers, posed no threat, she was wrong, however. She was a Jew of Polish origin, and a few months after the scene described by her son she and her husband were arrested by French policemen, deported and killed.

DEMARCATION LINES

Geography was the most obvious thing that governed Franco-German relations. German troops penetrated a long way into France in 1940. The armistice pulled them back behind a 'demarcation line' that ran from Dole in Burgundy across France and then down the Atlantic coast (see Map 3). The line existed on paper until May 1943, but in practice it lost most of its significance in November 1942 when the

Germans, responding to the American invasion of Algeria, sent troops into the southern zone of France. The line itself was an important feature of France during the occupation. It cut across towns and villages: the town of Bléré managed to get the line moved in August 1940, so that its cemetery was no longer located in the 'free zone'; before this, funeral cortèges had been obliged to cross the line.[4] Elsewhere, inconvenient divisions remained. Areas cut off from their normal departmental capital by the line (which divided thirteen of the ninety departments in mainland France) were then allocated to new departments; mayors found that they could no longer reach the suburbs of their own towns.

The Germans devised the line with military matters in mind; they wanted to control the Atlantic and Channel coasts and also to control the regions where the greatest concentrations of French industry were to be found. For French observers, however, the line assumed a more symbolic importance. Jacques Laurent, who stood guard on the French side as a corporal in the small army that France was allowed to retain after the armistice, wrote:

The demarcation line was a peculiar frontier which made one tremble at its frailty – all it took was a German punch to break it – and above all at its incongruity. It twisted among the most sensually French names of our land; ran blindly, traced in haste between invisible historic frontiers, those of the *langue d'oc* and the *langue d'oïl* ... it crossed lands where the political frontiers had been only sketched out between the fifth and the fifteenth centuries.

The demarcation line was not entirely static. French and German authorities negotiated about its impact. Some towns, such as Loches, that were initially placed in the occupied zone were subsequently moved into the unoccupied one. There were adjustments to the line that were sufficiently radical to bring towns into the 'free zone' up until August 1941. The Germans sometimes used mines or barbed wire, or felled trees in order to give themselves a clear field of fire. These measures, however, were unusual. Generally, the line was not well guarded. A German commander estimated that it would have taken fifteen divisions to guard the line properly; in practice, the Germans never devoted more than two divisions to the task. In February 1941, most German soldiers, particularly those whose youth fitted them for more active duties, were removed from the line and replaced by customs officers. These were more flexible and ingenious in guarding the frontier than the soldiers had been, but they were still in no position to seal it hermetically. In April 1941 about 2,500 Germans guarded the line. This meant that there were two men for every kilometre. Given that they worked in groups of four, most parts of the line were out of sight of guards for most of the time. Professional *passeurs* guided people across the line. Most *passeurs* were young men from humble backgrounds; many of them lived on the fringes of criminality (poachers were especially adept at finding ways through woods at night). Crossing the line could become a large-scale enterprise, and at least one firm (Thomson et Bellenger of the Rhône) employed a *passeur* to convey their staff in and out of the occupied zone.[5]

On the French side, the line was guarded by troops from the armistice army, policemen and gendarmes – the three groups not always being very well co-ordinated. French efforts were slightly farcical because the French authorities knew that they could not afford real confrontation with the Germans: French soldiers on the line were sometimes given no ammunition.

The Germans used the demarcation line to put pressure on Vichy. This meant that they controlled official passages across the line most severely at moments when Vichy had annoyed them, and particularly in the aftermath of Laval's dismissal in December 1940 (between November 1940 and January 1941 less than a third of the 5,100 requests for passes made to the German authorities in Bordeaux were granted).[6] At first, most movement, both official and clandestine, across the line involved people who wished to move from the southern to the northern zone. People who had fled during the *exode* wished to rejoin their families or protect their property.[7] Some Jews wished to return to the German occupied zone, and many of these had to cross the line illegally because the Germans would not allow them in. As time went on, the balance between those heading north and those heading south shifted; increasing numbers of those who crossed the line (especially those who did so clandestinely) wanted to escape from the Germans.

Crossing the demarcation line was not equally easy for everyone. The Germans excluded 'gens de couleur' from the start. The French also differentiated amongst those trying to cross and, perhaps more importantly, amongst those who had been caught after crossing illegally. Some categories, particularly escaped prisoners of war, were positively welcomed. North Africans and Jews (especially Jews who did not have French nationality) were less likely to find a warm reception from the French authorities.[8] Even the *passeurs* distinguished between different clients. Jews, the people most desperate to cross the line, were usually charged more than others.

The demarcation line became a centre of Franco-German cohabitation. Germans who were posted there stayed in the same place for a long time. They lived in relatively small groups away from the distractions – cinemas, military brothels – to be found in areas where Germans were more concentrated. The area through which the line passed was an agricultural one where food, for those with the right associates, was relatively plentiful. French people needed to cross the line for all sorts of reasons, most of which had nothing to do with their attitude to the occupation. The Germans also found it convenient to have access to resources that could be found in the southern zone: sometimes they connived in French smuggling operations designed to extract goods that the Vichy government wanted to keep in its zone. In November 1940 French officials intercepted a lorry near Bourges; it turned out to belong to the German commission on the control of aviation. It had come from Marseilles driven by a Frenchman under the command of a German civilian, and it contained six tonnes of soap, six tonnes of rice and 500 kilograms of ham.[9]

Mutual interest could bring French and Germans into working relations of various kinds. Germans sometimes intervened to help their French associates who had been arrested close to the demarcation line by the French authorities. In December 1940 French gendarmes confiscated butter and chickens from a grocer in Vierzon; the Germans stopped anyone crossing the demarcation line in the area until the grocer was compensated.[10] When a woman from Faverolles known for the 'commerce de ses charmes' lost her pass to cross the demarcation line the local German commandant asked about her at an official meeting with his French counterparts.[11]

Germans were often persuaded to loosen the restrictions of the demarcation line, especially with regard to the agricultural population living immediately around the line. In August 1941 German guards were allowed to let farmers cross the line at their discretion; in some places farmers had their own keys to gates through the barbed wire. Often such arrangements seem to have been rooted in the common interest of Germans and French. In Bourges, Germans allowed boar hunts to cross the line: ostensibly this concession was made to protect crops, but the German officers themselves were often keen hunters and, presumably, hunts would have generated supplies of meat to be distributed to anyone who had helped the huntsmen.[12]

The demarcation line was not the only formal division in occupied France. The Germans annexed Alsace and the department of Moselle in Lorraine on 16 July 1940. The German language was imposed in most of Alsace and inhabitants of those villages recognized as francophone had to obtain special cards to permit them to speak their native language. The Hitler Youth was instituted in these regions, as was, from the spring of 1941, the German compulsory labour system for young people. The village of Bennwihr, with a population of 880, saw 48 boys and 7 girls sent away to perform compulsory labour service. In the summer of 1942 young men from Alsace and Lorraine were forced to join the German armed forces. Around 130,000 of them served in German uniform.

The life of Marguerite Poiré gives some indication of what German action in Lorraine did to the inhabitants of the area. Her family was one of ten thousand or so who remained, rather than fleeing to France, but who refused to accept German nationality. In January 1943 the family was deported to the Sudetenland. Marguerite, eleven years old when she went, grew up speaking Czech and German. One of her brothers was killed fighting with the German army on the Eastern Front, the other fought with the Free French. Her grandmother was raped by Russian soldiers in 1945. Poiré, by now thirteen years old, wrote with glee of the German suicides that accompanied defeat.[13]

The Germans created a 'forbidden zone' in the north and east of France. Part of this zone, that made up of the departments of the Nord and Pas-de-Calais, was ruled by the German high command in Brussels, and some feared that it was being prepared for annexation by the Germans. The German army, rather than German civilians, always dominated the Nord and Pas-de-Calais. Indeed, more than any other part of France, these departments remained a war zone throughout the period from 1940 to 1945. There was a heavy German presence from the beginning: 120,000 troops were in the region as the Germans considered invading Britain in the summer and autumn of 1940. Thereafter this became the front line in the German air war against Britain, which also meant that it was a target for Allied bombing and for early British commando raids.

The line around the forbidden zone was more ruthlessly enforced, at least for the first year of the occupation, than the demarcation line that separated occupied France from the rest. French civil servants found it almost impossible to get into the forbidden zone and the frontier between it and the rest of France was not completely abolished until 1943. Many natives of the region had trouble in getting home. Pierre Malle, father of the film director Louis, stayed to manage the family sugar refining business near Lille while his wife and children went to Paris. Malle was sufficiently influential to obtain a regular German pass but he still saw comparatively little of his children for almost two years.[14]

Coastal areas in the German occupied zone were dealt with in special ways, and a 'coastal zone' was established in October 1941. Eventually the Germans removed most French inhabitants from near the Atlantic and Channel coasts. The Italians occupied a small part of south-eastern France from the summer of 1940, an occupation that, initially at least, caused more resentment than the German occupation. In November 1942 the Italian zone was expanded to take in Nice, Toulon and Corsica.

The most incongruous frontier in wartime France was that with the principality of Monaco, an independent state ruled by Prince Louis II of the Grimaldi dynasty. The prince was no great admirer of democracy – he had suspended the constitution in 1930 and asked for French help in suppressing demonstrations – and, as a former officer in the French Foreign Legion, he admired Pétain. Initially, the principality survived the defeat of France well. Vichy's rationing and its bans on dancing and gambling all increased the attractions of Monaco for wealthy people. The only cloud on the horizon was Italian interest in the area, which was partly due to the large Italian population of Monaco. In November 1942 the Italians occupied Monaco, but, after Mussolini's deposition in September 1943 they were replaced by the Germans. The prince and his entourage felt more comfortable with the Germans. They seemed to have no long-term ambitions in the area. The prince himself had grown up partly in Germany and was already well used to German occupation because he spent much of his time hunting at his property in the north of France. His grand-daughter, Antoinette, even fell in love with a German lieutenant but the prince, no stranger to imprudent liaisons himself,[15] put a stop to the romance when he realized that the officer was the son of a railway crossing keeper. The Wehrmacht helpfully posted the lieutenant to Russia.[16]

All the new administrative divisions in occupied France were, like almost everything else, refracted through a prism of rumour and false information. In late July 1940, Paris police reported that maps were being sold that gave inaccurate versions of the divisions imposed by the invaders. One map showed Marseilles, Toulon and Nice to be occupied by the Italians. The map had been seized and its publisher, Alphonse Cohen, had fled.[17]

THE GERMAN PRESENCE IN FRANCE

Who was in charge in German-controlled France? Answering this question is harder than it might seem. On being told that Germany was an authoritarian state, Laval is said to have remarked, 'Yes, but what a lot of authorities.' The armistice commission at Wiesbaden handled official negotiations with the French, though its powers (par-ticularly with regard to economic matters) diminished as time went on. Otto Abetz's mission in Paris was upgraded into an embassy in November 1940, but the status of an embassy away from the official capital city was always slightly odd and, in any case, it was hard to know how far Abetz's strategy was supported in Berlin. The German high command in France had surprisingly circumscribed powers. The high command in Brussels controlled the Nord and Pas-de-Calais; the main German command in the west controlled assault troops (as opposed to those assigned for keeping order within France), and exercised authority in the southern zone after the Germans took it over in 1942. The barons of the Nazi regime all had their representatives in France who answered directly to their masters in Berlin.

The first German commander in Paris was Alfred Streccius but he was replaced in October 1940 by Otto von Stülpnagel. Otto von Stülpnagel was, in turn, replaced in 1942 by his cousin Karl-Heinrich von Stülpnagel, who had been head of the German delegation at Wiesbaden before serving for a time on the Eastern Front. Both the Stülpnagels were Prussians and veterans of the First World War. Both seem to have disliked certain aspects of Nazi policy in occupied France. Control of policing in France was taken away from the military authorities in the spring of 1942 and given to the SS under Karl Oberg.

Ernst Jünger, an officer in German headquarters in Paris, made much of the anti-Nazi sentiment amongst his colleagues. In 1941 he wrote: 'We have formed here, in the middle of the military machine, a sort of shining cell of spiritual chivalry, we meet in the belly of the Leviathan and, furthermore, we look out for those who are weak and without protection.'[18] A few months later, he said of his brother officers in the Hôtel Raphaël: 'For the first time, I saw that I could trust the inhabitants of this hotel. This is only possible nowadays if one chooses a circle that is intimate and invisible. A mischievous and funny remark by Philipps about Kniébo [Jünger's code name for Hitler] launched the conversation.'[19]

The main issue over which army officers argued with Nazi party authorities was the shooting of French hostages in reprisal for Resistance attacks on Germans. However, officers seem to have disliked the shooting of hostages most when it concerned Frenchmen for whom they felt particular sympathy (that is, middle-aged notables, who were often themselves veterans of the First World War). They were less interested in the fate of Jews and Communists; a number of officers in France, including Karl-Heinrich von Stülpnagel and Jünger, had served for a time in Russia, where the Wehrmacht committed atrocities against civilians. Furthermore, the practical effects of German army distaste for Nazism were limited. Jünger's opposition to Nazism seems mainly to have been confined to the pages of his diary and to private conversations.

In December 1941 there were 100,000 German troops charged with maintaining order in France, but their number then dropped to 40,000 in March 1942 before rising again to 200,000 at the end of 1943. Other troops, often stationed along the Channel or Atlantic coasts, were designed to fight against foreign enemies rather than to maintain order. There were 400,000 of these troops in France in 1942–3, and their number rose to a million just before the Allied invasion of 1944.[20]

German troops in France were not all the same. In the summer of 1940, France was full of young soldiers brimming with the self-confidence that came from their recent victories: these were the kind of men who lay naked in the grass on Jacques Le Roy Ladurie's farm studying maps of England.[21] After plans for the invasion of England were abandoned, and especially after the invasion of the Soviet Union, the number of German soldiers in France dropped. France was sometimes a posting for men considered suitable for non-combat duties. Such soldiers were often posted to the same place for long periods, and had time to develop relations with the local population. Increasingly, Germans posted to France were grateful that they were not enduring the harsher conditions on the Eastern Front and occasionally French people could exercise power over German troops by threatening to denounce them for offences that were likely to incur a transfer to the east.[22]

The German high command in Paris had two civilian subdivisions. The first handled administrative matters and was headed by Werner Best, a jurist born in 1903 who had begun his career campaigning against the French occupation of the Rhineland in 1923 and who had joined the Nazi party in 1930. Best advocated a policy of 'surveillance' over French institutions as a means by which the Germans might control France with the minimum of effort, but Best's policy was rendered increasingly unrealistic by French Resistance attacks and savage German repression. In 1942 he was transferred to Denmark. The second office, headed by Dr Elmar Michel, handled economic matters, and its activities increased when it took over economic negotiations from the armistice commission at Wiesbaden. By 1941 the German command in France employed around 1,500 German civil servants who had been delegated from ministries in Germany. Building works, particularly the construction of the Atlantic Wall, probably brought around 80,000 German civilians to France, many of them part of Fritz Saukel's labour agency, which was only partly under the control of the German authorities in France.

The duration of the German occupation, the interest that the Germans took in civilian, especially economic, matters and the German taste for bureaucracy all meant that it began to impinge more and more sharply on the everyday lives of the French. By the beginning of 1941, Edmond Duméril recalled with nostalgia the time when it had seemed that 'As long as one respected the military authorities ... it would be possible to live in peace'. Duméril, as official interpreter, now spent much of his time helping his compatriots with complicated forms that they needed to submit to German officials.[23]

Paris had a particular part to play in the German rule of France. Here the Germans established their main headquarters as well as their embassy. It was reckoned that there were 40,000 Germans in Paris in 1940 and 15,000 in 1943;[24] the number dropped a little after this date as men were sent to the Eastern Front. Paris was also used as a centre of recreation for German troops who were brought to the city under the 'Jeder einmal nach Paris' (everyone to Paris once) programme, which subjected them to a brief tourist visit that included standard attractions (a ride on a *bateau-mouche*, climbing the Eiffel Tower). Hitler himself had set the tone of such visits when, on 23 June 1940, he spent two and a half hours in Paris (the only visit of his life). He arrived at Le Bourget airport at five in the morning, accompanied by Albert Speer and the sculptor Arno Brecker; he hoped that the visit would provide ideas about how German cities might be rebuilt on a grander scale. He began by visiting the Opéra at six in the morning before moving on to the Arc de Triomphe. He saw the Place de la Concorde, where he was annoyed by the statue of Charles Mangin who had commanded the French forces that occupied the Rhineland after the First World War.[25] The tour finished with a visit to the Sacré Coeur, and Hitler flew out of Le Bourget at half past eight the same morning. Hitler did not speak to a French person during his visit and indeed saw almost no one except a few policemen and a terrified concierge at the Opéra who refused to take a tip from Speer.

Some notable meetings between French and Germans took place in Paris. In April 1942 Hermann Goering summoned the actor Sacha

Guitry to see him at the Quai d'Orsay, where the Luftwaffe in Paris had its offices. Guitry was alarmed, but, as it turned out, the Reichs-marschall merely wished to discuss Guitry's films – he was a particular admirer of *Le Roman d'un tricheur*.[26] In his autobiographical novel *La Fin des ambassades*, Roger Peyrefitte describes a dinner in 1944 that brings together Frenchmen – a smart diplomat, a bishop and a barrister who represents the Gestapo – and a number of German officers; the party dines on caviar, brought back from Russia.[27]

Meetings of Parisians and Germans were usually more mundane. Ordinary German soldiers often felt the shortage of food and fuel almost as acutely as the French, and sometimes simple material interest brought the two together. In September 1940 a German NCO handed sacks of coal (presumably from requisitioned French stocks) to three young French girls. When the French police intervened, the girls attacked them; the NCO was later punished by the German authorities.[28] On 12 August 1944, just before Allied troops arrived in Paris, German soldiers joined several hundred French civilians pillaging a tanker of white wine near the Gare de l'Est.[29] Some encounters between French and Germans turned nasty. Alongside, and mainly separate from, the war between the Germans and armed resisters, were outbursts of low-level violence produced by drink and squabbles over girls.[30] German troops, usually drunk, fired their guns without authorization on several hundred occasions in Paris between 1940 and 1944.[31]

Germans in Paris were concentrated in the smart western quarters – indeed, part of this area was closed to all French people who did not have a pass. The main German headquarters were in the Hôtel Majestic in the Avenue Kléber. Best's offices were in the Hôtel Claridge on the Champs-Élysées. German counter-intelligence was based in the Hôtel Lutetia on the Boulevard Raspail. The Gestapo took over the Ministry of the Interior in the Rue des Saussaies, next door to the Élysée Palace. The German administration of Paris itself was based in the Palais Bourbon (formerly the site of the National Assembly) and in the Hôtel de Ville. The Germans had their own cinemas, such as the Rex in the Boulevard Poissonnière, and five or six nightclubs were reserved for their use.

German presence in the east and north of the city, and in the industrial suburbs that surrounded it, was relatively slight. These areas had few of the grand public buildings that German authorities liked to colonize. Anyone who wanted to hide from the Germans was better off in the winding streets of Belleville than in the wide open spaces of western Paris. It is no accident that the first Resistance assassination in Paris (that of a German naval cadet, Alfons Moser) took place in the Barbès Rochechouart metro station, in a working-class quarter of north-eastern Paris.

The intensity of the German presence was a matter of time as well as place. The curfew had important effects, especially since the Germans enforced central European time (an hour earlier than French time) in the occupied zone. Frenchmen were required to be off the streets by eleven o'clock. Sometimes the Paris police took French people in to prevent them from falling into the hands of the Germans: in 1940, a bourgeois lady and her daughter spent a night in a police station in the company of tramps and petty criminals.[32] Eleven o'clock was also the curfew hour for German private soldiers and for German women. Midnight was the curfew for German NCOs. Officers were allowed to roam the streets all night, a privilege worth having because the blackout lent the city a sombre charm. In the small hours of the morning, Paris streets belonged to German officers, French policemen and those people, often criminals in the eyes of French law, who had managed to obtain special passes from the Germans. There were some incongruous incidents in these dark empty streets: in November 1943 a French policeman complained that his 'parties sexuelles' had been touched by a German soldier in the Avenue Foch. The French authorities admitted that they had received similar complaints in the recent past.[33]

All big towns in occupied France had areas in which there was a heavy presence of Germans. In Rennes, for example, they concentrated in an area south of the centre of the city bounded by the canal, the station and the Place de Bretagne.[34] They wanted billets where they could find running water and reasonable space. Sometimes this meant imposing themselves on private houses. Very few French people, however, had houses big enough to accommodate significant numbers of Germans.[35] Mostly, German soldiers took over public buildings; schools were a particular favourite.

The German army in France was highly motorized, whilst even those few French people who had had access to cars before 1940 were generally forced onto bicycles, public transport or foot after the defeat. This fact had an effect on relations between the two. One of the simplest favours that the Germans granted to their French associates was to give them lifts; one of the most common sources of conflict between French and Germans came when German cars ran over French pedestrians or cyclists.[36]

The Germans clustered around ports, railways and main roads. They avoided places where access for their cars and lorries was difficult. They particularly disliked hills. Jews, political refugees or young men who might be sent for labour service in Germany quickly learnt that the best way to avoid meeting Germans was simply to climb. The town of Roussillon d'Apt in Provence became a sought-after location for many people on the run because it was unattractive to Germans: it was inaccessible to heavy vehicles and had few buildings that would provide suitable billets (only one house had a bathroom).[37] Equally, the village of Saint-Martin-en-Haut, a hill village about thirty kilometres from Lyons, attracted a population of Jews drawn by its inaccessibility to Germans.

TALKING TO THE GERMANS

French people often discussed how they should deal with the Germans. They laid a heavy emphasis on silence (interestingly, silence was a great virtue for Pétainists too) and on the need to avoid meeting the eyes of Germans. Even collaborators, such as Jacques Benoist-Méchin, thought that there should be limits to the intimacy between victor and defeated. Real encounters with Germans, however, did not always fit into any preconceived code of etiquette. Liliane Schroeder was a middle-class Parisian of anti-German and pro-English views (her father was of Scottish descent and she sometimes made her diary entries in English). In the summer of 1940, her family took refuge in Rochefort (in the south-west of France), where they shared a house with eight German soldiers – including, as she noted, Albert, Frantz, Karl, Gustav and Willy (nicknamed 'the redhead'). She wrote:

We started off by not wanting to look at them and still less to talk to them. But little by little 'relations' became more polite and almost amicable. For sure, when one thinks about it, it is not normal to live with eight German soldiers . . . Personally I accepted the idea very quickly and very simply. I did not even have to adapt myself. Where does this state of mind come from? It is not cohabitation with these wretched soldiers that is going to worry me when so many more important things are happening, and are going to happen.[38]

Relations between French and Germans could escape from formal etiquette entirely. Schroeder reported a conversation between a six-year-old boy, Philippe Giraud, and a German who lived next door to the boy's aunt:

The other day, he [the boy] said through the fence with a firm but friendly air: 'Germany Kapout'. At which his interlocutor, entering into the game, replied, 'Philippe Kommandantur, bang, bang, bang!!!' But the prospect of being shot did not upset the young Philippe and the conversation finished on the best of terms.[39]

The conversation would have seemed different four years later when Germany really was 'Kapout' and when boys, not much older than Philippe, were being shot quite frequently.

Simple questions of language governed many relationships. A large proportion of the educated classes in France spoke German. Most ordinary French people, however, conducted their relations with the Germans on a simpler level. In his prisoner of war camp, Jean-Paul Sartre, who had spent a year in Berlin, lectured on Rilke, but one of his comrades in captivity, a poacher and agricultural labourer, insisted that he needed only four words to understand German society. Those words were *Kartoffel* (potato), *Arbeit* (work), *Geld* (money) and *verboten* (forbidden).

When dealings between the two sides had to be conducted at a formal level, people who spoke both languages were found to translate. Translation could be a delicate business. German was full of *faux amis*. When the Germans described a French person who had gone to work in Germany as a 'Freiwilliger', they meant that he or she was not confined when they got there; they did not mean, as the French did when they used the word 'volontaire', that he or she had chosen to go.[40] The German word *Kollaboration* (it was said that Hitler had difficulty in pronouncing it) implied a politically motivated desire for German victory; the German equivalent of the French word *collaboration* (which, initially, had no political connotations) was *Zusammenarbeit* or 'working together'. A German officer lost his patience with a translator who handled his conversation with a French prefect – 'the prefect "demands" but I merely "desire"', he complained.

Interpreters were not necessarily sympathetic to the German cause. Many of them had been schoolteachers or academics before the war (professions generally associated with left-wing, or at least republican, views). Some French interpreters were specifically anti-Nazi. One man who volunteered his service as a translator in Paris in 1940 had previously campaigned against anti-Semitism.[41]

Edmond Duméril was chief official interpreter for the prefect of the Loire-Inférieure, and had four men working under him. He got on well with his German interlocutors, with whom he dined on at least one occasion.[42] He developed a particularly close relation with Lieutenant Colonel Karl Hotz, the German commander in Nantes. Once Hotz confided in him that he wished to avoid confrontation with the local population.[43] On another occasion, Hotz mentioned that he was reading Bainville's biography of Napoleon: the works of Bainville, a nationalist and anti-German historian, were forbidden in the German occupied zone.[44] Duméril was angry when the Resistance assassinated Hotz.[45] However, Duméril did not see his relations with the Germans as having any political implications. He refused to join the Collaboration movement,* saying that his position required him to maintain a stance of political neutrality,[46] and was to claim, after the war, that he had provided information to the Resistance.

At lower levels, translation was sometimes a more improvised affair and often involved people from less privileged backgrounds than Duméril. This was especially true of female interpreters. Nine out of ten women in Brittany who worked for the Germans spoke no German, but those who picked up a few words of the language

---

* The Groupe Collaboration was the political party established by Alphonse de Châteaubriant.

were sometimes transformed into interpreters. 'I was hired through the labour exchange in Quimper as charwoman at the base of Camaret. A few days later, knowing a few words, I was engaged as an interpreter,' one reported.[47] Another woman picked up German talking to the clients in her mother's restaurant in Saint-Malo before being hired as an interpreter.[48] A variety of informal intermediaries also managed relations between the French population and the Germans. Often such intermediaries worked with comparatively low-ranking German soldiers in pursuit of aims that would not have been approved of by the German authorities. In the small town of Sucy-en-Brie, a naturalized Hungarian, Ladislas Frank, volunteered to translate for the Germans and soon, with the aid of corrupt German officials, he began to sell petrol on the black market.[49] In the Landes, a Frenchman, who had learnt German during his time as a prisoner of war between 1914 and 1918, pimped local women to German soldiers.[50]

WORKING FOR THE GERMANS

Work was the single thing that brought the largest number of French people into contact with Germans. Construction was particularly important. On their arrival, the Germans needed to get ports (often damaged by fighting) and aerodromes back into operation, and they needed to build facilities to prepare for their planned invasion of England. The need for labour was particularly acute on the Channel coast and in Brittany. Labour was, at first, not hard to find. The French economy had been disrupted by the defeat and there were almost a million people unemployed. Sometimes, the German presence in an area destroyed existing sources of employment and created new ones. This was particularly true in ports, because fishing and civilian trade diminished as opportunities for employment on German military projects increased. Fécamp in Normandy was a fishing town. In the autumn of 1940 there were 900 unemployed there, out of a population of 16,000. Two years later 900 people were directly employed by the Germans and it was estimated that a third of all households drew their income from working for the Germans.[51]

The number of people employed by the Germans in France increased sharply when Hitler decreed, at the end of 1941, that fortifications should be built on the Atlantic coast to resist any future Allied invasion of Europe. The Todt organization, responsible for large-scale construction projects, was the largest single employer of labour, but the army, air force and navy continued to employ workers on their own behalf too. By the summer of 1944 at least a quarter of a million people worked for the Todt organization in France, and a further half a million worked for other German agencies.

Finding workers in France became more difficult as time went on. The unemployment that had marked the early stages of the occupation was replaced by labour shortage. The Germans paid higher wages than French employers, who were constrained by legal regulation of salaries, and the Germans sometimes simply closed down enterprises (especially those in construction) that competed with them for labour. Employment by the Germans, however, meant long hours of backbreaking work. It also increasingly meant the risk of being killed by Allied bombing, which was directed at the very sites where the Germans employed most people.

Sometimes the Germans employed groups that were in no position to resist. People from outside France were one such group. Spanish Republicans and North Africans could rarely return to their native countries. Many of the former were already organized into work groups by the Vichy government and were simply handed over to the Germans. In December 1942 the Todt organization in western France employed 87,257 people, of whom 29,132 were foreigners and 2,614 were Algerians. Jews were another vulnerable group, especially when Vichy stripped some of them of their nationality. In the Nord and Pas-de-Calais, the Todt organization employed 2,000 Jews before they were deported to Auschwitz in October 1942. Ordinary prisoners were also handed over to the Germans: 800 inmates of Loos prison were sent to build bunkers in the summer of 1943.

Increasingly, the Germans abandoned all pretence of seeking volunteer workers. A French law of September 1942 allowed workers to be drafted into employment 'in the national interest'. Some were sent to work for the Germans (though the risk that they might ultimately be drafted to Germany encouraged many to desert). Local commanders exercised their right under the Hague Convention to conscript labour for their purposes.

Those who worked for the Germans often caused social upheaval in the areas to which they were sent. Men were piled into crowded lodgings. Large groups were sometimes concentrated in relatively underpopulated parts of the country. The fact that many who worked for the Germans were drawn from backgrounds which the French authorities regarded with disdain caused problems. Mayors in Brittany complained about the presence of foreigners and criminals close to their villages.

Some people from France went to work in Germany itself. A report to the French consul-general in Germany of April 1942 estimated that 157,000 French citizens had gone to Germany and that 96,000 were still there: 50,000 had not renewed their contracts; 8,000 had returned to France without fulfilling their contracts; 2,500 had returned after injury and 500 had died in the Reich. One German source estimated that around 250,000 people volunteered to work in Germany during the course of the occupation.[52] As far as the French authorities were concerned, those who volunteered to work in Germany (as opposed to those who were compelled to do so under the terms of French legislation in 1942 and 1943) were drawn from a lumpenproletariat marked by immorality, dirtiness and criminality. This view was not just expressed after the liberation; it can be found in documents produced by the Vichy government itself. The report of April 1942 suggested that 'around 15,000 [of the 96,000 people in Germany] are of good quality; the rest are not worth much, especially the women'.[53] Volunteers were often treated with disdain when they returned to France. In 1943, the Secours National refused help for a woman who lived with a man who had volunteered to work in Germany. It was reported that he was a Belgian national and that both he and his lover were drunks (a drunken foreigner who lived with a woman outside marriage was the archetypal volunteer in the eyes of Vichy officialdom).[54] When large numbers of young Frenchmen were compelled to go to Germany under the Service du Travail Obligatoire programme, Vichy officials were keen to protect them from the 'lamentable influence of volunteer workers'.[55]

Explicit political commitment amongst those who worked for the Germans was rare. Paris police investigating returning workers after the liberation found only tenuous links to collaborationist politics: one couple who had gone to Germany were known as 'quiet but pro-German';[56] another volunteer was said to be the son of a woman who supported the Parti Populaire Français (PPF).[57] In Calvados, only 357 people (about a tenth of returning volunteers) were investigated. Those investigated were usually perceived as the most political of the volunteers, but, even in this unrepresentative minority, only forty people were identified as having been members of collaborationist parties.[58]

Indeed, the most marked correlation between politics and volunteering to work in Germany concerned, not members of collaborationist groups, but Communists. The report to the consul in April 1942 recognized that the collaborationist parties – the PPF, the RNP (Rassemblement National Populaire) and the MSR (Mouvement Social Révolutionnaire) – had sent militants to Germany but argued that the Communists had done so on a larger scale and with more effect. It was suggested that a quarter of all French workers in Germany in April 1942 were Communists.[59] Among a hundred and ten volunteers returning to the Meurthe-et-Moselle at the liberation, only six appeared to have had political connections and only one of these was a 'fascist'; the other five were Communists.[60] In November 1942 the Renseignements Généraux were asked for information about fifteen French volunteer workers in Germany. Only one of these was reported to have any political affiliation: he was a Communist, son of a Communist and a former member of the Red Falcons.[61]

Industrialists or prefects sometimes forced Communist militants into 'volunteering' as a means of removing a potentially troublesome presence. In some cases, Communists were already in prison and, like other prisoners, were offered release if they signed a contract engaging them to work in Germany. The prefect of the Meurthe-et-Moselle suggested that 165 'more or less Communist' individuals from the internment camp at Écrouves should be sent to Germany (eventually 120 of them went).[62] Some Communists may have decided that they would be safer if they removed themselves from communities where they were known, and where they might face the wrath of old enemies or, given the fact that the Communist Party itself was divided after the Hitler–Stalin pact, their former comrades. A twenty-four-year-old man returning to Paris from Germany in 1945 told police that 'being a member of the Communist Party and fearing that he would be deported, he signed up voluntarily to go to work in Germany on 15 October 1942'.[63]

It may also be that Communist leaders incited some militants to go to Germany. In 1940 French Communists were keen to maintain contacts with the French working class and to make contact with the German working class. One Frenchwoman in Germany recalled meeting a French worker who had gone to Germany as a Communist agent in 1940. On his return to France he found that he was re-proached by some for having been a Communist in 1939–40, and by others for having volunteered for work in Germany. Eventually, fearing assassination, he returned to Germany.[64]

Most volunteers for work in Germany, however, had no political affiliations.[65] The authorities sometimes reported on the politics of volunteer workers who applied for passports. Most of these reports were bland: 'this worker is not political',[66] or 'no unfavourable re-mark'.[67] Occasionally, it was reported that a worker was 'good' from the political point of view,[68] or good with regard to the 'national ques-tion'.[69] Sometimes volunteers were seen as belonging to a world where revolutionary politics and criminality blended into one another.[70] More commonly, Vichy officials regarded volunteers as being beneath poli-tics. They reported that one volunteer was of 'passable' morality and conduct and 'indifferent' political opinions.[71] One official lost patience with questions about politics on the standard form. Faced with a man of twenty, of uncertain origins, brought up by the *Assistance Publique*, sacked by seven employers in three years, convicted of two serious offences in the same period, and dismissed from the French army after four days, the official suggested: 'In view of the deplorable record of this young man, I do not think that there is any question of worrying about his political attitude.'[72]

The lumpenproletariat that attracted so much scorn from Vichy officials had not emerged out of thin air. In some respects, it was rooted in pre-war social and economic conditions, but in some ways it was also rooted in the specific circumstances of the war. Indeed,

Vichy's disdain for certain kinds of people was often part of a vicious circle by which such people were forced out of respectable society and then forced to survive by expedients that confirmed their 'non-respectable' status. The high unemployment of the period immediately after the defeat forced some to go to Germany. In the Nord, the Germans sometimes compelled the unemployed to work in Germany.[73] Unemployment was the most common reason given by people who volunteered to go to Germany. Of the sixty-two volunteers returning to the area around Nancy, twenty explained their departure with reference to unemployment whilst another twelve referred to the possibility of earning higher salaries in Germany.[74] Unemployment was also the reason most commonly cited by returning volunteers who were interviewed by the Paris police.[75] Most volunteers came from the most marginal part of the working class and simple economic constraint often seems to have governed their decisions. The Eure-et-Loir was very different from either Paris or the east in that it was a primarily agricultural area, and in that comparatively few volunteers left during the period of high unemployment in 1940–41. In spite of this, some volunteers justified their departure in economic terms.[76] Eleven out of 211 returned volunteers had been unemployed when they went; five referred to poverty;[77] two said bluntly that the Germans paid better than the French; one said that he had gone to Germany in order to be able to work in his own profession;[78] one man left when he was unable to continue commuting to Dreux because he could not obtain new tyres for his bicycle.[79]

People who worked in light industries or services or who were not well established in the French workforce were particularly likely to be affected by unemployment. Women and the very young were also vulnerable. Most of all, large numbers of foreigners lost their jobs during the occupation and, in some cases, seem to have been prevented from working in France by the French authorities. Police enquiries at the liberation recognized that some foreigners had had no choice but to go to work in Germany during the early stages of the occupation. At first, almost all volunteers were immigrants: only about 15 per cent of the 12,000 people who went from France to work in Germany before the end of October 1940 were French, and French citizens were still a minority (42.5 per cent) of those who had gone to Germany by the summer of 1941.[80] Many of the volunteers who returned to France in 1945 were foreigners.[81] The 323 volunteers who left the Var in the first two months of 1943 included seven North Africans, one Chinese, one Armenian, one Belgian, two Spaniards, seventeen Italians, three Poles, one Russian and three Serbs.[82]

Foreigners made up a notable proportion of the working class in France (especially in the north and east) and were vulnerable to particular pressures. They were less likely than their French colleagues to have families to fall back on if they lost their jobs and were probably less likely to be supported by the French authorities if they resisted going to Germany. One volunteer returning to Paris in 1945 argued that he had had no choice but to go to Germany in 1941 because, as a foreigner, he had no right to work in France.[83] A man and his fifteen-year-old son were said to have gone to Germany for the same reason.[84]

Some who went to Germany came from groups that did not have complete legal independence. The very young were one such group. Technically, no minor could be sent to Germany without parental authorization. In practice, absence of parental authorization rarely prevented anyone from going to Germany,[85] and, in any case, the authorities often said that very young people who 'volunteered' to go to Germany had no traceable parents.[86] Some returning volunteers claimed that their parents had obliged them to go by signing authorizations.[87] Children from the *Assistance Publique*, on whose behalf civil servants signed authorization forms, were particularly likely to 'volunteer' for work in Germany.

Some who volunteered to work in Germany were either in prison or facing the prospect of prison. Thirteen of the 211 volunteers who were investigated by the *Comité Départemental de la Libération* of the Eure-et-Loir were said to have gone to Germany in order to escape prosecution in France. Almost a fifth of French volunteers in Bremen already had criminal convictions before they left.[88] The judicial authorities in Dijon reported that, between June 1942 and June 1944, 159 French prisoners had been freed in order to work in Germany and that another 280 had benefited from suspended sentences on the same grounds.[89] Releasing prisoners so that they could go to Germany became so common that in May 1944 the authorities considered it worth comment that Santé prison had refused to release a man who had volunteered for work in Germany.[90] The prison population expanded during the occupation years, which no doubt increased the enthusiasm of prison governors to reduce the number of their inmates, and mortality rates in prisons rose steeply (especially in early 1942), which no doubt increased the enthusiasm of inmates to accept any expedient that would get them out.[91]

Sometimes the very means by which people were recruited to work in Germany were those that blended criminality and collaboration. The Germans had the right to recruit workers from the occupied zone in France, but before April 1942 they were not supposed to do so in the southern zone. In practice, however, Vichy recognized that official recruitment offices in the occupied zone existed alongside *bureaux officieux* (unofficial offices) and *officines louches* (shady agencies). Recruitment in the southern zone was conducted exclusively through *bureaux officieux* and *officines louches*.[92] Private enterprises which recruited workers for Germany could earn bonuses and this encouraged criminality amongst both the French and the Germans. German entrepreneurs were continuing to claim bonuses even when they were handling workers who had in fact been conscripted under French legislation.

Adrien L. was characteristic of those who presented themselves as German agents. A failed businessman, who had become an official of the collaborationist Parti Populaire Français after 1940, he turned up in a small town in 1942, announcing that he was a representative of the 'Société des Ateliers Mécaniques de la Seine' and that he was authorized to requisition a building in order to recruit workers for dispatch to Germany. This provoked a flurry of angry letters from local officials. The regional prefect of the Gironde wrote: 'The regional representative of the Service de la Main d'Oeuvre Française en Allemagne informs me that L. exercises no function in that body. He thus has no authority to ask for premises.'[93] The prefect of the Landes complained about the propensity of men such as L. to act 'on the margins of administrative rules'.[94]

FIGHTING FOR THE GERMANS

Vichy was a neutral government and, except for some confrontations in Algeria, Madagascar and Syria, regular members of the French army did not fight against the Allies during the Second World War. However, some at Vichy did sponsor new agencies, the members of which came to fight alongside the Germans. Some at Vichy also sponsored increasingly vigorous forms of policing, directed especially against the Resistance.

In 1941 Marcel Gombert created a small inner group in the Légion Française des Combattants in the Alpes-Maritimes that was designed for 'missions of order and protection'. The new body attracted the interest and support of the leader of the Légion in the Alpes-Maritimes – Joseph Darnand – and obtained official recognition from Vichy in January 1942 as the Service d'Ordre Légionnaire (SOL). Although the SOL was theoretically a part of the Pétainist Légion, in practice it marked a break with conservative Pétainism (see p. 68). *Légionnaires* shunned the SOL (only a quarter of them turned up when it was presented with colours in Haute-Savoie). Members of the SOL were aged between twenty and forty-five (younger than the average age in the Légion); they had to be French, gentile and not to have been freemasons. The SOL's mission was to protect the 'National Revolution' against subversion from within France. The SOL was not initially collaborationist. Darnand had fought against the Germans in 1940 and escaped from German captivity. The success of the section of the Légion that he led in the Alpes-Maritimes owed much to anti-Italian feeling in this area and desire to maintain some military organization that might protect French sovereignty. Darnand's position was changed by anti-Communism. In July 1942 he invited members of the SOL to join the French volunteers fighting in Russia against the Soviet Union, an invitation that provoked some members of his movement to resign.

In January 1943 Laval entrusted Darnand with the creation of another body, the Milice. The most important elements of the Milice were the militarized *francs gardes*, some of whom were paid professionals. The Milice marked yet another step away from the Légion, in which Darnand had originated. The Milice, unlike the Légion, explicitly excluded Jews from membership and its members were younger than the *légionnaires*, having an average age of thirty against the Légion's average age of fifty. The Milice also drew its recruits from cities to a greater extent than the Légion – the countryside was becoming a dangerous place for anyone likely to be a Resistance target.

The Milice became more and more closely associated with the Germans. Darnand himself was commissioned into the SS in August 1943, and in November of that year the Germans began to give the Milice weapons. This association, however, never meant that Darnand entirely abandoned his anti-German nationalism, and even just before joining the SS he seems to have talked about the possibility of supporting the Free French.

There were about 35,000 *miliciens* by the liberation, of whom around a quarter were in the *francs gardes*. Some *miliciens*, such as Henry Charbonneau or Christian de la Mazière, were upper-class young men driven by anti-Communism and the search for adventure. Increasingly, however, recruits to the Milice had more obviously material motives. Many were young, urban and poor. Some wished to secure exemption from labour service in Germany. Others were attracted by the relatively high salaries paid to full-time *miliciens* (a member of the *francs gardes* could earn 2,500 francs per month, at a time when a factory worker earned 1,300 francs) or by the opportunities for pillage. Quite large numbers of *miliciens* were regarded as suffering from mental instability.[95]

The Légion des Volontaires Français contre le Bolchevisme (LVF) was founded by Jacques Doriot, Eugène Deloncle and Marcel Déat, after the German invasion of the Soviet Union in June 1941. Unlike the Milice, it was meant to fight outside France's frontiers (against the Red Army and Soviet partisans) rather than to police France. Vichy gave the LVF official sanction in August 1942 and urged men to join it. Laval hoped to gain credit from the Germans for the LVF and perhaps to take it over. In practice, many Pétainists felt uneasy with the LVF. It compromised Vichy's neutrality and did so at a time when most people in France knew that Germany would lose the war. More importantly, perhaps, the recruits to the LVF were conspicuously drawn from outside respectable society. Almost half of those who joined in Marseilles were unemployed and 40 per cent of them had criminal records.[96] When Paris police arrested eight members of the LVF after a brawl in 1944, they found that three of them already had criminal records: one for fraud, one for receipt of stolen goods and one for murder.[97]

The main LVF barracks were in Versailles and its members were not supposed to go into the capital without special permission, but many drifted into Paris. Members of the LVF often set themselves up as a police force and punished those that they regarded as anti-patriotic. They were particularly exercised by *zazous*, young bourgeois Parisians who dressed in a self-consciously dandyish fashion and listened to jazz. In February 1943, 'several members of the LVF wanted to throw some young *zazous* out of the Paris Swing Club on the boulevards'.[98] In June of the same year, fifty members of the LVF attacked a group of *zazous* on the Champs-Élysées.[99] A month later the LVF were in conflict with 'some young men aged from sixteen to nineteen who were walking around in slightly eccentric dress (striking straw hats, canes etc.)'.[100] Members of the LVF themselves were often young and usually drawn from underprivileged backgrounds. It is easy to understand the hostility that they – in their uncomfortable military uniforms and probably aware that their lives might well end in a battle with the Red Army or in front of a firing squad – felt for those who had been insulated from the horrors of war by black-market chocolate and powerful fathers.

The LVF and the Milice were both, at least nominally, loyal to Vichy. The Germans also employed French people directly to police France for them. In the film *Lacombe Lucien* (1974), Louis Malle gives a picture of people who worked for the German police that seems to have been based on real documents from the occupation. Lucien himself is a poorly educated teenage peasant. His colleagues include a delinquent aristocrat, a policeman ('sacked in 1936', the year of the Popular Front government), a corrupt hotelier, an obsessive anti-Semite (the only man in the band to show any sign of political commitment) and an elegant black man (the German police in Bordeaux had, apparently, really employed two black men).[101]

Some of those who worked with the Germans had criminal records before 1940. The most spectacular example of such criminality was to be found in the Bonny–Lafont gang. Henri Lafont (aka Henri Chamberlin or Henri Normand) was born in Paris in 1902. He was orphaned at thirteen and convicted of his first crime at seventeen. He performed his military service in the 39th regiment of the Tirailleurs Africains (North Africans were to play an important part in his later career). During the 1930s he continued a life of petty crime. He also developed close relations with parts of the Paris police force, and even ran the club of the Paris prefecture of police for a time. In 1940 he was in prison in the south-west of France. In the confusion of the *exode*, he escaped. He was accompanied in his escape by three men who had spied for the Germans, notably the Swede Max Stocklin. He was also accompanied by four French veterans of the Bataillons d'Afrique – the punishment units of the French army – Henri Chevalier (aka Riri Tête Dure), Pierre Loutrel (aka Pierrot le Fou), Jo Attia (aka Jo le Boxeur) and Charles Le Guen (aka Charles le Nantais).

Stocklin introduced Lafont to Radecke, a German army officer attached to the Abwehr, and Hermann Brandl, also known as Otto. Lafont persuaded these men that he was a well-connected figure in the Paris underworld, which at this stage he was not, and that he would be able to provide them with information and access to goods that could not be obtained on legitimate markets. Senior Wehrmacht officers did not always approve of Lafont or his methods, and the German high command in Paris ordered his arrest in the summer of 1940. However, Lafont had two advantages. First, a group of Germans who were relatively low down in the formal hierarchy (often NCOs rather than officers and sometimes men who themselves had criminal records) were willing to protect him and often to conduct mutually beneficial transactions with him. Secondly, Lafont could undertake operations that were difficult for the Germans; in particular, he could arrange kidnappings and assassinations in the unoccupied part of France.

On 6 July 1940, accompanied by two German NCOs, Lafont arrived at Fresnes prison and obtained the release of five convicts; over the rest of the month a total of twenty-one convicts were released at the instigation of Lafont, who soon became known as someone who could extract criminals from almost any difficulties. Paris gangsters arranged to have their own criminal records destroyed: the Corsican De Palmiéri bought his *casier judiciaire* from the head of German liaison with the Paris prefecture of police for 800,000 francs.

Lafont's gang was completed in 1941 when he was joined by Pierre Bonny, a former police inspector who had been dismissed in 1935. At first, the gang devoted most of their energy to procuring goods for the Germans from the black market. In this task they were aided by Joseph Joinovici, a Romanian Jew who had arrived in France in 1925 and who had made a fortune in scrap metal despite being almost illiterate. Some Germans were willing to protect Joinovici as long as he was useful to them – he survived the war and, thanks to some prudent investment in Resistance funding, survived the liberation too.

The Bonny–Lafont gang also helped the Germans to hunt their enemies and, as the Germans turned away from black market activities in 1943 (because they believed that the black market was undermining their own war economy), this became the gang's major purpose. Lafont illustrated the blurring of the line between policing and crime during the occupation. Some of his associates were gangsters with names that seemed to come from a Jean-Pierre Melville film – 'le Manchot', 'Riri l'Américain' – but others had had previous experience of police work: four out of five of the men whom Lafont liberated on his first visit to Fresnes were former policemen.

Lafont spent money on fast cars and women – his mistresses included a black singer with a false Irish passport and a German Jewess. His involvement with the Germans became ever more direct. He took German nationality in 1941, joined the SS and eventually led a 'Brigade Nord-Africaine' (made up mainly of Algerians recruited from the margins of the Paris underworld), which fought against the Resistance in south-western France. After the liberation, the leaders of the Bonny–Lafont gang were executed.[102]

RIVAL POLICE FORCES

The existence of parallel police forces backed, officially or not, by the Germans put the regular police in an awkward position. They had no control over German protégés and little knowledge about where or how they operated. German-sponsored agents often behaved like gangsters – often were gangsters. In the blacked-out streets of Paris after the curfew, French policemen encountered mysterious armed Frenchmen who turned out to possess German credentials. Sometimes the French police were warned off, and sometimes Germans intervened to prevent investigation of the activities of their employees. In 1943 Paris policemen heard a gunshot and found a man lying in the street, apparently having accidentally shot himself in the foot with his own revolver. The man, André C., born in 1908, insisted that he worked for the Gestapo and had been watching a building on their behalf. The French police delivered the wounded man to hospital under guard, but soon his chief arrived and insisted that this was a 'purely German matter', though neither the wounded man nor his chief seem to have been German.[103] In March of the following year, police heard shots near the Gare Saint-Lazare, but, on going to investigate, they were told by two Frenchmen working for the German police that this was 'a German matter'.[104]

Forces that worked for or with the Germans sometimes treated French law and regular French policemen with contempt. Celebrations in Paris in August 1943 to mark the second anniversary of the LVF's creation left seventy-four casualties amongst Paris policemen.[105] A couple of months earlier, members of the LVF had beaten a policeman with his own truncheon.[106] A policeman who went to investigate suspicious noises was greeted by 'five or six men' who said: 'You looking for something, Mr Policeman? We are the Légion, do you want something to remember us by?'[107]

The French police were lightly armed. Most of them had just a revolver and five bullets.[108] Yet they found themselves up against men with sub-machine guns and hand grenades. In 1944 a Paris policeman had to ask a group of members of the LVF to leave their machine guns in a coat rack before going into a Paris cinema. The LVF men agreed but only after making a sinister threat: 'You will be in Germany before us,' they told the policeman.[109]

There could be real ambiguity about who did work for the Germans. Criminals claimed to be German or to work for some German-sponsored agency in order to enrich themselves. The thousand or so reported cases of 'false policemen' who extorted money in wartime

Paris (see Chapter 7) mainly involved people who claimed to be part of the German police. The circumstances of the occupation – with deserters, criminals and men on the run desperate to make a living – often provided the incentive to commit such crimes. Sometimes such circumstances also made it easier to do so. Lack of alternative clothing meant that discharged members of the LVF, for example, were often allowed to keep their military coats and could thus still present themselves as soldiers.[110] Sometimes the Germans distanced themselves from crimes committed by their employees. However, at other times, the Germans found it useful to employ people they knew to be criminals, and at least parts of the German hierarchy encouraged or tolerated certain kinds of crime. In 1941, French police arrested Alfred Spielman (born in the Haut-Rhin in 1875) for telling gullible clients whom he met in the Terminus du Nord that he could obtain the release of French prisoners of war for 75 francs per head. Spielman claimed to be a German national and was turned over to the German authorites. But, in spite of the fact that he had previous convictions for fraud and threatening violence, the Germans released him.[111]

People who claimed to work for the Germans sometimes seem to have been motivated by a desire to deceive, perhaps including a desire to deceive themselves. It was hard to know where the fantasy or con-artistry ended and the reality began. In the Landes, police investigated a man calling himself Villy Van B. who lived in a café in the village of Morcenx. Van B. sometimes gave his address as a chateau in the Vienne and claimed that he had fought with the LVF on the Eastern Front. He frequently brandished a cutlass saying: 'This has already opened many Russian bellies.' Not surprisingly, Van B.'s behaviour aroused comment. However, the French police reported: 'It seems nonetheless that Van B. does really belong to a service dependent on the occupation authorities and that, if necessary, confirmation can be asked from that authority.'[112]

Many authorities tried to lay down rules for the conduct of Franco-German relations during the occupation. In some ways, the *raison d'être* of the Vichy government was to ensure that relations were regulated and channelled through appropriate institutions so that individual French people should not come to terms with the Germans on their own. Vichy was often hostile to those who worked most closely with the Germans.

The Germans also had rules. They wanted their soldiers in France to be disciplined and distant from the French population. They discouraged black market dealings with French citizens, sexual relations with French women and uncontrolled violence against French people. Some representatives of the Resistance also tried to lay down rules about how the French should behave, or to make generalizations about how they did behave, that stressed the need to maintain dignity and distance, and to avoid eye contact or casual conversation. None of these rules was very successful. Much Franco-German contact involved individuals brought together by chance or the search for some mutual benefit.

French people tended to think of a German rather than Nazi occupation. Nazism may have dictated overall German policy towards France and it obviously had a dramatic impact on the lives of some people in France, especially Jews, Communists and Resistance activists, but relatively few French people had much contact with specifically Nazi agencies. For most, the quintessential German was a middle-aged corporal in a non-combat unit rather than a Gestapo man. The French often thought about the occupation in terms devised to deal with the First World War. *Anciens combattants*, and especially men who had been prisoners of war in Germany, sometimes mediated between the Germans and the French. The term 'boche', which had come into use during the First World War, was used by French people, even those who supported Vichy or collaboration, to describe the occupiers. The fact that French people did not experience or appreciate the most radical aspects of Nazism does not, however, mean that their experience of the Germans was benign. 'Boche' may sound a rather twee term in retrospect, but the Germans repeatedly punished French people who used it. In Brittany, a typist hired by the Germans spent much of her time reading plays to be performed in village halls and crossing out the word 'boche'.[113]

Public memories of the occupation in France have tended to concentrate on spectacular acts of large-scale violence: the massacre of civilians at Oradour in 1944 or the deportation of Parisian Jews during the summer of 1942. Sometimes attention devoted to such incidents can give the impression that German behaviour towards French people who did not belong to particularly victimized groups was generally 'correct' or that French and Germans cohabited with relative amicability. It is true that there were occasions when French and Germans co-operated in the pursuit of simple mutual interest, but it is also true that even in relatively quiet periods the French often experienced the occupation as a time of low-level humiliation and the constant threat of violence.

4

Jews, Germans and French

Admittedly Monsieur Moszkowski has a Jewish ancestry, but he is not legally [a Jew], because he fought in the war of 1914–18 in which he was mentioned in dispatches, won the *croix de guerre* and *médaille militaire* and lost an arm. (Letter from French official protesting at the arrest of a subordinate, January 1944)[1]

Our enemies are strange: you ask a Frenchman and he says that it is the German who has sent you to the camp; you ask the German and he says that he has nothing to do with it. The truth is that they both do it, and the Frenchman seeks to surpass his master and does it all too well. (Letter from Isaac Schoenberg, interned in the camp at Pithiviers, to his fiancée, 2 October 1941)[2]

Until Vichy and the Germans began to count them, no one really knew how many Jews there were in France; indeed, there was no unanimity about who should be defined as Jewish. The Third Republic did not distinguish between its citizens on the basis of race or religion. Only 20,000 religiously observant Jews were registered with the Consistory of Paris. Anti-Semites claimed that the country contained up to 900,000 Jews. The various censuses carried out during the war itself suggested that, at the beginning of the occupation, there were around 330,000 Jews in France, of whom 190,000 were French citizens. About 200,000 Jews lived in Paris.

Everyone knew the German invasion was bad news for Jews. Some German Jews had already fled to France during the 1930s, and around

4. (overleaf) *The sign reads: 'Reserved for children; forbidden to Jews.'*

20,000 Dutch and Belgian Jews had come into France as they tried to get away from the German army in 1940. Initially, however, the Germans took little direct action against Jews in France. There was no killing spree of the kind that had accompanied the invasion of Poland. Far from hunting Jews down, the German authorities sought to exclude them from the zone of France that they occupied.

The Germans sponsored French anti-Semites in the occupied zone, notably those of the Institute for the Study of Jewish Questions. They also shot Jews in France in reprisal for Resistance attacks. Mainly, however, from 1941 onwards, the Germans deported Jews in France to Auschwitz where they were either gassed or worked to death. Deportation was a German policy but it was sometimes implemented with remarkably little direct participation by the Germans. Until 1943, French Jews were arrested primarily by French policemen and all but one of the seven internment camps in which they were placed were run by the French.

French Jews also suffered at the hands of the Vichy government, which introduced anti-Semitic legislation from 1940 onwards. The law of 27 August 1940 removed penalties instituted in 1939 for anti-Semitic defamation. The first Jewish Statute was promulgated on 3 October 1940. Jews were excluded from holding most sorts of public office, including teaching in schools, and from running newspapers or cinema companies. Jews who had fought in the First World War, those who had been decorated or mentioned in dispatches in the war of 1939–40 and those who were recognized as having rendered 'exceptional services to the French state' were excused from the provisions of the Statute. The Statute anticipated the imposition of quotas of Jewish participation in the liberal professions. A second Statute of 2 June 1941 was more specific in its definition of Jews and listed further professions (notably banking) from which they were to be excluded. The law of 7 October 1940 removed citizenship from Jews in Algeria; the law of 29 March 1941 created the General Commissariat for Jewish Questions. The Commissariat was first headed by Xavier Vallat, a crippled veteran of the First World War and right-wing member of parliament, notable for his savage denunciation of the Jewish Prime Minister Léon Blum in 1936. Vallat was, as he always insisted, a particularly French kind of anti-Semite: he made at least theoretical allowance for the possibility that Jews could prove their loyalty to France by fighting for her in war. In April 1942 Laval replaced Vallat with Louis Darquier de Pellepoix, a more violent anti-Semite and one whose rhetoric more closely matched that of the Nazis. In 1944 Darquier was in turn replaced by Charles Mercier du Paty de Clam.

Anti-Semitism was not a defining feature of Vichy, in the way that it was a defining feature of the Third Reich. Some who supported the Vichy government were not anti-Semitic and some Jewish members of parliament had voted in favour of granting full powers to Marshal Pétain. On the other hand, many people who supported the Resistance were anti-Semitic. When the opinions of Resistance organizations were canvassed in 1942, five out of thirty-five of them alluded to the 'Jewish problem'. One respondent described the Jewish politician Pierre Mendès France as 'Jewish, too clever by half', whilst another wrote: 'The Jews should be kept out of public functions . . . if there is some disapproval of the harassment, deportation etc. to which they have been subjected, no one wants to see them reappear as before the war.'[3]

Vichy legislation was not driven by the same logic as German measures. Vichy aimed to exclude Jews from public life rather than to kill. French and German measures may have had different ideological roots but they did not function independently of each other. The French responded to German moves. Thus, when the Germans began to 'aryanize' Jewish property in the occupied zone in October 1940, the Vichy government introduced its own rules on the appointment of administrators of Jewish property in the hope that this would prevent businesses from falling into German hands; in July 1941 the French began to 'aryanize' businesses in the unoccupied zone too. Vichy's measures sometimes made the German project easier to realize. This was most obviously true of the direct co-operation of French police in the arrest and deportation of Jews, but it was also true of less direct measures. The census of Jews carried out in the non-occupied zone in July 1941, and the requirement in December 1942 that all Jews should have a special stamp on their identity papers, made it easier to hunt them down.

Public perceptions of Vichy anti-Semitism were influenced by the distinction that many French people made between Marshal Pétain and his government. It was widely, and wrongly, believed that Pétain would protect Jews, especially those who had fought in the French army. Raoul Girardet recalls his father comforting Hermann, an old family friend who had won the *croix de guerre* during the First World War and who now feared deportation, with the words: 'The Marshal would never permit it.' Hermann hanged himself with his belt in a French internment camp whilst awaiting deportation to Auschwitz.[4] When Mendès France was convicted of 'desertion' from the French air force (he was in fact trying to rejoin his unit in Morocco), Edmond Giscard d'Estaing, an official in the Finance Ministry, asked his defence lawyer for papers relating to the case so that he could show the Marshal how unfair the verdict was. Mendès' conviction stood. It was rumoured that, when a Jew, presumably an ex-serviceman, wrote to Pétain complaining about anti-Semitic measures and returning his ribbon of the Légion d'honneur, the Marshal wrote the word 'patience' on his visiting card and sent it back.[5]

In August 1942, someone who described himself as 'an old primary school teacher of sixty-nine . . . of the old school [who had] always taught the love of France' wrote to Pétain in the following terms: 'I go to you, Monsieur le Maréchal, as an upright and revolted conscience and I come to cry to you my disappointment and disgust.' The teacher was horrified by the treatment of Jews (for whom, he insisted, he 'had never had much sympathy') who were 'wrenched savagely from their homes, marched crying in the streets like dogs, like bandits, by gendarmes . . . some of whom were ashamed of the ignoble task imposed on them'. The teacher stressed that the events he described occurred in the free zone, where the word French was said 'to retain a meaning and a value', and pleaded: 'Act, Monsieur le Maréchal, before it is too late.' Clearly, this old man, who presented himself as a conservative, still had some faith in Pétain as an individual, though the fact that he concluded his letter by noting that French people could no longer register protest through the ballot box, and the fact that he did not sign his letter, suggests that he had limited confidence in the Vichy government.[6]

As far as French gentiles were concerned, understanding of anti-Jewish measures varied greatly. A small group of highly educated

French people (particularly lycée teachers) understood the implications of legislation quickly. This was not just because such people were well placed to see the importance of a move that struck at republican universalism. It was also because Vichy's anti-Semitism struck at people they knew. Jean-Paul Sartre, for example, could hardly fail to be aware of Vichy's policy because the job that he obtained at the Lycée Condorcet was vacant after the forced resignation of Henri Dreyfus-Le Foyer, a nephew of Alfred Dreyfus.[7] The majority of the French population, however, did not know many Jews and did not have much reason to think about the conditions under which *l'Éducation Nationale* employed academics. Not all French people even necessarily knew what a Jew was; throughout the war, the population of one provençal village referred to all the outsiders who took refuge there, a group that included two upper-class Irish Protestants, as 'the Jews'.[8]

The complexity of French attitudes to anti-Semitic measures was illustrated by reactions to the obligation, imposed on Jews in the occupied zone in 1942, to wear a yellow star. This was not a Vichy policy and it was not enforced in the unoccupied zone. However, Vichy could not dissociate itself from the yellow star either. French police had to enforce the wearing of yellow stars, and they provided a striking symbol of Vichy's collaboration with the Germans. The yellow star often seems to have encouraged displays of sympathy for the Jews, especially children. Annie Kriegel remembered 'discreet' signs of sympathy that greeted her when she wore a yellow star to her Paris lycée. Maurice Rajsfus recalls that few pupils at his school joined the boy who mocked him for wearing one, and that the headmaster, a fervent Pétainist, told the boys to 'leave your unfortunate classmates alone'.[9]

The yellow star could be turned into a weapon against Nazism and Pétainism. Sometimes this was done in a very explicit fashion. A Paris priest pinned a yellow star to the baby Jesus in a crib at Christmas 1942. Sometimes the significance of a yellow star could be less clear. Micheline Bood wrote of it: 'Apart from the fact that it is ridiculous and ugly, the Germans are stupid to do this [impose the star], because I know lots of people who hated the Jews but who now think well of them, because they are "martyred".' She said that some of her non-Jewish classmates in her Paris lycée planned to wear yellow stars.[10] Their action does not seem to have had any explicit political context – indeed, it seems to have been a gesture of rebellion comparable to that made by the very anglophile Bood when she pinned a German imperial eagle to her dress.

Wearing the yellow star sometimes went with the cult of the *zazous*, young and self-consciously louche admirers of American jazz. The collaborationist press was bitterly hostile to the *zazous*, and often contrasted them with the short-haired, virile and self-sacrificing members of the Légion des Volontaires Français contre le Bolchevisme. *Zazous* embraced a hedonism that subverted Pétainist and collaborationist desires for a youth movement of cold showers and communal singing. Not many *zazous* were Jewish: young Jews would hardly have been keen to draw attention to themselves on the streets of Paris. However, attacks on *zazous* often went with anti-Semitism because the *zazou* culture – urban, cynical, sexually immoral – seemed to have all the qualities that Vichy anti-Semites attributed to Jews. Jazz, which the *zazous* admired, was often dismissed as 'Jewish', though some earnest jazz fans defended it as being 'authentic' negro folk music (Vichy, unlike the Nazis, did not necessarily dislike negro culture), or even argued that jazz, because of its origins in Louisiana, was actually French.

Some *zazous* seem to have picked up the Jewish label that was applied as a term of abuse and worn it as a badge of pride. However, this response was not rooted in any thought-out rejection of Vichy values nor, for that matter, in any concrete provision of help to Jews. The smart suits, rolled umbrellas and dark glasses of the *zazous* would not have fitted into the Maquis any more than they fitted into the Chantiers de la Jeunesse, and *zazou* attitudes were as inimical to most Resistance ideologies as they were to Pétainism or collaborationism. *Zazou* politics were mainly about mocking politics – 'une France zazoue dans une Europe swing'. The fact that some *zazous* fastened yellow stars to their clothes seems to have been part of a general desire to shock bourgeois convention rather than a specific protest against a particular Vichy or German policy.[11]

The Paris police were faced with a curious dilemma. If they had to arrest Jews who refused to wear the yellow star, what were they to do with gentiles who did wear it? Some policemen tried to dissuade people from showing ostentatious sympathy for Jews or drew up reports in which they explained away the wearing of yellow stars as being due to a mistake.[12] Some French policemen, however, arrested gentiles who wore the yellow star. A dozen gentile women were interned in 1942 for this offence. Laconic police notes hint at the range of their motives. One woman, who had superimposed a Star of David onto a cross, seems to have been a Christian. Another, who carried a run of stars on her belt each one of which contained a letter of the word 'victoire', was presumably a Gaullist. Most of the women, however, had less obviously political motives. They were mainly young (six of them were in their early twenties and one of them was nineteen). Some of them seem to have associated the wearing of the star with the expression of sympathy for an individual (three had attached names or initials to their stars, and one woman, born in 1913, admitted that her star had been given to her by a Jewish 'camarade'). Other women seem to have given their stars meanings that were not apparent to the police (what did it mean to attach the number '130' to a yellow star?) or to have used them as gestures of fashionable rebellion. In three cases, police reports referred to an 'insigne fantaisiste', a term often applied to *zazous*. One young woman had attached a star to her dog.[13]

Gentiles who wore the yellow star were often themselves in some doubt about the precise significance of their act. Interviewed by historians sixty years after the event, some simply described themselves as motivated by youthful rebellion. Solange de Lipkowski, an eighteen-year-old girl of Russian but not Jewish extraction, was a student at the chic École Alsacienne in Paris. Furious at the imposition of the yellow star on Jews, she made her own and wrote the word Buddhist in French and German on it. She was arrested by a French policeman and placed in the cells of a police station but during the night other policemen took her out of her cell, played cards with her and told her that they would deal with the man who had arrested her after the war. The following day she was handed over to the Germans. A Gestapo officer rebuked her sharply but, when she continued to defy him, he patted her cheek, told her she was a 'good girl' and released her. When she returned home, her father, a 'real' Resistance fighter, was furious with her for drawing attention to the family. Later he was arrested and died in Buchenwald.[14]

Who was a Jew? Vichy defined anyone with three Jewish grandparents, or anyone with two Jewish grandparents who was married to a Jew, as Jewish. Their definition was slightly more all-embracing than that of the Germans, though Vichy, unlike the Germans, allowed some people to escape the full consequences of its anti-Semitic policy. Vichy's policy was based on race rather than religion; it made no provision for those who had converted to Judaism and Vichy officials insisted that baptism, indeed ordination to the priesthood, did not mean that someone ceased to be a Jew. There were, however, no records to establish who had Jewish ancestry. In the first instance, Jews simply declared themselves in the censuses conducted by the Germans and Vichy. The great majority of Jews seem to have registered with the authorities, perhaps because many of them felt that there might be serious consequences from breaking the law and because few of them yet realized how serious the consequences of obeying the law might be.

Some people who had been long established in France, and who had long abandoned all religious practice, genuinely did not understand that they were to be defined as Jewish. Some assimilated Jews defined themselves as *israélites* rather than *juifs* (the latter had a pejorative tone) and were hostile to more recent immigrants to France. People who did not register as Jews were sometimes asked to prove their gentile credentials. The singer Charles Trenet, much admired by the *zazous*, had to assemble a dossier to prove his case, as did the actor Sacha Guitry. People's names, or the names of their ancestors, could be used as evidence. Baptismal records going back for generations might be investigated. Increasingly, physical examinations sought to determine whether men had been circumcised or whether people had 'Jewish' features.

Identifying Jews could be harder than it seemed. Abraham Goukassov was arrested in the south of France. His name sounded Jewish, and, on examination, he turned out to have been circumcised. Only when he reached an internment camp was he able to explain to his captors that he was in fact a wealthy Armenian who had funded a pro-Tsarist newspaper.[15] Some people owed their survival to the strangely rigorous bureaucracy of the German killing apparatus. Marie Reille was arrested by French authorities in Bordeaux in 1942. She had two Jewish grandparents but she should not have been defined as a Jew because her husband was a gentile. In spite of this, she was deported and sent all the way to Auschwitz. However, by the time she got there, the German authorities had discovered the mistake. They separated her from the crowd of terrified and starving people, put her on another train and transported her back across the Third Reich to France.[16]

Some Jews in France were already in camps when the Germans invaded. The French had interned foreigners, particularly Spanish Republicans and German refugees. From October 1940 prefects could intern foreign Jews, and 40,000 had fallen victim to this measure by the beginning of 1941. The camps were designed for different kinds of people. Some were intended to punish as well as contain: that at Vernet was 'repressive' and that at Gurs was 'semi-repressive'. Those at Bram, Argelès and Saint-Cyprien were holding camps. Milles, in the south of France, was a transit camp designed for those who stood a good chance of being allowed to go abroad. All camps were unpleasant. They were made up of hastily erected structures exposed to wind and rain. In the winter the ground around the huts was often a sea of mud. In Gurs, the authorities eventually worked out that 'Uncle Raaf' was a slang word for hunger and banned reference to this relative from all correspondence. Around 3,000 Jews died in the camps from cold or hunger or disease.

Arrests of Jews in Paris began in May 1941. The arrests were alarming but they seemed to be relatively restricted in their scope. Most of those arrested did not have French citizenship; they were all adult men and they were mainly drawn from those parts of north-eastern Paris in which large numbers of Jews – especially foreign and relatively poor Jews – lived. At first the police simply summoned Jews to police stations and then arrested them: of 6,494 summoned in May, 3,747 were interned. Jews were assembled in two camps near Orléans – Pithiviers and Beaune-la-Rolande – that had originally been constructed by the French in order to accommodate the German prisoners they had anticipated capturing. The Germans inspected both camps but did not directly control either of them.

On 18 August 1941 French policemen sealed off the 11th arrondissement of Paris. They checked papers at the exits to metro stations and prevented Jews from leaving. They then raided flats and seized every Jewish man between the ages of eighteen and fifty that they could find. They eventually arrested 4,242 men, about half the adult Jewish male population of the district.[17] The raid, extended to neighbouring arrondissements, continued until 23 August. The arrests were carried out mainly by French policemen. Those arrested were taken to Drancy. Here a half-finished block of four-storey buildings (originally intended to be apartments) formed a squared-off U shape. This camp, too, was run by French policemen, and was to become the most notorious in France. It was from here that the first deportation convoys of Jews left for Auschwitz in March 1942: of roughly 76,000 Jews deported from France, 67,000 went via Drancy. Few preparations had been made for the sudden influx of people into the camp and there was not enough food or clothing. Conditions there were so bad that in October 1941 a German inspection ordered the release of 900 sick inmates.

The largest round-up (code named Operation Spring Wind) occurred on 16 and 17 July 1942. This round-up involved an important novelty. Until then, arrests had involved adult men, but Laval now suggested that the Germans should take children too. This had horrible consequences: men who had hidden to avoid arrest emerged to find that their children had disappeared. It also blurred the distinction between foreign and French Jews, because many children of foreign Jews had French citizenship. Most importantly, the round-up of children was sinister. As long as arrests had concentrated on adult men, it had been possible for Jews to convince themselves that those arrested were being taken away to work. This explanation was less plausible now. In total, 3,031 men, 5,802 women and 4,051 children were rounded up in July 1942. Of these, 6,900 were held, with little food or water, in the Vélodrome d'Hiver, a cycling stadium on the smart Boulevard Grenelle, for a week before being transferred to internment camps and then on to Auschwitz. Deportation to Germany became increasingly common. Before 16 July 1942, four convoys of Jews had left Drancy and, in the year that followed it, forty convoys were to leave. Around forty thousand Jews were deported from France in this one year.[18]

In 1943 the Germans themselves increasingly undertook the arrest of Jews in France and also took control of the Drancy internment camp. Vichy was more reluctant to participate in anti-Jewish arrests, perhaps because public opinion was against them, perhaps because the Church applied pressure or perhaps simply because it seemed less likely that Vichy would obtain anything in return for its co-operation.

In all, 75,721 Jews were deported from France, of whom 2,500 returned alive. A further 4,000 Jews died in France itself (mostly as a result of poor conditions in camps). More than three-quarters of Jews who had been in France at the time of German invasion survived the war. What determined whether they survived or not? Jews who were French-born stood a better chance than recent immigrants. Of the 190,000 Jews who were French citizens, about 13.5 per cent were deported; of the 140,000 Jews in France who did not have French citizenship, about 42 per cent were deported. This was partly because the Germans themselves concentrated on foreign Jews in their first deportations. It was also because the French authorities offered more help in the arrest of foreign Jews, though the Vichy government did not have any organized plan to save French-born Jews or, for that matter, to destroy foreign-born Jews.

The division between foreigners and French-born Jews went with social and cultural differences. French Jewry encompassed those who owned banks and those who were desperately poor; those who were members of the Académie Française and those who could barely speak French. Once a Jew fell into German hands, these social differences counted for little. However, the wealthy, assimilated and well-connected stood a much better chance of avoiding falling into German hands in the first place. Highly assimilated French Jews were less easy to identify. They were less likely to have accents and were less likely to live in those heavily Jewish areas of eastern Paris that were raided first by the police. Possession of a country house, especially one located in the 'free zone', was useful because it provided a means of obtaining food and of escaping from the urban centres where the Germans were most concentrated.

Money and contacts mattered. Escape overseas was an expensive luxury. Tickets to America, which had cost $80 in 1939, cost $400 in 1940.[19] A place on a boat was a huge privilege. The anthropologist Claude Lévi-Strauss got across the Atlantic on board the same boat on which he had previously, at French government expense, travelled to Brazil. The ship was crammed with 350 people, including André Breton and Victor Serge.[20] Lévi-Strauss himself was granted the special favour of a cabin, which he shared with the ship's three other privileged male passengers: an Austrian metal dealer, a mysterious character from North Africa with a Degas painting in his suitcase and a rich Creole from Martinique (the only passenger who was not presumed to be a 'Jew or an anarchist').[21] Getting tickets or finding space on boats was not the only problem. Travellers needed visas to leave France and visas to enter other countries. Visas for Panama or Cuba could be bought from corrupt consular officials but there was no guarantee that they would be honoured. Those wishing to enter Colombia had to be baptized. The most attractive destination for most Jews was the United States, but American officials usually required Jews to demonstrate that they had means of supporting themselves and that they had American guarantors. Vichy was keen to speed departures of Jews. It sought to make the process quicker, but there were limits to what it could do. Currency restrictions prevented anyone from taking more than 25,000 francs out of the country. The Germans insisted that Vichy keep men of fighting age (defined as those younger than forty-eight) from leaving the country. Thus, for example, Marc Bloch was able to secure permission for himself, his wife and his aged mother to leave the country so that he could take up an academic post in the United States, but he was unable to obtain exit visas for his sons and therefore decided to stay in France.[22]

Jews without money faced an increasingly desperate situation. As Jewish businesses were aryanized, their employees were thrown out of work; by the summer of 1941 more than half the Jews in Paris had virtually no means of support. They were dependent on charity and desperate expedients. Some foreign Jews protected themselves from deportation by working for the Germans; this sometimes meant that adult men stayed behind whilst women and children were deported. However, any Jew who worked for the Germans was vulnerable to future measures and in February 1944 the Germans deported all the Jews who were working for them in Paris. All sorts of circumstances could expose Jews to risk. From 1943, for example, they were only allowed to receive medical treatment at the Rothschild hospital, and any patient at this hospital was very vulnerable to deportation.

Schools offered protection to some young Jews. The French state education system had been meant to treat people without distinction of race or religion, and academic success had provided a means by which some Jews integrated into French society. In spite, or because, of this, some of the most ferocious anti-Semites in France – Robert Brasillach, Abel Bonnard – were graduates of the École Normale Supérieure. Generally speaking, however, French teachers seem to have disliked anti-Semitic policies, or at least disliked having them applied to their own pupils. Sometimes the privileges of French elite schooling could create incongruous contrasts in the life of a young Jew. One girl recalled that her examiners in the oral of the baccalauréat examination went out of their way to be helpful when they saw the yellow star pinned to her coat.[23] Sometimes schools offered more direct practical help. Stanley Hoffmann's history teacher forged papers for him and his mother. Father Jacques, the Carmelite head of Louis Malle's boarding school near Fontainebleau and a man whose motives were presumably rather different from those of teachers in the state lycées, hid three Jewish boys in his school.[24]

No single category of Jew was guaranteed to survive. Guy de Rothschild was well connected (he knew Pétain from pre-war shooting parties) and wealthy. He was able to travel freely in the 'free zone' of France and in Morocco, and he was treated with respect by most of those he met (including those nominated to run his business). He had no difficulty in securing a visa to enter America (his parents, who were already in New York, knew Eleanor Roosevelt) and in November 1941 Pierre Pucheu, the Vichy Minister of the Interior, granted him permission to leave France.[25] However, even this supremely powerful family was not able to protect all its members: most of Guy de Rothschild's mother's relatives who stayed in France died in Auschwitz. Equally, some people without money or connections survived through a combination of luck or ingenuity. Sometimes the authorities failed to enforce their own rules for reasons that were not easily explicable. Maurice Benhamou owned a pharmacy near the Parc des Sources in Vichy. He never hid the fact that he was Jewish and registered when required to do so. He managed to remain after the decree of 6 June 1941 banning almost all Jews from the town of Vichy. Most Jews in

the medical profession were put out of business by the quotas that
followed the Jewish Statute of 2 June 1941, but Benhamou seems not
have been affected. His business should have been taken from him
under Vichy's aryanization laws but, for some reason, the provisional
administrator appointed to run it was removed. He should have been
arrested during the round-up of Jews in the department of the Allier
carried out by French gendarmes in February 1943 (as a result of this
and other measures 132 Jews from Vichy died during the occupation).
He should have attracted the attention of the Germans who arrived
at Vichy in November 1942 and who might have been expected to
take a particular interest in a pharmacy, in case it was providing
medical supplies to the Maquis, but he did not, apparently, do so.
Maurice Benhamou was, in fact, arrested three times during the occupation but released every time. He plied his trade throughout the war,
and Xavier Vallat, head of the General Commissariat for Jewish
Questions, sometimes patronized his shop. Benhamou was still living
in Vichy at the age of a hundred and six in 1998.[26]

To understand the ways in which Jews in France survived the
occupation, we may look at three contrasting cases. Annie Kriegel,
Georgette Elgey and Maurice Rajsfus were around the same age
(they were born respectively in 1927, 1929 and 1928) and all became
historians after the war. Beyond this, their lives were very different.
Elgey was the most privileged of the three. Her father was not Jewish
(though it was impossible to prove this during the occupation because
she had been born outside marriage and he had never acknowledged
his paternity) and, though the great-granddaughter of a rabbi, she was
raised as a Catholic. She came from a wealthy and well-connected
family who had fled to the south-west during the *exode*. Georgette,
her mother, sister and grandmother returned to Paris, and hence to
the occupied zone, in the autumn of 1940. They did not even think
of themselves as Jewish and simply ignored the legal requirement
that they should register as Jews. Indeed, Elgey remembered that her
grandmother

belonged to that section of Jewish high society that was profoundly chauvinist
and xenophobe – even, I now have to admit, anti-semitic, at least towards
Jews only recently settled in France. Nor was she aware of running any great

risk in refusing to comply with the occupying power's legislation. What could possibly happen to her? At the very most she might be fined. Could she not show proof of several generations of ancestors who had rendered distinguished service to France, as the saying went? Didn't she know the Marshal personally?[27]

On 13 April 1942 Elgey's mother was visited by French policemen acting on a tip-off who demanded that she produce proof of her non-Jewish origins. She consulted the mother of one of Georgette's classmates (herself the daughter of a Vichy minister) who assured her: 'The anti-Semitic laws are not meant for French people like yourself . . . the Marshal would never put up with it.' Elgey's mother, however, was not entirely reassured. She told her daughter that she should go to her godmother's if she (the mother) was ever absent when she returned from school. She had formerly had little to do with 'foreign' Jews, but now began to give food to a Jewish family from the Levant.[28] The two policemen returned but, presumably informed of the family's powerful contacts in Vichy, they remarked that the Germans would soon force them to act and hinted broadly that the family might be safer in the non-occupied zone.[29] Family doctors gave Elgey's mother a certificate saying that her health required a visit to a spa in southwestern France. A police superintendent gave them identity papers even though he cannot have failed to notice that some of their ancestors had Jewish names; Elgey believed that the policeman acted from pure altruism, though perhaps an experienced policeman did not need to be told that a family with a huge flat in a smart district were likely to have the power to make his life difficult if they were crossed. Elgey's mother paid an intermediary 100,000 francs to obtain four German passes (for herself, her mother, and her two daughters) to cross the demarcation line.

On the line, the family were stopped by German soldiers who searched their baggage and found an illegal horde of gold coins. The soldiers realized that the family were Jews and arrested them. However, both the police superintendent and the German officer who had provided documents in Paris backed up the family's story, and they were eventually released. They found refuge in a small hilltop village outside Lyons. It was an ideal place for refugees, almost never visited by the Germans and relatively well supplied with food, and for this reason had a large population of Jews, who were not always popular. However, Elgey and her family – perhaps because they were so conspicuously French, or perhaps because they were so wealthy – were accepted by the locals. Back in Paris, German soldiers tried to requisition the family apartment but they were driven off by the concierge who insisted, truthfully, that she had attended the baptism of the children, and by the building's owner, a wealthy man who threatened to call the French police.

Annie Kriegel's origins were more modest. Her father was a salesman. Her parents were French citizens and indeed her father, a veteran of the First World War with origins in Alsace, was particularly conscious of the difference between himself and 'polacks'.[30] Her family lived in the east of Paris. They did register as Jews and did, much to their disgust, wear the yellow stars enforced in the occupied zone from June 1942. By 1942 the family knew that they were under threat but they were protected to some extent by their neighbours. Annie's father, believing that men of his age were more threatened than their wives or children, began to sleep in a different building; when it was raided, the concierge concealed his presence from the French police. The fifteen-year-old Annie met an earnest eighteen-year-old boy, Roger, from a Catholic Breton family who proposed to marry her because the spouses of aryans enjoyed some protection from anti-Semitic measures: the proposal horrified both families. Annie took refuge from the hard circumstances of the time in education. She was well treated at school and, on a more practical level, her brother was taken in as a boarder at his lycée – Louis-le-Grand – thus reducing the chances that he would be arrested in the street. Educational success and racial persecution came together on 16 July 1942. Taking the first round of her baccalauréat examinations, Kriegel was warned by her mother not to return home. She took refuge with friends and the following morning in the Place des Vosges saw a column of Jews being led away by a French policeman with tears running down his cheeks. She recalled the wails that came from the column being like those of a woman in childbirth. Kriegel and her family were hidden by their neighbours the Poublans. They paid 10,000 francs to a *passeur* to get them into the free zone. He took them to the demarcation line where he left (or abandoned) them and they swam across the Allier river.

Maurice Rajsfus was less privileged than either Kriegel or Elgey. His parents came from Poland and did not have French citizenship. Maurice was at school during the first two years of the occupation, and was well treated there, but his school was a less prestigious institution than those attended by Kriegel or Elgey. On 16 July 1942, at half past four in the morning, French police arrested Maurice's parents. Maurice and his sister, who were French citizens, were not taken, in spite of Laval's request that children should be deported with their parents. The two children were left to fend for themselves. Maurice left school and found a job; his sister wrote to their landlord and asked for a reduction in rent but he said that 'cases such as hers were not foreseen by the law' and refused. Eating little and keeping away from public places as much as possible, Maurice and his sister managed to survive in occupied Paris.

For Kriegel and Elgey, the occupation was not an entirely negative memory. Kriegel remembered that her departure from Paris in July 1942 was 'exciting', like the *exode* of 1940. School provided them with a refuge and this contributed to an interest in academic work that persisted for the rest of their lives. Family loyalties, too, were strengthened by their experience of the occupation, though it provided both of them with a means of obtaining some autonomy from families that would otherwise have been suffocatingly close. Kriegel and Elgey were helped by those around them. Elgey's landlord prevented the Germans from sequestrating her apartment; Kriegel's neighbours took her family in at the moment when they were most threatened. Kriegel recalled the occupation as a time of increased solidarity:

In a working-class area of Paris at that time . . . conscious of a levelling of conditions, faced with a common misfortunes of various aspects, everyone was prone to tighten the links of neighbourliness. This was certainly true of the Jews amongst themselves . . . but also of the Jews with their non-Jewish neighbours . . . For our part we had always maintained cordial relations with our neighbours the Poublans, as is normal between good people, but the relations had never become intrusively familiar. These limits fixed by the Parisian *petite bourgeoisie* . . . exploded [and] from then on the left-hand side of the fifth floor of our staircase became as though the two apartments were just one.[31]

Rajsfus's memories, by contrast, were bitter. The policeman who came to arrest his parents on 16 July 1942 was a neighbour, and his landlord treated him and his sister with contempt when they were desperate for help. Elgey's experience of the Paris police was benign. At the very moment when their colleagues in the east of the city were arresting poor foreign Jews, a policeman in the smart west of Paris went out of his way to help her family. For Kriegel, the Paris police were victims of the situation, though her choice of a crying policeman as a symbol of suffering humanity may have owed something to her desire to annoy the post-1968 French left (she had moved a long way to the right by the time she published her memoirs in 1991). Rajsfus hated the police and spent much of the rest of his life denouncing them.[32]

The differences between these three people were partly rooted in simple matters of wealth and social position, but their retrospective accounts (and the mere fact that they wrote such accounts makes them unusual) also raise questions about cause and effect. Their post-war careers were products of their wartime experience but also provided prisms through which they looked back on that experience. Rajsfus in particular was a lifelong rebel against authority. Whilst Elgey became a loyal and valued member of de Gaulle's entourage and Kriegel moved from Stalinism to conservative Zionism, Rajsfus has always been an eccentric and libertarian left-winger who, in recent years, has supported the Palestinian cause.

Jewish experience of the occupation cannot, of course, be described in terms of a simple dichotomy between 'victims' and 'survivors'. Those who remained alive in 1945 had rarely escaped without paying some long-term cost. Even though deportation had hit one section of Jewry harder than another, many survivors had lost relatives. Rajsfus had lost both his parents (as had, for example, the Resistance fighter Claude Aubrac or the historian Pierre Vidal-Naquet). Kriegel's immediate family survived but some of her relations died in a particularly horrible way in the summer of 1944 when *miliciens* buried them alive. Laure Michel survived the occupation but her brother

Hans-Helmut (one of the boys sheltered in Louis Malle's school) was arrested on 15 January 1944 and gassed at Auschwitz on 6 February. The historian Jacques Adler survived the occupation, as did his mother and his sister, but he saw his father for the last time in June 1941, standing behind barbed wire in a camp; his father died in Birkenau three years later. Adler's mother did not die until many years later but she was, in her son's words, 'a broken human being'.[33]

The Jews in France endured huge material losses. The Rothschild family were able to take back possession of their luxurious house which had been kept in good condition because it had been used by the SS (when Jean Cocteau attended a party there during the occupation, the butler told him that the SS had the same guests as 'Monsieur le Baron'). They got their racehorses back from the German stud farms to which they had been sent and found their pictures at the bottom of a salt mine. Very few families were so lucky. From 1941 onwards, the Germans seized property in apartments vacated by Jews. Initially, it was intended that this property should go to German colonists being settled in Russia; in practice, most of it went to people, some of them French, whose homes had been destroyed by Allied bombing. The French authorities resented these seizures, partly because they hoped to sell off Jewish goods in order to pay outstanding debts. By December 1942, 220 million francs' worth of goods had been seized. By July 1944, 69,619 flats (38,000 of them in Paris) had been requisitioned, and over four hundred train-loads of goods had left France for Germany. One hundred and twenty Jews were taken out of the Drancy camp simply to sort the property that had been taken from their co-religionists.[34] After the war the French state made some effort to restore property to its rightful owners, but these were often hard to find. Over 2,000 pianos were exhibited in Paris but almost half of them remained unclaimed. The historian Marc Bloch heard in 1942 that the SS had taken all the books in his Paris apartment. The Germans seized a total of over half a million books.

Many Jews had lost money or property in ways that gave them no chance of compensation. They had paid huge sums to get false papers, to be guided across the demarcation line or to obtain food on the black market. They had been forced to rent uncomfortable and expensive rooms in godforsaken villages in the Massif Central that had nothing to commend them, except the fact that they had nothing to commend them to the Germans either. They had been blackmailed and robbed by 'false policemen', who knew that they could not afford to complain to the authorities.

The deportation of Jews from France ripped families apart. In Nice in 1943 the seven-year-old Serge Klarsfeld heard his father Arno being taken away by the SS as he and his mother hid at the back of a cupboard: Arno was gassed at Auschwitz. Georges Gheldman, aged ten, returned home on 16 July 1942 in Dax to find a note from his mother saying 'come and find me at the police station darling'. He went and spent the night in a cell with his mother, ten other adults, and a small girl. The following morning he was thrown out of the police station and saw his mother being taken away under German guard. He found refuge with 'le père Cougouille', a friend of his mother's, who placed him in hospital for two weeks, and then arranged for him to cross the demarcation line into the southern zone where he eventually found refuge with a peasant family. After the war Georges testified at the trial of Maurice Papon who had organized the deportation of Jews from the region. He also wrote a book based on his archival researches. He discovered that his Aunt Hélène and Cougouille had both intervened in an attempt to save his mother. They had pointed out that she was a Hungarian national and Cougouille had said that he was due to marry her. The French authorities had said that Hungarians enjoyed no protection (in any case, when she was deported, Berthe was incorrectly described as being of Polish origin) and that an intention to marry, as opposed to a marriage, made no difference to a Jew's status. Georges found that his mother had been taken to Drancy on 18 July and from there sent straight to Auschwitz, where she arrived on 21 July. He also discovered that his father (divorced from his mother in 1940, and not seen by either mother or son since he joined the Foreign Legion in 1939) had been on the same convoy from Drancy to Auschwitz as his mother. He never found out whether his parents had seen each other again before they died.[35]

One case of family separation became notorious. Dr Finaly arrived in France from Austria in 1939. He had two sons (Robert and Gérald) who were born in April 1941 and July 1942. In spite of the dangers of the time, Finaly had his sons circumcised and seems to have assumed that they would be brought up as Jews. In April 1944, shortly before being deported, he and his wife confided their sons to Madame Brun, a devout Catholic. Madame Brun, in turn, placed the children in a series of religious institutions. Dr Finaly and his wife never returned. The boys' aunts in New Zealand and Israel tried to get the children back but Madame Brun claimed that she had made them into 'little Catholics' and refused to return them. In 1952 a court ordered her to do so, but instead she arranged for the children to be hidden in a Catholic school in Bayonne and then taken to Spain. The boys were returned to their relatives in Israel in 1953. The return was considered a triumph for many in Israel and a defeat by some in the Catholic Church. What it meant for the boys and their surviving family is less clear. The boys can have barely remembered their parents, and they had spent nine years in the care of strangers. Madame Brun seems to have played little direct role in caring for them.

Some Jews who were too young to remember much of the occupation grew up haunted by the sense that their lives should be defined with relation to events of 1940–45. Sometimes this meant a preoccupation with violent conflict. Michelle Fark was born in 1937 of Polish Jewish parents living in France. She grew up in an atmosphere of suffocating fear: 'Learning to speak, we learnt to keep quiet.' In 1969 she shot herself in Guatemala in order to avoid being captured with a group of left-wing guerrillas who had assassinated the American ambassador.[36] Pierre Goldman was born on 22 June 1944. He wrote later that he was 'too young to fight but old enough to die in the Polish crematoria'. He sometimes swore oaths on the 'six million' and said: 'I thought that it was important that I die before I was thirty.' He was murdered, in mysterious circumstances, at the age of thirty-five, shortly after he himself had been released from prison.[37]

Of course, only a small proportion of Jews who survived the occupation were so anguished, or at least so prone to give political expression to their anguish; Pierre Goldman's half-brother, Jean-Jacques, for example, became a successful pop singer. However, many tragedies were played out in the private sphere. An Austrian Jew entrusted his infant daughter to a French family. Father and daughter survived but he returned from a concentration camp to find that his daughter had grown up speaking only French, a language that he did not understand.[38] Another father's last letter from Drancy expressed the hope that his son might learn to play the violin. As an adult, the son constructed a violin with his own hands and learnt to play it. He practised every day – though he always hated doing so.

5

Frenchwomen and the Germans

In his absence [the absence of a Frenchman in a prisoner of war camp], his wife, in the company of her sister, took in numerous soldiers day and night. I, with the authorization of her husband, invited her to resume the life that she had led honestly beside her husband, but this was no use, she said the Germans were much nicer than the French and that her husband could go back to Germany . . . It is a secret to no one that when a new German military unit arrives in Léon, the first person that the new arrivals ask for is Madame B. (Letter from conservative bourgeois Frenchman to prefect of the Landes, April 1944)[1]

I find it unacceptable that this girl, having prostituted [herself] to the Germans, having displayed an openly provocative attitude, having directly threatened me, having, in France as well as in Germany, worked for the enemy, having been guilty of infanticide, is now at liberty and even allows herself to take a provocative attitude. (Male forty-seven-year-old member of the *Comité Départemental de la Libération* of the Eure-et-Loir, June 1945)[2]

The French population during the occupation was predominantly female (because so many men had died in the First World War or been captured in 1940), whilst the German occupying forces were overwhelmingly male. The contrast seemed even more striking because those areas where Germans were most present (towns in the north and east of France and along the Atlantic coast) tended to be the places where young Frenchmen were most absent. The extent to

5. (opposite) *Some Frenchwomen took great risks to remain with their German lovers. Here a French girl insists on being taken prisoner along with defeated German soldiers.*

which all French people had relations with the Germans varied with location, age and social class but this variation was particularly marked amongst women. A 'respectable' gentile woman of forty-five from a small town in the Auvergne was unlikely to have much to do with the Germans. On the other hand, a girl who had been born in 1923 of an unmarried mother, and who worked as a waitress in a café near the station in Lille, would be in regular contact with Germans from June 1940 onwards. She would, in all likelihood, be regarded as a legitimate target for the sexual attentions of soldiers and possibly for recruitment to work for the Germans.

Not surprisingly, therefore, relations between France and Germany during the occupation were often described in sexual terms. The Resistance saw the defence of French honour as being bound up with the behaviour of French women. Adrien Texcier's clandestine pamphlet 'Advice to the Occupied' of July 1940 told Frenchmen how they should treat Frenchwomen who seemed too close to Germans: they should wait until the German had gone and then slap the woman. Vercors's novel *Le Silence de la mer* (1942) presented a young French woman, who refused to speak to the German soldier billeted in her house, as an icon of French dignity. Collaborationists used sexual metaphors too. Marcel Déat wrote that 'rapes sometimes lead to marriages', whilst Robert Brasillach remarked at his trial that 'we have slept with the Germans and the memory is sweet'.

Present-day views of relations between Frenchwomen and German men are refracted through the prism of the liberation, when some women had their heads shaved, and refracted again through the prism of the sometimes fictionalized accounts that outside observers wrote of these events. The punishment of Frenchwomen at the liberation went with sweeping condemnations that often blended specific allegations about political help to the Germans with more general condemnation of 'immoral' and 'scandalous' behaviour (see Chapter 10).

In view of the hysteria that came to surround Frenchwomen's relations with Germans, it is worth making an obvious point. Every German who walked into a shop or café was almost certain to speak to a Frenchwoman. There were times when Frenchmen regarded such relations as unthreatening. Charles Rist thought it normal that his wife should have a friendly talk with 'soldats allemands très convenables'.[3] More surprising, perhaps, was the attitude of Maurice Rocqueil, a young man from the Aveyron who was sent to work in Germany. We might expect such a person to be preoccupied with the fidelity of his fiancée; Vichy officials became agitated on behalf of French prisoners of war who were allegedly cuckolded in their absence. However, far from seeing such relations as threatening, the young man welcomed the fact that his fiancée made friends with German railway workers in France while he was in Germany. She showed the German workers postcards that she had received from her lover, and she passed on to him the advice that the German workers gave her about how to survive in a German factory.[4]

FILLES AUX BOCHES

What of sexual relations between Frenchwomen and German men? Objective evidence about this subject is scarce, although occasionally official investigations into some other matter give a brief glimpse of such relations. Thus the French Service Diplomatique des Prisonniers de Guerre, which kept a watch over the wives of French prisoners, reported on the case of Madame C. in 1942. She had been born in 1915 and in the absence of her husband, imprisoned in Stalag VIA, she ran the family hairdressers. For the first year of the occupation, her conduct gave rise to no comment. After this, it was noted that she had begun to frequent French non-commissioned officers attached to the armistice commission. In the winter of 1942, saying that she needed to be somewhere warm, she began doing her accounts in a local bar, owned by another woman. On 28 February 1942, German military policemen charged with the repression of prostitution arrested her in the company of German soldiers, subjected her to a medical inspection and then detained her in hospital from 4 to 26 March. On her release, she left Bourges and had not been heard of since.[5] Similarly, French police became intrigued by an eighteen-year-old girl from Nîmes who had begun to make frequent visits to Lyons. They concluded that she was conducting a 'sentimental liaison' with a German officer attached to the armistice commission there.

The girl's patriotic and bourgeois father would almost certainly have disapproved of the affair. Her brother went on the run in order to avoid being sent to work in Germany and, after capture in May 1944, was shot by the Germans.[6] In August 1944 French gendarmes reported that a French girl of sixteen had been killed along with three German soldiers in a Resistance attack on an isolated German base near Cholet. According to the gendarmes, the girl had 'sung, amused herself and eaten with the Germans'.[7]

Historians have made much of an estimate by the German authorities that their soldiers fathered between 50,000 and 75,000 children in France.[8] But Jean-Paul Picaper and Ludwig Norz's recent study suggests that the real figure was 200,000.[9] Statistical certainty is probably impossible. The Germans established a Lebensborn nursery in Chantilly to raise racially desirable children born in France of German fathers,[10] but only a tiny number of children were taken into the institution, and the Germans themselves had little idea about how many children might have been fathered by their troops – they estimated around 3,000 or 4,000 in Rouen.[11] Women may have had an interest in claiming that their children had German fathers during the occupation, when the German authorities might provide money. However, large numbers of children fathered by Germans were actually born after the Germans had left, and, after the liberation, women who had associated with the Germans often denied that their children had German fathers.

Whatever the validity of their statistics, Picaper and Norz's case studies provide suggestive evidence about relations between French-women and German men. Most information about women who had relations with Germans comes in snapshots; a Vichy report or an account of punishment at the liberation gives us a picture of a woman's life at a particular moment (usually in 1943 or 1944), but we rarely know much about what had happened to such women before they came to the attention of the authorities or anything about what happened to them after 1945. Picaper and Norz draw their information mainly from interviews with the children, on one occasion a grandchild, resulting from liaisons between Frenchwomen and German men. Consequently, they put such relations into the context of longer-term family history.

The thirteen mothers they studied were all young – only one was over twenty-five – and all were from humble origins. Several were themselves the children of unmarried or separated mothers. Most children were born towards the end, or after the end, of the occupation (two in 1943, four in the summer of 1944, one in November of that year, one in 1945 and one in January 1946). All thirteen mothers lived in areas with a high concentration of German troops (mainly on the western coast). The German fathers were all older than their lovers. Mostly, they were low-ranking soldiers. Their affairs did not meet with the approval of their superiors. Only one of the women felt political sympathy for Nazism – though her German lover seems not to have had any particular ideological convictions.

Some women knew relatively little about their German lovers. Most of the women spoke no German: military rank or the geography of German towns cannot have meant much to them. Relations on both sides were marked by a certain amount of deception and self-deception. One woman believed that her lover was an airman and an officer. Post-war investigations showed that he served in the Hermann Goering regiment of the army. He was probably not an officer and possibly not even a combatant soldier. He seems to have been a fantasist who had been married four times by the time he committed suicide in 1958.[12] Another woman believed that she had herself been married to her German lover, though the German army would never have permitted such a ceremony.[13] One German soldier deserted from his unit and sought refuge in Switzerland with his lover. The couple eventually married, had children and returned to (East) Germany after the war. On arrival in Switzerland, he gave details of his name, rank and occupation but lied to his Swiss interrogators, as he had presumably lied to his lover, about his age. He claimed to be thirty-three; he was actually thirty-eight, almost twenty years older than her.[14]

None of the women studied by Picaper and Norz managed to stay in touch with their lovers, though some children were later able to contact the German parts of their families. Women who had had affairs with Germans, and the children who issued from those relations, had harsh lives after the liberation. Many children were badly treated by grandparents or stepfathers; some of the families in which they grew up would have been unhappy even without the special tensions introduced by 'l'enfant du boche'. Some children only found out about their real fathers later in life. Some were mocked by their classmates and neighbours, or even by their teachers.

On the whole, the women most closely associated with Germans came from sharply defined groups. Often they were drawn from families that were seen as non-respectable: sometimes sisters or mothers and daughters were simultaneously accused of having associated with Germans. Bitter mutual recrimination hints at the links between family tension and relations with the Germans. A woman from Morbihan who had gone to work in Germany said that her husband had beaten her and that she had left him when she heard he had joined the German police in Bordeaux.[15] Two men from the Eure-et-Loir claimed that they had volunteered to work in Germany because they feared denunciation by German soldiers who were having affairs with their wives.[16] In Brittany, a girl who had gone to work in Germany at the age of fifteen blamed her father for signing the authorization papers; the father said he knew nothing of it and blamed the girl's mother.[17] A girl claimed that her mother had forced her to volunteer to work in Germany at the age of sixteen so that the way was open for the mother to have affairs with German soldiers, the girl's sister having also gone to Germany.[18]

Class and employment were important. Waitresses, shop assistants and chambermaids were all likely to come across Germans in the course of their work (and were often regarded as legitimate sexual targets by both French and Germans). In the Maine-et-Loire, the proportion of typists and cleaning women prosecuted in civilian courts after the liberation was three times higher than the proportion of the general population who suffered this fate, and women were overwhelmingly accused of crimes that involved association with the Germans.[19] Primary school teachers (*institutrices*) were sometimes accused of having had sexual relations with Germans. German troops were often billeted in schools and no doubt some primary school teachers – young women free of the constraints that might normally have been imposed by economic dependence on, or cohabitation with, their families – did flirt with German soldiers. It also seems, however, that independent women who did not conform to village conventions provoked fantasies of sexual abandon. At the liberation, a woman in the Var, talking about the case of three teachers who were disciplined for having been too close to German soldiers, recalled: 'One evening, passing very late by the school, I heard laughter and cries that made one think of an orgy.'[20] In villages, state schools were often seen as agents of anti-clericalism and sometimes discussion of 'immoral teachers' fitted into religious disputes. A priest in Figeac wrote to the prefect of the Lot insisting that an *institutrice* be transferred: 'She almost continually gets up from her desk to sit at the table of a pupil and puts her feet on another table in front . . . and she is very lightly dressed.'[21] In the village of Cheviré-le-Rouge (Maine-et-Loire), the anti-clerical town councillors accepted that a schoolteacher, a woman of thirty-two, should be sacked without pension, and sentenced to four months in prison and twenty years of *indignité nationale*, for having associated with German soldiers, but they complained that the priest, whose conduct during the occupation had been equally reprehensible, had escaped all punishment.[22]

Some women worked for the Germans. Such work could range from taking in washing, a common means of earning money in areas where Germans were garrisoned, to going to work inside German bases. The work that Frenchwomen did for the Germans was almost always menial. With the exception of a few interpreters, they worked mainly as cleaners and cooks. Working for the Germans often over-lapped with sleeping with them, sometimes because Germans seduced their employees and sometimes because women who were having affairs with Germans found it convenient to enter German employ-ment (either to stay close to their lovers or in order to escape the disapproval of their neighbours). Only 16 of the 198 women who were tried in front of the Chambres Civiques of the Morbihan at the liberation for having worked for the Germans had not also had a German lover.[23]

'VOLUNTEERING' TO WORK IN GERMANY

It is not quite clear how many Frenchwomen went to work in Germany during the occupation. German records suggest that there were around 80,000 and that they made up about a third of all French volunteer workers in Germany.[24] A few kept women went back with their lovers. A seventeen-year-old Parisian went to Germany in the summer of 1944 with a German officer, and subsequently lived with friends of his while avoiding being conscripted to work in a German factory (a considerable achievement for an able-bodied person during the last months of the Third Reich).[25] Ordinary German soldiers, however, would have found it difficult to protect foreign lovers even if they had wished to do so. More commonly, women volunteered to work in Germany because they had got into the habit of working for the Germans, or because their association with Germans had become so notorious that return to their home communities would have been intolerable.

In defiance of official rules, some women were simply compelled to go to Germany. In particular, some who worked for the Germans were removed by force with the departing army in the summer of 1944. Some women were told, perhaps correctly, that they would be at risk of attack if they stayed behind in France; others were told that they were being taken to prevent them from providing the Allies with information they had gleaned whilst employed by the Germans.[26] Some who were taken back to Germany with the German army were uncertain of, or misled about, their ultimate destination.[27]

Most importantly, women worked in Germany simply because they needed money. Economic pressures often interacted with family ones. Mothers sometimes went to Germany because they needed to support children. Young girls sometimes went to avoid being a burden on their parents ('my parents had eleven children. I had to work').[28] Many women were running away from a family in France. Some sought to escape their 'fate as a servile wife'.[29] In the Eure-et-Loir, a woman left 'because her husband drank and was cruel to the children', and she wanted to pay to put them 'with a foster family'.[30] Two girls (of sixteen and seventeen) left because their stepfathers repeatedly threw them out of the house.[31] A mother left with the eldest of her six children. One of her sons remained in the care of his grandmother; when she died he too went to Germany.[32] A woman left shortly after the death of a child and explained that she needed to get away because 'she thought she would die of grief'.[33]

Two young women from the Eure-et-Loir went because they were pregnant, one by a Luxembourger and one, she claimed, by a French-man. They had been abandoned by the fathers of their children, they needed money and, perhaps, needed to remove themselves from local disapproval.[34] Another woman went to support a young baby; she admitted that she had frequented German soldiers and refused to name the father of her child.[35] A large proportion of Frenchwomen who went to Germany were either pregnant when they left or fell pregnant soon after arriving. In December 1944 the French authorities anticipated that 3,000 children would soon be born to Frenchwomen in the Reich,[36] and 1,970 children had been born just a month later.[37] The Germans eventually refused to allow the repatriation of pregnant women, and Nazi Germany in the closing stages of the Second World War was hardly an ideal place to give birth. The French struggled to create and equip crèches. Infant mortality rates were high. One woman gave birth early and in secret in Berlin in 1943. The child was dead and, when her landlady reported her, the woman told the German police that she had strangled the baby because she did not want to have the child of a 'boche'. A post-mortem revealed that the baby had been born dead, but the Germans still imprisoned the mother and the French blamed her for infanticide, amongst many other things, when she returned in 1945.[38]

Odette Chambroux volunteered to work in Germany and sub-sequently published an account of her experiences. Her account was not written until decades after the events it described, and the very fact that she published a book suggests that she was different from most women who went to Germany. In spite of this, it is worth discussing her account at some length, partly because there is not a comparable degree of evidence about any other woman volunteer, and partly because the very ambiguities in her recollections are sugges-tive. In some ways, Chambroux seemed typical. She was born in 1918 in the Corrèze, a poor area of the south-west. Like many women who went to Germany, she came from an unhappy family. Her drunken father raped her at the age of fourteen and her family sent her to a convent in Bordeaux (which was, to all intents and purposes, a prison) to prevent her from talking about the incident. However, Chambroux's departure for Germany was not a direct attempt to flee from this background. She had, in fact, moved to Paris in 1933 and taken a job that made her financially independent. She acquired some education and, in particular, learnt English and German at the Berlitz school (she belonged to that small minority of Frenchwomen who would have been able to communicate easily with their German employers). Unusually for a woman who went to Germany, she had strong political views. She had befriended German Jewish refugees in Paris, had worked to help Spanish Republicans and had Communist sympathies.

The precise circumstances in which she went to Germany are somewhat unclear from her autobiography, and may have been unclear in her own mind. She began working for the Germans near Chartres after being arrested for infringing blackout regulations. She then went to Chartres, apparently in a bid to meet a Resistance contact, was arrested in a German raid on a cinema and told to go to Germany. This order seems to have been linked to the fact that she had a criminal record, or simply that she was out late at night without apparent reason, rather than to any German suspicions about her political views or Resistance contacts. She remembered that the other 'volunteers' who accompanied her to Germany had had problems with the police, though she also described herself as a victim of Service du Travail Obligatoire, a programme that was never applied to women. She worked in Germany as a childminder and then in a shell factory. Unlike many women who returned from Germany, she suffered no reprisals at the liberation – perhaps because her anti-Nazi feelings were so transparently sincere, perhaps because she was more 'respectable' than most female volunteers (she had never been involved in prostitution and, apparently, never slept with a German), or perhaps just because she was lucky.[39]

OFFICIAL DISAPPROVAL

Women who worked for, or slept with, Germans (in practice, the two often went together) were the object of much contempt. This contempt was not just expressed after the liberation and did not just come from people who regarded themselves as supporters of the Resistance. Pétainist emphasis on women's role as wives and mothers went with condemnation of women who were seen as unpatriotic or immoral. A policeman in Dax wrote the following report:

I believe that it is useful to indicate that the six women who have agreed to go to the Reich [*ont accepté de se rendre dans le Reich* – not, incidentally, a choice of words that suggests an exercise of completely free will] are all prostitutes, known to have had relations with the soldiers of the occupation forces. One of them has a husband who is a prisoner of war in Germany and is the mother of two young children; another aged seventeen and a half has already prostituted herself, along with her mother, to French soldiers and then to soldiers of the Reich; another is an unmarried mother whose conduct is scandalous, her sister left several months pregnant by a soldier of the Reich; finally two others have been selling their charms since the arrival of soldiers.[40]

A report by the Vichy Mission to prisoners of war referred to the scandalous conduct of women who had volunteered to work in Germany in the region around Stalag XA: 'All display swastikas on their clothes. In their dormitory, by each bed there are portraits of the Führer alongside the photographs of German soldiers known in France.'[41] Women who returned were treated with disdain by the authorities in France: in May 1944 a woman was refused a milk ration by the mayor of a Breton village on the grounds that her child was an 'enfant du boche'.[42]

Official attitudes to Frenchwomen's associations with the Germans tied in with the more general way in which such relations were structured by class. Bourgeois women were likely to be 'protected' from such associations. The diaries of Micheline Bood are revealing in this respect. Bood, a schoolgirl from a bourgeois background, was thirteen in 1940. She was an adventurous and rebellious girl who had like-minded friends. She lived in Paris, where there were many Germans, and the anonymity of a big city gave a young girl greater freedom than she would have enjoyed in the provinces. She got to know a number of German soldiers during the occupation, and part of the attraction of consorting with them seems to have come from the disapproval that such relations excited from 'respectable' society. However, Bood was careful not to let her mother know too much about her acquaintances, and careful not to let them go too far. She visited Germans in their hotel rooms (behaviour that could have got her into a lot of trouble in a small town), but she regarded kissing a German as shameful. She thought Jacqueline, who planned to have a baby with 'the most recent of her Germans' in order to go to Germany, imprudent,[43] and she disapproved of Monique, who took a secretarial course in the hope of working for the Germans.[44]

If her diaries are to be believed, Bood herself never hid her pro-English views from her German suitors and she mixed flirtation and patriotism in ingenious ways. When she met a young German soldier at a swimming pool, she took out a pencil and wrote 'Vive de Gaulle' on the wall. The German, perhaps aware of the terrifying penalties that might be imposed on him for complicity with such an act, claimed not to understand the words that she had written.[45]

Social distinctions were important for Bood. Her German friends were frequently officers, and she enjoyed the frisson of being saluted by soldiers when she walked with them.[46] The German officers seem to have understood that their relations with young bourgeois girls were governed by a certain etiquette, and one of them suggested that a mother should get the French police to prevent her daughter, a legal minor, from joining a lover in Germany.[47] Bood knew that relations further down the social scale were less influenced by gallantry and restraint. Her family were amused to hear that two German soldiers had visited their maid and pushed her towards a bedroom saying: 'Venez un peu sur le lit, cinq minutes.'[48]

Ernst Jünger's diaries provide an interesting accompaniment to those of Micheline Bood. He was in his mid-forties when he arrived in Paris (though most Frenchwomen with whom he associated were not much older than Bood). Jünger's attitude to Frenchwomen resembled his attitude to the butterflies, books and autographs he collected. He commented on his conquests – a doctor, a shop girl, an 'amazon' – with detached amusement.

Jünger was unusual. An officer attached to the German military headquarters in Paris, he was also a famous writer and a cultivated man who spoke good French. He was in a position to secure benefits for his French contacts that ranged from extra food to help in finding an imprisoned husband. He was also free from some of the disciplinary constraints imposed on ordinary soldiers. His diaries, however, reveal much about the lives of less privileged people. In April 1941, along with other German officers, he watched naked girls dance for his entertainment. He concluded that girls whom he met in a club were 'almost all the daughters of Russian émigrés', and he had a long discussion with one of them, a girl of twenty, about 'Pushkin, Aksakov and Andriev, whose son she had known'.[49] He talked to an *entraîneuse* who explained that she needed to support her sick mother.[50] The following month he presided over a firing squad that executed a German NCO who had deserted and spent eight months living secretly with his French lover.[51] Jünger also commanded the night guard in central Paris and dealt with forty or so German soldiers who had been arrested drunk. Those who had been found with French-women were given a medical examination. A raid in Montmartre picked up 'a little prostitute of eighteen who stood to attention like the soldiers to salute'. Jünger concluded: 'Since this little miss was very gay and high spirited I made her sit down in the office and talk to us. I kept her like a canary in this awful place.'[52]

The diaries of Bood and Jünger both show how class influenced relations between Frenchwomen and German men. It also influenced discussion of whether women should be compelled to work for the Germans and, most importantly, whether they should be obliged to work in Germany. Conservative opinion in France, particularly expressed by the Church, was keen to prevent Frenchwomen from being compelled to go to Germany, and the Vichy government repeatedly insisted that no such compulsion existed. In practice, some women were effectively forced to go, and such compulsion was especially likely to be applied to particular kinds of women: prostitutes, foreigners, criminals, inmates of internment camps or simply the poor.

Two incidents in the Landes hint at the varying extent to which women of different social backgrounds were 'protected' from contact with Germans. Two German civilians arrived in the town of Montfort and demanded a list of all women aged between twenty-one and thirty-five. They ordered five of these women to Orthez. However, the women were able to defend themselves, helped by the fact that the mother of one of them, who was related to the mayor of Orthez, accompanied them. Eventually the women were able to make the Germans 'recognize that going to Germany was not obligatory and that it was up to the French administration to take all necessary measures for the girls to be able to go home'.[53] The French authorities conducted an extensive investigation into how the Germans had exercised pressure on these women to go to Germany.

Yolande H. from Tosses was very different from the women of Montfort. She was born in February 1925, an illegitimate child of a 'feeble' mother. She had been 'a girl of limited intelligence, a liar with hardly any friends'. She was said to have had 'very reprehensible male associations' since the age of thirteen, and, when she should have been at work, 'she was pleasantly passing her time with soldiers from the occupation army'. No one bothered to enquire into the circumstances under which she 'volunteered' to work in Germany in November 1942. Minors were not supposed to go to Germany without parental authorization,[54] but after the war even Yolande's mother claimed that she had not been aware of her daughter's departure until the end of January 1943. One imagines that an ostracized and poorly educated girl of seventeen would have found it hard to defend herself against German coercion.[55]

PROSTITUTION

Discussion of women's relations with Germans overlaps with discussion of prostitution. Prostitution in France was, in theory, tightly regulated. Prostitutes were officially registered (put *en carte* and declared to be *filles soumises*), and subjected to regular medical inspections. *Maisons closes* or *maisons de tolérance* were officially permitted as places where prostitutes could ply their trade. Vichy tightened regulation of prostitution and, in December 1940, gave proprietors of *maisons closes* even greater powers over their charges. This regulation was part of Vichy's desire to draw clear lines between respectability and non-respectability.

Regulation also suited the German authorities. They were keen to ensure that their soldiers should only have relations with particular kinds of women: Jews and *filles de couleur* were excluded. The Germans were also obsessively concerned to prevent the spread of venereal disease amongst their soldiers.[56] Both German soldiers and women found in their company were liable to medical checks by German doctors.

Some prostitutes were specifically intended for the German market; in Paris they were equipped with cards that stated their terms of business in both French and German. The Germans established brothels in France that were reserved for their soldiers. There were three such enterprises in Reims and at least seventeen in Paris. The six brothels reserved for German soldiers in Angers served 8,000 clients between February 1941 and February 1942.[57] German officials approached prostitution with a seriousness that sometimes amused their French interlocutors. In Nantes, the Germans suggested that the *police des moeurs* might indicate known prostitutes to a woman who was to establish a brothel, and were indignant when the French did not co-operate, especially because the woman to whom they refused help was a '*patronne* from Paris duly authorized by the Feldkommandantur to organize a brothel'.[58] Sometimes brothels were seen as part of the German war economy: a German official suggested, without success, that the inmates of such places should receive the special rations granted to workers fulfilling German contracts,[59] whilst the French authorities in Rennes insisted that the Germans provide brothels reserved for their soldiers with supplies of coal.[60]

The only people who were unhappy with the regulation of prostitution were the prostitutes themselves. They hated interference by the *police des moeurs*, hated medical inspections, hated the prospect of being shut up in hospitals that resembled prison camps,[61] and hated the authority exercised over them by the proprietors of *maisons closes*. In the Eure-et-Loir, a *fille soumise* claimed to have gone to Germany partly in order to escape from the *maison de tolérance* and the 'assiduités de son ami'.[62] Another woman went to Germany to escape harassment by a member of the *police des moeurs*,[63] and a third abandoned prostitution in her own locality in order to avoid being put *en carte*.[64]

The regulation of prostitution ran into other problems. At the very moment when Vichy and the Germans were seeking to define and control prostitution more rigorously, new, often very young, girls entered into it. Poverty and unemployment increased, especially during the first year of the occupation; many women's husbands or lovers were in German prison camps and there were large numbers of German soldiers in some French towns. In these conditions, it is not surprising that some women traded sex for money or favours. Sometimes, the circumstances under which they did so were desperate. Odette D., born in 1927, was the daughter of a retired post office worker. In January 1943, after the suicide of her mother, she left Paris and went to Rennes. She was prosecuted for vagabondage (sleeping rough in Brittany in midwinter cannot have been easy), and soon began to support herself by sleeping with Germans, sometimes for money and sometimes for food.[65] Informal or, as the French put it, 'clandestine' prostitution flourished during the occupation. In Angers, in February 1941, a police sweep found thirty clandestine prostitutes at a time when there were 120 registered prostitutes (half of whom worked in brothels).[66]

Attempts to stamp out clandestine prostitution were vigorous. The French authorities forcibly put women *en carte*; the Germans sometimes moved women known as prostitutes out of areas in which their troops were based.[67] The German destruction of the *Vieux Port* in Marseilles in 1943 seems, in part, to have been motivated by the desire to 'clean up' an area associated with prostitution – it was widely reported that the women taken from the *Vieux Port* had mostly been dispatched as 'volunteer' workers to Germany.[68] The effect of these measures was often to make women even more marginalized and desperate than they had been before. Women attempting to avoid repressive measures moved away from their homes and increasingly congregated in towns where they might hope for some protection in anonymity.

As the authorities attempted to define and regulate prostitution more clearly, the circumstances of war and occupation were blurring the boundaries between prostitutes and other women. There was a gulf between Vichy's prescriptions for how women ought to behave – staying at home to bring up large healthy families of children fathered by their husbands – and the reality, in which many women found themselves separated from their husbands and forced to work to support themselves or their families. Furthermore, whilst the formal policy of Vichy sought to define prostitutes more clearly as a small group of full-time professionals, Pétainists often labelled any woman who did not live in accordance with their moral dictates as a whore.

Prostitutes, or women of ill-repute, were particularly likely to end up working for the Germans. Sometimes the Germans deliberately sought out women in France to provide sexual services for foreign workers in Germany. There were sixty official brothels for such purposes by the end of 1943, and they employed a total of 600 prostitutes.[69] Sometimes the French authorities pushed prostitutes, along with other criminals and 'undesirables', into working for the Germans, presumably because they regarded such women as more dispensable than 'respectable' people. When Germans in the Loire asked for eleven women to work in their mess halls, the French provided three who were ill, one who was pregnant, one who was syphilitic and three who were prostitutes.[70] Among twenty-eight women from one French internment camp who were listed by the French as 'suited to go to work in Germany', six were said have been prostitutes (mostly clandestine, that is, unregistered). Two others were said to have been abortionists.[71]

The French believed that prostitutes made up a large proportion of women who volunteered to work in Germany. A report to the French consul in Germany of April 1942 suggested that there were 19,000 Frenchwomen there:

Many of these women, without defined professions, attracted by the publicity, have arrived here [in Germany] with the firm intention of working as little as possible and of earning their livings by prostituting themselves. One should say that, not having any special skills, the majority of women get pitiful wages and that their vital needs push them to prostitution. It is also true that the Germans are extremely partial to Frenchwomen and that makes things easier and many of our women workers are now installed in their lodgings by civil servants or industrialists.[72]

The following year, another Vichy official suggested that there were 30,000–40,000 Frenchwomen in Germany and that, of these, 10–15 per cent were 'éléments sérieux', 20–25 per cent were prostitutes and 'the rest are becoming [prostitutes] by choice or by force'.[73]

Police statistics provide a less lurid picture of female volunteers in Germany. Only 3 of the 182 women known to have left the Ille-et-Vilaine between 1940 and 1942 were 'officially recorded prostitutes'.[74] None of a group of twenty-nine women investigated by the Paris police was a registered prostitute, though one of them had worked as a maid in a *maison de tolérance* and been implicated in several abortion cases.[75]

The gap between estimates of the number of 'prostitutes' among Frenchwomen in Germany and police records of the number of such women who were actually registered as prostitutes seems to be rooted partly in the fact that some women who went to work in Germany were 'clandestine' prostitutes, or at least women who had lived on the margins of prostitution before their departure. It may also be, as some observers suggested, that women resorted to prostitution as a means of survival once they got to Germany. Finally, perhaps, many women who went to Germany belonged to social groups that were likely to be labelled as prostitutes regardless of their behaviour; one Frenchman in Germany recognized that some of his compatriots would put any woman who accepted factory work in this category.[76]

WHAT DID RELATIONS MEAN?

Occasionally, there is evidence about the intimate feelings of women who had affairs with German soldiers. In Finistère, the *Comité Départemental de la Libération* seized the private diary of a seventeen-year-old girl, to be used as evidence in her trial.[77] The diary describes her feelings for her German lover and her bitterness at the abuse that she received from her compatriots. There is evidence that other women regarded their relations with Germans as something other than commercial transactions. One woman from Morbihan, most unusually, admitted to such feelings and took full responsibility for her actions when interrogated at the liberation: 'I left my home on 3 March 1943 with the sole aim of joining my fiancé and marrying at the end of hostilities . . . A short time after my arrival in Germany, I learned of the death of my fiancé when a letter that I had sent was returned with the words "died for Germany".'[78] The feelings of other women can be inferred from the risks they took to stay with Germans at a time when German defeat was inevitable. Some of them helped their lovers to desert, or hid them when the Allies arrived. In Lorient in the west of Brittany, a besieged German garrison held out long after the rest of France had been liberated. The town was bombed and starved. Most French people moved out of it before the Germans made their last stand, but around two hundred Frenchwomen chose to stay with their German lovers.

From the German side, too, there was sometimes an emotional content to the affairs they had, or wanted to have, with Frenchwomen. A German major commanding a camp for French prisoners of war near Reims tried to secure the release of a French prisoner in Stalag VIIA, who was the brother of an assistant in a sweetshop that he frequented 'assiduously'.[79] Sometimes German passion was comic: in Chinon a German officer was outraged when the French police put his French lover *en carte* as a professional prostitute; the French wearily pointed out that the German was merely one client on a 'long list'.[80] Sometimes German obsessions with Frenchwomen could be tragic. Early one morning in January 1943, a German NCO turned up on the doorstep of Madeleine J., a twenty-five-year-old dancer at the Cabaret Mon Jardin. In spite of her opposition, he forced his way into the apartment saying that he intended to shoot himself: when the military police broke down the apartment door he did so. Similarly, a German soldier shot himself in the corridor of a building inhabited by Raymonde B., a twenty-four-year-old woman who apparently had said that she no longer wanted to see him. French police concluded that his act was provoked by a 'chagrin d'amour'.[81]

After the liberation, many Frenchmen regarded women who had worked for or slept with Germans as 'collaborators'. Women themselves rarely thought in this way. Often they saw their relations with Germans as similar to the relations they might have had with soldiers of any other army. Women who consorted with Germans had often already been known for their relations with French soldiers before the defeat. A woman watching girls accused of *collaboration sentimentale* having their heads shaved in Chartres in August 1944 remarked: 'These are soldiers' women: tomorrow they will be with the Americans.'[82] A number of women prosecuted in 1945 for their relations with Germans seem already to have been closely associated with English or American soldiers. Lucienne See had married an American soldier after the First World War and had three daughters by him before divorcing. During the occupation she ran a café frequented by German soldiers and pushed at least one of her daughters into prostitution. After the liberation, she worked in a hotel run by the American forces.[83] Women who had gone to Germany with German lovers returned with French prisoners of war (some of them seem to have hoped that such companions would serve as evidence of their patriotic credentials).[84] Odette Chambroux, though emphatically not a 'soldiers' woman', cooked for American soldiers after they arrived in the town where she was working in a German shell factory. She believed that the Americans had offered to make her a member of their unit and even to take her with them to the Philippines. One of Micheline Bood's German suitors complained that she would have been equally willing to associate with English or Russian or Chinese soldiers. She told him briskly that she would much prefer English soldiers.[85]

For all the denunciation of women who had slept with German soldiers as 'unpatriotic' that followed the liberation, very few of them saw their affairs as having any political content. Few women who were associated with the Germans were members of collaborationist movements.[86] The Vichy authorities who commented on women volunteering to work in Nazi Germany often drew attention to their low morality, but rarely suggested that they had any ideological commitment: 'A woman of mediocre morality and conduct, the above-named D. is not politically active.'[87] Post-liberation investigations also stressed that women could have 'very loose morals . . . without political concerns'.[88]

Many French people believed that women were particularly prone to denounce their compatriots to the German authorities. One of the most famous French films of the occupation, though one that makes no specific reference to the circumstances of the war, is Clouzot's *Le Corbeau* (1943), which concerns the havoc wreaked in a small town when an elderly spinster writes anonymous letters accusing her neighbours of crimes. Philippe Burrin draws attention to the fact that large numbers of those prosecuted for denunciation at the liberation were women and suggests that denunciation may have provided women, particularly those who were normally excluded from respectable society, with a means of revenging themselves on their social superiors. This interpretation is open to some important questions: it is not clear that the areas studied by Burrin are representative, and, in any case, the fact that women were prosecuted for denunciation at the liberation may reflect the prejudices of men in authority as much as women's behaviour.

Investigating authorities after the war were particularly concerned to establish whether or not women involved with Germans had denounced Frenchmen involved in the Resistance. On the whole, they found little evidence that women who had slept with Germans had passed information to them. The mayor of one Breton village explained the absence of denunciation in a contemptuous way: 'Denunciations had little effect and women of international morals [that is, those who slept with foreigners] noticed how little attention was paid to what they said, because of the contempt they inspired even in the Germans, who, having satisfied their passions, considered them as simple females and did not listen to their talk, [which was] as vulgar as themselves.'[89]

Policemen, conducting more detailed investigations, commented on women associated with the Germans in less hostile terms.[90] The police also sometimes remarked specifically that women who slept with Germans had not been informers: 'This woman of loose morals whom one might describe as an international woman has never denounced anyone.'[91] Police enquiring into a woman who had taken a German lover and eventually gone to Germany reported that people had been made nervous by this affair because the woman's father was known for being too talkative but that, in spite of this fact, no one had been denounced.[92] A police report on a woman who had followed her lover to Germany remarked on her 'dubious morality and conduct' and her 'scandalous' public displays of affection for him, but the same report admitted that she had known about the Resistance network led by Captain Altenburger and that she had not given the Germans any information about it, even when they encouraged her with threats and promises.[93]

Denunciation can, in any case, be a misleading term. It conjures up images of Resistance fighters being dragged away to concentration camps by the Gestapo. Occasionally women did denounce men for political crimes that got them deported. More commonly, however, female denunciation to the Germans involved less serious crimes. Sometimes women denounced people involved in the black market, or wives of prisoners of war who were having affairs (these crimes would have been handled by the French authorities rather than the Germans). Even when women did tell the Germans about 'anti-German remarks', the statements they reported were rarely expressions of support for the Resistance. More commonly, denunciation seems to have been part of low-level local conflict. Often it involved women who were working for or sleeping with Germans, who had been abused by their more respectable neighbours, usually other women, and who sought to defend themselves by enlisting German support. In the Eure-et-Loir, a woman attracted the disapproval of fellow lodgers who insulted her in the streets. She warned her landlady that she would send 'the German police' if the insults directed at her did not stop. There was no evidence that she would, or could, deploy such power, but the landlady persuaded her other lodgers to keep their opinions to themselves, at least until the liberation, when they were free to tell gendarmes, 'I saw the Germans queuing outside her door'.[94] When a landlord complained about his tenant receiving German guests or getting behind with her rent, she told him: 'I know what to do and you have only to shut up.'[95] In the Maine-et-Loire, more than half the forty-three cases of denunciation for 'anti-German remarks' investigated after the war involved such disputes. Women complained that they had been described as 'more boche than Hitler' or a 'putain des fridolins'.[96] In many cases, the victims of denunciation were merely summoned to the Kommandantur for a rebuke and required to present their excuses.

French treatment of women who had had any kind of relationship with the Germans revealed double standards. Women were punished for sleeping with German men, though Frenchmen were almost never punished for sleeping with German women, something which many prisoners of war in Germany had done (see Chapter 9). Women were more likely than men to be punished or investigated for the same act. Thus, though women made up around a third of those who volunteered to work in Germany during the occupation, they often made up more than half of those who were investigated by the police on their return (see Chapter 10). Attitudes to women's relations with Germans were marked by prurience and intrusiveness. One woman, who had had a child by a German and subsequently tried to hide her lover when Allied troops arrived, recalled that her French interrogators repeatedly slapped her, asked about her lover's performance in bed and even produced a ruler so that she could tell them about the size of his penis.[97]

The Frenchwomen most associated with the Germans, or at least the ones whose association with them aroused most comment, mainly came from the most underprivileged part of society. They were often very young, almost always poor and poorly educated. Many of them were badly treated by their communities, their employers and even their own families. Some women felt that they were responding to economic or family pressures. A significant proportion of Frenchwomen associated with Germans belonged to groups – minors, foreigners, *filles soumises*, criminals and internees – that were subject to explicit formal limits on their freedom. Many women who ended up in close association with the Germans were fleeing from brutal fathers or husbands or from the attentions of the *police des moeurs*. To what extent, for example, can a Polish prisoner on parole, who volunteered to work in Germany in 1940 partly in order to escape from a brutal employer, be said to have made a free choice?[98] Some women were victims of more direct forms of coercion. Frenchwomen were sometimes put into the hands of Germans by others. One recalled that her mother and sister had thrust her, a sixteen-year-old virgin, into a room above the family café with a brutal, middle-aged German soldier. Frenchmen pimped women to the Germans: a girl from Rennes recalled that her 'ami' had told her, 'I do not want you to do any more civilians – just German soldiers.'[99]

The Germans coerced Frenchwomen too. Bourgeois observers made much of German 'correctness'. They knew that French girls from 'respectable' backgrounds were generally treated with consideration and that the German army punished rapists severely. However, girls from lower-class backgrounds were raped by German soldiers.[100] The women most likely to come into contact with Germans – those who worked for them directly or those who worked in cafés or hotels – were particularly vulnerable. Pressing a complaint against a German soldier would have been difficult for an isolated and poorly educated young woman who spoke no German. Such women were not likely to get much help from the French authorities, which often regarded them as little better than prostitutes. A laconic note in the French archives gives a hint of what could happen. A girl of twenty who worked for the Germans was travelling in a railway compartment with seven German soldiers in February 1944. When she rebuffed the attentions of one of them, he killed her with a blow from his rifle butt. The German police identified the culprit but, apparently, let him go on his way.[101]

Though 'respectable' French people often reproached women for their association with Germans, those associations were, in effect, encouraged by elements of 'respectable' society. Sometimes 'non-respectable' women were handed over to the Germans; some women, especially prostitutes, felt that they were constantly on the run from controls imposed by both the Germans and the Vichy authorities. French authorities deployed great energy to 'protect' bourgeois girls from contact with Germans, and especially from being sent to work in Germany, but they never took a comparable interest in the fate of women seen as non-respectable. Association with Germans could get a woman into a vicious circle. Such association could confirm a woman's non-respectable status which, in turn, made her ever more dependent on German support to protect her from the disapproval of her own community. Young women from small villages who became known as 'filles aux boches' were increasingly likely to move into the larger towns, where the German presence was greater and the weight of neighbourly disapproval less onerous. Some of these women ended up going to work in Germany.

The shaving of women's heads is normally seen as a punishment imposed on women after the liberation for having been too close to the Germans (see Chapter 10), but it could also be a means of exclusion, applied during the occupation, that marked some women out as 'non-respectable' and thus pushed them into ever closer association with the Germans. In November 1943 seven armed men broke into a café in Plouhinec in Brittany. They disarmed a German officer and shaved the head of a woman with him. The next day the woman went first to Quimper and then to Paris in an attempt to find a wig. Returning home, she was laughed at by her neighbours, so she went back to Quimper and got herself hired as a cleaner by the Germans.[102] Another woman from Brittany later claimed that she had not had sexual relations with Germans *before* her head was shaved in March 1944.[103]

Association with Germans could offer women who were excluded from respectable French society a kind of revenge. For a short time they could display themselves with people who were considered powerful by the French (though the German associates of Frenchwomen rarely had much real power in the German hierarchy). Women who volunteered to work in Nazi Germany could imagine themselves to be travelling to exciting destinations and boast to their neighbours about the luxuries obtainable in Germany (though their boasts would not have sounded very convincing to anyone who knew much about factories in the Third Reich). Women could try to frighten their neighbours with threats of denunciation – though the Germans did not always take denunciations by lower-class Frenchwomen very seriously.

The revenge that underprivileged women were able to take during the occupation was short-lived. One of the most common allegations about such women made at the liberation was that they had shown themselves 'arrogant' and 'provocative'.[104] Such women were seen to have escaped from their natural place in society; public humiliations were designed to put them back in it.

6

Captivity

French Prisoners of War, 1940–1942

On all sides, on the walls, little photographs, of women, of children, of the Marshal. Everywhere the Marshal. Sometimes as leader. Sometimes as a father. He at least thinks of us.   (Jean Guitton, on his fellow prisoners of war)[1]

The prisoner, national martyr, expiatory victim, suffering Christ . . . The prisoner, tall emaciated figure with a gaze that was full of silent reproach . . . The Marshal talked of nothing else, on every occasion, with tears in his eyes. The whole of France suffered . . . through its two million prisoners . . . Every family had at least one 'over there'. The whole of France communed in the religion of the wounded fatherland. The Marshal is God the father, the prisoner is the suffering son. As a symbol, barbed wire was worth as much as the cross.   (François Cavanna, on meeting prisoners of war when he was sent to Germany as a forced labourer in 1943)[2]

Barbed wire was an icon in early Vichy propaganda. Prisoners in Vichy posters were almost invariably shown standing behind barbed wire (partly, perhaps, because it evoked the battlefields of the First World War). When Edgar Morin, a Communist resistant on the run, wished to impersonate a recently released prisoner in 1943, he impressed his fellow passengers on a train by muttering 'les barbelés' over and over again.[3] Pictures of prisoners stressed solidarity, suffering and inactivity. Gaunt, unshaven men (again reminiscent of *poilus* in the First World War) were shown standing together with stoical resignation. Prisoners were an obsession for the new regime; Pétain's

6. (opposite) *A German photograph of French prisoners of war. German propaganda made much of the presence of 'racially inferior' elements in the French army.*

chef de cabinet reckoned that a third of the Marshal's time, and a quarter of that of members of his entourage, was devoted to prisoners.[4]

Prisoners had a special role during the first two years of the Vichy regime. This was a period when they seemed the most important victims of the war, and it was still possible that the government would succeed in negotiating the release of all prisoners. It was also a period when a certain number of prisoners, usually those from the most privileged social backgrounds, did return to France. Some of these men – Jean-Paul Sartre, Robert Brasillach and François Mitterrand – were influential in their respective circles, and they ensured that prisoner experience, or at least their version of prisoner experience, was widely discussed.

However, the image of prisoners spread in Vichy France was a deceptive one – as Cavanna found out when, during his own enforced sojourn in Germany, he met prisoners who turned out to be relatively well-fed and bad-tempered men rather than suffering martyrs. Prisoners were not a united group. The divisions of rank, class, race and political opinion and the separation between reservists and professional non-commissioned officers[5] interacted with new divisions imposed by captivity; divisions that, for example, separated different kinds of camp. Most strikingly, nineteen out of twenty prisoners were not behind barbed wire, but spent most of their time in work Kommandos in factories or farms. Each work Kommando was formally attached to a prison camp but they were rarely located inside the perimeter: some were two hundred kilometres away from the camps to which they were attached. Prisoners in work Kommandos often lived without guards and without any obvious signs of their captivity. Indeed, when French prisoners were offered 'transformation' into civilian workers in 1943, many of them considered they would gain nothing by accepting such a status.

ARRIVAL AND SORTING

The one time when almost all French prisoners of war did find themselves in camps came immediately after their arrival in Germany. The camps into which they were put varied greatly. Officers went to

Oflags, whilst other ranks went to Stalags. Officers' camps were more comfortable than those reserved for other ranks and, on the whole, no attempt was made to force their inmates to work. Those who held the rank of colonel and above were usually kept in a special prison at Koenigstein, a gloomy place in which bitter old men spent their time blaming each other for the defeat of 1940.[6]

The Stalags, in which the majority of prisoners were placed on arrival, varied greatly. Some had previously been lunatic asylums, cadet schools or barracks. Stalag IID was a specially constructed model camp with a number of brick buildings, which was used to train camp commandants. Other camps were improvised at short notice. A group of prisoners slept on the track of a cycle-racing stadium; others were obliged to construct their own accommodation. Prisoners in Stalag VIG were still living under canvas in October 1941.[7]

Arriving prisoners had their first contact with German bureaucracy. New arrivals were disinfected and had their heads shaved. They were photographed, and acquired the serial numbers that, from then on, provided them with their identity. The Germans often sought to divide their captives up. Sometimes the attempt to find which prisoners were Communists, Jews or Bretons was linked to a desire to identify potential collaborators or enemies of the Reich. Sometimes, though, the Germans seem to have been motivated by simple tidy-mindedness: in Stalag XVIIA, for example, particular barracks were reserved for priests and intellectuals. Sometimes the Germans used prisoners as laboratory specimens who might reveal things about the French mentality. In March 1941 inmates of one Oflag were given a questionnaire by a 'commission of psychological enquiry'. They were asked, among other things: 'What race do you think you belong to?'; 'What do you think of granting rights of citizenship to negroes?'; 'What are the motives for birth control in France?'; 'Why do so many French people live on *rentes*?'; 'Why do the French make such great efforts to obtain the Légion d'honneur?'; and 'Are French marital relations as free as one might suppose from innumerable erotic comedies?'[8]

The French population contained a large proportion of immigrants and many men captured in 1940 were of foreign, especially Italian or Polish, origin. In addition to this, other nationals had been captured fighting with the French in 1940. Some Spanish Republicans ended up in prisoner of war camps. Some of these were simply refugees (many of whom had been imprisoned by the French before being taken by the Germans), but some possessed valid French papers (given the confused circumstances of 1940, this is not quite the same as saying that they had actually fought with the French army). The Germans treated Spaniards with particular contempt. Many Poles were also caught fighting with the French in 1940 and were treated in the same way as their French comrades; this distinguished them from 'Poles of the east' who had been captured in 1939 and the great majority of whom had yielded to German pressure and accepted a change in status that made them civilian workers. Francis Ambrière worked in the Foreign Bureau, responsible for sorting the post of those foreigners taken with the French army, at Stalag XIIC, at Wie-belsheim. He recalled dealing with letters for Poles, Italians, White Russians, Turks, Spaniards, Hungarians, Swiss, Yugoslavs, Belgians, Portuguese, Bulgarians, Danes, Norwegians, Slovaks, Greeks and Armenians, as well as South Americans and several men whose origins were so vague that they were simply classified as 'Heimatlos'.[9]

Substantial numbers of prisoners came from the colonial regiments, and some French units contained non-white soldiers. The Germans treated these men with ostentatious brutality,[10] and kept most black, North African and Vietnamese soldiers in separate camps. Most of them were returned from Germany to Frontstalags in France, where some of them were eventually guarded by French soldiers.[11] Soldiers from colonial units suffered severely from cold and hunger (they were less likely than their white comrades to be able to supplement their rations with food parcels from home). In May 1943 a prisoner from Madagascar died in the Frontstalag in Épinal: the authorities were unable to trace any of his relatives or indeed to identify him by any name other than 'Boto'.[12]

THE ESTABLISHMENT OF ORDER

Stalags were chaotic during the summer and autumn of 1940. Prisoners' lives were still governed by rumours about imminent release,[13] some later believing that the Germans had deliberately fostered such rumours in order to pacify their captives.[14] Hope of release was focused around significant dates: 14 July, 11 November and Christmas Day. It was probably in the bitterly cold January of 1941 that most prisoners finally accepted that there was not going to be a large-scale release. Some groups had particular reason to expect that their confinement would not last long. Fathers of large families or veterans of the last war assumed, rightly, that the Vichy government would be keen to secure their freedom and, wrongly, that it would soon succeed in doing so.

Letters and parcels from France took a long time to reach prisoners of war. Gustave Folcher did not receive news from his family for the first eight months of his captivity.[15] Yves Bourges did not receive a letter from France until 24 October; he learnt that his first child had been born ten days previously.[16] Camps were overcrowded. Inmates competed for inadequate supplies of food. The separation of officers and men, the frequent refusal of the Germans to recognize the special status of non-commissioned officers and the general disorientation that followed a spectacular defeat all undermined discipline. Many prisoners recalled this period as being marked by the 'law of the jungle',[17] or the 'government of the knife'.[18]

Soon, however, a kind of order was established. One prisoner, who returned to a camp after six months in a work Kommando, recalled:

Six months before I had left an overcrowded and chaotic Stalag . . . I came back to a camp where everyone knew his place. The barracks were disciplined, formed into companies with their heads, their deputy heads and other people who had got a cushy billet. But everyone had his place, his allotted function. Life was organized there, with the cunning, the not so cunning, those who got by, and the passive. In the end, a society had been created as it is created everywhere when men live together starting out from nothing.[19]

Probably the most important change in the life of the Stalags sprang from the simple fact that their population diminished as men were sent to external work Kommandos. Camps became less overcrowded and the reign of the strongest that had characterized many of them was ended when the Germans sent the strongest out to work. A degree of order was also brought by the Red Cross, which supplied parcels, thus making competition for food less savage, and gave prisoners information about their rights and duties.

The Germans sought to put some prisoners in authority over their fellow inmates. In theory, the Geneva Convention allowed prisoners to elect their own *hommes de confiance*; in practice, the Germans often imposed men during the first year of captivity. However, even these nominated men provided a channel for discussion with captors, and increasingly *hommes de confiance* were genuinely elected. By 1942, many were respected by their fellow captives, so much so that the Germans liberated them in the hope of making French prisoners of war more malleable (see below).

Prisoners who rebelled against German authority were sometimes sent to special camps. The most notorious of these was Rawa Rawska in Poland, which took in 26,000 French prisoners at one time or another. Prisoners convicted of certain offences were tried by military courts and sent to civilian prisons. The most common of these offences was having sexual relations with German women (see Chapter 9). However, prisoners were also frequently prosecuted for violence against their employers, theft, poaching and even cruelty to the farm animals in their care (an offence that must have seemed incongruous to men who knew how Polish labourers on German farms were treated).[20]

The French government also tried to exercise some influence over prisoners of war. It established an office to keep records on their prisoners in 1939. During the German invasion of 1940, this body was withdrawn from Paris and eventually, after a brief sojourn in Vichy, installed in Lyons. The most determined attempt to keep records relating to the hundreds of thousands of Frenchmen taken prisoner during this period was made by an ad hoc agency established by the prefect of the Seine, though the French never had complete records about all their prisoners of war. All combatant powers nominated a neutral government to look after the interests of their prisoners, and the French had chosen the United States. However, negotiations relating to prisoners of war were increasingly undertaken by French officials themselves. In particular, Georges Scapini, a fifty-year-old former conservative deputy who had been blinded in the First World War, was appointed as first minister plenipotentiary and then as ambassador with a special brief to look after prisoners. In November 1940 France announced that it would now take over from the

United States and look after the interests of its prisoners directly; other French interests in Germany, such as property and volunteer workers who went there after the summer of 1940, continued to be the business of the United States until Germany declared war on it in December 1941. The agencies established by Scapini to deal with prisoners of war were known as the Scapini Mission. This had offices in Paris and Berlin and sent representatives to visit prison camps,

The Scapini Mission had an uneven impact on the lives of prisoners. Many men in work Kommandos had no contact with its representatives and probably never knew of its existence. Men in Stalags and Oflags were more likely to come into contact with it, but were often hostile to its representatives, especially later in the war. From about 1942 onwards, the Scapini Mission, faced with the difficulty of persuading men from France to come to Germany, recruited most of its staff from camps (mainly the Oflags). The Mission was never a united or homogeneous body. Scapini himself was against escape attempts by prisoners and wished to encourage non-commissioned officers to work (he believed that work would be good for them and that they would provide leadership for the other ranks in the work Kommandos). Many of his staff disagreed with him on both these points.

ESCAPE AND REPATRIATION

Around a third of prisoners returned to France before the end of the war. How did men get out? Escape was widely discussed; indeed, some prisoner autobiographies are written as though the history of imprisonment is almost the same thing as the history of escape attempts. The Ministry of *Anciens Combattants* reported that 70,000 men had escaped from Germany (although only 31,248 of these had been awarded the *médaille des évadés*). Overall, about 5 per cent of prisoners seem to have escaped, though for every successful attempt there were numerous failed attempts and many prisoners made several bids to get away.

Defining escape is harder than it might seem. Things were most clear in the Oflags, where officers had formal committees that authorized escape attempts and a clear sense of what constituted an escape: getting over or under the perimeter fence. Alain Le Ray, the first man out of Colditz, was an example of a clear-cut escape. He eluded his guards during an exercise outing, knocked down a man to steal his wallet (an offence that could have earned him the death penalty) and finally crossed the Swiss frontier stowed away on a train.[21]

However, even for a man like Le Ray, the meaning of escape could be unclear. Any British soldier who escaped was obeying military instructions and such men aimed to rejoin the fight against Germany. French soldiers were not obeying orders and did not have any fight to join. Alain Le Ray returned to the unoccupied zone of France after his escape in April 1941, but did not join the Resistance until almost eighteen months later. The attitude of the Vichy government complicated matters further. Vichy did not encourage escapes (though some individual Vichy officials did), but it did not return prisoners who reached the southern zone before the end of 1942.

In the early years of the war, before their need for labour made them desperate to keep men in Germany, even the Germans sometimes seemed to have ambivalent attitudes to French escapes. Prisoners were often threatened with punishment if they attempted escape, but Germans also connived in certain kinds of attempt. On Christmas Day 1941 a French policeman reported the following incident. A Frenchman had escaped from a prisoner of war camp and reached the unoccupied zone where he was safe from recapture. However, his fiancée remained in Paris. When the man returned to the city to visit her, he was denounced, arrested by the French police and taken to the German authorities. The German police commissioner (no doubt sodden with schnapps and sentimentality) told his French colleagues that he did not like denunciations and that he himself had been a prisoner in the First World War. The French policeman seized his chance and persuaded the Germans to give the prisoner a Christmas present of his freedom.[22]

Men who tried to escape were usually dealt with inside the camp system. This meant that they were subjected to a relatively brief period in a punishment block. They were not tried in court and were not, on the whole, sent to civilian prisons or concentration camps.

Frenchmen who were accused of other offences often sought to defend themselves by arguing that, for example, the use of a stolen bicycle was not a crime in itself but merely part of a 'legitimate' escape attempt.[23] Equally, the German authorities sometimes tried to obtain more severe penalties against would-be escapers by prosecuting them for some other offence. A prisoner caught trying to stow away on a boat to Sweden was punished for 'attempting to export currency from the Reich'.[24]

The fact that most French prisoners were in work Kommandos rather than in camps had important implications for would-be escapers. For most of them, there was no perimeter fence to mark the frontier between freedom and captivity. Some left their normal place of work in order to see comrades or simply to enjoy a period of idleness rather than because they hoped to make it back to France. Families back in France were sometimes pained that their loved ones seemed so unenthusiastic about escape. However, the choices facing a would-be escaper from a work Kommando were more difficult than those that faced someone escaping from a camp. Getting out of the Kommando was easier than getting out of a camp, but the penalty for being caught trying to escape could be worse. An escaper might find that he was transferred from a comparatively benign agricultural work Kommando into a coal mine or a factory.

Escape was an absorbing activity. Fernand Braudel refused the chance to join an escape team on the grounds that an escape attempt would require six months of concentrated activity, and that this would distract him from his academic work. Some escapers believed that even unsuccessful attempts were worthwhile. Such attempts could restore dignity to defeated soldiers and earn them a few days of respite from the routines of imprisonment. Francis Ambrière's account of his first attempt to escape is interesting. It was a hopelessly botched operation. He and three comrades left their work Kommando on 16 December 1940 hoping to walk the two hundred kilometres to the French frontier and get home for Christmas. They endured a week of hunger, cold and exhaustion before being recaptured and spending Christmas Day in a German prison. Yet Ambrière looked back on this episode with pleasure. The attempt to get away restored his pride. Furthermore, recapture meant imprisonment with a group of men who were also committed escapers, men who saw themselves as an elite.[25]

More common than successful escapes were releases that the Germans permitted. Sick prisoners were often sent home. Some categories of prisoner were repatriated because they were seen as useful back in France. Medical workers not needed in the camps were released in the autumn of 1940. Gendarmes and postmen were also released. Renault sent lists of workers in prison camps that it needed to fulfil German orders.[26] Veterans of the First World War were ordered to be released in 1941, as were fathers of four children and eldest sons in families with more than four children in which the father was dead. Flemish-speakers were released in February 1941, because the Germans assumed that they would be hostile to French unity. Camp life was dominated by rumours about which category was going to be freed next.

The definitions around which formal release schemes revolved were as blurred as those that governed escape. Deciding who was an *ancien combattant*, a postman or the father of a large family depended on the production of documents, and ingenious prisoners were able to forge or alter papers to their benefit. In the early stages, the German authorities seem to have regarded this practice with amused tolerance (perhaps because the non-working populations of Stalags were not particularly useful to their economy).[27] Louis Althusser later claimed that he had no difficulty in altering his papers to make himself appear to be a nurse (and thus eligible for repatriation). Only a careless mistake, which he later attributed to a subconscious desire to stay in the Stalag, prevented him from being released. Many who were repatriated with false papers later defined themselves, or were defined by their friends, as escapers, although their 'escape' sometimes seems to have involved a degree of complicity from the German or Vichy authorities. Often releases involved manipulation, by the prisoner himself or his contacts back in France, but sometimes prisoners themselves were confused by releases.[28]

The complexity of the mechanisms by which men were released, and the extent to which those mechanisms could be manipulated, was illustrated by the release of Flamands in February 1941. In extending the definition of Flamands to those from northern France who spoke

Flemish, the Germans created a new category that did not bear any relation to prisoners' existing bureaucratic status. Men had to prove that they spoke Flemish by appearing in front of a 'linguistic commission', which contained a Belgian civilian (presumably one who was politically sympathetic to the Germans) and a German officer. This opened opportunities for enterprising prisoners. Jean Legros, a French speaker from Belgium, was able to learn enough Flemish to pass the test. His brother, who spoke no Flemish, came into the room immediately after him and Legros got his release simply by saying, 'That is my brother.' Legros also gave language lessons to prisoners from northern France who hoped to secure their release in the same way.[29] At the other extreme was a Flemish-speaking prisoner from northern France in a work Kommando of Stalag XVIIB in Austria. The prisoner in question was illiterate and spoke poor French.[30] It is easy to see why he had not been repatriated. Isolated in a work Kommando and unable to read circulars or to understand much of what his comrades said, he probably had no means of knowing about the possibility of repatriation.

The French sometimes regarded those who returned from German captivity with suspicion. In 1946 police in the Gironde wrote a report on two candidates who had recently been defeated in municipal elections. One of them had been repatriated from a German prisoner of war camp: 'This return created an unfavourable prejudice with regard to him in the mind of the population of Ludon.' The other had escaped, been recaptured after a month, then been released and apparently thereafter enjoyed good relations with the Germans.[31] The two men, known to be supporters of the extreme right, had not been convicted of any offence at the liberation, but the local population believed that their relations with the Germans had been excessively close. The most vocal collaborationist to have been captured by the Germans, the writer Robert Brasillach, returned to Paris in 1941; Jean Guéhenno described the book that Brasillach subsequently published, *Notre avant guerre*, as 'the price of his release'.[32]

Sometimes the Germans did release men from prisoner of war camps because of their collaborationist views. A Breton autonomist was released (ostensibly as a nurse) in 1941, but he admitted to his French interrogators that he had in fact been freed because of his political views.[33] Some prisoners joined collaborationist movements to facilitate their release, and some women in France joined such movements in the hopes of helping imprisoned husbands. However, collaborationists could never have made up a majority of those released (most prisoners would not have been in a position to perform any useful service for the Germans even if they had been willing to do so).

More generally, early release often went with social privilege. A disproportionate number of those who were seen as useful to the French economy were from wealthy backgrounds: the Duc de Brissac, an important figure in the electrical construction industry, was released within weeks of his capture. His account of his release illustrates how a mixture of economic usefulness and social privilege could secure freedom. He suggested that a 'commander of a prison camp had for several weeks [in the summer of 1940] the enormous power to liberate anyone who seemed likely to him to put the French economic machine back on the road'. In order to benefit from this power, Brissac had to make contact with the world outside his camp. A brother of one of his fellow inmates owned a business near the camp. He persuaded his friend's brother to tell the iron mine at Droitaumont close to Jarry about Brissac's imprisonment. The iron mine then obtained the support of the town mayor and the local German commander for Brissac's release. In fact, Brissac was not really a specialist in mining iron and did not stay in his new job for long. He explained the willingness of the company to secure his release by the fact that he had been enrolled in the École des Mines in 1918 and 'could claim to be a mining engineer and furthermore, and this was the most important thing, I had had Droitaumont under my authority when I had been head of the mining business for Schnieder for four years from 1935 to 1939'.[34]

Some releases of men from the *grande bourgeoisie* cannot be explained in terms of their uses to either German propaganda or the French economy. It was widely believed that some releases were bought from corrupt officials, but probably more important was the pulling of official strings by well-connected families. The importance of such machinations is reflected in the fact that the release rate from the special camp for *aspirants* (a particular kind of junior officer in the French army) was higher than the release rate from ordinary Stalags.

This cannot be explained in terms of any of the officially admitted reasons for release. *Aspirants* were generally young men, unlikely to be fathers of large families or veterans of the First World War and less likely than other prisoners to be sick, and they seem to have been particularly hostile to German attempts to enlist them in the collaborationist cause. The only explanation for the high release rate is that large numbers of *aspirants* came from wealthy and powerful families.[35]

Connections secured release in all sorts of ways. Sacha Guitry's theatrical career brought him into contact with the Germans and he was later to claim that he had obtained the release of eleven young men through these contacts.[36] Charles Rist's activities as a banker brought him into contact with the Germans, too. He would, however, have been outraged by the suggestion that these contacts made him into a collaborator. One of his sons resigned from the civil service rather than serve the new regime and another died fighting with the Maquis. His third son, Léonard, was a prisoner of war who took a strongly anti-collaborationist line in his camp. In spite of his own and his family's anti-German sentiments, he was released in October 1941, and Charles Rist took it for granted that the release owed something to his business contacts: 'We suppose that he was liberated as a result of the intervention of Grobkop and Wagemann.'[37]

Repatriation could be facilitated by contacts back in France, but some prisoners could also advance their cause through their own initiatives. Sometimes these initiatives involved forged documents. Sometimes they involved negotiating with the authorities to prove a case. Most importantly, prisoners in camps stood a better chance of repatriation than those in work Kommandos. Stalags contained the administrative offices and medical services which had to process any application for repatriation. Furthermore, the German authorities were more likely to release one of the relatively idle inhabitants of a Stalag rather than one serving the German economy in a Kommando. Generally, the Germans were more willing to release men who did office jobs back in France (and who were therefore of limited value to the German economy) than they were to release manual workers. By 1941, the prefecture of Arras had obtained the return of half of its employees, at a time when only 6.4 per cent of those working in agriculture in the Pas-de-Calais had returned home.[38]

In the end, distinctions between the various ways in which prisoners got back to France are artificial. Retrospective accounts tend to distinguish between heroic exercises of will that brought escapes, simple adherence to the rules that brought 'legitimate' repatriation and dishonest manipulation of the rules that brought 'illegitimate' repatriation. The truth is that most releases did not fit neatly into any single category. The potential complexity of repatriation is revealed by Henry Charbonneau. He was released as the eldest son in a large family, but his own account concedes that his release did not come automatically. He had to get himself removed from his work Kommando and sent back to the Stalag 'on an administrative pretext'. From the Stalag he went as an interpreter to Breslau station and there he almost immediately received his liberation papers. No doubt Charbonneau's release owed something to his own initiative: he was an educated man who spoke good German and had shown himself willing to co-operate with his captors. It is hard to believe that his release did not owe quite a lot to strings being pulled in France, too: Charbonneau was the son of a general and, most importantly, he was in regular contact with Deloncle and Darnand, two of the most important collaborationists in France.[39]

The case of Jean-Paul Sartre illustrates how uncertain people could be about the distinction between escape and repatriation. Sartre returned to France in early 1941. Two different versions of his return circulated after the war. One, repeated in some biographies and apparently propagated by Simone de Beauvoir for a time, suggested that Sartre had escaped in disguise. A second suggested that the collaborationist writer Pierre Drieu la Rochelle had obtained his release, and that Sartre might even have promised some favour to the Germans in return. The reality seems to have been that in 1941 the Germans released a number of civilians who had been taken prisoner by accident. Sartre was able to obtain forged papers suggesting that he had been classed as unfit for military service on account of poor eyesight, and thus persuade the Germans that he should be released.

THE *RELÈVE*

On 22 June 1942, Pierre Laval made a speech in which he announced the institution of the *relève*. Under this scheme, French workers were to be encouraged to volunteer to go to Germany. In return for every three workers who went, one prisoner of war would be released. The *relève* was a quintessential Vichy programme. It purported to defend the interests of prisoners of war and to extract benefit for French people from dealing with the Germans. It also fitted in with Vichy's social agenda: Laval suggested that the majority of prisoners released would be farmers whilst the majority of those who went to Germany would be industrial workers. However, the *relève* programme also marked a new step in Vichy's relations with Germany. For the first time, Vichy actively encouraged men from all over France to go to Germany (up until this point it had merely allowed the Germans to recruit and had often regarded those who yielded to German blandishment with some distaste). More importantly, in his speech announcing the *relève*, Laval uttered the most notorious sentence of his career: 'I wish for German victory, because, without it, tomorrow Bolshevism will be installed everywhere.'

The numbers of prisoners released disappointed the French. In total, around 100,000 men were released under the scheme; this meant that the rate of release was actually less than it had been in 1940 and 1941 when no formal scheme had been in place. The disappointment at the small number of men on the first *relève* trains turned to farce when 1,000 rations of red wine were issued on a train that contained only a little over 600 men; a number of the men, used to weak German beer, acquired several rations of wine and arrived at Compiègne drunk.[40]

Further problems were created by the choice of men to benefit from the scheme. The French government was only able to choose between 15 and 20 per cent of those released, the remainder being designated by the Germans.[41] The French had anticipated that peasants would be the main beneficiaries; in fact, only around a quarter of released prisoners were farmers.[42] A large number of those released were sick men, of whom the Germans were glad to be free.[43] Some simply belonged to categories that should have been released under the terms of earlier agreements relating to *anciens combattants* or fathers of large families; the French reckoned that 23,103 out of 95,095 men released under the *relève* should in fact have been released under earlier agreements.[44] Even after the *relève*, however, the French were shocked to note that old men and fathers of large families remained in prison camps at times when the Germans were releasing young men.[45]

Some men were released under the *relève* scheme because they were required by factories working to fulfil German orders in France. One metallurgy firm had secured the return of thirty specialist workers by February 1943 and was working to obtain the release of three men who remained in Stalag IA.[46]

As with previous release schemes, the *relève* tended to benefit the most privileged and articulate prisoners. A disproportionate number of those released under the scheme came from camps rather than work Kommandos. An ability to handle paperwork, good contacts back in France and regular dealings with the camp authorities (dealings that did not necessarily imply political sympathy) all made it easier to get released. Quite large numbers of men who held positions of authority – *hommes de confiance, officiers conseils* – in the camps were released. Men from twenty camps had arrived back in France by July 1943. In four of these camps, the *homme de confiance* was released, and in three of these cases, the Vichy authorities believed that the release sprang from the fact that the men had been too good at defending their compatriots: 'The Germans, finding him to be awkward, have liberated him.'[47] Some *hommes de confiance* refused liberation in order to continue their work.[48] Men in prominent positions in the camps could be liberated for both pro- and anti-German behaviour. The collaborationist *officier conseil* of the Wehrkreis XI had the *hommes de confiance* of both Stalag XIA and XIB first transferred and then repatriated 'because he reproached them for not favouring his policy of collaboration enough', but was then himself sent back to France, presumably because the Germans were grateful to him, or keen to use his services in France.[49]

The *relève* quickly became unpopular with prisoners, their families and the French population as a whole. *Hommes de confiance*, at least those who had not themselves been released, wrote to complain: 'In the convoys of the *relève* that I have seen pass, all places are reserved either for the sick or for comrades who have been called back to France, on the orders of the OKW [German military authorities]; [the returned men are] too often very young and are often not even specialist workers (students, teachers etc.).'[50] The wife of a prisoner wrote: 'This *relève*, about which there is so much talk, will, as my husband writes, doubtless bring us a little more disillusion.'[51] Gustave Folcher, a prosperous peasant and father of a family, was exactly the kind of man who was meant to benefit from the *relève*, and exactly the kind of man from whom the Vichy government hoped to get support. But he believed that the *relève* only advantaged 'fils de famille'.[52]

Officials of the Scapini Mission to prisoners of war themselves believed that the *relève* was being conducted 'in an atmosphere of intrigue and favouritism'.[53] When Marcel Déat's collaborationist newspaper *L'Oeuvre* organized a celebration to mark the return of the 100,000th prisoner, the Mission wrote to the paper pointing out that 100,000 men had not in fact yet returned under the *relève*, and suggesting that it might be unwise to draw attention to such an unpopular programme.[54] However, for all its efforts, the Mission was blamed for the choice of men who returned under the *relève*. One *homme de confiance* said that the Mission's lists were composed 'of those with connections'.[55] The *relève* caused division in the camps themselves, where Pétainist leaders were often believed to have secured their own release (see below), and even amongst the various official bodies of the Vichy government itself; the Ministry of Agriculture's desire to obtain the release of peasants caused particular tension. Indeed the *relève*, which was presented in France as a policy to benefit prisoners, was probably the biggest single cause of disillusionment with the Vichy government in prisoner of war camps. An aide-memoire for the Mission to prisoners of war summed up the impact of the programme:

Consequences. The French judge the *relève* according to the particular cases that they see around them. Disunion amongst prisoners. A fall in morale in the camps ... Severe verdict on the government which is accused of having let it happen.[56]

WORK

Those formally released were a significant minority of French prisoners, but the majority did not remain in the camps. What took them outside the wire was not repatriation or escape but work. Under the Geneva Convention, private soldiers, but not officers or NCOs, were obliged to work. In practice, NCOs often did work. Even François Mitterrand, an exceptionally well-informed, determined and patriotic sergeant, spent six months in a work Kommando. At first, many NCOs simply did not know about their rights. Only when the Red Cross told them the terms of the Geneva Convention and, paradoxically, when Vichy authorities urged them to work, did NCOs realize that they had the right not to do so.[57]

The Germans made life difficult for NCOs who refused to work. They were often threatened, and sometimes set to doing menial tasks in camps. Around 5,900 NCOs, of the 150,000 who had been captured in 1940, were sent to Kobierzyn, a camp established in Poland in January 1942 where conditions were particularly harsh.[58]

Curiously, the very men who had been most vigorous in defence in their right not to work in 1940 and 1941 often agreed to work later in the war. Some justified this decision in retrospect by saying that they hoped that escape would be easier from work Kommandos. It also seems that the relative advantages of Stalags and work Kommandos changed over time. A great attraction of the Stalags in 1940 was that men in them were well placed for repatriation: they were in contact with the French and German bureaucracy and with the doctors who might be able to certify their unfitness to remain in captivity. As time went on, repatriation became less common while the inconveniences of camp life – boredom and poor food – became more evident: René Dufour admitted that an invasion of lice induced him and his 350 comrades to agree to leave their camp and go to work on farms.[59]

Prisoners who worked went to Kommandos. They were kept in smaller units than in the camps (sometimes they were lodged on their own) and they were under less strict supervision. Industrial work Kommandos were usually harsh. By February 1944, almost two-fifths of French prisoners worked in industry and almost one fifth worked in enterprises – metallurgy, mining or chemical plants – where conditions were particularly hard. A Kommando from Stalag XIIA worked in a lead mine 1,200 metres underground in temperatures of up to 40 degrees.[60] Towards the end of the war, the pace in factories was ever faster, with catastrophic consequences for safety. Factories were also subject to close surveillance, sometimes exercised by the SS, and were increasingly likely to be targets for Allied bombing raids.

Most prisoners, especially in the early years of the war, worked on farms. Jean Brustier seems to have been typical in working on four agricultural Kommandos and one industrial one.[61] As late as February 1944, more than half of French prisoners of war worked on farms and almost a tenth of them worked in forestry. Most prisoners saw agricultural work as attractive. Many of them were peasants or agricultural labourers in civilian life. Even those with no previous links to agriculture recognized that life on a farm was likely to be more pleasant than life in a factory. The selection processes by which men were chosen for different kinds of work were rather haphazard. Sometimes the Germans simply allocated people at random. Sometimes they misunderstood what was said – one man who described himself as a *miroitier* (a mirror-maker) was sent to work as a *menuisier* (carpenter).[62] Most of all, prisoners themselves sought to manipulate the selection process. Almost all of them did so with a view to avoiding industrial work and obtaining work on farms. A prisoner was struck by 'the number of French and Belgians who were, or more precisely who claimed to be, farmers, gardeners and cooks . . . the shortage of quarrymen'.[63] Usually groups of prisoners who had been allocated for work on farms were taken to villages where a second selection took place as individual farmers tried to pick those they believed would be the best workers. Many prisoners found this 'slave market' humiliating and German farmers, who sometimes discovered that the robust young man they had chosen was actually a bank clerk, were disappointed.

Generally, prisoners on farms had a remarkable degree of freedom; during the working day they were usually under the supervision of no one other than the civilian farmer, and, as the war drained the male population of the German countryside into the army, prisoners often worked independently.[64] The French Mission to prisoners of war believed that some of them lived in a state of semi-liberty, trading a promise not to escape for the removal of the guards.[65] This informal arrangement was different from the formal change by which some prisoners were transformed into civilian workers in 1943 (see Chapter 9). Some prisoners could arrange their lives more or less as they wished so long as they got their work done. Maurice Duverne in eastern Prussia went around neighbouring farms to collect milk and would then sometimes relax with other prisoners of war (including English ones) over a beer at the station bar.[66] René Dufour in the Sudetenland was able to continue his civilian career as a poacher,[67] an especially rewarding activity because strict German regulation of hunting ensured that game was much more plentiful than it would have been in France.[68] Gustave Folcher hunted for mushrooms.[69]

German farms were not always easy places. The work was hard for those unused to physical labour and poorly maintained agricultural machinery could be dangerous: a disconcertingly large number of Frenchmen who had worked on German farms were repatriated with missing hands. There were, in any case, considerable differences between different kinds of assignment – picking grapes in the Moselle was better than digging an irrigation ditch in Prussia. Many prisoners established good relations with their employers but some farmers treated them harshly. A few prisoners were beaten and, when one was prosecuted for having fought back against his employer, his defence lawyer pointed out that the farmer in question had employed fifteen prisoners of war, one after the other, and that none of them had stayed.[70]

Farm work came easiest to peasants or to those who had grown up in the country.[71] However, peasant proprietors sometimes had mixed feelings about working in agriculture because they resented working on someone else's property at a time when they knew that their own farms were not being kept up.[72] Agricultural labourers from the poorest regions of France adapted best. Often unmarried men with no property, they had left little behind in France. They were used to hard work and harsh words from their employers.

LIFE IN STALAGS

Most prisoners passed back through the Stalags when they moved from one work Kommando to another or when they were ill. The Stalags, far from being simple places of confinement, became administrative centres for the work Kommandos in the surrounding area. Huge bureaucracies grew up: in Stalag XVIII between 120 and 150 men were employed in simply sorting out parcels addressed to the prisoners in the camp and its work Kommandos.

Who exercised power in the Stalags? In part, the answer to this question lies with the formal military hierarchy. Non-commissioned officers, or at least those NCOs who had refused to go to the work Kommandos, made up a good proportion of the camp populations. More generally, educated people tended to stay behind in the camps. Stalags were not, on the whole, places for the highly privileged, who would have been in officers' camps or would have enjoyed an early release secured by their relatives. The classic figure of power in a Stalag was from the lower middle class, a teacher or a clerk in civilian life.

Networks of influence developed in the camps. Records were kept there, and often the posting that a French prisoner obtained would depend on the goodwill of his own comrades who processed his papers. One man, who had made the mistake of annoying a German doctor by pretending to be ill at his work Kommando, was saved from being sent to work in a salt mine when the French prisoner in charge of his file turned out to be a fellow Vendéen, who helpfully lost the relevant paperwork.[73] Joseph Raoux attributed his escape from a harsh work Kommando to the 'mafia of primary school teachers' that operated in his Stalag.[74]

Men from the work Kommandos sometimes regarded the Stalags as centres of corruption in which their more clever and manipulative comrades had found comfortable *planques*. Camps could be corrupt places. Black marketeering was rife. Prisoners in the Stalags had parcels from France or from the Red Cross that contained goods – especially chocolate – that were hard to get in Germany. Prisoners in the camps got more than their fair share of supplies because they intercepted parcels that ought to have gone to their comrades in work Kommandos.[75] The German guards were relatively old men, neither crack troops nor committed Nazis, who were often willing to trade with their captives. In Stalag IXA prisoners stole fat and potatoes from the camp kitchens and then sold plates of chips to their guards for 50 Pfennigs a time.[76]

Léo Malet's fictional detective Nestor Burma began his career in a camp that resembled Stalag XB, where Malet himself had been imprisoned, and his first novel says much about the atmosphere in prisoner of war camps. Burma has found himself a perfect *planque* as a clerk responsible for registering new arrivals in 1940. He and his colleagues are rewarded for their labours with an extra allocation of tobacco, confiscated from the very men they are processing. When new arrivals cease, Burma finds a new *planque* working in the infirmary until he himself, a man of famously robust health, manages to be repatriated for health reasons in December 1940. Malet himself got repatriated by faking a heart murmur.

Relations between the Stalags and the work Kommandos reflected an interesting dichotomy, a dichotomy that was perhaps typical of wider French life. The camps were about literacy, formality and official bureaucratic regulation. The work Kommandos were about warmth, community and, often, being in a position to ignore formal rules. Jean Moret-Bailly, who became *homme de confiance* of Stalag XVIIB in 1943, likened the work Kommandos to provincial towns and the Stalag to 'a capital city without women or external contact'.[77]

The dichotomy between Stalags and work Kommandos was sharpened by the fact that the majority of prisoners who spent most of their time in the Kommandos had a difficult time when they passed through the Stalags. They were often lodged in inferior quarters and they lacked the contacts that regular inmates of the Stalags had established to make life bearable. Moret-Bailly suggested that most men who passed through the Stalags during their transfer from one Kommando to another 'were horrified by the capital, its disinfection, its searches, its hunger'.[78] Vichy officials reported that men from work Kommandos passing through Stalag VID had lost poker games, 'se fassent littéralement sucer par leurs camarades'.[79]

Whereas men in the work Kommandos tended to recall the intimacy of friendship and the relative abundance of food as being among the main compensations of their life, men in the Stalags took refuge in more organized entertainments. Bernard Fay, director of the Bibliothèque Nationale, organized a programme to send books to prisoners. In Stalag IXA there were 7,000 books and a further 28,000 that circulated among the camp's satellite Kommandos. Louis Althusser's diary of his time in Stalag XA was full of entries on Lawrence, Mauriac and Roger Martin du Gard. By April 1944, he was able to write: 'More than ever, I understand Proust.'[80]

Books were written in captivity. Fernand Braudel's thesis on *The Mediterranean in the Age of Philip II* (which was to revolutionize historiography when it was published) was written in Oflag XIIB in Mayence and then at Oflag XC at Lübeck. Braudel sent chapters, handwritten in school exercise books, to his supervisor Lucien Febvre in Paris. It is interesting to speculate on how captivity marked this work. Was Braudel's approach influenced by the access to German history books, brought to him from the town library by a sympathetic German guard? Was it the chance to escape from academic routines that turned Braudel away from what had previously been orthodox historical writing? Was Braudel's determinism and emphasis on the *longue durée* characteristic of one who was leading a life of enforced passivity controlled by inscrutable forces? Does the vividness with which the material richness of the Mediterranean is evoked owe something to the deprivations of a German winter?[81]

Concerts, plays and football matches helped pass the time in camps. Prisoners gave lectures to their comrades: Mitterrand on 'Les lettres de cachet sous l'ancien régime',[82] Sartre on the idea of death in the work of Rilke, Heidegger and Mauriac.[83] Jean Guitton's *History of French Thought from 1870 to 1940* was first composed as a series of lectures to be delivered in his Oflag.

Prison camps often brought into intimate contact men who would have been unlikely to encounter each other in civilian life, and this was especially noticeable before the reassertion of social hierarchy that took many of the most well-connected prisoners back to France, while the least privileged went to work Kommandos. Jean-Paul Sartre became friends with a man known as the poacher (a peasant and ex-convict). More unexpectedly, Sartre developed a respectful and affectionate relationship with the priest Marius Perrin.[84] François Mitterrand, a student from a Catholic and conservative background who had dabbled with the politics of the right-wing leagues in the 1930s, got to know Roger Pelat (a Communist and a former worker at Renault who had grown up in extreme poverty as a *pupille de la nation*) and Bernard Finifter (a White Russian Jew, who had been a boxer in Berlin and stowed away on a ship to New York before joining the Foreign Legion in 1939).[85] Louis Althusser, a neurotic and unworldly twenty-year-old, who had just finished his studies at the Lycée du Parc when he was called up in 1939, and who would spend the rest of his life in the École Normale Supérieure, believed that he had developed a close friendship with Clerc, the footballer who had played for Cannes when they won the Coupe de France in 1932. History does not record what Clerc thought of Althusser.[86]

POLITICS

Political organization played an important role in some prison camps (more than in work Kommandos where men were generally kept in small groups and were always busy).[87] In some ways, prisoner of war camps preserved a political culture that was suppressed in France itself. Most political activity in France had been a male preserve (particularly the preserve of men who had proved their right to be citizens by performing military service), and Vichy often presented the population over which it ruled as female or infantile. The population of the prison camps was entirely made up of adult men, all of them soldiers. A prisoner protected by the Geneva Convention in Germany could express his opinions more freely than a civilian in France. Prisoners were the only group of French people who still voted, because they elected *hommes de confiance*. The Germans sought to propagate collaborationist sentiment among prisoners. They provided a newspaper, *Le Trait d'union*, that took a pro-German editorial line. Some collaborationist *cercles européens* were founded in the camps.

More common than *cercles européens*, however, were *cercles Pétain*. These *cercles* were founded in 1941 and seem, eventually, to have operated in all camps. Pétainism had particular resonance in the camps. Prisoners knew that their fate recurred regularly in Pétain's speeches. Groups who were very active in the early organization of the camps – Catholics, former Boy Scouts – were especially susceptible to certain aspects of Vichy rhetoric. A report on prisoners returning to France in March 1942 suggested: 'The great majority are ready to follow blindly the doctrine of the Marshal.'[88]

Pétainism in the camps, however, as everywhere, could have more than one meaning. Some *cercles Pétain* were simply advocates of collaboration. The *cercle* founded in an Oflag by Georges Soulès was so overtly pro-German that eventually Eugène Deloncle, head of the collaborationist Mouvement Social Révolutionnaire, asked for Soulès to be repatriated to work with him in Paris.[89] More commonly, Pétainists in the prison camps seem to have defined themselves in terms of a conservative patriotism that made them favourable to Pétain and hostile to Laval or to the Paris-based collaborationists. Aspects of life in the prison camps fitted in with a certain kind of conservative Pétainism. The Germans with whom prisoners dealt were mainly soldiers (often, given that camp guards were usually old, veterans of the First World War). Relations between the German authorities and prisoners were more restrained by formal rules than relations between the Germans and civilians in France.

Even more than people in France itself, prisoners focused their loyalty on Pétain as an individual and often rejected 'political Pétainism', by which they meant collaboration. In Stalag VIA, 'the *cercle Pétain* which, from its creation, tended to become a political group, failed for this reason. Reformed as an organ of information, it has regained a little of its activity.'[90] In Stalag XIB it was reported that a doctor ran the *cercle Pétain* 'to the satisfaction of everyone, limiting the action of the circle to literary and scientific conferences'.[91]

Prisoners may have believed in the possibility that relations with the Germans could be governed by military etiquette in the short term, but they also had more reason than any other group of Frenchmen to be aware of the difference between an armistice and a lasting peace and to be sceptical about whether lasting peace with the Germans was possible. In Oflag VIA, 'the majority of officers have rallied to the movement of the Marshal. These officers, however, find it difficult to understand how the salvation of France can come from German goodwill.'[92] Prisoners often assumed that loyalty to Vichy could go hand in hand with a desire to see German defeat. Employees of Vichy's official mission to prisoners of war, which was itself riven by political division, seem to have encouraged this assumption. One delegate apparently told prisoners that collaboration was an 'astuce du maréchal'.[93] In Stalag VIIA, the *cercle Pétain* worked well: 'There was never any question there of sincere collaboration with Germany' (prisoners in this camp seem to have believed – a surprisingly common view amongst conservative Pétainists – that the most abject collaborators were Jews).[94] Inmates of Stalag IXC were 'clearly for the programme of National Revolution', but they also had good relations with their English fellow prisoners and were sympathetic to the English cause.[95]

It is notable that those who were most Pétainist in terms of social conservatism, anti-Semitism and opposition to the Third Republic were also most prone to do the one obviously anti-German thing that lay within a prisoner's power: escape. The most high-ranking escaper from a German camp was General Henri Giraud.[96] Giraud, born in 1878, was a conservative officer who had commanded the seventh army (the one that advanced into Belgium) in 1940. Maurice Martin du Gard wrote of him: 'He is very "National Revolution". He was even *avant la lettre*: father of seven children, the model of an honest man and a man of order.'[97] Giraud was captured in June 1940. In July, in his prison camp, he drafted a long note for Pétain about the causes of the defeat that could have come straight from one of the Marshal's own speechwriters. Giraud blamed defeat on the British army: 'Friendship gave way to egoism. There was Arras, there was Dunkerque, there was Cherbourg, there was, alas, Mers-el-Kebir.' He then turned to the general decline of France: 'In a race formerly robust, rustic, hardened to fatigue, but in which alcohol and syphilis have opened flowing wounds, the frame has shrunk, tissues have become flabby.' He talked more specifically about the damage done by the Popular Front, 'the fatal association which united under the same banner the bourgeois freemason, the convinced syndicalist and the Bolshevist', which meant that 'authority [was] flouted, order destroyed, laws and regulations violated; these were common coin from 1936 to 1938'.[98]

Giraud's escape from the Koenigstein prison camp did not mark a break with Pétainism; on the contrary, it was helped by elements of the Vichy intelligence service. Some at Vichy would have liked Giraud to return to captivity but he was not compelled to do so, and Marshal Pétain received him cordially. Giraud remained loyal to the Marshal – though ever more hostile to Laval – until his departure to join the American landings in Algeria at the end of 1942.

François Mitterrand was another example of prison camp Pétainism. He too tried to escape from his prison camp (his return to France in 1941 was the result of the last of his three escape attempts). Thereafter he worked for Vichy agencies and in October 1942 received the *Francisque*, a Vichy decoration, from Pétain's own hands. In the body set up to organize prisoners of war, he combined work for Vichy with work against the Germans. Mitterrand turned against Laval's protégés in the prisoner of war movement in 1943 and went to London at the end of that year. However, it is not clear that he ever turned against Pétain. He was on good terms with Jacques Isorni, Pétain's defence counsel and apologist, in the 1950s.

The links between Pétainism and escape affected the atmosphere in some Oflags. Colditz Castle was for a time home to the most determined escapers among French officers, but the attitudes of these officers to political questions, particularly anti-Semitism, shocked those British servicemen imprisoned with them. The paradoxes of positions among French prisoners were exposed when the Germans began to put all French officers who were 'enemies of the Reich' in a single camp at Lübeck. As far as the Germans were concerned, 'enemies of the Reich' was a category that embraced Jews, left-wingers and persistent escapers, but in fact these three categories had little in common other than hostility to the Germans, or German hostility to them. The escapers were often reproached by their new companions for their Pétainist opinions.

The politics of the prison camps did not remain the same throughout the war. Many prisoners remained loyal to Pétain, but increasingly they distinguished him from the Vichy government. Laval's return to government in April 1942 was badly received. Laval, a conspicuously non-military figure associated with the subjugation of France to Germany, was unpopular amongst prisoners – the report of the Mission to prisoners of war remarked dryly that prisoners considered Laval to be a 'skilful politician'.[99]

Laval's *relève* programme did much to undermine Pétainism amongst prisoners of war. This was partly because they disliked the programme and blamed Vichy for the way in which it was implemented. It was also because some men who benefited from the *relève* had been the heads of *cercles Pétain*. Their departure deprived the Pétainist movement of its leadership and also contributed to a general sense that Pétainism was corrupt: 'The Pétain circle of IIIC . . . has lost its influence following the liberation of all the leaders of the circle. This has created a very bad impression on all the members.'[100] In some cases, heads of *cercles Pétain* seem to have believed that displays of pro-German feeling would increase their chances of freedom and such displays undermined their credibility with their own fellow captives:

The Pétain circle has lost much of its activity. The men complain that the leaders seek above all to get a personal advantage from their situation. A prisoner sold out to the Germans [*acquis aux allemands*] was placed at the head of the circle and a little while after his appointment was liberated, which provoked a lot of resignations amongst the members.[101]

The American invasion of French North Africa in November 1942, and the subsequent German invasion of the non-occupied zone of France, was also important in alienating prisoners from the Vichy regime.[102] The anti-German variety of Pétainism that many prisoners had espoused was similar to that cultivated in Algeria under General Weygand in 1940 and 1941. It seemed less plausible when Algeria ceased to be under Vichy rule and when France had lost its last vestiges of real independence. Besides, the American-sponsored leader of the Free French in Algeria was, for the first six months of 1943, France's most prominent escaped prisoner, Henri Giraud. Jean Guitton wrote that life in the Oflags was divided into 'geological eras': 'The time of Pétain before the landings in Algeria, the time of Giraud after the landings and the time of de Gaulle.'[103]

Laval and his associates tried, without much success, to associate themselves with prisoners, as did supporters of the collaborationist Marcel Déat. In January 1943 Laval sacked Maurice Pinot, who ran the Commissariat Général aux Prisonniers de Guerre Rapatriés et aux Familles de Prisonniers de Guerre (CGPGR) that organized released prisoners of war. Pinot was replaced by André Masson, who had made himself notorious amongst prisoners for writing collaborationist articles in *Le Trait d'union* and who had been released from Stalag VC in December 1942. Masson's appointment was resented by prisoners and also by other Vichy bodies that concerned themselves with prisoners (particularly the Scapini Mission). Those who claimed leadership of repatriated prisoners in France itself struggled fiercely with each other. Five men who had been dismissed from the CGPGR in January (of whom the most notable were Pinot and Mitterrand) began to operate with the Resistance.

Ceremonies to greet repatriated prisoners of war often became occasions for struggle between the varieties of Pétainism. Matters came to a head in April 1943 when the first prisoners to be granted leave to visit their families arrived in France. Many officials seem to have expected that they would be grateful and that their reception would provide good propaganda for the collaborationist cause. The French organized a ceremony at Compiègne. Masson, Bruneton (the French official responsible for civilian workers in Germany), Chambrun (Laval's son-in-law) and de Brinon (the French representative in Paris) attended, as did high-ranking German officials. Masson was accompanied by an entourage of 250 people wearing the *complet Pétain* (the suit issued to prisoners who had been 'transformed' into civilian workers).

The prisoners' response to this display was described, with ill-disguised glee, by an official of the Scapini Mission: 'Not a cry, not a single manifestation of joy. On the wagons, written in pencil ... provisionally liberated, no volunteers. Everyone was stupefied and Monsieur Masson, among others, seemed absolutely shocked and did not cease to repeat: "But I do not understand. They should be happy."' When Masson made a speech, the only applause came from his own entourage. During the meal that was laid on for the prisoners, an orchestra played, but the atmosphere remained 'painful'. The prisoners only showed enthusiasm when the musicians agreed to play the

'Marseillaise' (theoretically forbidden in the occupied zone), at which point everyone stood up and many cried.[104]

Prison camps changed over time. Some of these changes affected prisoners on both sides of the wire. Generally, they were hellish places in the summer of 1940 and difficult in the harsh winter of 1940 – when food, clothing and accommodation were still often inadequate. They became more civilized as they became less heavily populated and more organized. Over the longer term, though, they tended to become less attractive. The huts in which men were usually housed aged quickly and the Third Reich had more pressing needs by 1943 than maintaining prison camps.

Most importantly, perhaps, the image of camps changed. For the first year or so after the defeat, French thinking about prisoners had concentrated on the camps rather than the work Kommandos. Captivity was presented as something between a religious retreat and a university course. Prisoners would return purified and ready to rebuild France. As time went on, this image became less plausible. As other young men returned to active fighting, either in the Resistance or in the Légion des Volontaires Français contre le Bolchevisme, prisoners ceased to be the focus of patriotism. As conditions in France got worse, they were no longer seen as the main victims of the war. Cavanna wrote that French people had considered that returning prisoners would be 'the future judge to whom we will have to give an account of ourselves'. But it became obvious that the judges of wartime France would really be drawn from the Free French forces or the Resistance – indeed, Robert Brasillach, one of the most famous released prisoners, was shot for collaboration in February 1945 before most of his former comrades had returned from Germany.

A large proportion of the most enterprising or best-connected French prisoners of war had either escaped or been repatriated by the end of 1942. Increasingly, it was felt that those who remained behind were inadequate in some way. The change was particularly sharp with regard to inmates of prison camps, once regarded as the elite of prisoners. Louis Althusser in Stalag XC already felt that those who expected prisoners to be philosopher kings, formed by suffering and reflection, would be disappointed when the prisoners returned. In fact, few people in France seem to have entertained such hopes after the end of 1942. Prisoners were increasingly seen as victims rather than heroes. Most importantly, perhaps, official discussion of them was conducted increasingly in terms that called their masculinity into question. They were seen as passive, sick, cuckolded or homosexual. One officer thought that '30 per cent' of the 25,000 officers in Oflags would return 'very diminished by the experience'.[105] A Paris police report, based on interviews with returning prisoners, suggested that morale in work Kommandos remained relatively high but that life in the Stalags was dominated by terrible food, poor hygiene and the black market. The report concluded: 'There results from this an almost universal amorality of which one of the most damaging consequences is pederasty which is practised almost openly.'[106] The last few words of the report were crossed out, as though the author found it unbearable to contemplate the extent to which prisoners had fallen short of the hopes once placed in them.

DU BEURRE POUR LES FRANÇAIS. DE LA MERDE POUR LES JUIFS

7

Survival

Clients ate what they liked, drank coffee with sugar and smoked foreign
cigarettes ... Most of them were not from society [*gens du monde*] but
seemed to belong to that business world, born from the economic circumstances of the present.   (Undercover police report on Maxim's restaurant,
October 1942)[1]

I am tired of standing in a line outside the market.   (Suicide note left by
mother of two who hanged herself in the Gard in April 1942)[2]

Food shortage in occupied France was never as severe as it was in
parts of the Soviet Union, Poland, Holland or Greece during the
Second World War. French people did starve to death – as an unemployed man from the Alpes-Maritimes did in 1942[3] or as four
women from Vauvert in the Gard did in February of the same year[4] –
but the event was sufficiently rare to arouse special comment.

However, if dearth did not have the very sharp physical effects that
it had in other occupied countries, it certainly had a cultural and
political effect in France. The French talked about food obsessively.
The banker and economist Charles Rist was a wealthy man, able to
avoid some of the hardships endured by his compatriots, and an
austere Protestant, not given to discussion of material comfort. None
the less, his diary is full of references to food. On 3 July 1944 he
wrote: 'People everywhere talk of nothing but provisions and supply.'[5]
The obsession with food filtered into the family's private language;

7. (opposite) *Thinking about food was intertwined with thinking about
almost everything else in occupied France. The inscription on the wall reads:
'Butter for the French; shit for the Jews.'*

when Rist heard that his son had 'gone to help uncle Loulou grow potatoes', he knew that he had joined the Maquis.[6] Preoccupation with shortage affected almost every person in France. It even affected domestic animals: dogs were killed or released into the wild in order to conserve food (the canine population of the Alpes-Maritimes halved[7]). The fate of other pets was more sinister: in October 1941 the prefect of Paris warned of diseases that might be transmitted by eating stewed cat.[8]

Shortages created a new sort of society. German power depended partly on the ability to control access to food and warmth. In July 1941 Ernst Jünger dined at the Tour d'Argent (an expensive restaurant on the top floor of a building overlooking the Seine). He wrote in his diary: 'One had the sense that the people sitting up there, consuming the famous soles and ducks, were like gargoyles, seeing below them, with a kind of diabolical satisfaction, the grey ocean of roof tops under which the starving tried to keep body and soul together. In such times, eating well and copiously gives a feeling of power.'[9] In 1942 the head of the SS in France told the French that Maxim's, Le Caneton, Lapérouse and the Tour d'Argent were under German control. Some people with no political sympathy for the occupying forces found it physically comfortable to be close to Germans. Simone de Beauvoir began to work at a table near the stove in the Dôme café in the winter of 1940–41. The Dôme had special supplies of coal because it was frequented by Germans. De Beauvoir's presence was not an act of collaboration, though perhaps the waiters were willing to let her stay at one of the best tables in the house for so long because they knew that their German clients would appreciate the presence of an elegant young woman.

People gathered wherever they could conserve energy, keep warm and, perhaps, get food. Cinemas were popular, though young men who might attract unwelcome interest from the Germans increasingly avoided such places. Library membership doubled. Many people simply stayed at home: Colette said that the best way to survive the occupation was to 'stay in bed'. Bourgeois Parisian families abandoned parts of their apartments to gather in a single heated room. Georges Simenon characteristically saw commercial possibilities opening up as people huddled together on cold, dark nights. He asked Gallimard to produce an advertisement that read: 'This winter you will reread all the Simenons.'

Urban consumers, especially women and children, spent hours queuing. On 13 December 1940 Liliane Schroeder queued for twenty minutes to buy some Brussels sprouts and then for another half an hour to buy a piece of black pudding.[10] In the provinces, people started queuing at three in the morning;[11] in Paris, some concierges rented out places in their courtyards or doorways during the night-time curfew to those who wished to be the first to queue outside shops in the morning.[12] It could be soul-destroying to wait for hours in the bitterly cold winters of 1940–41 and 1941–2 only to find that there was nothing left in the shop. In 1943 Marcel Aymé published a story entitled 'En attendant'. It is set during 'the war of 1939–1977'. It concerns fourteen people queuing outside a grocers in the Rue Caulaincourt: they include an old man, whose wife has just died; a woman of twenty-five, whose husband of twenty-eight is a prisoner of war; a mother of four, whose fifth child has just died and who remarks that there will be revenge against those with 'their bellies over their belt' when the Germans leave; a prostitute, whose career has been hampered by her failure to learn German; a Jew, whose misfortune is summed up with the words ' "Me I am a Jew", said the Jew'; and a girl of sixteen, who wistfully recalls the days when 'all the men were twenty'. There is also a character who does not speak. She is described thus: 'husband a prisoner, three children, misery, anguish exhaustion', and she dies waiting.

Some made queuing a profession. Often this was a family business: mothers would queue for seven francs an hour and then send their children to deliver the provisions to clients. People who had special rights to go to the head of a queue, such as a tramp with a card that defined him as 'severely handicapped', were the elite of this new profession.[13] Established social hierarchies were reversed in wartime queues. In Marseilles, Italian women, normally the lowest in the working class, were said to have pushed to the front of queues saying, 'Priority to the victors.' In Brittany, women who cooked for the Germans were given special rights to go to the head of queues. Since women who worked for the Germans were usually poor and often regarded as little better than prostitutes, housewives from 'respectable' families resented making way for them. When Madame L., who bought provisions for the Germans, went to the front of a queue in November 1940, 'there was general discontent and muttering could be heard'.[14] In a food queue in Beauvais, an argument that began when one woman accused another of 'sleeping with boches' finished with the accused woman having her head shaved at the liberation.[15]

People talked in queues, spreading the gossip that was so important in occupied France, and, sometimes, they began to protest. On 22 December 1940 there was a near riot in the Marché de Buci when five Germans went to the head of a queue of 2,000 people who were waiting to buy 300 portions of rabbit.[16] The Paris police became uncomfortably aware that every queue was a political demonstration waiting to happen and, in December 1940, they sought to regulate queues by insisting that shoppers collect a ticket and come back at an appointed time. On 28 June 1941 (perhaps anticipating the ways in which the Communist Party might exploit discontent after the invasion of the Soviet Union), the Paris police tried to forbid the formation of queues more than half an hour before shops opened.[17] They were right to be worried. On 31 May 1942 a queue in the Rue de Buci gave rise to a riot in the course of which Communist militants killed two policemen.[18]

The absence of petrol made bicycles important. They were especially valuable for town dwellers who needed to get into the countryside to buy provisions. On his way back to Dijon in September 1941, Henri Drouot noted 500 bicycles coming in the opposite direction, including ten ridden by grocers pulling small carts.[19] André Montagnard, who wrote 'Maréchal nous voilà', also composed a song entitled 'Pédalons' about a couple who spill a bag of onions while cycling back from a provisioning trip. Bicycles themselves became sought-after items on the black market: in Rennes, a city of 100,000 inhabitants, about 1,000 bicycles were stolen per year during the occupation.[20]

Keeping track of consumption in occupied France was hard. Prices rose so fast and so unpredictably that, in 1943, school mathematics textbooks ceased to ask students to compute specific prices and suggested instead that they should assign commodities prices that seemed realistic to them at the time.[21] Official rations were barely enough to support life; the philosopher Simone Weil is said to have starved to death in 1943 because, as an exile in London, she tried to live on the official rations that were permitted to her compatriots who stayed in France. However, it was not always easy to obtain even minimum rations, because shopkeepers were unable, or unwilling, to honour ration tickets: a Paris police report described ration tickets as 'uncovered cheques'.[22] Furthermore, many could not afford to buy, with their official wages, even the meagre goods that they were permitted by their rations.[23] Inevitably, people were forced into informal and illegal transactions.

Informal channels were themselves complicated. There was no single black market. Prices might vary according to who was buying, and how risky the transaction seemed to be. Often exchange replaced simple cash purchase, and sometimes the exchange involved an unspoken assumption of favours to come. The very goods that were exchanged changed in nature. The underfed cattle of July 1944 were not the same as their fat relatives of 1940: it was estimated that 130 beasts in 1944 would provide the same amount of meat as 70 in 1940.[24] The government sponsored ersatz production so that state-manufactured cigarettes contained one part 'odourless leaves' to two parts of tobacco. Bakers were permitted to include maize as well as wheat in their bread. Black marketeers watered milk and mixed butter with margarine.

Consumption was never, however, just about grams and calories. The very basis of the Vichy regime was linked with food. In his message of 13 August 1940, Pétain said: 'The first task of the government is to ensure an adequate supply of food for everyone.' Jacques-Alain de Sédouy recalled of his schooldays: 'I was not surprised that the distribution of the vitaminized biscuits and pastilles that took place each morning was staged in front of the portrait of the Marshal, as though he himself presided over a sort of communion.'[25]

THE BEGINNING OF SHORTAGE

The armistice imposed conditions on France, in particular the payment of occupation costs, that drained the country of goods. The Germans seized large quantities of food. Problems were particularly severe in Paris, which contained many Germans and which was dependent on 'imports' of food from agricultural areas; in one week in December 1940, the Germans were said to have taken 80 per cent of all cattle brought into Paris.

Alongside formal requisition, the Germans also bought up goods on the black market, thus generating more shortages and forcing up prices. Officially sponsored German purchases on the black market stopped in 1943, because the Germans feared that they were forcing prices up too high. However, relatively junior Germans continued to dabble in the black market, either for their own benefit or in order to serve some particular German agency. French officials sometimes found it hard to know how far Germans who worked in the black market were working on their own account and how far their actions were sponsored by higher authorities. In March 1943 inspectors in the market at Les Halles in Paris found a merchant who had 310 kilograms of beef, 173 kilograms of veal, 210 kilograms of eggs and 45 kilograms of cheese, none of which had been acquired through legal channels. The merchant insisted that he was buying for German agencies and, at the request of the SS, the goods were left in his possession.[26]

Agriculture was disrupted by the war. Not surprisingly, the harvest of 1940 was not collected efficiently. Huge numbers of farm animals that had been abandoned by fleeing farmers had died. The two million prisoners who were taken back to Germany in 1940 included around 450,000 men who worked in agriculture. For a time, in the autumn of 1940, French experts feared famine and this threat was only averted because the Germans were willing to make concessions, allowing prisoners of war still in France to help collect the harvest, and sometimes giving horses to farmers.

Coal was scarce in wartime France, because imports ceased and because the Germans used much of France's own production. The winters of 1940–41 and 1941–2 were particularly severe. Temperatures dropped below freezing in Paris on 39 days in an average winter, but during that of 1940–41 the city froze on 48 days and in the following winter on 51 days.[27] In December 1940 Paris models were thrown out of work as painters gave up painting nudes in their freezing studios and resorted to still lifes,[28] though one assumes that bowls of fruit were not easy to come by either. Jean Guéhenno made long diary entries throughout the occupation in which he discussed literature and politics, but on 21 January 1942 he wrote just one sentence: 'It is so cold that I hardly think of anything but that.'[29]

The French suffered increasingly from the extension of the war. The British blockade cut off a large part of French imports. The Germans became ever more ruthless in their drive to take resources from France. America, which had provided food to France in the first couple of years of the occupation, was at war with Germany from December 1941 and broke off diplomatic relations with Vichy a year later. The American invasion of Algeria in November 1942 cut France off from her most important sources of goods outside Europe. Coffee and chocolate became almost unobtainable in France.

Shortages varied from one part of the country to another, because transport was difficult and because prefects were often reluctant to let food go outside their own department. Most of all, France was divided into zones by the Germans. The most important supplies were located in the northern zone, under German occupation. About three-quarters of French wheat and all her sugar beet came from the occupied zone. Even within the occupied zone, there were pockets of abundance and pockets of shortage. Georgette Elgey, a Jewish girl on the run from the Germans in 1942, was astonished to find that in the streets of Orthez, in the south-west, one could buy real ice cream openly and legally for the same price as one paid for an ersatz ice cream in Paris.[30] Shortage also varied across any single year. The spring, just before the arrival of the first vegetables, and the middle of winter, when shortage of food was accompanied by bitter cold, were the worst periods of the year. Infant mortality peaked in the first three months of each year, because of the cold, and again in the autumn, because of the declining quality of milk.[31]

Food distribution in occupied France was inefficient. Price controls sometimes meant that food was supposed to be sold in Paris for less than it would fetch in the areas where it was produced. The difficulties of transport, disputes between local authorities and the general confusion caused by rigid bureaucratic systems meant that much food simply rotted. Goods that before the war had been moved out of the port of Le Havre in a week or two could now be blocked there for anything up to six months.[32]

Everyone improvised in an attempt to get enough food. Pétain's address on 31 December 1940, a day on which people would have been painfully aware of how their meals differed from those they had enjoyed a year previously, asked the French to 'improvise for themselves the means to complete their food supply'. People in towns tried to keep animals for food. There were said to be 400,000 rabbits kept on Parisian balconies.[33] Generally, however, attempts to feed animals on scraps soon ran up against the problem that French people ate the scraps themselves.[34]

The French authorities tried to manage shortage by rationing. The population was divided into categories. E contained children under three years old; J1 encompassed children of three to six years old; J2 took in children of between six and thirteen; J3 was a category created in 1941 to take in those between thirteen and twenty-one; A was for people between twenty-one and seventy; T was for those between twenty-one and seventy who did heavy manual work; C was for all who worked in agriculture and V was for people over the age of seventy who did not belong to any other category. Children got special rations, notably of milk. So too did men doing heavy manual work (usually in industries judged useful to the German economy). Consumers were also grouped according to where they lived, so that those who lived in the countryside received smaller rations even if they did not work in agriculture because it was assumed that they would have means of getting extra food. Special rations were given to the sick and to pregnant women and nursing mothers.

The rationing system produced odd results. Wealthy people with helpful doctors were often able to obtain certificates entitling them to the special allocations of milk supposedly reserved for the sick. Frontiers between different kinds of consumer were drawn in arbitrary ways. People given rural rations sometimes lived very close to those defined as town dwellers. Young children seem to have been the one group provided with rations adequate to their needs (though it was often hard to get milk rations honoured in cities). Families with young children had useful extra supplies of luxuries, such as chocolate, which could then be distributed to relatives or, perhaps more usually, seized by fathers.[35] The J3 category did not provide most adolescents with enough food, but it did give them more generous rations than those afforded to adults. Partly for this reason, the number of people in the

J3 category grew from just over five million in 1941 to just over six million in 1945. The expansion did not reflect a real demographic change but rather the fact that people continued fraudulently to draw J3 rations after they had ceased to be entitled to them.[36]

Rations blurred ordinary social distinctions. Men doing heavy labour, who obtained extra rations, could be better off than people in white-collar occupations that would have been more highly regarded in peacetime. Employers tried to provide extra food for their workers. Factory canteens were particularly useful: absenteeism was a big problem during the occupation and canteens ensured that workers could only obtain food by turning up to work. Only firms working for the Germans, however, were usually in a position to stock such canteens.[37] Industrialists went to ever greater lengths to get food for their workers. In July 1944 Charles Rist's son Mario, who worked for Ugine, took a lorry and went foraging.[38]

BLACK MARKETS

With rationing went the black market. The phrase 'marché noir' came into widespread use in December 1940 and entered into the Larousse dictionary in 1942, though it was one that many French people preferred to avoid. Almost everything was for sale during and immediately after the occupation. In August 1942, forty-two black-market cases tried in Paris involved soap, pastis, cigarettes, beef, pears, oysters, potatoes, oranges, artichokes, leeks, pork, tomato purée, Bhyrr (an aperitif) and onions.[39] Pierre Mendès France claimed that tickets for his trial for desertion from the French army could be bought in 1941, and, as late as 1946, the baccalauréat papers were on sale. In 1942 an employers' organization talked of a 'parallel economy'. A quarter of all letters intercepted by the contrôle postal in Saint-Étienne in 1942 mentioned the black market.[40]

The black market did not just concern individual consumers. Large firms needed resources that could not be obtained through official channels. Companies kept two sets of accounts, one of them mirroring the real prices paid. Insurance companies developed techniques that allowed them, in effect, to insure illegal black-market stocks.[41]

The black market was not always more efficient than the bureaucratic system that it sought to circumvent. Only certain kinds of goods flowed through black market channels. Black marketeers disliked heavy, perishable food that was hard to transport. A great deal was simply thrown away. One French peasant reckoned that he had buried enough hide from illegally slaughtered cows to provide boots for a battalion.[42] In 1942 the Vichy government tried to prevent such waste by allowing hide from cows slaughtered 'in clandestinity' to be handed in with no questions asked.

The morality of black marketeering was interesting. Almost everyone in France practised it to some extent, and almost everyone in France condemned it, or at least condemned certain kinds. Accusations of black marketeering often went with other forms of hostility. People in the cities blamed peasants, workers blamed the rich, and the grande bourgeoisie blamed parvenu shopkeepers.

The black market epitomized everything that Vichy disapproved of. It went with selfishness, materialism and indifference to the authority of the state. Denunciations under Vichy often concerned black-market matters, and were couched in interesting terms. Someone describing himself as 'an average Frenchman who suffers from restrictions'[43] blamed the black market on Jews. In the south-east, black markets were often blamed on the Italians.

In practice, most Pétainists used the black market. Sometimes Pétainist officials were blatant practitioners: the Graeve family in Chinon trafficked wine at a time when both the son and daughter of the family held positions in the Vichy administration.[44] Vichy bodies and local authorities often used unofficial channels in order to get food for their own employees. The Vichy government itself came to recognize that suppressing the black market entirely was not possible or desirable. A law of March 1942 regulating the black market specifically excluded transactions to cover personal needs,[45] and a circular to prefects in the summer of 1942 talked of 'struggle against all traffickers of the black market but complete freedom left for family supply'.[46] Policemen turned a blind eye to small quantities of illicit goods.[47] Even the Church, normally marked by intense moralism and asceticism, did not wholly condemn the black market. In December 1941 Cardinal Suhard stressed the need to obey the law but then distinguished disobedience from 'the modest extra-legal transactions by which the extras judged necessary are procured and which are justified both by their small scale and the necessities of life'.[48]

Black markets were not, in any case, wholly black. Transactions did not always involve strangers selling goods in a completely free market for cash, and they did not always involve people who thought of themselves as criminals. Money did not necessarily mean much during the occupation. At a time of rapid inflation, everyone preferred goods with a more tangible value. The coupons that gave particular companies the right to buy certain raw materials were traded, illegally. The barter that might normally have operated at village level became institutionalized. One firm advertised a swap of typewriters for bicycles.[49] Cigarettes acquired particular importance, both because nicotine-starved smokers wanted them and because they provided a convenient unit of exchange. Both Micheline Bood, the Parisian schoolgirl, and Charles Rist took a touching interest in the cigarette value of books. A peasant boy in the Corrèze bought an hour of violin lessons for a pound of butter.[50]

Black marketeers sold primarily to people they knew and usually varied their prices according to how close the association was. This was not simply a matter of affection. Anyone doing business with a stranger was running a greater risk of denunciation. The black market divided the French into insiders and outsiders in ways that were not just to do with money. Often the beneficiaries of the black market were those whose official position gave them the power to cover up illegal transactions. Policemen, customs officials, railway workers and members of the *Contrôle Économique* all featured amongst black-market networks. In December 1942, in a town in the north of France, ten people were arrested for trafficking ration cards. They included the head of the *Service du Ravitaillement*, his assistant and his assistant's secretary.[51]

Those who had no access to either money or power were outsiders in the black and grey economies. Prisoners depended on official rations and rarely had the means to supplement their diet from the free market. In the prison in Riom, an average of four prisoners had died per year before the war; in the first few months of 1942, 120 died there.[52] Inmates of mental hospitals were also obvious losers in this system. Unlike many other hospital patients, they were not given additional rations, and they rarely had the means to buy food on the black market. Mortality rates in mental hospitals rose sharply. It has been estimated that the number of deaths during the occupation exceeded that which would have been expected in the same period before the war by 48,000. Vichy officials were slow to respond to warnings by psychiatrists and they may, perhaps, have been influenced by the eugenic thinking of Alexis Carrel, whose work attracted Pétain's interest. Generally, however, the death of mental patients does not seem to have been the result of any planned policy; indeed, the wife of Max Bonnafous, Vichy Minister for Food Supply, got rations increased at one mental hospital. Rather, mental patients died in such numbers because of low rations combined with bureaucratic indifference and, sometimes, with the corruption of officials, who sold part of the food intended for patients on the black market.[53]

Some people were turned into outsiders by the circumstances of the occupation. Anyone on the run had to feed himself without recourse to official channels. Stolen ration cards were valuable, and by 1943, when large numbers of young men were seeking to avoid compulsory labour service in Germany, the Resistance organized attacks on places where such cards could be obtained. Tobacconists were the single most common target for Maquis attacks in Haute-Savoie, not only because tobacco had an intrinsic value, but also because tobacconists often distributed ration cards.[54]

Jews in France were mainly concentrated in cities (especially Paris). Many of them were recent immigrants, or the children of immigrants. They did not have the contacts in the countryside that sustained many other inhabitants of French cities. They were often discriminated against in the distribution of food. As German persecution in the northern zone became more severe many Jews moved south, which meant again that they lost contact with informal networks that might have helped them get access to food.

THE REVENGE OF THE COUNTRYSIDE?

The peasant Ephraïm Grenadou recalled in his autobiography: 'With all those people who were hungry and who talked about food, we ate half as much again as before the war. We got fat.'[55] Grenadou's account has contributed to the perception that the countryside benefited at the expense of the city during the occupation. There was an important element of truth in this perception, but Grenadou was not entirely typical and his case hints at the fact that not all farmers benefited to an equal extent. Grenadou was lucky in the area where he lived. The Beauce in western France is fertile land and it supports several different kinds of farming. Grenadou's farm produced wheat, vegetables, pork, poultry, mutton and milk. He could sell whatever fetched the best prices and was not obliged to buy food. Furthermore, the Beauce was well placed for farmers who wanted to trade with city dwellers. It is flat country easily accessible from Chartres by bicycle and accessible from Paris by train. Most of all, Grenadou was a particularly enterprising man.

Some peasants in some regions made gains similar to those of Grenadou. An official reported of the Eure in 1942: 'The rural part of the population, which the scarcity affects little as far as farmers are concerned and which earns more money than ever, does not seem unhappy with its fate, but the suffering of the towns leaves it indifferent.'[56] Mortality rates rose in cities (by 24 per cent in Paris, 29 per cent in Lyons and 57 per cent in Marseilles), but they dropped in some agricultural areas (by 11 per cent in the Indre, 10.9 per cent in the Mayenne and 10.4 per cent in the Orne).[57] Some agricultural departments saw big increases in savings during the war (partly because there was little on which money earned through the black market could be spent). In 1948 the French government took 5,000-franc notes out of circulation, and it was agricultural departments (headed by the Mayenne) where the largest number of such notes were traded in.[58]

However, not all agricultural areas gained from wartime conditions. The southern departments were generally less fertile than those of the north and west, and they suffered particularly during the drought of 1942–3. They were also more dependent on single types of cultivation, particularly vines. Farmers in such regions did not have the option of living from their own resources, nor could they trade extensively with their immediate neighbours, who mostly had the same commodities to sell.

Even those farmers who lived in fertile areas of polyculture were subject to pressures that were not always obvious to urban observers. French farms were not comfortable, as many bourgeois young men found out when they fled into the countryside to avoid being drafted to work in Germany in 1943. Life on farms was particularly hard during the cold winters of 1940–41 and 1941–2. The perception that peasants did well during the occupation came partly from the simple fact that peasants had lower expectations than many city dwellers; they were less likely to complain about the absence of coffee or tobacco.

Resources – agricultural machinery, horses and fertilizers – were all scarce and expensive. The number of tractors in France dropped from 35,000 in 1939 to 28,000 by the liberation.[59] The agricultural committee of the Légion Française des Combattants reported in the Puy-de-Dôme that the price of agricultural produce sold by farmers had risen by 216.9 per cent but that the price of goods that farmers needed to buy had risen by 308 per cent.[60] Basic commodities were hard to come by: farmers found it difficult to collect wheat because they lacked sisal string with which to bind bundles together.

A group of French schoolchildren from a village in the Aude left an interesting account of life in an agricultural community seen from the inside. Far from being beneficiaries of the black market, they saw themselves as its victims because agricultural raw materials were scarce and expensive. Fodder for horses had to be bought on the black market. Shortage of sulphur (needed to protect vines from parasites) was a particular problem: 'It is said that rich landowners have given 10,000 francs for 100 kilos of sulphur.'[61] In June 1941 Janine Roux recorded the circumstances of her classmates and their families. The horses were so underfed that some were held up by ropes attached to stable ceilings and almost everyone in the town had killed their dogs in order to conserve food. She also listed things eaten by children she knew: these included a hedgehog, a large grass snake, a fox, frogs, a squirrel, a cat, a falcon and a badger.[62]

Often farmers paid a long-term price for the short-term gains of the occupation. Equipment deteriorated because it was not maintained, and soil was over-farmed. Land was put to inappropriate use as, for example, winegrowers tore up vineyards, which produced profitable crops in peacetime, in order to grow food. The damage done to French agricultural productivity was reflected in the fact that agricultural production recovered much more slowly than industrial production after the war. Laurence Wylie, who lived in a village in the Vaucluse in 1950, was struck by the 'irrationality' of peasant economic choices and explained things thus:

During the last war, the people who were best off in the commune were not those who had the most modern farms producing the best adapted crops. There was little use for quantities of asparagus and table grapes when the express trains were not running to Paris. The farmers who were best able to care for their families were those who had departed least from the old self-sustaining economy of the Peyrane of 1801. Wheat and sheep, even though they were produced inefficiently, gave bread and cheese and wool for the family or for barter. This was not an economy of prosperity but an economy of survival, and if a crisis threatens one must think first of surviving. In 1950 fourteen per cent of the best soil of the commune was still planted in wheat. Everyone knows that this soil could be exploited more efficiently than by growing wheat, but on the other hand a field of wheat is a kind of disaster insurance.[63]

Calculating profit and loss for French farmers was, in any case, more complicated than it looked. Farmers were not economically rational, or at least, their rationality was different from that of the cities. They did not necessarily want to sell their produce, however high a price they were offered. For example, *vignerons* around Montpellier, who produced a few litres of olive oil, were said to refuse to sell this oil for 1,000 francs a litre on the grounds that they needed it for their own use, though the same winegrowers would almost certainly have refused to buy the oil for such an extortionate price.[64] Certain kinds of farming were seen as more dignified than others. Farmers often liked working with horses, which was why they particularly resented the wartime requisitions of such animals; the killing of pigs was an important festive occasion, which was why farmers resented having to do so in secret, even when secret slaughter was highly profitable.

Farmers aimed to build prosperity over a lifetime, or even over more than one generation, rather than over a financial year. The provident farmer knew that the most prosperous years of his life would probably be those when his son or son-in-law was old enough to help on the farm, and that, in due course, the son would take over the business as the father withdrew from the heavier work. The absence of young men during the war broke this cycle. Old men and women struggled to keep farms going and, often, to send food parcels to a young man who was spending the best years of his life tending a farm in Pomerania.

For decades before 1940, French people had been moving from the country to the town. In the 1930s something new had happened as women became particularly keen to leave the land: the proportion of women in the working agricultural population fell from 46 to 40 per cent between the wars. The mechanization of agriculture created a domain from which women were often excluded, whilst the consumer culture in the city was often seen as particularly attractive to women. The films of Marcel Pagnol, films that anticipated certain aspects of Vichy ideology,[65] made much of how the provençal countryside was being deserted as women were lured away to the city. During the occupation, things changed. The city was less attractive. Young men were no longer pulled away from the country by military service; on the contrary, the need to escape from compulsory labour service in Germany made the countryside particularly attractive for some of them. Young women had fewer opportunities in towns, and the particular opportunities offered by serving the occupation army were not welcomed by respectable families. The terms of trade in marriage markets changed. Peasant girls were less likely to be seduced by smooth young men in urban dance halls (dancing was illegal during the occupation). Rather, courtship was conducted at *bals clandestins* in isolated barns, where peasant girls put galoshes over their clogs and danced with their neighbours. Bourgeois women even married peasants: in the Loire, one farmer won the heart of a judge's daughter with rillettes and pork chops.[66] Weddings became occasions on which farmers could display their new-found wealth. In March 1943, a bourgeois Parisian, living at his country house in western France, attended the wedding of a shepherd's son; seventy guests feasted on twelve rabbits and seven lambs.[67]

However, as the marriages between city dwellers and peasants suggest, separation between town and country was not clear-cut, and, in some ways, the occupation made it less so. City dwellers found, or revived, ways to establish contact with the countryside. Sometimes these contacts involved violence. Townspeople scouring the countryside for food were sometimes angry with peasants who refused to deal with them; farmers sometimes shuttered their windows and bolted their doors when parties from the city arrived. Late in the occupation isolated farms were attacked by armed gangs who stole sums of up to 300,000 francs.[68] However, more commonly, contact between countryside and city took place in less tense circumstances. Some rekindled their affection for long-forgotten country cousins. Wealthy Parisians hired maids from Brittany who could be relied on to bring food parcels as well as domestic labour to the family.[69] The provision of parcels from rural areas became a huge operation: 6,700 parcels containing a total of 13 tonnes of goods left the Côtes-du-Nord every day in October 1941.[70] A Parisian doctor who studied nutrition estimated that in 1942 the average Parisian got 1,725 calories per day from their official rations, 200 calories from the black market and 200 from food parcels.[71] Many people from the cities spent time in the countryside during the summer simply in order to be close to food supplies; it was estimated that the population of the Mayenne increased by 50,000 in July 1942.[72] City children were sometimes packed off to live with family friends or relations in the country. The collaborationist writer Claude Jamet returned to his beloved Paris during the occupation, but he sent his baby daughter Marie-Claude to a family in the country near Poitiers. She returned in 1944 – healthy and plump but also illiterate and speaking nothing but patois.[73]

The wealthiest spent more time in their country houses. Indeed the *vie de château* that had been undermined by the charms of urban life for the last century underwent a revival under Vichy. Though he was an industrialist who had married into the Schneider family, the Duc de Brissac spent a good deal of time at his chateau in the Anjou during the occupation. The German ban on hunting, in the occupied zone, often revived the privileges of the *ancien régime*, because the Germans could grant their aristocratic protégés special licences to hunt in return for access to their estates. Poaching sometimes blended into Resistance, if only because both involved the illegal possession of guns. Equally, those who had been given official permission to hunt during the occupation were often regarded as collaborators after the war.[74]

Even for those who did not belong to the privileged classes, the division between countryside and city was not always as clear as it seemed at first. City dwellers went out into the countryside to buy food directly from farmers. Police who inspected passengers at Versailles station on 29 December 1943 found 57 kilograms of meat, 28 kilograms of butter and 50 kilograms of beans.[75] Labour shortage also helped bring countryside and city together. Urban workers sometimes worked on farms during busy times of year – in Saint-Étienne, workers were explicitly encouraged to take holidays at harvest time.

The potential complexity of town–country relations was illustrated by the schemes to send city children to the countryside at state expense during school holidays. Between 5,000 and 10,000 children were sent from Bordeaux to the Tarn-et-Garonne in a single summer.[76] Reports by Vichy officials suggest that relations between the families of the children and the peasants who took them in were tense. Some peasants believed that the parents had deliberately provided their children with inadequate clothing in order to arouse the charitable instincts of their hosts. Parents who visited their children seem to have expected that they themselves would be provided with food – 'rabbits, chicken, eggs and butter' – and to have protested 'noisily' when such goods were not available.[77]

The question of how far the countryside benefited from the occupation, and how far the city lost, is tied up with the nature of the rural black market. Throughout the war many peasants sold directly to consumers and evaded official requisitions. However, such actions did not necessarily mark a sharp break with accepted morality or even with pre-war customs. Some peasants had always poached game or distilled spirits in defiance of the law. A whole range of regulations had simply been disregarded in many parts of the countryside. Peasants, interviewed many years after the war, rarely talked about the 'black market'. Instead they described 'helping out', 'working with friends' or 'doing favours'. Yves Durand, a historian who grew up on a farm in the Creuse during the war, talks of a 'pink market' that was, he insists, less lucrative than is generally assumed.[78] During the occupation, the Institut National de la Statistique conducted discreet studies of the official market, the black market and what it labelled the 'marché amical'. Its results are shown in Table 1. René Limouzin recalled his wartime dealings thus: 'It was not the black market properly speaking. We sold at a normal price and bought likewise. But, when our tickets had run out, we still had a little bit of meat, a little coffee.'[79]

Table 1. Prices paid to producers in 1943

Products market	Official price	*Marché amical*	Black market
Butter	59	125	217
Eggs	24	53	76
Pork	25	97	126
Chicken	26	59	84
Rabbit	15	39	52
Potatoes	148	562	767
Dried beans	11	59	49
Lentils	11.6	54	77
Beef	12	23.9	29.7
Veal	15.6	30.1	35.4
Mutton	14.2	31.2	39.5

Note: eggs by dozen; potatoes by quintal; prices in francs.
Source: Michel Cépède, *Agriculture et alimentation en France durant la IIème guerre mondiale* (1961), p. 334.

Calculations of profit and loss were made more difficult by the fact that peasants rarely lived in a cash economy.[80] Often such exchange went with an element of trust, with the expectation of returned favours that was not made fully explicit, and with a certain haziness about precise measurement (many farmers did not, in any case, have the means to weigh their goods).

More than a quarter of French agricultural produce, even in peace-time, was simply eaten on the farm from which it came. During the war this increased: in the Aveyron, 10 per cent of peasants reckoned they had produced 80 per cent of their needs during the war; 7 per cent of them claimed to have provided for all their own needs.[81] Beyond this, a great deal of food went to family and friends. Depart-mental authorities in the Cantal estimated that a quarter of all butter was eaten by the producers and that a further 15 per cent went to friends; this left 40 per cent to be distributed through the official ration system and 20 per cent to be sold on the black market.[82]

The complexity of the rural economy was illustrated by the case of Henri Paillard, a thirty-year-old railway worker with two children and a total income of 2,780 francs per month. As someone who lived in the countryside, and hence had reduced rations, but who was not himself a farmer, Paillard might have been expected to do badly during the occupation. In fact, he grew food in his own garden but also got bread and butter from an acquaintance and most of his vegetables from members of his own family. Perhaps Paillard's benefactors were motivated by altruism or affection, though it may also be that a railway worker was able to provide them with reciprocal favours; the ability to move food was a crucial advantage for anyone who hoped to trade on the black market.[83]

Farmers lived in webs of mutual dependence, in which the frontiers of friendship, family and business association blended into each other. For all his business acumen, the peasant Ephraïm Grenadou did not conduct all his dealings according to purely financial criteria. He sold much of his produce to a young archivist from Chartres, who was also the son of his own former schoolteacher (eventually the archivist recruited him into the Resistance).[84] His neighbour, Monsieur Richer, was a business associate but also an old friend and his daughter's future father-in-law.

The fact that the rural black market was outside official regulation did not mean that it was unregulated. The Maquis punished farmers who were believed to have drawn unfair profits from the black markets. *Maquisards* confiscated money and goods from farmers whom they regarded as dishonest. Such confiscations could be driven by self-interest but *maquisards* sometimes went out of their way to stress the disinterested character of their action. Often they gave receipts for goods they requisitioned; *maquisards* in the Maine-et-Loire returned 75,000 francs that they had confiscated from a farmer after deciding that the money had in fact been earned 'honestly'. On several occasions, *maquisards* burned banknotes that they had taken from profiteering farmers: in an attack on the night of 21/22 June 1944, they burned 30,000 francs (fifteen times the monthly wage of an agricultural worker).[85] Often people who had roots in the countryside without being farmers themselves were accepted as judges of what was fair. The family of Denise Guillaume, a bourgeois girl from Montpellier, were asked by the leader of the Maquis in the village where they had their summer house to help set fair prices in June 1944. Denise and her mother drew up a list halfway between official prices and those charged on the free market and pinned it up outside the village hall.[86]

Even state employees often exercised an influence that did not simply derive from the law. The gendarmes who policed the French countryside had always based their relations with the rural communities in which they lived on discreet co-operation as much as control. Their complicity, or their benign indifference, was useful to anyone who wanted to do business outside the law. The gendarmes were often beneficiaries, and sometimes regulators, of the black market. Grenadou's account of his farm in the Beauce shows how the process worked. Grenadou's neighbour Richer asked the gendarmes how much he should charge for the beans that he began selling to visiting Parisians in the autumn of 1940: 'It was they who set the price.'[87]

Primary school teachers were another group that exercised influence in the countryside. Teachers frequently got food from former pupils or the parents of pupils.[88] They were also sometimes recognized as village elders with authority over important matters; frequently they served as secretaries to mayors. Georges Guingouin was a primary school teacher, and Communist Maquis leader, in the Limousin. When he pinned up a notice in which he, as 'prefect of the Maquis', fixed 'fair' prices for food sold by peasants, he claimed that many locals would recognize his handwriting.

The politics of the countryside were tied up with food and the black market. The Vichy government made much of the role that the peasantry were to play in the resurrection of France. Quite quickly, however, Vichy's desire to extract food from the countryside brought it into conflict with the peasantry. Official requisitioning of food was resisted. The government was blamed for its regulations and its failure to provide agricultural materials. Official publications directed at the peasantry were full of weary exhortations to obey the law. Prefects' reports were often hostile to peasants: Fernand Carles, the prefect of the Nord, who talked of peasant 'egoism', was typical.[89] The prefect of Vienne was one of the rare officials who did take rural concerns seriously. In October 1941 he wrote a long report on the lack of sisal string, problems with onion production and the protection of hen houses. He was rebuked by Admiral Darlan for raising 'trivial matters', and subsequently sacked.[90] On 20 April 1941 Pétain addressed French peasants directly, urging them, 'having assured their own needs', to deliver all their remaining produce 'for consumption and consumer' (an interestingly imprecise formulation by which Pétain avoided admitting that he was asking peasants to give up their produce to state bodies).

Official injunctions were almost useless. Attempts to impose control ran up against the problem that always dogged Vichy in the countryside. Either it used officials who did not know the area or its agriculture, in which case its representatives would be deceived, or it used men who did have good local knowledge and contacts, in which case its representatives were likely to be locked into networks of complicity with the peasants:[91] the gendarmerie in Brittany were embarrassed in March 1942 when one of their vehicles crashed at night, and was found to be laden with black market goods.[92] René Limouzin described the problems of the village commission established to manage requisitions. Peasants used requisitions as a means of disposing of poor quality goods. Such goods were accepted, either because the members of the commission were simply ignorant ('just about capable of telling the difference between a donkey and cow'),[93] or because of collusion with well-connected local people ('since it was rare not to have, here or there, a friend on the commission, things always got fixed up').[94] The Germans were more ruthless and more effective at squeezing resources out of the countryside. In late 1942 and early 1943, the German authorities took over the collection of butter in seven departments of the west of France and they obtained a marked increase in deliveries, even though production at that time of year was normally low.[95] However, the Germans were reluctant to waste men on rural policing, and often found it easier to pay black-market prices.

Peasant evasion of rules mocked Vichy's ruralist rhetoric. Grenadou was deeply hostile to the Pétainist mayor of his village, who sought to suppress both the black market and the Resistance, and named one of his horses Pétain. In his second speech as head of state, Pétain had talked of the virtues of 'the earth that does not lie' (the speech had been written, in part, by a half-Jewish Parisian intellectual). One peasant remarked: 'I like the Marshal because he is like me . . . a good liar.'

AU BON BEURRE: SHOPKEEPERS

Jean Dutourd's novel *Au Bon Beurre* (published in 1952) purported to draw on a real family of shopkeepers in Le Havre. It describes the rising fortunes of a *crémier* in the 17th arrondissement of Paris. The novel gave currency to the phrase BOF (*beurre, oeufs, fromage*), which French people still use to describe particularly crass materialism.

It is easy to see why consumers who queued for hours to obtain meagre rations or paid high prices on the black market believed that shopkeepers were growing rich, but it is not always obvious that such allegations were well founded. Those, like Dutourd's anti-heroes, who were provident enough to build up large stocks before shortage hit, or who had good contacts with the German or Vichy authorities, may have done well. However, the great mass of shopkeepers were in an awkward position. They were not, unlike farmers, primary producers. Everything they sold had to be bought. Supplies to be sold at legal prices were often unavailable, and supplies to be sold under the counter were expensive. Most importantly, large parts of the market economy just disappeared. Shopkeepers in small towns were damaged by the growing tendency for peasants to eat all they produced, which meant that they neither bought nor sold. Even Parisian shopkeepers had to contend with the fact that part of their clientele was going to the countryside to obtain their provisions directly from farmers. The increasing importance of factory canteens damaged shopkeepers, and brought protests from those who claimed to represent them.[96]

In the countryside, black marketeering was often conducted by people who were otherwise eminently respectable. People who indulged in such activity were not seen as criminal. In the cities, by contrast, black marketeering often involved people who were already seen, in one way or another, as outside respectable society. Paris police uncovered a black-market ring centred on the provision of forged ration tickets for a restaurant. None of the members of the ring were big-time criminals but several were known to the police. One was an Algerian, one was a woman who had been convicted for bouncing cheques, one had been declared bankrupt in the 1930s, and two were described as being of 'dubious morality'. Perhaps most significantly, the members of the ring denounced each other as soon as they were caught.[97]

Shopkeepers who traded on the black market were more likely to be victims of hostility than farmers who did so. Many people railed against profiteering peasants in general, but most had quite good relations with the particular peasants with whom they did business. By contrast, much hostility to shopkeepers was focused against particular individuals. In Paris in the Rue Daguerre in the summer of 1943 a crowd of a hundred and fifty attacked a shopkeeper whom they accused of selling rotten peaches.[98]

The political connotations of black markets involving shopkeepers and of those involving peasants were different. The peasant black market was often seen as a means by which Vichy and German requisitions could be evaded. Increasingly, this blended into resistance activity. Amongst shopkeepers, by contrast, black marketeering was more likely to be associated with collaboration than resistance. The Germans were more present in the towns: the gulf between the two widened as the Maquis took over parts of the countryside in 1944, and as German rule became stricter in the towns. The Germans, or their French associates, provided the most lucrative clients for the shopkeepers and, increasingly, German complicity was useful for anyone who wanted to conduct black-market operations in the towns. In the Landes, a police report of February 1942 remarked: 'The population is, above all, hostile to the local shopkeepers whom it accuses of preferring to serve the occupation troops.'[99]

However, dealing with the Germans was a dangerous game, for two reasons. First, it excited hostility from other French people (which became increasingly important as the liberation approached). Secondly, the Germans were awkward clients who had the means to ensure that the terms of trade were weighted in their favour. In the Landes, a tyre merchant developed a lucrative trade with the Germans. Perhaps feeling that it had become too lucrative, the Germans arrested him and only released him when he paid them 50,000 francs. After the liberation, the tyre merchant asked for the return of his money: the request was not well received.[100] Other tradespeople had worse fates. In the Maine-et-Loire, only one person in every three hundred was prosecuted after the war. However, in Saumur, home to the greatest concentration of Germans in the region, about one in every eighty butchers and bakers was prosecuted.[101]

FAUX POLICIERS

One of the most curious features of the black economy of the occupation was 'false policemen'. Throughout the occupation, criminals impersonated policemen as a means to steal or extort bribes. False policemen were reported in cities across France – a Rennes newspaper, *L'Heure Bretonne*, carried an article entitled 'Attention aux faux policiers'[102] – but they seem mainly to have been a Parisian phenomenon. Marcel Aymé, so often the chronicler of the Paris black economy, published a short story entitled 'Le Faux Policier'. It concerns Martin, who makes 3,500 francs a month as a book-keeper. During the occupation he finds himself unable to support his wife and three children from his legitimate income and notices the gulf between 'the market value of food and the market value of morality'. To increase his income, he takes to impersonating a policeman in order to rob people or to extract bribes. After the liberation he continues with his operations, though now targeting collaborationists rather than resistants and now killing his victims as well as robbing them.

The Paris police investigated more than eight hundred thefts and frauds attributed to *faux policiers* between 1941 and 1945. The cases illustrate several important things about the urban, especially Parisian, black economy. They show the simple fact that illegal relations in the city involved an element of anonymity, which, in turn, generated chances for fraud and extortion. Posing as a false policeman in the countryside, where peasants generally knew their local gendarmerie, would have been more difficult.[103] The Germans were more present in the cities than in the countryside. Most false policemen posed as Germans; some really were Germans. Four men arrested by French police were German nationals: two had deserted from the German army and two were Germans normally resident in France (one had already been arrested in Lille in June 1942).[104]

The French authorities themselves seem to have been uncertain about the links between the Germans and the *faux policiers*. Many *faux policiers* had worked for a German agency, but most had done so at a low level, usually as labourers in the Todt organization or the NSKK (the Nazi organization responsible for motorized transport). Such men had no real mandate from the Germans. They had probably just acquired a uniform, or an official-looking piece of paper, or the ability to mutter a few words in German.

Faux policiers illustrate the blurring of the lines between police and crime that occurred during the occupation. Some were simply criminals who impersonated policemen: some had bought their identity cards in bars; others, however, had, or had had, a real link with some police agency. The occupation meant the creation of new parallel police forces responsible for fighting against enemies of the Vichy regime or enemies of the Germans. Some, such as the members of the Bonny–Lafont gang (see Chapter 3), worked directly for the Germans. Others were answerable to Vichy. Some of the new police agencies, especially those closely associated with support for the Germans, recruited many of their members from people with criminal backgrounds. This was particularly true of the Légion des Volontaires Français contre le Bolchevisme (LVF). Strictly speaking, the LVF was not meant to be a police force at all: its members were supposed to fight on the Eastern Front alongside the German army. However, members of the LVF did often try to repress those they regarded as opponents of Vichy, and 'policing' by the LVF spilled over into thieving, especially when they came across people involved in the black market. In August 1943 a police patrol met a railway employee who revealed that members of the LVF had just searched him and requisitioned a shoulder of mutton that he had been carrying in his case.[105] A butcher was shaken down for money by two members of the LVF, who accused him of dealing on the black market and added: 'We are above the police and endowed with special powers.'[106]

Gangs of false policemen sometimes involved odd mixtures of people who had various kinds of official status and others who had none. A single gang contained a man, born in Tunisia, who was 'an inspector delegated to the Gestapo', a *milicien*, a trainee gendarme, a secretary to the LVF and an Algerian boxer.[107] Experience of various French agencies seems to have given Frenchmen the knowledge or contacts to prey on their compatriots.

The black economy blurred distinctions between respectable and non-respectable society in ways that opened up new opportunities for blackmail and extortion. One case investigated by the Paris police concerned a priest from the Mayenne, a wealthy agricultural area, who brought ham and butter to sell in Paris, and who then took clothes back to his parish. He also used his visits to the capital, and, presumably, the profits of his transactions, to engage prostitutes with whom he stayed (notably in the Hôtel Fairyland in the 9th arrondissement). The priest had come to live on the margins of a world where collaboration and crime overlapped (the brother of his mistress was serving with the German army). In February 1944 the priest arrived at the Hôtel Fairyland, where the proprietor paid him 14,000 francs for butter. However, on the evening of 18 February the priest had an 'animated conversation' with a known criminal and a prostitute who demanded that he give them butter and suggested that a priest ought not to be frequenting this kind of hotel or trading on the black market.[108] Members of the LVF then extorted money from him. The Paris police heard about the incident from the proprietor of the hotel. The priest made no complaint and was not traced.

Occasionally false policemen hunted big prey. In 1942 three men claiming to be German policemen raided a large private house in the 6th arrondissement and extracted thirty million francs' worth of jewels from the secretary of a former minister.[109] A countess lost jewels worth three million francs in 1943.[110] *Faux policiers* were often inspired by fantasies about hidden Jewish wealth; one gang said that they were looking for the 'Rothschild stamp collection'.[111] Generally, however, the victims of the *faux policiers* were poor and often drawn from the most desperately vulnerable parts of the Paris population. About two-fifths of victims were Jews, mainly foreign-born Jews. Jews had every reason to fear German policemen and every reason to avoid going to the authorities. The hauls produced by extortion of victims who were themselves poor were usually pitifully small. In January 1944 men in German uniform stole 'a fox fur, a small empty box, a pair of new shoes and an electric lamp'.[112]

'MON FILS SERA CRÉMIER'

One feature of the occupation was the sense of social inversion. 'Respectable' people were seen to have lost out to parvenus and opportunists. Dutourd's *Au Bon Beurre* is partly about the family of profiteering *crémiers*, but it is at least as much about the social decline of a young man from a more respectable bourgeois background. He becomes a lycée *professeur* and gains that supreme accolade of the French education system by becoming an *agrégé des lettres*. However, the young man is unable to feed his family properly or to protect his own professional interests against the scheming of his enemies. The novel finishes with him finally recognizing the uselessness of his educational distinction and vowing 'mon fils sera crémier' (my son will run a dairy).

The occupation upset social hierarchies based on income and education. Parts of the respectable middle class saw their incomes eroded by inflation. Equally, many believed that the brutal economics of the occupation had changed attitudes to schooling. Dr Alfred Brauner studied children who had grown up during the war, and believed that respect for education was particularly low among them. He reported one as saying: 'It is easy to earn money without knowing Racine.'[113] Jean-Louis Bory's novel, *Mon village à l'heure allemande* features a scene in which a young man is told by his girlfriend: 'You do not need to pass the *bac* to run a garage.'[114]

Certainly, there is some evidence that educated professions, and particularly teachers, saw their living standards decline relative to people whose economic value was more tangible. Alongside the sense of material deprivation went humiliation. Dominique Jamet was the son of the *normalien agrégé*-turned-journalist Claude Jamet, who might almost have served as a model for the hero of *Au Bon Beurre*, except that he was an unworldly collaborationist rather than an unworldly resistant. Dominique had bitter memories of the new power that Monsieur Brisquet the grocer had acquired over him and people like him:

What were they just two years earlier, him and his wife? . . . Little local grocers, clean and humble, toughened to hardship, without importance. That sort of vermin proliferated at the time. They reigned over the Rue Vavin, and were feared. They watered the milk, they cheated on weights and prices, they secretly sold the goods that they did not put in the window . . . Minor civil servants, office workers, the population of garrets, that did not interest Monsieur Brisquet. Controlled portions, controlled prices, captive clients, that was not commerce, but administration or apostolate, a social service . . . They knew, on the other hand, how to be all sugar and honey, the cream of men with certain clients who spoke to them in low voices.[115]

Accounts such as this illustrate the sense of social inversion that went with the black market. One should, however, take the supposed suffering of the French educated classes with a pinch of salt. The very fact that teachers and academics were particularly prone to write memoirs and diaries means that historians are particularly aware of their suffering. However, there is no proof that their suffering was uniquely terrible. Teachers may have been for a time worse off than, say, grocers or butchers, and they may have found their dependence on people they regarded as inferiors to be particularly humiliating, but they were certainly better off than many lower-level public sector employees. Besides, the educated, especially celebrated intellectuals, usually had contacts that made their lives more bearable. For all his son's complaints, Claude Jamet did in fact obtain food parcels from his admirers in the countryside and, as someone with good contacts in collaborationist circles, he could presumably have made life very unpleasant for the grocer who was so rude to his children if he had chosen to do so.

In any case, the insistence that the status of the educated elite in

France was irredeemably damaged by the war sits oddly with the prestige enjoyed after 1945 by Sartre or Althusser. The son of the unworldly teacher in Dutourd's novel may have become a *crémier*, but the real-life son of Claude Jamet became director of the Bibliothèque Nationale.

WOMEN AND CHILDREN

Vichy's rationing system did not just have implications for relations between rich and poor or between countryside and city. Rations were different for men and women: the latter were deprived of tobacco but given extra food if they were pregnant or nursing. Women's responsibility for feeding their families meant that they spent enormous amounts of time in towns queuing and searching for supplies. The most common demonstrations in many cities consisted of women showing their discontent about food shortages: there were forty-six demonstrations by women about food in the Paris *banlieue* in 1941.[116] The sale of food was often segregated by sex. René Limouzin, who lived with his father after the death of his mother and grandmother, sold his butter to a local grocer rather than selling it directly himself: 'Selling butter and eggs in the market at Ussel is an essentially feminine task. What man would be brave enough to dare face the loud-mouthed dressed-up women of Ussel?'[117] Similarly, the sale of cattle and horses was a male preserve. During the occupation, there was a sharp decline in the number of horses and tractors in use on French farms (traditionally, men had occupied themselves with these), but an increase in the production of butter (a female domain).

Women were involved in the black market as buyers because they were usually responsible for providing food for their families. This created an interesting situation in which a Pétainist patriarch could pontificate over dinner about the importance of observing laws on rationing whilst failing to notice that his plate contained food that exceeded the maximum legal ration.[118] Women were also involved in the black market as sellers because more than a quarter of a million were left running shops and farms. Shopkeeping became an ever more female-dominated profession because male shopkeepers were rarely given exemption from military service or labour service in Germany or early release from prisoner of war camps. Women's black-market activity was often highly visible: they sold goods directly to the consumer. It may also have put them in a particularly vulnerable position. Women who worked in restaurants, cafés and bars (where black marketeering and contact, especially sexual contact, with Germans were seen to overlap) were especially likely to attract the hostile attention of their neighbours.[119]

Food and the black market also tied in with ideas of youth. Pre-school children seem to have been the one group who did not suffer unduly from shortage of food. However, children above this age were obsessed by hunger. Like women, children were often sent to queue, and several of the fourteen characters in Marcel Aymé's *En attendant* are children or adolescents. One of them says simply: 'I am hungry, I am always hungry.' When schoolchildren were asked to write an essay on what wish they would ask to be granted by a fairy, one little girl wrote simply: 'Never to be hungry.' Hunger undermined Vichy's rhetoric about a hardier race, as malnourished children in urban schools found physical exercise almost impossible.

Adolescents felt the lack of food with particular sharpness. Many French people of a particular generation went on identifying themselves by the name of the wartime ration category 'J3' for some time after the liberation. Hunger was a constant feature of even bourgeois childhoods: boys at the Lycée Jean-Baptiste Say had their own scales to measure the food they were given.[120] Further down the social scale, hunger had ever more serious consequences. Children often became involved in petty crime as a means to obtain food. Children grew more slowly; puberty was delayed. Even Vichy's textile rationing helped to prolong childhoods: boys under the age of fifteen were forbidden to wear long trousers.[121]

It is misleading to look too hard for winners and losers in occupied France. German requisitions, loss of imports, absence of men in prisoner of war camps and declining efficiency all meant that there was less of almost everything. In these circumstances, most people were losers. Urban consumers, particularly the bourgeoisie, may have been shocked to find themselves dependent on vulgar shopkeepers but that did not necessarily mean that the shopkeepers did well. All sorts of prosperity could turn out to be illusionary as inflation ate into carefully hoarded savings or as short-term profit created long-term problems.

Most importantly, perhaps, the wartime black-market economy was associated with high levels of uncertainty and suspicion. There was mistrust even in those fertile parts of the French countryside where food was relatively plentiful, and such mistrust may have been particularly painful precisely because the illicit economy depended on long-established relationships that were corroded by new economic pressures. In the cities things were often bleak. Dominique Jamet recalled his Parisian childhood thus: 'The fact is times were hard. People too. Reserves of altruism were at their lowest, stocks of compassion had run out. People pressed up against each other in homes that had reverted to being lairs. Each for himself or for the few people he cared about. Generosity did not flow in those dark streets.'[122]

8

Stolen Youth

Service du Travail Obligatoire

Service du Travail Obligatoire (STO), instituted on 16 February 1943, was, as far as most French people were concerned, the most important single Vichy policy. It required men of an age that would normally have made them eligible for military service (those born between January 1920 and December 1922) to perform two years of compulsory labour service (in theory, they were granted remission for time already spent in the army or in the Chantiers de la Jeunesse). Students were initially allowed to defer their departures until they completed their examinations in September and farmers were initially exempted. Both these provisions were abolished in the summer of 1943. It was widely understood that most young men affected by this scheme would be sent to work in Germany. In July 1943, STO was extended to a small group of slightly older men. More significantly, in view of the frequency with which STO is assumed to have been an experience that only affected young men, a circular of 23 April 1943 stressed that *oisifs* (that is, the idle) from amongst all age groups could be sent to Germany.[1]

STO did not, in fact, mark the beginning of compulsory labour in Germany. Workers who 'volunteered' for work in Germany during the first two years of the war had often been subjected to various forms of compulsion. In the summer of 1942 the *relève* scheme aimed to trade three French workers for every released French prisoner of war; in practice, many of these workers were coerced into going. A law of 4 September on 'the use and direction of labour' made this

8. (overleaf) *Young men leaving Nice station for compulsory labour service in Germany.*

coercion explicit. Almost half of the 650,000 workers formally required to go to Germany went before the institution of STO in February 1943.[2] However, workers who went before STO belonged to restricted sections of society. 'Volunteers' were mainly from the lumpenproletariat. Many of them were foreign immigrants or criminals. Those compelled to go under the law of September 1942 before February 1943 were mainly workers (the Germans were particularly interested in skilled metallurgists).[3]

STO hit a broader swathe of society. In theory, every man in his early twenties was eventually liable to go (though, in practice, some social groups went in much larger numbers than others). STO was bitterly resented. For the first time, Vichy had an obviously malign effect on the lives of millions of French people, not just on those who left but also on those who endured risk or hardship in order not to go, and on the relatives of both these groups. The historian Yves Durand, referring to his own wartime adolescence in the Creuse, wrote: 'The problem of STO affected the whole population and assumed an important place in the existence and the representations of the war and occupation of the French. This was not just because physical contact with the victims of STO was inevitable but also because they were easy to integrate into [our] consciousness.'[4] STO continued to dominate French people's perceptions of the occupation generally and of labour deportation to Germany in particular: people often referred to all French workers who went to Germany as 'partis au titre du STO'.[5]

STO features in standard accounts of Vichy as marking a stage in public disillusionment with the regime, but it is generally studied only as part of this wider process. Emphasis is normally placed on those who remained in France rather than on the men who went to Germany. The primary significance of STO for historians of France is the role that it played in increasing popular opposition to Vichy, and in providing young men for the Maquis.

In fact, evasion of STO could take many forms. Some escaped from France altogether: two particularly enterprising boys stole a boat in Le Havre and managed to reach Sweden.[6] More commonly, men took to the hills and woods and lived illegally. Vichy initially labelled men who took this route as *défaillants*, or *insoumis*, a term normally applied to those who evaded military service.[7] Gradually, *réfractaire*, a term that implied a conscious decision to rebel and that was favoured by the Resistance, became applied to those avoiding STO and eventually came to be used by Vichy officials themselves. After the war, around 180,451 men who could prove that they had lived illegally for at least six months whilst avoiding labour service were given cards that entitled them to certain benefits. Historians estimate that, allowing for those people who did not claim a *carte de réfractaire* or who failed to meet the precise formal requirement of such status, there were 260,000 *réfractaires*.[8] However, only a minority of *réfractaires* were active *maquisards*.[9] Furthermore, many young men avoided STO in ways that did not involve living outside the law.

French attitudes to STO have always been double-edged. In public, victims of labour deportation are regarded as victims of the war, though they lost the right to refer to themselves as 'deportees' after a legal case in 1979.[10] In private, however, many people felt suspicious of men who had been sent to work in Germany. The fact that so many did not go seemed to suggest that obligatory labour service was not, in fact, very obligatory. STO was often discussed in terms of individual choice, as though the decision about whether to obey a government order or to take to the hills was simply a matter of personal temperament. Little attention was devoted to the ways in which French society, rather than just the French state, pressed some men to go to Germany.

A *RÉFRACTAIRE*

Before looking at the general contexts that governed people's reaction to STO, it is worth looking at a single case of a man who managed to avoid going to Germany, a case that reveals how complicated and difficult such evasion could be. Jean Guibal from Nîmes was not a *maquisard*. He stressed that the Maquis barely existed in his region when he was first called up for STO, and he later refused to join it when he was given this chance by a priest linked to the Resistance in Haute-Savoie. He was bitter about the extent to which he had been obliged to act on his own without help from people in authority:

Unfortunately, the people who, by their position and their authority, were marked out to group young men and arrange an organized escape for them, failed. Oh, certainly, at the liberation, once the danger had gone, advisers were not hard to find. But when young men were lost, what did they find? Nothing or almost nothing . . . In the southern region, the Maquis did not exist. It was premature to take the enemy on with arms in hand. For various reasons and, above all, so as not to break the law, many parents who were worried about the fate of their sons did not have the courage to stop them responding to STO. One cannot blame them. They thought they were acting in the interests of their own people.[11]

Guibal's first thought was to get across the Pyrenees, and he talked to a woman who seemed able to organize such escapes. However, increased controls made escape to Spain impossible. He then consulted friends and also 'some of my old teachers whom I knew to be "Gaullists"'.[12]

He then went to Haute-Savoie by train, spending much of the journey in the toilet to avoid inspection of his papers. In Haute-Savoie, his sister got him a job at a youth camp for children of railway workers. Haute-Savoie had advantages for a *réfractaire* in that it was a relatively sparsely populated region with plenty of food and it bordered on Switzerland. However, Guibal's need for a ration card brought him to the attention of the authorities, and he was called to Annemasse for a medical examination, at which he was declared 'good for Germany'.[13] Subsequently the *garde champêtre* (village constable) brought him a summons but said with an air of complicity that he would declare him 'absent' when Guibal refused to sign the receipt. Guibal then tried to cross the Swiss frontier with the aid of a tobacco smuggler and of the director of his youth camp, who gave him some Swiss money. He was caught by the Swiss police and forced to go back to France, though not handed over to the French authorities. He was helped by a café owner, whose son was also on the run from STO, and by a hotelier, whose son was a recently repatriated prisoner of war. He obtained a series of jobs with local farmers.

The secretary of the village mayor then told him that the situation was becoming too dangerous to provide a ration card for a *réfractaire*. The farmer who was employing him, fearing denunciation, asked him to leave, and other farmers were reluctant to employ him in view of the fact that it was now the 'empty season'. He considered walking to the Saône-et-Loire, in order to avoid inspections that might have taken place on a train, but his shoes had no soles and he had no money to replace them on the black market. For several days he was very discouraged, but a peasant whose own son had been called up for STO gave him food, and he found work with another peasant. Guibal's sister obtained another false identity card for him and he went to Paris, where a Resistance doctor provided him with a ration card, and then to a school in the Seine-et-Marne. However, the school was under heavy German surveillance. He went back to Paris and got a job as a *valet de chambre* in Pigalle, but the Gestapo turned out to be interested in the hotel where he worked. Guibal then met an industrialist with interests in forestry and he went to work on one of this man's properties in the Nièvre, where he was ruthlessly exploited.

Guibal returned to Nîmes for personal reasons but was reproached by his own former neighbours: 'According to the sacred formula of the time, I was reminded that if all the young men had acted like this, the old would have been called up.'[14] He was also told that parents whose own sons had gone to Germany were prone to denounce *réfractaires*. He worked on a farm; he had come to like rural work and he was now accustomed to the odd life of a man on the run: 'I had now lost all notion of my real identity. In the area, I was called the refugee, but my southern accent that I had not been able to shake off deceived no one and, when talking of me, the peasants spoke of the *marseillais*, a title that they readily accorded to any southerner.'[15] Finally, a friend got him a job working in a vineyard, and another well-connected associate got him a false identity card and ration tickets, 'indispensable in this area of monoculture'.[16]

Guibal had had at least eight different employers and lived in five different regions with three different false identity cards. He had benefited from the tacit complicity of at least one mayor, at least one policeman and every single pupil at the youth camp in Haute-Savoie (the children queued up to shake his hand and wish him luck on the night he tried to get over the Swiss frontier). Guibal himself obtained a *carte de réfractaire*, though some of the expedients by which he lived involved complicity by the authorities as much as rebellion against them. Some of those who helped him – such as the woman who tried to get him over the Spanish frontier – specifically denied being resistants. At least two of his employers – one of the Savoyard peasants and the headmaster of the school in Seine-et-Marne – were Pétainists.

Guibal was a determined man who enjoyed good luck and benefited from the support of his family (especially his resourceful sister), but successful evasion of STO did not just depend on strokes of luck. Certain categories of men stood a much better chance of evading than others.

CONTEXTS

Place was the first and most obvious context in which STO must be understood. Departures of labour deportees (*requis*) were more common in some areas than in others. Men stood least chance of evading STO in areas where there was a heavy German presence; this meant, in particular, the north and east of France. They stood the best chance in sparsely populated wooded countryside where, in the last resort, groups of *réfractaires* could hide. Agricultural areas were generally better than urban ones, partly because peasants were, initially, given exemption, and partly because agricultural regions, especially those of polyculture where food was plentiful, could sustain *réfractaires*.

Heavily policed cities were difficult places to avoid STO. Though there was debate about the extent to which French police were supposed to enforce summonses for STO, as opposed to hunting down men who had refused to respond to such summonses, Paris police prepared to enforce STO ruthlessly from the beginning. As early as 25 February 1943, a prospective holding centre was surveyed. Officials concluded that it was badly placed because it was too spread out and because it was surrounded by the houses of workers, which would make escape into a 'hostile population' too easy.[17] Three days later plans were discussed for dealing with young men who had failed to respond to summonses for STO. It was proposed that teams of armed policemen in plain clothes would raid their houses early in the morning and take them to centres; families would be invited to bring their clothes later.[18] In August 1943 a *réfractaire* who tried to escape from custody was reported to have broken two legs jumping from an upstairs window.[19]

Timing also mattered. STO departures were most common in 1943. In March of that year, immediately after STO was instituted, 126,000 men went to Germany and in June, immediately after exemptions for students and peasants were abolished, 84,000 men went. By contrast, only around 10,000 went in each of the last few months of 1943. Surprise facilitated early departures. In Villefranche-sur-Saône, 243 men were called for medical inspections between 2 and 4 March 1943; only four did not turn up, and the men were then sent rapidly to Germany. One boy from the Rhône who had been registered for STO on 25 February was on his way to Germany by 7 March.[20] These men had little time to prepare any means of avoiding departure; similarly, around three-quarters of all peasants who went to Germany did so in June 1943, immediately after the abolition of exemption for those who worked in agriculture.[21] As time went on, young men began to anticipate their summonses for STO and to prepare their strategies of evasion. In the coal mines of the Rhône, between October 1943 and March 1944, 36 per cent of all men hired belonged to the age group most affected by STO (miners were usually exempted), but a further 42 per cent were slightly younger men who had, apparently, anticipated their future call-up.[22]

The law of diminishing returns also governed departures for STO. Those most vulnerable to STO left first, and those who remained were more able, or more determined, to resist being sent to Germany. STO may also have seemed a less daunting prospect in its early stages than it did later. Those who left early could still believe it possible that they would be allowed home when their terms of service expired, or that they would be granted leave. Some did benefit from leave, and by September 1943 the French authorities estimated that 60 or 70 per cent of French *requis* who returned to France on leave used the opportunity to desert.[23] As time went on, it became more obvious that STO was a one-way ticket. Leave was almost entirely abolished. Allied military success made resisting STO easier, because young men knew that they would only have to hold out for a short period, but it also made going to Germany even more unattractive; workers there would have to endure Allied bombing, and would be cut off from France by Allied advances.[24]

Time and place interacted in determining responses to STO. In Lorraine, large numbers of men were called up early, went to Germany, and subsequently deserted. In the Rhône, most men were called up later: this meant that the proportion of those who failed to turn up was high, but also that the proportion who managed to desert once they had been sent to Germany was low.[25] Shifts in German policy over time meant that circumstances in 1944 were very different from those of a year earlier. On 17 September 1943, Albert Speer, the German Armaments Minister, agreed with Jean Bichelonne, the French Minister of Industrial Production, that workers in factories serving the German war effort should be spared from labour service in Germany. More than a million French people worked in such factories. Fritz Saukel, responsible for German labour policy, did not share Speer's view about the benefits of keeping labour in France; one of Saukel's officials described the protected factories as constituting 'a legal Maquis'.[26] However, the following month, even Saukel agreed to relieve pressure on the French labour market for a few months and after this deportations never returned to their previous pace.

Perhaps even more important than the formal shift of policy in Berlin was the increasingly sharp competition for labour among German agencies in France itself. Some Germans in France had an interest in preventing workers from being sent to Germany. The Wehrmacht and the Todt organization (the German agency responsible for large-scale construction works) employed at least a million French people by the summer of 1944. German agencies also intervened at local level to protect labour supplies for French companies with which they did business. In October 1943 a Vichy official complained that young men who should have been sent to Germany were being hired in France with the complicity of German engineers.[27] German agencies even competed with each other in France. In Saint-Nazaire, young men arrived under armed guard but most of them had disappeared within a week. A Vichy official suggested that a few of these men had gone into the 'brousse'; most, however, had simply been hired by rival firms.[28]

The complicated divisions among, and within, French and German agencies meant that the conflict between the two was always confused. In general, the Germans pressed for more labour whilst the French attempted to retain the largest number of workers possible in France. Even Laval, the architect of Service du Travail Obligatoire, tried to persuade the Germans to satisfy themselves with fewer workers. In addition to this, some at Vichy disliked the whole idea of compelling Frenchmen to go to Germany and attempted to impede departures as much as possible. Jacques Le Roy Ladurie, Minister of Agriculture from April until September 1942, established large numbers of men as woodcutters in order to get them exemption from labour service in Germany.[29]

There were times, however, when Vichy officials pressed for particular men to be sent to Germany, and Laval complained that 'some German officers practise an excessively gentle collaboration'.[30] Conflict between Vichy and the Germans over STO reflected wider differences of approach. Vichy officials saw STO in political and social terms. They were most enthusiastic about sending foreigners, criminals and *oisifs* (idlers) to Germany. They wanted STO to be seen as 'fair', or at least to be seen as fair to groups, such as rural artisans, of whom Vichy approved.[31] Vichy officials were worried when, for example, married men were sent to Germany at the expense of single men, or when Frenchmen were sent to Germany whilst foreign workers remained in France.[32] German officials, by contrast, were concerned with economics: they wanted STO to contribute to the German war effort. Where Vichy was keen to protect rural artisans from being sent to Germany by the Germans, the Germans were keen to prevent steelworkers from being sent to Germany by Vichy.

The authority of the Vichy government broke down as time went on. The imminence of liberation deterred civil servants and gendarmes from participating in labour deportation. The increased power of the Resistance, itself related to the impact of STO, made local authorities frightened of reprisals. The Germans responded to this breakdown of authority with acts of arbitrary violence that sometimes included the more-or-less random seizure and deportation of young men to Germany. But the era of systematic, bureaucratic deportation was over, and German intervention was often a sign of weakness rather than strength. Such acts made it seem that there was no middle way between resistance and collaboration, and made the French even less willing to entrust their young men to the care of the Germans. Men had been most willing to go to Germany when they felt that German rule was sufficiently well organized to track down particular individuals and take sanctions against particular families. But the generalized violence of 1944 was not accompanied by much targeted reprisal against those associated with resistance to STO.

Most importantly, the Maquis expanded. It is a commonplace that young men fleeing from STO fuelled this expansion; in fact, the process operated both ways. *Réfractaires* may have helped create the Maquis but the Maquis also helped to create *réfractaires*. More people were able to run away from STO when they knew that there was a structured movement in the countryside that was willing to shelter them. As we saw with Jean Guibal, a number of those who went to Germany in 1943 stressed that the Maquis simply did not exist in their region when they left.[33] André Delapierre wrote: 'In 1943, the Resistance was not organized as it was the following year, the Maquis was small. And then, one had to know people.'[34] Anyone seeking to join the Maquis, or simply to hide in the hills, faced an easier task in 1944 than their counterparts the previous year for a simple reason. They did not have to endure a winter of living in a damp cave,[35] or trying to get work from peasants during the 'empty season'.

LEGITIMACY

Timing affected perceptions of STO's legitimacy. Many communities, even families, encouraged some of their young men to obey instructions that required them to go to Germany. Most did so because they feared German reprisals, but, at first, some people also saw STO as a justifiable imposition, or at least as something natural and unavoidable, 'like hail'.[36]

The most explicit discussion of the legitimacy of STO took place inside the Catholic Church. By 1943 the French Church was no longer as Pétainist as it had been in 1940. The Vichy minister responsible for STO, Pierre Laval, was a secular figure who enjoyed no particular admiration amongst Catholics. Bishops were careful in their discussion of STO. Most of them refrained from condemning it, but made it clear that they did not regard evasion as a sin. A Catholic language of sacrifice and duty was often well suited to the justification of departure for Germany. Many priests expressed the fear, widespread in French society, that women might be taken if men did not go. Catholic leaders were also concerned to nurture contacts with the working class that they had worked hard to build before the war. For this reason, they often advised Catholic militants – members of the Jeunesse Ouvrière Chrétienne or Catholic scouts – to go to Germany when called up, or even to volunteer for work there.

There were other reasons why STO seemed legitimate to some. Perhaps most importantly, it conformed to a French tradition. Many justified labour service on the grounds that it replaced military service, and that it was only fair that young men of this generation should undergo some *corvée* that matched the one imposed on their elders by the army.[37] André Delapierre recalled: 'People said at the time, obligatory labour service in place of the regiment.'[38] Like military service, STO was sometimes seen as a form of initiation into adult life and masculinity,[39] and, in its early months, some argued that STO would be good for young men. François Cavanna wrote that old men said: 'Since they [the Germans] have been here, there is no longer an army . . . that means men without balls, youth needs discipline and adventure, kicks up the arse and drinking sessions, otherwise there will be no one with a bit of backbone.'[40]

More particularly, STO was compared to the experience of two cohorts of Frenchmen: *anciens combattants* of the First World War and prisoners of war. Those called up for STO were often the sons and nephews of men who had fought in the war of 1914–18. To most French people in 1943, that was still *the* war. Its horror overshadowed anything that came later and gave middle-aged men rights over their juniors. The men called up for STO had often been brought up on stories of Verdun,[41] and this seems to have given some of them a sense that they had no right to complain much about their own lot. Marcel Ayot recalled: 'My father had done seven consecutive years for France, from 1911 to 1918 [that is, his father had finished three years of peacetime military service when the First World War began] . . . one day, not without bitterness he said to me: you must go.'[42]

Even more importantly, there were still more than a million prisoners of war in Germany. There was no direct link between STO and the fate of prisoners, but some families felt that STO might help prisoners or simply that it was unfair that young men should be free in France while prisoners endured a fourth year of confinement. Men who tried to evade STO in 1943 particularly feared denunciation by the wives of prisoners of war.

INSTITUTIONAL STRUCTURES

Young men faced with the decision about whether or not to go to Germany often operated in wider structures. The Jeunesse Ouvrière Française Travaillant en Allemagne (JOFTA) was established to provide some *requis* with training for work in Germany, and to give them some degree of organization when they got there. Some young men seem to have assumed that a period in JOFTA would supply a means of delaying their departure to Germany. In practice, things were more complicated and, as ever, some seem to have derived advantages at the expense of their less privileged contemporaries. Victor Savary went to a JOFTA centre in Paris, where he hoped to spend some time in relative tranquillity before, or instead of, being deported to Germany: he found that he was almost imprisoned and that, within two days, he was on a train to Germany.[43] Yves Laurent also investigated the possibility of joining JOFTA as a means of delaying his departure to Germany, but he ultimately felt too suspicious to do so.[44] Laurent noted that the young men at JOFTA were mostly bourgeois, a view that seems confirmed by the post-war testimony of the head of JOFTA.[45]

Most importantly, many of those called up for STO were already in camps set up by the Chantiers de la Jeunesse, which had been established by Vichy in the southern zone of France in the autumn of 1940 to provide young men who were no longer subject to compulsory military service with a period of discipline and training. Young men were taken to remote camps (usually in woods or mountains), where they endured a mixture of hard work and patriotic education. The Chantiers were almost invariably run by men who thought of themselves as Pétainists; they were heavily influenced by the army and the Boy Scout movement. However, like many conservative Pétainists, the leaders of the Chantiers were also often anti-German.

The Chantiers could make it more difficult for young men to escape STO: they were already concentrated, in uniform and under the command of Pétainist officials. Anyone wishing to desert from the Chantiers needed transport and civilian clothes. The Chantiers became unpopular as deportations to Germany began. An official warned: 'On the level of internal politics, the measure would be badly received. The Chantiers will seem from now on like assembly points for STO and no longer as a stage in the training of young Frenchmen.'[46] Another noted: 'There certainly exists propaganda tending to show the Chantiers as the antechamber for dispatch to Germany: it seems above all to affect parents.'[47] Desertions from the Chantiers, or failures to turn up at all, increased as STO began. General de la Porte du Theil, the head of the Chantiers, reported that the number of *défaillants* had been negligible before 1943 but that 8,000 of the 63,000 men called to the Chantiers in July 1943 did not turn up.[48]

The leaders of the Chantiers de la Jeunesse were divided. Many of them believed that young men under their command had a duty to go to Germany, and some of them believed that they had a duty to accompany their subordinates. Men from the Chantiers were allowed to leave in uniform under the command of their existing leaders. Other Chantiers seem to have impeded departures to Germany. Camp leaders sometimes warned young men in advance so that they had the chance to desert; some Chantiers passed more or less directly into the Maquis, a move that was easiest for camps that were already based in mountainous areas such as those around Grenoble.[49]

EMPLOYMENT

Whether or not men called up for STO went to Germany also depended on their jobs. The initial legislation granted exemptions or delays to certain categories of men. These exemptions were eventually revoked though the fact that young men had legal reasons for avoiding departure early on meant that they stood a better chance of remaining in France until illegal means of avoiding STO became more available. Gendarmes, policemen, members of the Milice, coal miners and men making charcoal could sometimes claim exemption.

The result of these rules was a rush of young men into professions that gave exemption. This rush could produce unexpected results. One historian has suggested that the treatment of juvenile delinquency was revolutionized in wartime France because young men found that working in centres of 'supervised education' could provide them with a means of avoiding STO.[50] The Vichy authorities struggled to prevent men who would normally have been required by STO from taking exempted jobs and sometimes argued that exemption did not apply at all to men of particular ages, but the very shrillness of their protests suggests that they were not very successful.

The exploitation of exempted professions shows that there was not necessarily any link between evasion of STO and resistance. Many professions were given exemption precisely because the Germans believed that they would be useful to their war effort. Some professions that offered protection from STO were directly involved in keeping order in occupied France and in the fight against the Resistance: this was the case of the gendarmerie and, more obviously, of the Milice.

An astonishing feature of the exploitation of exemption was that young men sometimes used employment by the very agencies that were meant to promote departures for Germany as a means to prevent their own departure. A French official complained in February 1944:

It seemed to me, on examination of the dossiers that were sent to me by the regional directors with regard to proposals to engage staff, that recruitment of agents needed to run the local services of the general secretariat had a frequent tendency to take place amongst the young men belonging to the three classes [that is, the age categories] affected by obligatory labour service.[51]

Sometimes officials were frank about the nominal character of jobs given to young men. In March 1944 an office charged with organizing the labour force asked to be allowed to move one of its employees to Paris or Toulouse so that he could continue his legal studies more easily.[52]

Who benefited most from exemptions from STO? Some Pétainists who supported STO believed that the bourgeoisie had exploited exemptions in order to avoid their sons going to Germany, and thus ensure that disproportionate numbers of less privileged young men were sent. The Germans, too, sometimes alleged that the bourgeoisie were being protected. A German officer wrote to a prefect: 'It seems more than obvious that a certain group of people . . . are exempt from requisition. It is not only the German services who have observed this, but the whole French population itself protests against this exemption . . . all so-called students who do not really take university courses must be called up for work.'[53] Many *requis* who went to Germany also believed that they had been sacrificed in order to protect more privileged men. Bourgeois young men often already enjoyed delays in being called up for STO because of the special provisions made for students. In addition to this, they sometimes became 'false farmers' in order to secure the exemption reserved for peasants; becoming a 'farmer' was a great deal easier for someone whose family owned land or exercised power over peasants.[54]

Wealthy and well-connected men were prone to sudden changes of status that protected them from all forms of compulsory labour. One such man in Saint-Servan in the Landes was initially listed as a 'proprietor'. When he was designated to work in the Todt organization in November 1942 he announced that he had in fact been an employee of a bank since the previous June (a claim that was supported by a director of the bank, the *chef du cabinet* of the prefect and the mayor of the town, though not, apparently, believed by the *inspecteur du travail*); for good measure, he added that he was also a 'student'.[55] A number of *requis* in Saint-Servan commented on the immunity enjoyed by this individual.

Most strikingly, many bourgeois young men became coal miners. It was estimated that around 20,000 young men evading STO became coal miners in the Nord and Pas-de-Calais (France's largest coal basin); in the Gard (where there were fewer mines and more alternative means of avoiding STO) the figure was about 600. The management of individual mines often determined the extent to which they welcomed men seeking to avoid STO: in the Cévennes, Rochembol and Le Grand Combe took large numbers of men; Bessèges, however, in the words of a resistant mine manager, 'did not do its duty'.[56]

Working in coal mines was a widely known means of escaping

STO. Philippe Ariès recalled that his father put his brother 'in a mine in Bruay-en-Artois so that he could escape from German STO'.[57] Bernard Pierquin, a medical student, recalled: 'In other faculties, our friends sought to hide in France in jobs that were more or less fictitious but considered useful to the German war machine. It was thus that my friend Monjin got himself hired in the mines at Montceau-les-Mines.'[58]

The effect of bourgeois young men seeking to evade STO could be seen in the coal mines of the Gard. In the last few months before the outbreak of the war, the mines had hired 234 people of whom 98 were Algerians and 17 women. Algerian labour remained important during the first two years after the defeat of France (the mines hired 493 Algerians in 1942). Everything changed with the institution of STO. New workers were now almost all young men and almost all French. The proportion of new miners who belonged to the age groups most affected by STO (which had stood at one in eight in 1939) was almost one in two by 1943. The proportion who lived outside the mining basin rose from less than a third to almost two-thirds. The proportion of those who had worked in a mine before (which had been more than three-quarters in 1939 and more than two-thirds in 1942) dropped to less than a quarter. Those hired in 1943 included men who had been engineers, bank clerks, garage workers, secretaries, students and civil servants. In 1944 the proportion of civil servants dropped (perhaps because they could find other ways to escape STO) while the proportion of students increased (presumably because student exemption from STO had been abolished). The proportion of recruits from within the mining basins increased: this seems not to have been because of a return of professional miners, but rather because only those with good contacts could now hope to get into mines (ten of the fifty-five men hired in 1944 were the sons of mining engineers or managers).[59]

The use of employment in coal mines to avoid STO aroused much official comment. A Vichy official complained: 'Students of medicine or law, or just young men belonging to the bourgeoisie, have thought that they can escape from Service du Travail Obligatoire by contracting engagements of this kind when nothing predisposes them to undertake this difficult profession.'[60] In September 1943 a civil servant in the Ministry of Education reported the rumour that only 10 per cent of students called up for STO had actually gone. The remainder had found jobs in the railways or coal mines.[61] A report of June 1943 estimated that more than half of those who had joined the mines since the law of 16 February 1943 had previously been members of the liberal professions, civil servants, artists or *oisifs*. Only 22 per cent of those who had joined the mines in this period had previously been manual workers.[62]

At a meeting between German and French officials in April 1944, one of the former alleged that some miners were only working two or three days a week underground. Déat, the Minister of Labour, admitted that students at Lille University were securing exemption from STO with part-time work in the mines, though he pointed out that this area was under the authority of the German command in Brussels.[63] Repeated attempts to remove men who were only in mines in order to avoid STO seem to have been unsuccessful.[64] Working in mines became such a well-known ploy that Jean-Louis Quereillahc was told that the mines of Carmaux were full when he tried to get a job there.[65]

'Real miners' were said to resent the influx of bourgeois men into their profession because their new colleagues, being less productive, lowered bonus payments. Vichy officials also hinted that the interests of bourgeois men were being defended at the expense of 'real miners' and that thirty of the sixty miners who had been sent from Carmaux to Germany had four or five years of work behind them[66] – though this seems to have been an unusual incident and, given the desperate shortage of coal in France, it is hardly likely that the Germans pressed for the deportation of experienced miners.

Evasion of STO through work in the mines was most systematic with regard to one highly privileged group of men: students at the École Polytechnique. The school was closely linked to the mining industry and to the industrial establishment generally; both Aimé Lepercq, the head of the committee that directed the coal industry, and Jean Bichelonne, the Minister of Industrial Production, were *polytechniciens*. Initially, *polytechniciens* were distributed amongst mines across the country. Finally, it was agreed that *polytechniciens* born in 1922 would go to Germany, where most of them worked as draughtsmen in aircraft factories.[67] Students from the school who were born in the other two years that would normally have made them subject to STO were placed in a variety of jobs: some worked in a special mine near Saint-Étienne, where they were able to continue their studies in return for spending a relatively short period of each week underground. *Polytechniciens* were privileged even with regard to other mining engineers: managers in one area complained that *polytechniciens* were being imposed on them in preference to graduates of the less prestigious local school who would be 'more suited to render immediate services'. Other *grandes écoles* seem to have made similar efforts to protect their students. Those from the École Coloniale were given the rank of sergeant in colonial units and then put to guarding African prisoners of war in France,[68] a task that the Germans had partly devolved to the French.

Social class mattered for STO, but this did not mean that the poor were invariably worse off than their betters. Real peasants and real miners benefited from exemptions even if some bourgeois young men managed to infiltrate these milieux. Vichy reports probably exaggerated the number of bourgeois recruits in these areas because nervous young men with soft hands and inexpert gestures would have been more obvious than men who had been recruited from less privileged backgrounds. In any case, privilege was a relative matter and choices often involved lesser evils. A French mine may have been preferable to a German factory, but it was still an uncomfortable and dangerous place. Jacques Dupâquier, a student at the École Normale of Saint-Cloud, was hired to work in an iron mine run by his uncle but found the work unbearable.[69] Agricultural work could also be very hard for those whose only previous experience of farming came from reading the pastoral novels of Giono. Jean Guibal recalled that a fellow *réfractaire* on an Haute-Savoie farm, a former bank clerk from Lyons, chose to return to the city, and almost certain deportation to Germany, rather than endure agricultural labour.

The worst off in terms of STO were neither industrial workers, who had suffered badly from the *relève* but stood some chance of exemption to work in France after September 1943, nor peasants, who benefited from early exemptions and good chances to evade later on. Three groups suffered badly. The first of these were members of the lumpenproletariat: casual labourers, domestic servants, criminals. Many men from this group had 'volunteered' for work in Germany (either to escape unemployment during the economic crisis of 1941 or to escape prison) before the institution of STO. Those who were affected by STO stood little chance of avoiding it. Their jobs were not seen as valuable to the German war effort, and they lacked the contacts or money that might have got them out of reach of the authorities. Only 8 of 129 *réfractaires* in the Var were labourers.[70]

The French authorities were also keen to track down those whom they regarded as being of no value to society. In Marseilles, an official wrote in March 1944: 'The conscription will focus in principle on idlers, foreigners, and those who are of no use.'[71] Hunting down young men who could be taken to Germany often meant checking cinemas, cafés, racecourses and other places where 'the idle' were expected to gather. Those hunting *oisifs* usually mixed moral and economic judgement. Thus a couple of travelling fairground workers living on waste ground were identified as being candidates for work in Germany.[72] Equally, the police in Bayonne commented on 'a mentally unbalanced man with the familiar physical marks', who was known to 'frequent the brothel in Bayonne'.[73] Another police report on the same man and a friend of his concluded: 'Many are astonished to see these two layabouts walking around and doing nothing when many farmers' sons, brothers or husbands have left for Germany or the Todt organization.'[74]

The second group to suffer from STO was made up of those who did jobs that the French regarded as respectable but were not useful to the German war economy. Artisans, shopkeepers and workers in luxury industries were all vulnerable. A characteristic victim of the 'combing' of 'useless' professions was René P., a grocer from Paris, born in 1903. In 1943 he was stopped by some Paris policemen who said: 'A grocer? That's no job', and promptly sent him to Germany. It was equally characteristic of the confused circumstances of occupied Paris that the French authorities were not able to identify the policemen who had intercepted P.[75]

The third group to suffer disproportionately was the urban lower middle class. Almost a third of departures from the Rhône were 'employees', especially bank clerks.[76] The lower middle class often did jobs that seemed more dispensable than those of, say, train drivers. Most of all, large sections of the lower middle class suffered from their visibility. Office workers left a trail of paper behind them. State employees were especially vulnerable (at least, if they did not belong to those groups that enjoyed the patronage of powerful elements in the state). Officials only had to refer to the voluminous files of the appropriate ministry to track down a teacher or a postman. Indeed, the French post office arranged for large numbers of its employees to be transferred straight into the German postal service.[77]

COMPLICITY

STO involved large numbers of people other than the young men who were called up. For the programme to work, Vichy and the Germans needed state employees: policemen and civil servants. Beyond this, they needed the co-operation of some people who were not state employees: mayors of villages were expected to provide information, doctors were needed to conduct medical inspections.

Even the state's own servants were not always assiduous in promoting STO. It was frequently alleged that those in authority were impeding STO, either out of generalized hostility to collaboration or to protect particular individuals. The authorities intercepted a letter sent by a deserter from the Chantiers de la Jeunesse who boasted: 'You have only to see the ease with which I move around the region. The police, the gendarmes, the civil authorities, everyone is for us. They pretend to act to obey government orders.'[78] A commissaire of the Chantiers de la Jeunesse reported: 'Dauphiné and Savoie seem overwhelmingly hostile to the work of the government . . . some parts of the administration have tried to wreck or at least limit the departure of young men to Germany.'[79] Gendarmes presented particular problems. In order to be effective at finding *réfractaires*, they had to have a good knowledge of the area in which they were operating. However, men who knew an area well had associations that made them reluctant to alienate part of the population they were meant to police.[80] Policemen frequently claimed that they feared reprisals or armed confrontation with *réfractaires*. Often, however, such claims were mere excuses for inaction. In the Auvergne, police claimed that 1,500 local *réfractaires* had weapons including anti-tank guns and were capable of holding a division at bay. An official who checked this claim concluded that the area contained two hundred young men, mostly living on farms, who were not yet the object of any political organization.[81] Generally, gendarmes feared boycott by their most powerful local associates rather than armed retaliation.

Mobile units who had no attachments in the area they were policing were more willing to act against *réfractaires* but less efficient at doing so.[82] Things were worst when the Germans themselves stepped in to take blind and violent reprisals, which alienated the population without doing anything to locate the people being sought. In September 1943 German troops killed seven unarmed *réfractaires* and then destroyed their bodies with hand grenades; they took six other *réfractaires* prisoner and also seized two agricultural labourers.[83] In 1944 German troops repeatedly burned houses and even entire villages that they believed to be concealing *réfractaires*. Their actions evoked despair from the Vichy authorities. On 17 February 1944 German police beat up a man in d'Albigny-Montrottier in the Rhône. Vichy authorities complained that the victim was the most reliable man in the region, and that the Germans had ignored a family in the same village who were known to be hiding *réfractaires*.[84]

Mayors turned blind eyes to the evasion of STO. A report on desertion from the Chantiers de la Jeunesse in 1943 complained: 'There is not a mayor who is not complicit.'[85] Those asked to administer STO often resigned, fearing, or claiming to fear, Resistance reprisals.[86] Resignations of mayors did not necessarily make things any easier for the authorities. In small towns, a mayor's authority rested on his reputation and contacts rather than on his formal position, and his real power might actually be enhanced by the perception that he was an opponent of Vichy and the Germans. Sacking a mayor, or allowing him to resign, could relieve him of responsibility for administering STO without depriving him of power to impede it. A particularly stark example of the gulf between the *pays réel* of notable influence and the *pays légal* of Vichy loyalty could be seen in a village in Burgundy in September 1943. The mayor of Cramans complained that two young men were not arrested by the gendarmes although they had blatantly avoided STO. One of the boys concerned was the son of the village's former mayor.[87]

Doctors could also impede STO. When conducting medical examinations, they sometimes certified every single man they saw as being unfit for work in Germany. The Germans noted with irritation the frequency with which doctors claimed that men presented for their inspection had 'diabetes'[88] – excessive sugar consumption was not, one assumes, a common cause of ill health among young men in France in 1943. In one town, doctors certified almost every young man medically unfit, only to be faced by German doctors who overturned their decisions.[89] In the Eure-et-Loir, the proportion of young men certified unfit varied from 4.78 per cent in Thiron-Gardais to 32 per cent in Authon-du-Perche (it was said that doctors in some cantons had certified everyone unfit).[90] The Germans and the Vichy authorities threatened sanctions against doctors who provided *certificats de complaisance*.[91] Increasingly, examining doctors were German or were chosen from collaborationist groups.[92] Medical examinations were sometimes conducted in German premises where fraud would be more difficult.

Doctors charged with medical examinations could be caught in awkward crossfire. In Dax, a doctor was charged with all medical inspections because the German medical authorities had come to trust his judgement when working with him on the inspection of prostitutes. The local inspector of health objected to this decision on the rather unconvincing grounds that other doctors in the town would be jealous.[93] After the liberation, a woman accused the doctor of having killed her husband by pronouncing him fit, and thus speeding his death from tuberculosis in Stettin. The doctor pointed out that he had in fact pronounced the man unfit but been overruled by a German doctor.[94]

Alongside general resistance to STO went more vigorous action when particular kinds of people were affected. As has been suggested, mayors were particularly recalcitrant when their own sons were involved. Medical inspections could also have a class bias. A mayor in the Eure-et-Loir complained that 'too many of the young men of the classes [that is, those whose age would have made them eligible for STO] have been recognized as unfit while they play football . . . on the other hand, forty-three-year-old fathers are called to go to Germany.'[95] Bernard Pierquin reported that 'patriotic doctors' provided certificates granting exemption from STO to many of his friends. Since Pierquin was himself a medical student and the son of an eminent Paris surgeon, his friends may have aroused the patriotism of Parisian doctors more than a collection of workers would have done. It was widely believed that medical students and the sons of doctors found it especially easy to get exemption from STO, and that, more generally, the bourgeoisie were more likely to be certified unfit than other young men.[96] Doctors in the countryside were often embedded in webs of influence that tied them to powerful families.[97] More simply, their interests were associated with those of their wealthiest and most lucrative clients.[98] On the eve of large-scale departures to Germany, one man turned up at a Chantiers de la Jeunesse camp insisting that his son was ill and asking to have him examined, 'with the support of a doctor of his acquaintance'.[99]

Doctors could not hope to extract every Frenchman from STO. They could only save the privileged few by condemning others. Not surprisingly, those who were sent to Germany often had bitter memories of their medical examinations. Many complained that these had been conducted in a cursory fashion (often men were not even required to remove their overcoats).[100] Pierre Bohin claimed that only venereal disease and tuberculosis were counted as reasons for avoiding STO, and that he underwent medical inspection along with a man of forty whose leg had been amputated below the knee and who was passed fit.[101] French doctors who examined workers when they arrived in Germany were often horrified by their state of health – of one group of thirty arrivals, it was said that five were seriously ill.[102]

Sometimes notables influenced resistance to STO in other ways. Some provided employment that allowed young men to get exemption. The radical politician Henri Queuille established a business making charcoal in Neuvic d'Ussel in order to provide the young men of the area with protected employment (fifty years later his next-door neighbour still remembered this activity, but had forgotten that Queuille had once been Prime Minister). Many businessmen sought to protect their workers from being deported to Germany and often, after the liberation, such businesses defended their wartime activity saying that working for the Germans had allowed them to save their workers from being sent to Germany. But, as ever, protection of some young men was usually at the expense of others.

The degree of local complicity in evasion of STO, and the complicated rivalries that lay behind struggles over individual deportations, was revealed by a case in the Nièvre in June 1943. The prefect heard that Lucien P., who belonged to the age cohort most affected by STO, was living in the village of Giry without being troubled by the gendarmes. The prefect fined the boy's employer and sacked the mayor who had issued him with a false identity card. However, Lucien was then released on the insistence of the Germans, who said that he was needed for economic reasons. They added that Lucien's mother had always welcomed German troops, and that his denouncer was a notorious anglophile. Most revealing of all, Lucien, who obviously came from a family of influence, was spared from deportation whilst a domestic servant, who was caught with him, was sent to Germany.[103]

If notables could provide protection for some young men against STO, they were conspicuously unable to provide protection for everyone. Labour deportees frequently recalled that they had consulted powerful local men before leaving for Germany. Generally, however, notables were able, or willing, to do little. Émile Nayrolles, for example, later recalled: 'Before the departure, I asked advice from the most important person in the area. He told me that for the tranquillity of my family and peace in the neighbourhood, it was better that I went. I did it under the pressure of fear.' Gérard Prosper went to see the head of the association of *anciens combattants* who told him that he had no choice but to go. Émile Sigaud went to see the husband of his primary school teacher, who was a captain in the army reserve and veteran of the 1914–18 war. Once again, no help was provided.[104]

STO AND THE BLACK ECONOMY

Evasion of STO tied in with informal economic networks as well as informal political ones. Vichy officials hunting for *réfractaires* recognized that the involvement of so many people in the black market made their task harder. *Réfractaires* were often both black market consumers, in that they needed to eat without possessing valid ration cards, and black market resources, in that they were available to work on farms and that much produced on those farms would itself have been sold under the counter. Employing men who might be vulnerable to STO brought risks but it also brought the possibility of increased profits. Labour was scarce in France by 1943, but young men on the run from STO could be had for the price of board and lodging. Only about a fifth of *réfractaires* who were employed seem to have been paid.[105]

Families who had power in the black market could use that power to protect their sons. Yves Durand recalled that his peasant father in the Creuse was part of a black market circuit that involved exchanging potatoes for wine with a winegrower in the Aude. This circuit eventually came to take in the son of the winegrower who was hidden on the Durand family farm from 1943, when he was called up for STO, until the liberation.[106]

Agents of the state could also be bought off with black market favours, especially in the countryside. The reluctance of the gendarmerie to arrest in some rural areas owed more to the fear that they would not be able to obtain butter than the fear that the Maquis would put a bullet in their back: a Vichy official commenting on the reluctance of the gendarmes to arrest the son of the former mayor of a Burgundian village commented: 'The gendarmes act gently in order not to risk closing doors that are useful for their own supplies.'[107]

FAMILIES

Most of all, the decision about whether or not to go to Germany was one that depended on the young man's own family. Most *requis de travail* were aged between twenty and twenty-five. They were probably, in comparison with their peacetime equivalents, young for their ages. The suspension of military service, the restricted possibilities for moving within France and the general fear that gripped occupied France meant that they had little experience of life away from home. Vichy's propaganda had stressed the importance of the family and, most importantly, restricted food supplies had made people ever more dependent on family support during 1943 and 1944.

The Vichy authorities repeatedly blamed parents for subverting

STO and encouraging their sons to desert. Fathers often turned up at the camps of the Chantiers de la Jeunesse to extract their sons when they believed that the young men were about to be sent to Germany. Fathers in positions of power were particularly prone to behave in this manner.[108] Sometimes the power that such men had came from their relations with the Germans. In August 1943 a man ran away from the Chantiers de la Jeunesse. His father, a garage owner, brought his son back but told the Chantiers that his son was a driver for the Todt organization and that he (the father) had 'a long arm' and would ensure that his son was placed wherever it suited him.[109]

Successful evasion of STO often depended on family support: in Calvados around half of all *réfractaires* said that their families had encouraged them not to go to Germany.[110] Some relatives intervened in the nick of time. Raymond Valette was at Caen station about to be put on a train for Paris and then Germany, when his uncle, a railway employee, found him and took him out through a back exit. Edmond Marie was put on a train at Caen. He rushed to the doors on the far side in the hope of escaping but found that the Germans had removed the door handles. At this stage, however, he was seen by his future father-in-law, a railway mechanic. The mechanic opened the door with a screwdriver, extracted Edmond and entrusted him to a group of colleagues who spirited him out of the station.[111]

Family support also mattered in the longer term. When Pierre Faraud joined the Chantiers de la Jeunesse, it was his first 'departure far away from paternal protection'.[112] His family had prepared for the worst; he left with a false identity card and a set of civilian clothes, which he deposited with a friendly peasant.[113] When he was called up for STO, his father came to collect him,[114] and subsequently hid him on farms belonging to his great-uncle and grandfather.

Even the most generous and resourceful families, however, did not find it easy to shelter men on the run. In 1943 René Limouzin's father agreed to take in one of René's cousins, Bernard, when he deserted from the Chantiers de la Jeunesse for fear of being sent to Germany. Limouzin's father was a farmer in the Corrèze. A farm in this hilly area of polyculture was an ideal place for a *réfractaire*, but life was not easy for Bernard or his hosts. The family insisted that Bernard should remain in a dark downstairs room for most of the time, and they hid him when friends came to visit. Everyone was relieved when Bernard left to join a Maquis group in the hills in the spring of 1944.[115]

Young men on the run sometimes developed intimate relations with their protectors. The singer Georges Brassens refused to return to Germany when he came back to Paris on leave from the BMW works in Berlin. However, he could no longer stay with his aunt, who had lodged him before his departure and whose flat would be raided by the police. He was taken in by a working-class couple (Jeanne Le Bonniec and Marcel Planche) who lived in the Impasse Florimont in the 14th arrondissement. Brassens remained permanently indoors in this tiny flat without running water until the liberation of Paris. This meant a hard life, though one apparently made easier, in this case, by the curious *ménage à trois* that developed with his protectors: Brassens did not, in fact, leave Jeanne Le Bonniec until 1966.[116] In Calvados, around one in ten *réfractaires* met their future wives whilst they were on the run.[117]

The case of Émile Salles illustrates the complex interaction of family, friendship and material interest in governing how potential protectors responded to a *réfractaire*. He was hidden first on a farm belonging to the Martels, friends of his nurse, but, since they were already hiding four *réfractaires*, he had to move on. A cousin of the Martels refused to take him because Salles was a schoolteacher and 'schoolteachers know nothing'. He was then sent to Saint-Aubin des Bois and hidden by a family who had nothing in principle against STO (their own son had gone to Germany) but needed extra labour. He was badly exploited and asked the Martels to find him another place to hide. He then moved to Mesnil-Caussois, but became too intimate with the farmer's daughter and was fired. He moved to an isolated farm in Landelles but was bored and moved to another farm nearby, from which in turn he had to move when work for him ran out. Finally, he moved back to Mesnil-Caussois, 'near to his future parents-in-law': presumably the farmer had now accepted that his daughter's affair with Salles had gone too far to be stopped.[118]

Equally, young men who went to Germany often attributed their decision to their families.[119] Many feared reprisals against their relatives. Jean Edmond was worried about the consequences for his father, who was only forty-three, if he evaded labour service in Germany.[120]

Families with more than one son were particularly fearful that failure of a *requis* to report for work in Germany might bring the deportation of his younger brother.[121] Such men recalled that they had been told by their own fathers that they should go to Germany in order to avoid sanctions that might be imposed on the whole family. Some young men who had reached the relative safety of Spain received letters from their fathers asking them to return to France.[122]

A radio broadcast by Laval threatening reprisals against the relatives of those who evaded STO had dramatic effects. Paul Fourtier-Berger recalled hearing the speech at the very moment when he was having dinner with a contact who might have been able to get him into the Resistance. Fearing the consequences for his father and brother, he decided to go to Germany.[123] Pierre Picard-Gilbertier was influenced by the same broadcast: 'In spite of his hatred for the Germans, under an intense moral pressure, Pierre, who refused to make his family run so many risks . . . turned himself in for deportation.'[124] Sometimes, the Germans or their allies did seize male relatives in order to put pressure on *réfractaires*.[125] But such reprisals never happened on the scale that some people seem to have feared when STO first started; indeed, declining fear of reprisals against relatives was one of the reasons why men became increasingly willing to avoid STO.[126]

STO could generate bitter divisions inside families. The eldest son of Raphaël Alibert, who had been Vichy Minister of Justice, was sub-prefect of Figeac, a good place for hiding *réfractaires*, and, when his younger brother was called up for STO, he offered to shelter him, but their father vetoed this suggestion either because of his legalism, as the older brother suggested, or because, as the younger brother suggested, he feared reprisals inspired by his political enemy Laval.[127]

André Noisette blamed his father, who was suffering from a degenerative disease that left him 'physically and mentally diminished', for having insisted that he go: his father died a few months after his return.[128] Yves Laurent's family blamed his Pétainist father and conformist stepmother for encouraging his younger half-brother to go to Germany:

Armand went to Germany, sacrificed by his mother who had a neurotic fear that deprived her of all capacity for thought. As for our father, a reserve officer of unconditional loyalty to the Marshal, judging collaboration as a necessary evil, he considered that it was his duty to obey and to bend to the decisions of the head of state. With that fear on one side, this conviction on the other, poor Armand, who up until then had never left his mother's skirts, was incapable of reacting and could not escape a trip across the Rhine.[129]

Laurent's opinion of his half-brother, who had 'never left his mother's skirts', and who eventually got himself repatriated from Germany by faking chronic incontinence, was not very flattering either.

Why were some families more able and willing to provide help than others? Some of the answers are relatively obvious. Rich families could provide more help than poor ones. The rich could use their contacts to get their sons jobs in protected sectors and they could provide them with money to live off the black market. Rich young men could travel more easily and pay *passeurs* who would take them over the frontier to Spain. The nominally independent state of Monaco also offered a degree of protection from STO. The principality had allowed the deportation of Jews from its soil in 1942, but a newly appointed French consul, Olivier Deleau (who seems to have been unsympathetic to Vichy), persuaded the government against deporting French citizens who were of an age to be affected by STO. Monaco also arranged for young men to be put into professions that might afford them some protection from STO (so many policemen were recruited that there were not enough uniforms to go round). Once again, the protection of the Monégasque authorities seems to have been most effective with regard to men from wealthy backgrounds; one newly recruited policeman had to be told that it was not normal for constables on traffic duty to kiss the hands of smart society ladies.[130]

Agricultural families were more helpful than urban ones. In a rural area of Normandy, more than half of *réfractaires* found shelter within 20 kilometres of their home and almost a quarter never left their canton; in Caen, almost two-thirds had to travel more than 20 kilometres.[131] One of the most important things that a boy contemplating evasion of STO needed was a link with a farm where he could hide and get access to food. Extended families were useful to would-be *réfractaires* because such families offered a wider range of options and because the authorities were less likely to search the houses of cousins and aunts than parents. There is also some evidence that female relatives were more helpful than male ones. Many *requis* escaped with the aid of sisters or aunts. STO was sometimes justified with reference to the supposedly masculine virtues that had previously been inculcated by military service, and women seem to have been less vulnerable to this rhetoric than men. The great majority of French people deported by the Germans for political crimes were men, but four of the eight people sent to concentration camps from the Saint-Étienne region for helping *réfractaires* were women.[132]

Different pressures operated on different families. Worst off were families trying to feed several children on limited money or families with more than one son. Collaborationist fathers sometimes urged their sons to go. In November 1943, Pierre Cathala, Minister of Finances, told a rally in Paris that his son and six out of nine of his nephews were working in Germany.[133] Fathers from certain sections of the lower middle class seem to have particularly feared the consequences for their own careers or pensions if their sons did not go.

Peasant families, by contrast, could be willing to stand up to the state because they were used to treating its representatives with some disdain. An example of the support that a tough-minded peasant woman could provide to a boy on the run was provided when gendarmes seeking to trace a *réfractaire* interviewed all the people who had served as witnesses at his baptism. One of these people was his aunt. She admitted that her nephew was close to his cousins but then insisted that she could not remember their addresses or their names or anything else about them. Helpfully she explained: 'I have been ill for a long time and I remember nothing.'[134]

What does STO tell us about the broader nature of the Vichy regime? Most obviously, it shows how resistance, collaboration, passivity and Pétainism always overlapped. Not everyone who evaded STO, or who helped others to do so, was a resistant. Some *réfractaires* specifically refused to recall their experience in terms of the Resistance or, like Yves Laurent, they distinguished between Resistance and resistance. Some people avoided STO in ways that involved serving the German war economy or even in ways, such as joining the Milice, that involved outright collaborationism. The very confusion of labour policy in

France in 1943 and 1944 makes it hard to classify actions in simple categories. Vichy was divided, as some officials sabotaged policies that were pursued by others. The Germans, too, were divided. Different leaders in Berlin had different views about how best to exploit French labour and, especially in 1944, German agencies in France were desperate to secure their own labour supplies even if they did so at the expense of other German employers. The result of this was that many people 'resisted' STO by 'collaborating' with some German agency.

Response to STO was not, however, simply a matter of institutions and political structures. Such responses were also rooted in French society. In important respects, the orders of Vichy and the Germans were mediated through French society. The direct use of physical force was rarely effective. Such force could frighten the whole community but it could not track down particular individuals, and violence by outsiders broke down the subtle networks of cohabitation on which the occupation rested. Vichy and the Germans could only make STO work by securing the co-operation of powerful individuals – not just, perhaps particularly not, people who held formal positions. This inevitably meant that the social hierarchies counted for much in the implementation of STO. Some of these hierarchies dated back before 1940. A young man who entered a *grande école* in 1940 stood a good chance of avoiding STO; a young man who entered Santé prison in 1940 stood almost no chance of avoiding it: it was highly likely that such a person would have 'volunteered' in order to escape the high mortality rates of Vichy prisons before 1943 and, if not, he would have been taken in handcuffs to the Gare du Nord.[135]

Pre-war hierarchies were, however, modified by the special circumstances of the occupation. Members of the grande bourgeoisie were protected from being sent to Germany but often had to endure considerable discomfort in order to achieve this. Members of the urban lower middle class were probably less privileged in the context of STO than almost any other social group, including those who would have stood below them before 1940. Agriculture, sometimes a poor relation before 1940, did well and young peasants were probably the only social group who sometimes managed to avoid STO without enduring any other serious inconvenience.

Rooting STO in its social context means recognizing the degree of complicity in its execution. This complicity did not just involve institutions and elites. The very people that *requis de travail* trusted – local notables and, most of all, their own fathers – often encouraged them to go to Germany. Men in authority (and it was mainly men who encouraged departures to Germany) felt that STO was a lesser evil. The departure of a particular cohort of young men, who had thus far avoided military service, was seen as a price worth paying to protect their communities and families from reprisals. As time went on, this calculation changed. The Germans and their French allies had more and more difficulty in tracing particular *réfractaires* or those who helped them and were increasingly prone to respond with random acts of violence. STO's legitimacy diminished as it became clear how harsh would be the fate of those who had gone to Germany, and the chances of avoiding it increased as the liberation approached and the Maquis expanded. By the summer of 1944, the circumstances that had made many feel that young men should obey orders to go to Germany in the summer of 1943 seemed remote. By the time the surviving *requis de travail* returned home in the summer of 1945, the logic that had seemed to require their departure no longer fitted into France's vision of herself. Some *requis* now found that they were blamed for going by the very men who had refused them help when they had tried to find escape routes, or that they were encouraged to keep quiet about their experiences by their own families.

9

The French in Germany, 1943–1945

Almost two million embittered men who, on returning to France, will become so many rebels. (Vichy report on French prisoners of war and civilian workers in Germany, January 1944)[1]

Until the end of 1942, official views of French people in Germany were simple. They were divided into two sharply contrasted categories: volunteer workers and prisoners of war. Prisoners were seen as men who had been taken to Germany against their will; volunteers were seen as people who had chosen to work for the enemy. Volunteers were viewed with contempt; prisoners with respect. Prisoners were the epitome of French patriotism and male honour; a high proportion of volunteers were foreign and/or female. The Vichy government stressed its desire to secure the return of prisoners of war. It had not succeeded in bringing them back as a block, but a large proportion (almost half the total) were released for one reason or another during the first two years after the defeat.

In June 1942, things began to change. For one thing, the movement of people between France and Germany switched direction. Until this point, it had been mainly from Germany to France, as prisoners came home. After this date, increasing numbers of civilian workers went from France to Germany. As we saw in Chapter 8, most of these workers went under the *relève* or STO schemes that involved explicit compulsion. Workers who had gone to Germany as volunteers lost their right to take leave or return to France at the end of their contract so that, in effect, they became forced labourers. French prisoners of

9. (opposite) *A German labour recruitment agency in France: around 250,000 people from France 'volunteered' to work in Germany.*

war became less separate from civilian workers. The number living in camps, always a minority, diminished further as the Reich, desperate for labour, pushed prisoners out of Stalags and into work Kommandos. Some French prisoners were invited to 'volunteer' for transformation into civilian workers. Boundaries between volunteers and press-ganged workers, or between soldiers and civilians, became increasingly porous, though in spite or because of this relations between the different groups of Frenchmen in Germany were often marked by suspicion and hostility.[2]

In September 1943 a Vichy official wrote an interesting report on the intercepted letters of Frenchmen in Germany. It expressed standard Pétainist assumptions about Frenchmen in Germany – it suggested that the 'militant patriotism' of prisoners of war was affronted by the left-wing views of French civilian workers, especially those from urban backgrounds. However, the official also admitted that it was, in fact, difficult to distinguish letters written by prisoners of war from those written by civilian workers.[3]

The status of the French in Germany changed in another way during the course of the occupation. In 1940, France's future seemed to lie in the Stalags and Oflags of Germany. The release of prisoners was seen to be the precondition of French revival. By 1943, France's future seemed to be in London, Algiers or, increasingly, the hills and woods of France itself. Men in Germany, whether they were prisoners who had accepted defeat and captivity or civilians who had accepted labour service in Germany, seemed passive spectators on the margins of history. This was particularly true of the young labour deportees (*requis*) who knew that their own contemporaries or juniors had often taken to the Maquis or joined the Free French forces. Jean-Louis Quereillahc recalled the words of one his companions on the train taking them to Germany: 'I think of my brother and my cousins who are fighting in Tunisia or somewhere. Yes ... they are lucky to be soldiers, they know why they are fighting and they have faith in something.'[4]

CIVILIANS

Men who were sent to Germany under the STO scheme (that is, after February 1943) were conspicuous for their youth. The majority of men who went were in their early twenties. Many had never been away from home until the moment when they were deported. The fact that the *requis* had not undergone military service meant that they lacked the veneer of ostentatious toughness that soldiers acquired. Many of them did not smoke – which meant that they were able to use their cigarettes as valuable items in trade – or drink much (one celebrated his return home with a Perrier and lemon).[5] Some regarded themselves as boys rather than men; one recalled that he wrote to Father Christmas in December 1944.[6] Michel Caignard wrote: 'From one day to the next, we had become adults, without any administrative formalities and without our consent by a simple decree of Vichy.'[7]

Experience varied with time and place. Early arrivals, especially those working in small enterprises, were often lodged with their employers. As time went on, special camps were constructed for foreign workers; the proportion of civilian workers who lived in camps was probably higher than the proportion of prisoners of war who did so. Like prisoners of war, *requis* were conscious of the difference the nature or location of their employment could make. Best off were workers who managed to pursue careers they had begun in France. Official schemes allowed postal workers and forestry officials to undertake such work in Germany. A few civilian workers managed comparatively easy placements as office workers or artisans. André Michel played the piano in a café orchestra, before deciding that he was willing to endure the discomforts and dangers of a German factory in order to stay with his friends.[8] Most *requis*, however, had no established profession. German selection techniques were, in any case, often haphazard: factory foremen, lacking any means of asking technical questions, sometimes felt the muscles of potential recruits.

Industrial work was hard for many labour deportees. Few of them had much experience of factories before they came (most French factory workers had been kept in France to work in their existing jobs). German factories were driven at a fast pace in 1943, equipment was poorly maintained, workers were often inexperienced and accidents were common. Some postings were particularly dreaded. Worst of all was the prospect of being sent to dig anti-tank ditches in eastern Germany. Work on these meant hard labour outdoors in the coldest and least welcoming part of Germany.

The best locations for *requis* were in western Germany, especially in the Rhineland. Such regions were seen as more physically comfortable (they were warmer) and more politically sympathetic to foreigners (Catholicism often created a bond between Frenchmen and the local population). Berlin and Vienna were also seen as good places to be. Timing made an important difference to civilian workers. Those who arrived early were sometimes able to establish relatively comfortable lodgings and to work in enterprises that suited them. Most importantly, perhaps, they were sometimes able to get back. Until 1942, volunteer workers were allowed home when their contracts expired. Men performing STO were at first allowed to go on leave, a chance that was removed when the Germans realized how few men were returning: by January 1944, French officials reckoned that only between 5 and 10 per cent of men given leave returned to Germany.[9] The sociologist Michel Crozier seems to have been one of the privileged few who had a relatively benign experience of STO. He spent ten months in Munich and Salzburg, working as a surveyor, a worker in a brewery, a hotel porter, an office worker and a scene shifter in the town theatre, before returning on leave, and deserting, in May 1944.[10]

Relations with other Frenchmen in Germany varied. Many deported workers came across prisoners of war, of whom there were over a million in Germany. Sometimes prisoners and *requis* worked alongside each other in factories. They had much in common; sometimes *requis de travail* managed to effect reunions with brothers in Stalags or work Kommandos.[11] Both groups thought of themselves as patriotic Frenchmen, both were detained in Germany against their will, both were sometimes bitter against those better connected men who had managed to evade STO or get themselves repatriated from prisoner of war camps.

Some prisoners gave *requis du travail* help, advice and, most importantly, a share of their Red Cross food parcels,[12] but there was also tension between prisoners and *requis*. Prisoners of war were, on average, about ten years older than civilian workers. Most prisoners had undergone compulsory military service in peacetime, fought in the war of 1939–40, and then spent three years in captivity. They sometimes looked down on men who had only just left home. The men deported under the STO programme, mostly born in the early 1920s, had a strong sense of generational identity that often turned into hostility to all middle-aged men. Georges Caussé wrote that the prisoners with whom he worked 'were probably good chaps, but moulded by long experience, they showed themselves to be . . . rather egotistic'.[13] Prisoners sometimes refused to believe that the *requis* had really come to Germany against their will. Caussé recalled a prisoner who said: 'And you were not capable of hiding [when called up for STO]? *Merde alors*, the blues [that is, the French team] are not too good this year. Me, my boy, I was taken with a gun in my hand.'[14]

There was a political gulf between prisoners and *requis*. As we saw in Chapter 6, respect for Pétain amongst prisoners was still strong even in 1943. Most *requis*, by contrast, had been adolescents in 1940. They had grown up after the initial wave of Pétainist enthusiasm had passed over France. For them, the Vichy government meant Laval (the man whose policies had sent them to Germany) rather than Pétain. Their attitude to the government, and often to all politics, was one of sullen nihilism.[15]

Relations between labour deportees and other French civilian workers were often strained. Deportees denounced almost all other French civilian workers as 'volunteers'. As far as public opinion in post-war France was concerned, volunteers and *requis* stood next to each other on the spectrum of resistance-collaboration: volunteers had chosen to go to Germany and *requis* had chosen not to resist going to Germany very hard. As far as the *requis* themselves were concerned, volunteers and *requis* stood at opposite extremes of a spectrum that measured altruism and socially acceptable behaviour. The *requis* were marked by their respect for rules and social convention. Many of them justified their acceptance of deportation on the grounds that it spared their families or communities from greater suffering. None of them regarded themselves as unpatriotic. They saw the volunteers, by contrast, as men who defied convention and who were motivated by the search for personal gain. The criminality of volunteers aroused much comment.

The labour deportees were often prim young men. They were shocked by the pimps, thieves and jailbirds they encountered among French volunteer workers.[16] Victor Savary recalled that he and his fellow *requis* needed to watch their bags carefully, 'because we had ended up amongst the dregs of the Old Port of Marseilles who were there to avoid being sent to prison'.[17] A French industrialist who visited workers in Germany spoke of the 'tattooed apaches' who had made up the early cohorts of volunteer workers. He described the damage done to German perceptions of French workers by these men and reported that canteens ordered Frenchmen to pay a deposit before they could take a knife and fork.[18] The belief that the behaviour of volunteers had caused all Frenchmen to be regarded with contempt was widespread.[19] Charles-Henri-Guy Bazin recalled that volunteers working at the BMW works at Eisenach had been ejected from their lodgings in town because of their fondness for 'poker, women and schnapps'.[20]

Divisions between volunteers and *requis* seem, in fact, to have been about many things other than the motives that underlay their presence in Germany. The victims of STO, all young men, were liable to label anyone over a certain age as a volunteer[21] (though in fact many volunteers were young, and some men who had been forced to come to Germany under the *relève* programme were relatively old). François Cavanna recalled his colleague Alexandre thus: 'He was over fifty, a very suspect age, but he was tearfully indignant when we called him a Nazi volunteer.'[22] Vichy officials, reporting on French workers in Germany, wrote that the atmosphere in one factory was damaged by the 'mixture of young and old', which produced 'ill-discipline and theft'.[23] It was clear that the division between 'young' and 'old' was also a division between *requis* and volunteers.

Misogyny also played a role in the attitude of *requis* to volunteers. All Frenchwomen in Germany were labelled as volunteers, and this was often associated with a more general denunciation of their morality. One returning *requis* said that Frenchwomen in Germany had been known as 'volontaires et vérolées' (volunteers and pox-ridden).[24]

RELATIONS WITH FRANCE

In March 1942 the Vichy government itself established a Service for French Labour in Germany under Gaston Bruneton. In February 1943 this body was renamed the Commissariat General for French Labour in Germany. Bruneton also came to lead a French delegation to the German Labour Front. Bruneton, born in 1882, was an industrialist who had done business with the Germans early in the occupation and visited Germany in 1941. His involvement with French workers in Germany, however, does not seem to be explicable purely in terms of self-interest. Bruneton was an Alsatian Protestant. He was the son of a pastor and deeply conscious of his Huguenot origins, and, in particular, of a pastor ancestor who had chosen to serve as a galley slave on a ship of Louis XIV in order to bring spiritual comfort to the other Protestants who had been sent there. Bruneton often talked a language of sacrifice and duty that resembled that of Catholic 'missionaries' in Germany (see below).

The Service had an office in Berlin and officials scattered across Germany.[25] It published newsletters and tried to intervene in favour of French workers in matters of health, safety, pay and the granting of leave. It was not very successful. Increasingly associated with the German Labour Front, from which he drew whatever powers he possessed, Bruneton had little impact on the lives of ordinary French workers. He had a small staff and little power to control the decisions taken by German industrialists. One *requis* recalled 'a sort of friendly association of French workers in Germany, an agency under government control, created by Vichy, designed to channel and control . . . having no real autonomy'.[26] Pierre Lagarde discovered the existence of Bruneton's organization, of which he had previously been unaware, when he asked for leave to visit his pregnant wife in January 1944. He was received by a French captain in an unfamiliar uniform in an office with a photograph of Pétain on the wall.[27] It was said that a thousand Frenchmen in one factory in Prussia had seen no representative of Bruneton for a year.[28]

The second group in France that tried to stay in touch with French workers was made up of Pétainist youth leaders. Official attempts to keep young men going to Germany organized and disciplined were first channelled through the Jeunesse Ouvrière Française Travaillant en Allemagne (JOFTA). This organization provided young *requis* with a blue uniform. It claimed to offer a four-month training period before departure and, a very important attraction, the prospect that young men might be permitted to remain with a particular group once they got to Germany.

Organization of young workers in Germany was, however, gradually taken over by the leaders of the Chantiers de la Jeunesse (the camp established by Vichy for young men). From 1943 onwards, increasing numbers of young men who had served in the Chantiers were deported. Some Chantiers' leaders, generally a few years older than the men under their command, wished to maintain contact with the groups they had led. To this end, a number of *chefs* accompanied their subordinates to Germany. Some kept the groups under their command in the green uniform of the Chantiers.

Gradually relations between the command structure of the Chantiers de la Jeunesse and the young men in German factories became formalized. Initially, leaders of the Chantiers who went to Germany were designated as 'enterprise guides' (thus benefiting from regulations that allowed firms to maintain contact with their workers in Germany in some circumstances). Later, the 'mission' of the Chantiers was given formal status through attachment to the French delegation to the German Labour Front. Individual Chantiers' delegates were sent to particular workers' camps. Great attention was given to the need to maintain the authority of these delegates, and to spare them from work. In some cases, delegates from the Chantiers replaced German officials and became responsible for the enforcement of discipline in camps.

The organization of the Chantiers in Germany was linked to a certain view of the Vichy government. It would be hard to find a more Pétainist figure than Paul Furioux, who headed the Chantiers' mission in Berlin. He was a soldier from a family of soldiers. He had served in the First World War. He had been a fifty-eight-year-old colonel at the beginning of the Second World War (the same age and rank that Pétain had had in 1914). The Chantiers' camp that he subsequently commanded was located in the Tronçais forest, where the 'Pétain oak' was to be found, and the company concerned was named the Pétain company.[29]

The Chantiers' leaders distinguished between Pétainism and collaborationism. They did not necessarily regard the attempt to maintain morale and order among Frenchmen in Germany as an act of collaboration. They often quarrelled with the collaborationist organizations that increasingly sought to exercise influence over French workers in Germany, especially after the departure of the Pétain government from French soil in 1944. As was often the case, Pétainist contempt for a certain kind of collaboration was expressed in moralistic terms. Louis Gilbert wrote that the official Delegation to French workers in Germany, before being 'purified' by himself and his comrades from the Chantiers, contained 'a delegate who got drunk in the name of the Marshal, a social worker who went back to France pregnant and an assistant who had his hand in the till'.[30] In January 1944 Furioux was returned to France, in part, it seems, because his nationalism had annoyed the German authorities.

The Chantiers' leaders saw their role as involving the diffusion of authority from above. They disapproved of volunteer workers, 'men who had left France to get away from prosecution',[31] and who lived 'in an indescribable moral and physical degeneration'.[32] They regarded the French conscripts with a mixture of fear and condescension, seeing them as rebellious young men who needed to have discipline imposed on them. One *chef* compared the conscripts to the recruits he had commanded in 1936 (the year of the Popular Front) who had arrived singing the 'Internationale'.[33]

The third body to interest itself in the lives of French workers in Germany was the Church and particularly the Jeunesse Ouvrière Chrétienne (JOC), a body established in 1927 to bring Christianity to young workers. A number of the JOC's members were called up for labour service and felt that their duty was to go in order to maintain a Christian spirit among their fellow workers. In some respects, the idea of a mission to workers in Germany fitted in well with the Catholic Church's preoccupation with gaining influence over the young and over workers. One priest who went to Germany wrote of 'this proletariat, so morally abandoned, so paganized'.[34]

Around two hundred priests, and a small number of nuns,[35]

volunteered to work in Germany – though they rarely applied to themselves the word volunteer, which in this context was associated with criminality.[36] In Nuremberg, one priest reckoned that there was a total of six French priests and sixty seminarians for a French population of 20,000, and that 50 out of a 1,000 French workers in one camp were practising Catholics.[37] Catholic 'missionaries' worked underground, especially after a decree of December 1943, which outlawed Catholic militancy amongst foreign workers in Germany. In spite of their illegality, French Catholics in Germany were sometimes given discreet help by German Catholic priests and occasionally by lay German Catholics. The Church's view of German factories was usually rooted in a predictable moralism. Priests disapproved of volunteer workers, particularly women: Paul Beschet recalled that female volunteers lived in 'the utmost indecency'.[38] A seminarian wrote of the 'repugnant promiscuity, accentuated by the presence of French volunteer workers'.[39] Victor Dillard, a forty-seven-year-old Jesuit who had been an important figure at Vichy until the summer of 1943, volunteered under a false name to work as an electrician in a factory in Wuppertal. Hoping to establish some contact with his French colleagues, he offered to give German lessons, and was depressed when his only clients turned out to be Frenchwomen who hoped to earn money prostituting themselves to Germans.[40]

There were differences of attitude amongst Catholic missionaries in German factories. Service in Germany sometimes attracted unconventional Catholics (the kind of people who would later join the worker-priest experiments of the late 1940s). Joseph Gelin even managed to turn his own vows of chastity into an occasion for self-mockery. He told a friendly German baker about his fiancée in France and suggested that the baker produce a cake with an abbreviated version of his girlfriend's name (Jocette) spelt out in icing. The priest's colleagues were astonished when he produced a cake with the initials of the Jeunesse Ouvrière Chrétienne on it.[41]

The Catholic Church was one of the few institutions that was at ease with discussion of STO. Where other bodies felt uncomfortable with an experience that could not be categorized as either resistance or collaboration, the Church had a vocabulary of expiation, obedience and mission that could be used to explain a decision to go to Germany. After 1945 a number of memorial volumes were dedicated to the achievements of Catholic priests and activists who had gone to Germany with young men deported under the STO programme.[42] Marcel Gallo, a JOC militant who had gone to work in the Walther armaments factory in Thuringia in 1943, was arrested along with six other members of the JOC and sent first to Flossenbürg and then to Mauthausen, where he died on 19 March 1945 at the age of twenty-four. After the war, he was beatified.

PRISONNIERS DE GUERRE TRANSFORMÉS

The Vichy government also launched a scheme to encourage prisoners of war to accept 'transformation' into civilian workers. Prisoners who volunteered for this scheme would have greater freedom, would have the right to unlimited correspondence and would be paid, but they would lose the protection that they enjoyed under the Geneva Convention. Transformation was advantageous to the Germans because it allowed them to economize on guards and because it gave them the right to post men to armaments factories. It was also attractive to some Vichy agencies, which believed that 'transformed prisoners' would earn them credit with the Germans. Vichy officials often also believed that *transformés* would exercise a good influence over young civilian French workers in German factories.[43] About 250,000 prisoners were transformed into civilian workers (almost entirely in the summer of 1943, although a few transformations occurred as late as December 1943).[44] This experience left few records. After the liberation, few Frenchmen wished to discuss an act that might have been seen as aid to the Germans. De Gaulle's provisional government treated all returning prisoners the same regardless of whether or not they had been granted civilian status in Germany.

The voluntary nature of transformation was often nominal.[45] Transformation was primarily imposed on prisoners who were already in work Kommandos. This meant other ranks, who had been cut off from their officers for the past three years. Some of the most privileged and highly educated prisoners had been repatriated to France; some

NCOs and some of the most educated prisoners to remain in Germany stayed in Stalags rather than work Kommandos. The prisoners in work Kommandos, especially unattractive industrial ones where pressure to accept transformation was highest, were likely to be ill-informed, and often cut off from contact with anyone except a few comrades for many years. Such men were not well placed to resist pressure from the Germans. Often whole work Kommandos, sometimes consisting of over a hundred men, were simply declared to be 'transformed'.[46]

Even Vichy officials recognized that prisoners had been pressured to accept the change in their status.[47] In Stalag IIIA it was reported that transformation 'operates by entire districts [that is, presumably whole groups of work Kommandos were transformed at the same time]. Around 30 per cent of the whole population of the camp had been transformed.'[48] Men who refused were threatened with 'sanctions',[49] with transfer to less desirable work Kommandos or with exclusion from the chance that they might benefit from the relève.[50]

Transformed prisoners were more common in industry than in agriculture: about a quarter of all transformed prisoners, as against more than half of prisoners as a whole, worked on farms. Agricultural wages were low so that men posted to farms had little to gain from becoming civilian workers (the advantages of being on the land derived from benefits in kind).[51] Men on farms also had little to gain from transformation in non-monetary terms. The right to go to cinemas or cafés meant little to men who were miles from the nearest town, and freedom from guards meant little to men who were sometimes living without guards already: the latter consideration was particularly important in east Prussia, where prisoners seem to have enjoyed considerable freedom without civilian status.[52] The Germans also had little incentive to press prisoners on farms to accept transformed status. The Geneva Convention imposed no particular constraints on agricultural work.

Transformation was soon seen as a 'marché des dupes'.[53] Integration into the civilian life of Nazi Germany was a grotesquely unattractive prospect in 1943. Prisoners lost the protection of the Geneva Convention at the very moment when Gestapo paranoia and repression made such protection most valuable. In Stalag IA it was reported that 'a plebiscite on the subject of transformation of prisoners of war into civilian workers only got a quarter of the vote. The prisoners of war fear the Gestapo more than their military guards, who are much more flexible when it comes to some lapse.'[54] The prospect of being posted to armaments factories was particularly unpleasant as Allied advances brought increasing numbers of factories within reach of American and British bombers. Transformation also had less directly material consequences. It deprived prisoners of their military status and consequently of their dignity; it associated them with the German war effort at the moment when the majority of the French population was getting ready to welcome Allied troops. Transformed prisoners sometimes felt despised by those of their comrades who had retained their prisoner status, and they particularly resented this contempt because they did not feel they had been offered any real choice: 'All protest at the idea that non-transformed prisoners in camps have of those who have been forcibly dispatched as free workers. The latter are, in general, seen by their comrades as bad Frenchmen and traitors.'[55] A Vichy official recognized that many *transformés* felt 'morally diminished', and that they would have preferred to have their status changed by force rather than in a way that appeared to involve their own complicity.

Many *transformés* were soon in desperate circumstances. The right to unrestricted correspondence with France was removed after the Allied landings in Normandy.[56] Most seriously of all, transformed prisoners suffered from a terrible lack of appropriate clothing.[57] Such men gave up their uniforms and were supposed to receive civilian clothes in return. But much clothing was lost in transit, stolen, or destroyed by bombing, and many men never received clothes designed to withstand the German winter.[58] In December 1943 Raymond D. wrote that he and his comrades had no shirts or underwear and were working outdoors dressed only in overalls.[59]

'Transformation' often fitted into the wider gulf between the Stalags and the work Kommandos. Even more than other working prisoners, *transformés* were vulnerable to exploitation by the prison 'bourgeoisie' who administered the camps. Men who retained prisoner status benefited from the 'transformation' of their comrades because they had the exclusive benefit of food parcels:[60] the total number of such parcels continued to be the same as it had been before transformation. A lucrative black market grew up as *transformés* traded whatever they could buy with their wages (not much, in practice) for the clothes, tobacco and chocolate that prisoners were able to obtain from the Red Cross. Sometimes men in the Stalags seem simply to have stolen goods that rightfully belonged to the *transformés*. It was said that many men in the Stalags were wearing clothes that looked remarkably like the civilian suits intended for the *transformés*.[61]

Transformés had few people to protect their interests. They were no longer in touch with the Red Cross, the Scapini Mission or the *hommes de confiance* of their own camps. In theory, they were subject to the Commissariat for French workers in Germany and to a new body, especially established to act as a link between transformed prisoners and the Reich agricultural office. However, these bodies were understaffed, riven by infighting and badly disrupted by the effects of Allied bombing. There was almost nothing they could do to help former prisoners, and officials often just wrote telling men to settle matters as best they could with their employers. It was intended that *transformés* who were prosecuted for crimes or who became unfit for work on medical grounds would be returned to Stalags, where they could be provided with appropriate legal advice, medical treatment, or, if necessary, repatriation to France. In practice, it was difficult for *transformés* to get back to Stalags. Men accused of crimes were sent directly to civilian prisons. Invalids who were unfit to work often found themselves in limbo as they were attached neither to their place of employment nor to their original prison camp: in one case, a man who had lost a hand in an industrial accident was classed as unfit to work by the civilian authorities but then found himself unable to return to his Stalag.[62] Some *transformés* were sent to build fortifications on the Eastern Front (in defiance of the original agreements about their status). In November 1943 a prisoner wrote to say that he and his comrades had not received the 1,000 francs that had been promised and felt that they had got nothing in return for their loss of prisoner of war status.[63] When a former prisoner complained that he and his comrades were lodged in atrocious conditions, denied the means of transmitting money home and deprived of their tobacco, a French official admitted that his complaints were well founded and that 'these men are treated like Poles'.[64]

FRENCHMEN IN GERMANY
AND WOMEN

French thinking about prisoners of war in particular was shot through with thinking about marital fidelity; almost half of all prisoners were married. Pétainists were obsessively concerned about the behaviour of the wives of French prisoners of war. They made it illegal to live with the wife of a prisoner of war 'in flagrant concubinage'. Infidelity by the wives of prisoners was to haunt French post-war culture. The unfaithful wife of the prisoner was almost a stock character in films about the occupation such as *Lacombe Lucien*, *Une affaire des femmes* and *Une femme française*. Boris Vian's song, 'Le Déserteur' (composed in 1954) contained the line: 'When I was a prisoner another man stole my wife.'

How did prisoners themselves feel about the fidelity or otherwise of the women they had left behind? Certainly, in Oflags and Stalags the matter was discussed at some length. A camp newspaper in Oflag XIIA contained an article entitled 'Solitude', which described a man lying on a bunk while his comrades played poker:

Poor woman! He had wanted to give her a happy life. Must destiny be so cruel as to separate them thus? What was she doing at this late hour? Was she asleep or bent over her sewing? Perhaps she was reading or perhaps she was writing her husband the letter for which he waited with such impatience. Or . . . no . . . that was not possible. Better not think about it. But the idea, confused at first, became precise, sharp, painful . . . His eyes, heavy with sleep, closed, and yet, the piercing thought was still there.[65]

In Stalag XIID, the priest Marius Perrin watched Sartre tease his comrades during a lecture: 'Sartre expressed a thought that should worry them [that] the women of France would now prefer the young German soldiers who had shown more courage.' Perrin had an interesting theory about the impact that such words had on their audience. He suggested that bourgeois prisoners were worried about the fidelity of their wives, whilst workers and peasants gave the matter little thought. There are some obvious reasons why this should be so. Bourgeois prisoners were more likely to be confined in Stalags or

Oflags, where they had little to do except brood on their worries: requests for divorce seem to have come disproportionately from men in camps.[66] Workers and peasants were more likely to be in work Kommandos, where they had the regular distraction of back-breaking work, and the occasional distraction of contact with German women. The American anthropologist Laurence Wylie had a conversation in a provençal village in the 1950s that hints at the matter-of-fact attitude that some French peasants took to sexual fidelity: 'I can't say I've always been faithful to my wife. During the war when I was in the army and then a prisoner on a farm in Germany . . . well, it was different. I think my wife has been faithful to me, but I don't want to know about it if she hasn't.'[67]

There may have been a more subtle reason for the difference in how men from different social classes thought about the fidelity of their wives. Bourgeois Frenchmen in general, and officers in particular, had grown up in a culture that emphasized seduction and sexual adventure. Colonel Christian-Marie-Ferdinand de la Croix de Castries, who escaped from Oflag IVD in March 1941, later became famous for naming his troop outposts during the battle of Dien Bien Phu after his mistresses: Anne-Marie, Gabrielle, Béatrice, Dominique, Éliane, Claudine, Françoise, Huguette, Guilleminot, Lily.

Whatever their private feelings, few prisoners availed themselves of the opportunity that the Vichy government offered them to have the lovers of their wives prosecuted. Some hoped to save their marriage.[68] They had strong incentives not to break with their wives, who provided material as well as emotional comfort. Those prisoners who did lose contact with their wives were sometimes more worried about food parcels or the state of their property in France than they were about fidelity,[69] and those who asked police to investigate the conduct of their wives were mainly concerned about the welfare of their children.[70]

Often the French authorities became intermediaries between prisoners and their wives, fiancées or families. A woman wrote explaining that she had broken off her engagement when she discovered that she had a lung disease (presumably tuberculosis). Now she regretted the breach and wanted the *homme de confiance* to effect a reconciliation.[71] Prisoners were often dependent on other people to give them information about their wives. Policemen and social workers carried out investigations into the conduct of the wives of prisoners on behalf of the Scapini Mission which, in turn, regarded itself as acting on behalf of prisoners. French officials began to intrude into almost all areas of the lives of French prisoners and their families. A woman wrote to the Scapini Mission because her husband said that he no longer wished to return home at the end of the war. She suspected that he was having an affair with a young widow on the farm where he worked. Officials investigated and concluded that the prisoner's reluctance to return sprang from the fact that he had contracted 'an intimate disease' in 1940.[72] Another woman wrote to her husband to say that she had been raped. The French police investigated and concluded that the woman wished to explain away the fact that she was pregnant, though officials stressed that this version of the facts was not to be communicated to the prisoner.[73]

Complicated local and family feuds came to light when the wives of prisoners were investigated. When the prefect of the Loire-Inférieure investigated the wife and mother-in-law of a prisoner, he concluded that rumours about their conduct were ill-founded. They kept a prosperous café, frequented by German soldiers, and it seemed that a letter denouncing them was motivated by jealousy.[74] Some families themselves were divided. A prisoner's father told him that his wife was having an affair with a seventeen-year-old petty criminal: the wife thought that the father wanted to break up the marriage so that his son would return to the family business.[75] A prisoner who asked why his wife had not written recently was reminded that she was illiterate and that his mother-in-law, who wrote letters on behalf of the wife, did not like him.[76]

Official concern about the fidelity of the wives of prisoners of war increased in the second half of 1942 (at the moment, perhaps, when it became obvious that there was no hope of early release for men who remained in German captivity). Scapini wrote of the 'malaise in the camps in the face of the increase, in worrying proportions, of cases of adultery and abandonment of which some women are guilty'.[77] Members of the Scapini Mission who visited camps talked of the need to increase penalties for adultery, though, as has been pointed out, such penalties were rarely applied. Official desire to deter women from adultery often went with flexibility when it came to dealing with real cases. A woman wrote to her prisoner husband that she had been engaged to keep house for a man who had seemed pleasant: 'You can guess the rest.' The prisoner tried to kill himself, but the French authorities urged the *homme de confiance* of the Stalag to do every-thing he could to save the marriage because the woman was 'honest' and had only ceded under pressure.[78]

Official treatment of adultery by prisoners' wives revealed some-thing interesting about attitudes to the prisoners themselves. Some-times the wives were depicted as victims of ruthless seducers who profited from the fact that women were 'less armed for life'.[79] Most strikingly, however, prisoners themselves were increasingly depicted as vulnerable men who needed to be protected, rather than as stern exponents of male authority. The authorities specifically suggested that prisoners' marriages should be saved 'sometimes, even often, against the prisoner's own will'.[80] Indeed, prisoners were rarely told the full truth about their families. Official reports on the conduct of prisoners' wives often asked that *hommes de confiance* should be careful what they told prisoners.[81] A report on a prisoner's wife who had been arrested for complicity in abortion, and who had admitted to having had an abortion herself in December 1941, suggested that the Scapini Mission should judge for itself the usefulness of telling the prisoner 'all or part of this information'.[82] When officials forwarded a police report on an unfaithful wife who had left her child to live with its grandmother in poor circumstances, they suggested that the *homme de confiance* should 'tone down the rather realistic terms' of the report.[83] In August 1942 the mayor of Le Mans wrote that he often got letters from prisoners of war and that enquiries revealed 'women of easy morals who had ceased to write to their husbands'. However, the mayor usually just told prisoners that their wives had changed address: 'I do not feel that I can allow myself to take from our unfortunate colleagues who are kept in Stalags the last illusions that they are able to maintain.'[84]

Some prisoners' wives volunteered to work in Germany as a means of staying in touch with their husbands. This was harder than it sounded. Fernande Dailly's husband was imprisoned in Stalag IB. Against the advice of the German authorities in Paris, she volunteered to work in Germany and extracted a written guarantee that she would be allowed to live with her husband. However, 'Stalag IB' was a term that concealed as much as it revealed. The work Kommandos associated with the camp were spread over a wide area. Dailly only found her husband after a month of searching, a sixty-kilometre bicycle ride, and some help from her German employer.[85]

The wives of prisoners of war who went to Germany posed interesting questions for French official morality. In theory, the French authorities sought to encourage people of both sexes to volunteer to work in Germany. In practice, most Vichy agencies went to great lengths to prevent 'respectable' women from going to Germany, and often portrayed those women who did go as prostitutes. There was also a tension in attitudes to wives of prisoners. In public, the state celebrated their faithfulness and patience. On the other hand, Pétainists often believed that many wives of prisoners had abandoned their husbands and fallen into a debauched life.

Sometimes the authorities could establish a clear division between the chaste loyal woman who went to Germany in search of her husband and the promiscuous woman who abandoned her prisoner husband. An extreme example of the latter case was found in Chartres. A woman returned to France in 1945, after having volunteered to work in Germany. Her husband was a prisoner but she had gone to Germany with her lover and without, apparently, any intention of finding her husband. She admitted that she had abandoned her prisoner husband, handed over to her lover a postal order that he sent her, and worked as a prostitute, having numerous relations with Germans, before following her French lover when he volunteered to work in Germany.[86] An extreme example of the chaste loyal woman was found in Paris when the secretariat of Stalag IIIB (a body representing the prisoners) sprang to the defence of a woman who had volunteered in March 1943 in order to be with her brother and fiancé.[87]

Many prisoners' wives, however, were hard to fit into neat moral categories. One woman conceived her third child after her husband's capture, but then sent him the birth certificate so that he could request repatriation as the 'father' of a large family; the Vichy authorities urged him to forgive her and suggested that she had experienced a moment of 'weakness' due to extreme poverty in the winter of 1940.[88]

Another prisoner found that his wife was committing an unusual form of 'adultery': sending food parcels to her lover, who was himself in a Stalag.[89] Women who had affairs with German soldiers subsequently volunteered to work in Germany in order to be with their husbands. A Breton woman went to Germany and joined her husband when she was pregnant with another man's child.[90]

Much was written, both during the war and after it, about the sexual activity of wives of prisoners of war, but very little about that of the prisoners themselves.[91] Prisoners, especially those who worked on farms, often lived in intimate circumstances with German women. Many prisoners recalled being told that sexual relations with German women were forbidden.[92] Most legal proceedings against French prisoners (nine-tenths of those in Stalag XVIIA)[93] related to sexual offences. In Stalag IA in a single month, twenty-two of twenty-six legal cases brought against French prisoners involved relations with German women.[94] Not surprisingly, given that sexual encounters often took place in woods or fields, offences were more common in the summer months than in the winter.

French prisoners tried in German military courts were advised by legal officials in their own camps and, usually, defended by German lawyers who seem to have taken their duties seriously. Sometimes cases hinged on distinctions that seem, in retrospect, farcical. Lawyers insisted that 'attouchements réciproques des parties génitales' should not be punished as severely as penetration;[95] they argued (sometimes with success) that transformed prisoners of war had been forbidden to have relations with 'femmes' but not with 'filles' and that they should not therefore be punished for affairs with unmarried girls.[96] Prisoners sometimes defended themselves by saying that they had believed their lovers to be Czech or Hungarian, though conversely a prisoner who had an affair with a Danish woman was punished because he had believed her to be German.[97]

Consensual sex was sometimes punished more severely than violence against women[98] or even attempted rape. Generally, a prisoner convicted of sex with a German woman was sentenced to three years in a civilian prison. Those who slept with women whose husbands were soldiers were punished more severely: they got slightly longer sentences and were often subject to more severe prison regimes.

German women involved in affairs with Frenchmen were tried in civilian courts and usually imprisoned. Often suggestions that the women were of 'loose morality' were advanced as mitigating circumstances by the defence lawyers of French prisoners.[99] Sometimes, French moral denunciations seem to have gone with Nazi categorizations of some women as 'degenerate'. Two Frenchmen from Stalag VIA argued that their former sexual partner was known to be a 'femme lubrique'; it emerged at the trial that she was seen as mentally ill and that her thirteen-year-old daughter had already been confined to an asylum.[100]

The evidence against prisoners often consisted of a confession by their lovers. Sometimes such confessions sprang from desire for revenge after the breakup of an affair, but sometimes women retracted confessions they had made in their own trials when they were produced as witnesses against Frenchmen.[101] One assumes that the German police found it easier to extract confessions from German women, often marginalized figures in their own community, than from French prisoners of war, adult men protected by the Geneva Convention.

'Forbidden' relations with German women did not, however, just mean sex. Prisoners were punished for 'relations amicales'. Men were sentenced for offences that involved kissing, exchanging gifts or going for walks with German women: one got four months for 'having exchanged *tendresses* with a girl'.[102] An officer was sentenced to two years for having drunk tea with two German women.[103] Another prisoner fell in love with a married woman, whom he met whilst taking a course in German literature. He gave her child chocolate and biscuits. He asked her for a photograph of her child and also stole a photograph of the woman herself. He wrote several letters to her but tore them up. Finally, he sent her a letter in which he declared his true feelings. For this offence, he was sentenced to a year in a civilian prison. The fact that he had referred to her as 'dearest' Ursula was held against him.[104]

Prosecutions of French prisoners of war give odd little glimpses of their relations with the German population. A prisoner returning from a fishing expedition met a German woman and exchanged one of his fish for some fruit. He also embraced her. At his trial, he insisted that the embrace was just a 'joke'. He was sentenced to five months for the embrace and six weeks for illegal fishing.[105] Another prisoner had spent the night in a German woman's house. The court seemed to accept that he had slept on the sofa, that he had helped the woman with various chores and that the prisoner was a friend of the woman's husband. In spite of all this, he was sentenced to six months.[106] A German woman invited two French prisoners into her house for coffee and cakes. When a patrol knocked on her door, the prisoners hid under her bed. They were found and both sentenced to six months; the woman was sentenced to four months.[107]

French prisoners were frightened of the reprisals that might follow an affair with a German. Joseph Raoux, who had had a brief fling with his employer's wife, faked conjunctivitis, even though he knew that this would mean transfer from a farm to the less congenial atmosphere of a factory.[108] René Dufour's friend Camille, who feared 'that I will be caught with my boss's wife', was one of a number of prisoners who tried to escape in order to get away from the consequences of an affair with a German woman.[109]

In spite of all this, numerous prisoners allude to the fact that Frenchmen did sleep with German women.[110] Indeed, the existence of such relations seems to have been taken almost for granted. Maurice Duverne wrote: 'On small farms (the husband often drafted), the prisoner of war was not badly off with regard to work, food, etc. Hum, I will say no more.'[111] When Duverne subsequently moved to an office job, one of his French colleagues had an affair with a German girl, who wore black when he was killed in an accident. Jean Brustier recalls teaching German to a peasant from the Aveyron who wished to be able to talk to his lover.[112]

Even back in France, people knew that prisoners of war were sleeping with German women. One prisoner wrote to his wife: 'I do not stint myself, if you want a photo I can even send you one. Yes, I have everything I need with a daughter of two, I will say no more.' The woman wrote to the French authorities seeking to establish whether her husband really did have a daughter in Germany – and the French authorities warned him to be more discreet if he did not want his wife to report him to his camp commandant.[113]

Some Frenchwomen asked to have their husbands moved to different work Kommandos in order to break up affairs.[114] One of the few direct references to the war in the novels of Georges Simenon concerns a prisoner who has fathered two children whilst in Germany.[115] A few prisoners seem to have seen the seduction of German women (or at least talking about the seduction of German women) as a means of continuing the war against German men.[116] One prisoner called his employer a whore and claimed to have slept with her. She first admitted the affair and then insisted that she had rebuffed his advances. At his trial, the prisoner admitted that he had been drunk and had recently received an anonymous letter alleging that his wife was frequenting German soldiers in Paris.[117] More commonly, prisoners recalled German women with amusement, mild embarrassment or wistful nostalgia. What is notably absent from any prisoner account is any sense that sex with German women might be seen as unpatriotic. No Frenchman had his head shaved for sleeping with a German woman.

Some sexual encounters between French prisoners and German women involved brief tussles in cowsheds or haystacks. Some relations, however, lasted a long time and involved real emotional commitment (a fact that German courts regarded as making the offences more serious). One girl of twenty-three hid an escaped prisoner in her bedroom for fifty-one weeks without even her own father knowing about his presence.[118] Those who slept together were usually working together and, in the case of agricultural Kommandos, often living together. Prisoners were sometimes in the same place and with the same woman for years. Sleeping together was often part of a wider relationship in which prisoners replaced absent or dead husbands.

Some relationships seem to have been tolerated by the local communities, if not by German officialdom. Henry Charbonneau suggested that the whole village knew that his fellow prisoner Edgard had seduced the two eldest daughters of the household in which he worked, but that these liaisons were tolerated because of Edgard's charms, and because the girls were known to have had many previous adventures. An 'almost conjugal' relationship between another prisoner and the wife of a soldier who was stationed in France was also tolerated because the absent soldier was known to be lazy while the prisoner was a good worker who had restored prosperity to the farm.[119] A prisoner who was repatriated to France in October 1942 from Stalag VIIA said that he had been in a Kommando making horseshoes, where it was accepted that 'chacun a sa chacune' and that his employers recognized this as the price of maintaining morale and work rates.[120]

Some French civilian workers also had affairs with German and Austrian women. The pattern of relations involving civilian workers seems, however, to have been rather different from those that involved prisoners of war.[121] Civilians were usually in factories rather than on farms and they usually lived in camps rather than lodging with their employers. The long-term affairs that developed between prisoners and German peasant women seem to have been rarer amongst civilian workers. Brief sexual encounters were more common.[122]

When civilian workers had long-term relations with German women, those relations were often not sexual at all. Young *requis* sometimes developed mother–son relations with middle-aged German women, particularly with women whose sons were absent or dead. One *requis* published an account of his relations with a German woman under the title *Tu es encore et davantage mon fils*.[123]

Not all the women with whom Frenchmen came into contact in Germany were German. German factories contained many workers from east European countries (Ostarbeiters), especially Russians and Ukrainians. The would-be moral guardians of French labour deportees were concerned by the presence of such women, whom they believed to be particularly prone to promiscuity. When the prefect of the Eure established a committee to discuss Service du Travail Obligatoire, a senior clergyman produced a dossier containing letters from Christian labour deportees and claimed: 'Our young men are obliged to sleep and live in mixed barracks along with Polish and Czech women of ill repute, whose presence is imposed by the Germans. These women have venereal diseases that our young Frenchmen catch.'[124]

Sometimes the hostility of the French authorities to workers from eastern Europe in Germany could have heartbreaking consequences. Louis M. began an affair with a Ukrainian girl whilst he was still a prisoner of war. When he changed his status to that of 'civilian worker', he assumed that he and his lover would be able to conduct their relationship more openly. He himself was not molested, but she was beaten and threatened with prison. At this point, M. suggested that the two might marry. The French authorities first tried to dissuade M. and then said that since the woman had no papers – it was hardly likely that a girl snatched from the Ukraine would have papers – the couple would have to wait until after the war.[125]

If the authorities were hostile to women from eastern Europe, French workers seem to have been almost universally favourable to them. The single most famous account of life as a *requis*, François Cavanna's *Les Russkoffs* (1979), is dedicated to Maria Iossifovna Tatartchenko, 'wherever she may be', and to twenty-four other Russian girls and twenty-one Frenchmen. Whilst Catholic and Pétainist leaders saw east European women almost entirely in terms of physical pleasure or danger, the *requis* themselves were keen to stress that their relations with such women had often not been sexual at all.[126] Jean-Pierre Ganter had a chaste friendship with Nadia, a Russian interpreter. Later he had an affair with Zina of Rostov. He wrote: 'I was never guided by desire, as everyone might suppose.' His parting from Zina was, he claimed, the most painful memory of his time in Germany, even more painful than that of the amputation of his leg after a bombing raid.[127]

Russian and Ukrainian women impressed Frenchmen by their strength, courage and independence. Cavanna recalled the Russian girls in his factory telling him how to work slowly without letting the German supervisors realize what he was doing and how they organized a strike under the slogan 'nicht essen, nicht arbeiten'. Pierre Thomas wrote: 'What a lesson in courage these Ukrainian women gave us.'[128] East European women were compared favourably with Frenchwomen, especially those Frenchwomen who had volunteered to work in Germany. Cavanna made much of the alleged contrast between idealistic 'Russkoffs' and the sluttish French. He wrote that Russian women particularly hated the 'poufiasses faschistes' in the Frenchwomen's camp. He himself told his Russian lover that French-women in Germany were 'all volunteers' and that they 'already had the revolting qualities of the old alcoholic tart who gives blowjobs to tramps for a glass of red wine in the Rue Quincampoix'. Talking to a prisoner of war, he agreed that both his own Russian lover and the prisoner's German one were better than 'those French girls . . . come to be a whore with the boches'.[129]

Evidence about relations between Frenchmen and east European women comes mainly from retrospective accounts composed decades after the events. It seems reasonable to assume that such accounts, sometimes written by men in their sixties or seventies recalling girls that they had known in their early twenties and whom they had not seen for forty years, are not simple records of fact. The existence of the Iron Curtain may have conferred a romantic distance on the whole of eastern Europe.

Not all evidence about relations between Frenchmen and Ostarbeiters comes from retrospective accounts, however. A few Frenchmen managed to bring women back to France in 1945. Authorities in the Landes investigated at least thirty-eight cases of young Frenchmen who had returned from Germany with foreign women.

Of women investigated in the Landes, twenty were Poles, eleven were Russians and three were Czechs. There was also one Austrian, one Belgian, one Dutch and one Turkish woman. All of them had, apparently, met their French lovers at their workplaces. One couple had been married in Germany under the aegis of French repatriation officials. Four couples already had children (always given French names) and eleven women were pregnant.

Peasants in one of the most backward parts of France seem to have been unexpectedly receptive to these alien women in their midst. Sometimes the women concerned spoke French: one Polish woman had actually been born in France when her father worked as an immigrant coal miner. On other occasions, Frenchmen learnt the language of their lovers. A prisoner of war, born in 1915, who had worked on a farm before his mobilization (presumably a man who would not have spoken very correct French), had learnt enough Russian to act as an interpreter for his lover during her interrogation by the French authorities.[130] His relatives had, apparently, accepted the arrival of a woman born in Kharkov who did not speak their language: 'The marriage raises no difficulty in the D. family which had spontaneously accepted this situation.'[131] A Polish woman who returned, pregnant, with her French lover was well received by her new family, 'où l'entente règne'.[132] A young man who had returned from Service du Travail Obligatoire with a Polish woman and their child was soon destined to inherit his employer's blacksmith's shop.[133] Even the one marriage that had been badly received by the family of the man involved was 'not considered badly by the population [of the village]'.[134]

Not all the love stories investigated by the authorities in post-war France had happy endings, however. Gaston C., a former prisoner, returned to Paris in 1946 and claimed to have been detained against his will in Poland. Police investigations revealed that he had in fact contracted a bigamous marriage in Poland in April 1945, presumably after being liberated by the Red Army, and that a child had been born to his new wife in January 1946.[135] Soviet citizens who had managed to escape from Germany came under the aegis of a commission containing both Soviet and French officers. Ten women from the Landes were investigated. Nine were allowed to stay, but one, who was not married to a Frenchman, not pregnant by one and not the mother of a French child, was sent back.[136]

LIVING IN NAZI GERMANY

What was it like for Frenchmen to live in Nazi Germany, particularly during the last two years of the regime as it became more radical, more violent and more conscious of its impending destruction? French prisoners of war were, in some respects, protected from Nazism because their captors more or less observed the Geneva Convention. Furthermore, most prisoners were either in camps, in which case they lived primarily amongst their own compatriots, or on farms, in which case they had dealings with a relatively small group of Germans whom they had come to know well over a long period. In some respects, a prisoner of war was less vulnerable to arbitrary violence by the Germans than a civilian in France itself.

French Jewish prisoners of war were in a particularly odd situation. The luckiest were those who were able to hide their racial origins entirely. Georges Musnik was a Parisian barrister, a man who would not have been marked out by accent or manner in the way that, say, a recent immigrant from Poland might have been. He was never identified as a Jew when in Stalag IIID and IIIA, and was even able to help his mother by writing her a letter in which he alluded to the work that he was doing with Germans; she was able to use this letter to allay suspicions about her own Jewish origins.[137] When he worked outside the camp, Musnik endured the curious sensation of being a Jew at the heart of the Third Reich who sometimes watched the persecution of other Jews but who never suffered from his own racial origins.

Jews whose families in France had not managed to hide their racial origins were in a horrifying situation. Though the Vichy authorities tried to protect adult men in prisoner of war camps, they could, or would, do nothing to help the women and children they had left behind. A Jewish lieutenant in Oflag XVIIA tried to find out what had happened to his wife and brother who had been deported by the Germans. Enquiries revealed that the prisoner's family had been arrested in Grenoble on 15 February 1944, sent to the Drancy holding camp and then, on 5 March, sent on to an unknown destination.[138] The Paris police archives contain a letter from a Jewish prisoner of war enquiring about the circumstances of his family. The police responded with the punctilious courtesy that they usually accorded to prisoners of war: the man's wife and daughter had been deported; his father had been spared immediate deportation so that he could work as a labourer for a German agency.[139] One assumes that the recipient of this letter would have been one of the many Jewish prisoners of war who returned to France in 1945 to find that their entire family had been wiped out.

Jewish prisoners of war themselves did not escape all persecution. They were harassed in many petty ways. They rarely benefited from repatriation under the *relève* scheme,[140] and it was not, in any case, clear that it was in the interests of Jewish prisoners to return to France and to civilian status.[141] Whether or not Jewish prisoners suffered in other ways depended on the attitude of the German and French authorities in their own camps. In Stalag IA, thirteen Jewish *aspirants* were separated from their gentile comrades and sent to a work Kommando (*aspirants* were not supposed to be made to work). The Pétainist French commander of the camp did little to prevent this improper treatment, but the German authorities in the camp seem to have been relatively lenient in their treatment of the prisoners. In April 1944 a new wave of anti-Semitism swept through the camps which led to physical examination of the *aspirants* and the separation of another three prisoners from their comrades. One of these men escaped and another managed to blend back into the rest of the prisoners after a period in a work Kommando.[142]

The Germans continually looked for Jews amongst French prisoners, and it was unwise for anyone who wished to hide his origins to draw attention to himself. In 1944 a Frenchman from Stalag IX was prosecuted for a 'flirtation' with a German woman. The French authorities asked for clemency in view of the fact that he had been a good soldier and that he had helped to put out a fire in Germany. The Germans, however, became suspicious of his origins (in Russia), his profession (a furrier), his appearance and manner. They also discovered that he was circumcised. In spite of his protests, the prisoner was classified as a Jew and sentenced to one year in a civilian prison.[143]

A characteristic example of the casual brutality with which Jews were treated in the camps was seen in Stalag XVIIB in 1941, when typhus swept through newly arrived Russian prisoners who were housed in a separate camp. The Germans responded by drafting four French Jewish doctors (men who had not previously been used by the camp hospital) to provide medical care. The Jewish doctors were not allowed the same degree of protection as German medical staff and, when one of them, Dr Rosenburg, contracted typhus and died, the Germans refused the military honours that were usually provided at the funerals of prisoners of war.[144]

Civilian workers had more direct contact with Nazism than prisoners of war. They were not protected by the Geneva Convention. They mixed more with the German civilian population, and particularly with the civilian population of large towns. Most of them worked in factories rather than farms, and consequently had more experience of Nazi labour discipline. Most civilian workers went to Germany relatively late in the war, at a stage when Nazi repression was at its height. Civilian workers were almost universally hostile to Nazism: an anonymous report (apparently written by French collaborationists) suggested that 45 per cent of Frenchmen in Germany were 'Communists, Socialists or sympathizers', that 35 per cent were 'Anglo-Americans or Gaullists' and that 15 per cent were 'attentistes'.[145] However, *requis* were sometimes less hostile to Germans as a whole than were French people who had stayed in France. *Requis* talked, ate, worked and, in some cases, slept with Germans. Whilst most French people in France saw only 'boche' troops, the French in Germany saw a wide variety of German civilians including women, old men and children. Most of those who worked alongside the *requis* were too old for military service. Such men, especially in Vienna, often had memories of the pre-war labour movement. Sometimes anti-Nazi Germans seem to have been more willing to talk freely with foreigners than they would have been with their own compatriots.

However nuanced their view of Germans as a whole, *requis* knew of Nazi brutality. Labour discipline in German factories could be horrific. In the summer of 1943 Frenchmen who had slept outside in order to escape from the lice that infected their dormitory were kicked awake by the factory police.[146] Men who worked slowly were sometimes beaten and those suspected of sabotage risked being sent to concentration camps. One French worker recalled seeing the body of a concentration camp prisoner, who had been shot for rebellion, hung over the factory wall.[147]

Many labour deportees had some contact with groups whose conditions were even harsher than their own, though not, on the whole, with Jews. French civilians often worked with people from eastern Europe in German factories. Many Frenchmen had some understanding of the racial hierarchy that operated in Nazi Germany, a hierarchy in which the French stood relatively high, and in which Russians, Ukrainians and Poles stood low. Air raid shelters were open to Germans and French but closed to Ostarbeiters. French workers were allowed to come up from a mine at the end of a working day while Russians were kept underground overnight.

French people in Germany provided an extreme example of something that was true for the French more generally during the occupation. They were isolated. They had no access to uncensored newspapers and what they heard of Allied radio broadcasts often came at second or third hand from people who had not always fully understood what was being said: Cavanna heard the rumour in 1944 that Paris had been burned down and that all the relatives of men doing compulsory labour service in Germany had been shot by the Communists. Each worker saw only the limited area around his or her own place of work. The result of all this was that many of them saw individual instances of Nazi brutality, but were not necessarily able to fit such instances into an overall picture.

French perceptions of Nazism were made even more complicated by the intervention of Vichy agencies and the Catholic Church. Some Vichy officials and most Churchmen were hostile to Nazism. Some officials of Vichy agencies, particularly the Scapini Mission to prisoners of war and the Chantiers de la Jeunesse, were members of the Front Intérieur resistance network that collected information to be passed back to the Allies. Around a third of people who worked for the Commissariat for French workers were arrested at one time or another.[148] Defining all conflict between French officials in Germany and German authorities as 'resistance' is, however, difficult. Sometimes, the Germans seem to have mistaken French patriotism, which often tied in with Pétainism, for anti-Nazism. Sometimes different French agencies were in conflict with each other and enlisted German bodies, themselves often divided by administrative conflicts, as supporters. Bruneton opposed Déat's collaborationist Rassemblement National Populaire, but he did so with the support of Darnand's equally collaborationist Milice. Bruneton's own position varied over time: sometimes he talked of the need to abstain from taking political positions; at other times he seemed to express the desire for German victory (at least on the Eastern Front). The London-based Gaullists recognized some virtue in Bruneton's actions whilst also regarding him as sufficiently dangerous to be considered as a target for assassination.

Even opponents of Nazism did not necessarily understand its nature. Churchmen, who risked their lives to bring spiritual comfort to French workers in Germany in defiance of Nazi edicts, also spoke about east Europeans in terms that seem disconcertingly similar to those used by Nazis. The attitudes of many Catholics and Pétainists in Germany were governed by traditional conservative assumptions about the need for 'discipline', 'hygiene' and 'morality'. Young Frenchmen were encouraged to be Boy Scouts in the land of the SS.

The clash between official French perceptions and Nazi realities was particularly striking in one place. The Camp Napoléon was a model of everything that the French authorities admired. A young man from the Chantiers de la Jeunesse, Georges Toupet, volunteered to work in Germany in order to accompany his charges. He found a camp dominated by louche and criminal volunteer workers and by corrupt German officials. He imposed discipline on the volunteers and arranged for corrupt Germans to be excluded from the camp. Young men under Toupet sang songs, saluted the colours and played games. Toupet stood for everything that Vichy admired (though he was, in fact, a Gaullist agent).[149] French officials in other parts of Germany regarded him as a model to be imitated. Frenchmen in the model camp, however, were disconcerted by the fact that they could sometimes smell burning flesh. The Camp Napoléon was in the Auschwitz-Birkenau complex.[150]

IO

Sunset of Blood

The Liberation

A sunset of blood came down. Ragged women rubbed shoulders with the bourgeoisie. Armed men went through the crowd. Everything was chaotic. It was like the end of the world.   (André Héléna on the liberation of Perpignan)[1]

What was France really like? . . . The average British soldier had been taught to believe that the French had 'let us down' in 1940 . . . The French were a weak and venal people . . . To the average American, France was simply another untidy, foreign country . . . He compared France to his own sane and much-desired world, where there was ice cream and decent plumbing.   (Alan Moorehead, British journalist accompanying Allied armies on D-Day)[2]

This refusal [to accept German victory] allowed us to look at a Russian, British or American soldier without blushing . . . Never have so many men consciously run so many risks for such a small thing; a desire to bear witness. Perhaps it is absurd, but it was by such absurdities that we restored our dignity as men.   (Roger Stéphane, French Resistance activist writing in 1952)[3]

From 19 August, it was the apocalypse. Seven of us had taken refuge in a room of three metres by five. We could not get out for three days. We had nothing to eat, just a pitcher of water to drink. The noise was incessant. At a certain point, we were no longer afraid.

We had gone into a sort of coma . . . During the night of 21 and 22 August, the noise stopped for five or ten minutes. We came out then, dirty and haggard. We could not believe that we were safe. The German who had

10. (overleaf) *Hair in a courtyard in Chartres after women have been punished for 'collaboration'.*

hidden with us started to cry. Outside, it was butchery. Thousands of German soldiers and horses swelled up and rotted. And then I saw a dead man who held in his hand the photo of his three children. The oldest must have been my age, fourteen.   (Jean-Pierre Philippe from the Orne, recalling his experiences sixty years after the event)[4]

I have to put up with the savage occupation of 300 Americans. The house is ransacked . . . everything is being stolen, there is no discipline whatever . . . during all this war never have I had a billeting that caused so much damage. (Intercepted letter from a Frenchman, 10 November 1944)[5]

 – Nous, libérer France.
 – Vous ne pouvez pas aller faire ça ailleurs.   (Exchange between a GI and a Norman peasant, reported by Franz-Olivier Giesbert, the son of an American soldier and a Frenchwoman)[6]

It has become a commonplace for historians to suggest that France underwent not one liberation but many different liberations. Liberation was spread out in time. The Americans invaded French North Africa in November 1942; the last parts of mainland France to be liberated were those 'pockets' where German soldiers did not surrender until 8 May 1945. Some French people in Germany who were liberated (or captured) by the Red Army did not get back to France until months, sometimes years, after the end of the war. Liberation varied with place; there was a world of difference between being in Saint-Lô, bombed flat by the Americans, and being in one of the south-western towns that was liberated by the Maquis. There could be big variations in small areas. In Paris in August 1944, Jean Guéhenno saw people gossiping on their doorsteps fifty metres away from a German tank that had just killed a Resistance fighter. German forces in La Rochelle surrendered after a deal with Free French forces. At the same time, a little way along the Atlantic coast, the town of Royan was the scene of a bitter battle, fought partly because de Gaulle wanted to prove the French army in action.

De Gaulle sometimes studiously ignored the presence of hundreds of thousands of Anglo-American troops in his country. In his first speech in Paris, on 25 August 1944, he remarked that Paris had

'liberated itself with the help of France'. The French never believed
this. Indeed, the Gaullist myth of a nation that had liberated itself
derived its power precisely from the fact that everyone knew it to be
untrue; if it had liberated itself, France would not have needed the
prestige of a general who had spent most of the war in London.

The liberation brought all sorts of meetings between different
groups that had previously been separated by the occupation. The
different Resistance groups inside France came into the open. Perhaps
more importantly, the leaders of each Resistance movement came into
sustained contact, for the first time, with rank and file members of
their own organization. French people saw Charles de Gaulle for the
first time. Many of them had heard his voice on the BBC but few had
much idea what he looked like. Parisians were surprised that he was
so tall (caricatures in collaborationist papers had portrayed him as a
short fat man).[7]

Young men and women met each other again during the liberation.
Dances, which had been forbidden under Vichy, were legalized for a
few months during the summer of 1944. Young men who had taken
to the hills in the spring came down into villages and towns. Men
who had avoided public places, for fear of being picked up by the
German sweeps for forced labour, showed themselves again. The
sense that 'normal' relations between men and women were being
restored may have had something to do with the fact that women
whose relations with men were seen as 'abnormal' were so often
punished during the liberation. Almost two million French men did
not join the happy reunions of 1944, however, because they were in
Germany.

TIME AND PLACE

The liberation of French territory began with Operation Torch, the
American invasion of North Africa, in November 1942. The Americans, who wanted to open a single second front with a big push
into occupied Europe, had initially been reluctant to launch such an
operation but were persuaded by the British. The assault was planned
in consultation with a number of Frenchmen in Algeria, mostly

supporters of the monarchist Action Française. The American government had poor relations with de Gaulle and did not wish to install him in power in Algeria. Instead, as we saw in Chapter 6, they made contact with Henri Giraud, a conservative French general who had escaped from a German prisoner of war camp.

The significance of American landings in North Africa, and particularly in Algeria, was complicated. Parts of the French Empire had rallied to de Gaulle or been conquered by Free French forces ever since 1940. However, these were mostly distant places with small French populations. Algeria was close to the mainland. It contained more than a million French citizens, including a large number of soldiers. Furthermore, Algeria was not a colony, unlike Indochina, nor a League of Nations mandate, unlike Syria where Free French and Vichy forces had fought in 1941, nor a protectorate, unlike Morocco. Algeria was part of France. It returned deputies to the French parliament, and its European population had resented Vichy moves that seemed to blur the distinction between it and the colonies or protectorates.

Operation Torch was, however, a funny kind of liberation. Landings in North Africa did not involve even the token Free French force that went to Normandy with the Allies in 1944. Furthermore, there were no Germans in French North Africa in 1942 and resistance to the American landings came from French forces loyal to the Vichy government. France was being liberated from the French.

Giraud, the Americans' candidate for the leadership of the French in 'liberated' Algeria, missed his rendezvous with an American submarine that was meant to pick him up from southern France, and was still on Gibraltar when the Americans landed in North Africa. If Giraud was unexpectedly absent, another conservative French military leader was unexpectedly present. Admiral Darlan was in Algiers visiting his son, who was seriously ill with polio. Darlan had no advance knowledge of the landings. Even as American warships approached North Africa, he insisted that the Americans would not break their promise not to enter French North Africa uninvited. When American troops landed, Darlan ordered the French to resist – 1,368 Frenchmen and 453 Allied soldiers died in the few days before Darlan changed his mind. Eventually, however, a ceasefire was arranged and the Americans suggested that Darlan himself might lead the French in Algeria. This was an attractive suggestion to an ambitious man who had recently been squeezed out of power in Vichy by Laval's return, and Darlan signed an accord with Clark, the commander of American forces in North Africa. The British were unhappy with Darlan's rule in Algeria as were American liberals: the journalist Ed Murrow suggested that letting Darlan rule Algeria was like letting Quisling rule a 'liberated' Norway.

Pétain was furious at the Clark–Darlan accords and denounced them six times in the week after they were concluded. Darlan did not denounce Pétain. On the contrary, he argued that he was acting in the Marshal's name and carrying out the policy that the Marshal was unable to announce openly. Darlan's suggestion that Pétain was not a free agent was made more convincing by the fact that the Germans invaded the free zone of France in response to the American invasion of Algeria.

Darlan's reign in Algeria ended on Christmas Eve 1942 when he was shot by a young royalist. The assassin was himself executed on Boxing Day, giving conspiracy theorists much food for thought. Now the Americans installed their original candidate, Giraud, in power in Algeria. Unlike Darlan, Giraud had never held office under the Vichy government and, unlike Darlan, he had always been anti-German. However, he had also expressed loyalty to Pétain and shared many of Pétain's beliefs. Giraud presented himself as a military figure who did not wish to play politics, a classic conservative stance that meant, in practice, that he would not overthrow much of what Vichy had established in Algeria. He had particularly strong views about one piece of Vichy legislation. He had spent his early life serving with North African units of the French army and had developed a deep admiration for Islam. This made him keen not to restore the Crémieux decree, which had given French citizenship to Jews in Algeria and which had been abolished by Vichy. Giraud believed that the Crémieux decree antagonized Muslims in Algeria, and, in fact, Jews in Algeria did not regain French citizenship until May 1943, six months after the Americans arrived.[8]

Charles de Gaulle played no part in the American invasion of North Africa and was still in London when Giraud was installed in office in Algeria. However, in both Britain and America, public opinion remained favourable to de Gaulle. The Americans pressed for some agreement amongst the potential leaders of the anti-German French forces. De Gaulle was brought to North Africa to attend the Casablanca conference in January 1943. Roosevelt described getting him to meet Giraud in terms that said much about his disdainful views of the Free French in general: 'General Giraud . . . cooperated very nicely on the proposed nuptials and was prepared to go through with it on our terms, I am sure. Our friends, however, could not produce De Gaulle, the temperamental bride. She has become quite high hat about the whole affair and doesn't wish to see either of us, and shows no intention of getting into bed with Giraud.'[9] When de Gaulle was presented to Roosevelt himself, their interview proved relatively amicable: de Gaulle was doubtless impressed to discover that Roosevelt was able to conduct a conversation in French. Roosevelt's adviser Harry Hopkins later reported, however, that the Americans were so nervous about the encounter that they placed secret servicemen with machine guns behind a curtain in case de Gaulle should attack the President of the United States.[10]

At the end of May 1943, de Gaulle returned to Algeria, and in June he and Giraud agreed to share the presidency of a Committee for National Liberation. Gradually, de Gaulle eased Giraud out of power. He was helped by the support of politicians from mainland France, who began to arrive in Algeria, and by the naivety of Giraud himself. In November 1943 Giraud was made military head of the Free French, an empty position since the most important military decisions were being taken by the British and the Americans, while de Gaulle assumed the political leadership. In April 1944 Giraud was excluded from the military leadership.

By the middle of 1943, for the first time, anti-Vichy forces controlled a large swathe of territory close to mainland France. For the first time, too, they had large numbers of troops: at the beginning of 1942 de Gaulle had had about 50,000 soldiers under his orders; two years later he had 550,000 (over half of whom came from the colonies).

De Gaulle's public image moved to the left, partly because working with left-wingers from mainland France helped him to outflank

Giraud. He established a Constituent Assembly in Algiers that contained many Third Republic parliamentarians. He restored republican institutions to Algeria. The Brazzaville conference in early 1944 brought together colonial governors and delegates to the Constituent Assembly. It laid down plans for reform of the French Empire (wrongly interpreted by some as plans for decolonization). Some people were tried for having supported Vichy. The most important of these figures was Pierre Pucheu. Pucheu had been Vichy's Minister of Industrial Production and then of the Interior. He had maintained contact with the Resistance, secretly meeting Henri Frenay in February 1942, but he had also been responsible for repression and particularly for the arrest of Communists, some of whom were subsequently shot by the Germans in reprisal for Resistance attacks. In 1943, Pucheu left France and made his way to North Africa. He was encouraged in this move by Giraud, who guaranteed his safety. However, on arrival in Casablanca in May 1943 he was arrested, tried and, partly as a result of pressure from Communists, sentenced to death. De Gaulle refused to commute the sentence: characteristically he believed that Pucheu had acted in good faith but that *raison d'état* was more important than justice. On 20 March 1944 Pucheu himself gave the command to the firing squad that executed him.

Punishment of Pétainists and collaborators in North Africa had dramatic effects in mainland France. Vichy officials noted, for example, that six leaders of the Chantiers de la Jeunesse in Tunis had been sentenced to death in their absence for encouraging Frenchmen to serve in the German army.[11] Notables, civil servants and businessmen became ever more keen to distance themselves from Vichy and the Germans. François Picard, a manager at Renault who was also a member of a Resistance group, made the following entry in his diary on 24 November 1943: 'René de Peyrecave, the director general, asked ... that a dossier be compiled showing that the factories [of the Renault firm] only worked for the German armies under compulsion and that they never initiated the slightest improvement in equipment. The purge in North Africa is bearing fruit.'[12] In July 1943 an official in the west of France noted: 'The population does not hide the fact that it is waiting for better days to settle accounts.'[13]

The eviction of German forces from Corsica in November 1943

illustrated the complexities of meaning that liberation could have. In one sense, this was a 'pure' liberation because only a relatively small group of American troops landed, and because local Resistance forces were involved in fighting. However, the liberation of Corsica also reflected political conflicts amongst the French. Giraud led Free French forces during this operation, and did not discuss his plans with the Committee of National Liberation until the last moment, though in practice his departure from Algeria served to exclude him from political power, rather than to exclude the politicians in Algeria from military decisions. Furthermore, though Giraud was a conservative, the liberation of Corsica gave a great deal of power to the local Front National resistance movement, which was dominated by the Communist Party. Finally, and most oddly, Corsica had been occupied by the Italians. When Mussolini was deposed, most of the Italians withdrew, leaving a German force of about 40,000 who controlled Bastia and the east of the island. However, some Italians took up arms against the Germans. A total of 245 Italians were killed in the subsequent fighting, as against 76 members of the local Resistance forces and 75 men from Giraud's expeditionary force – a fact that was not much discussed in the violently anti-Italian climate of 1944 and 1945.[14] The German decision to withdraw from Corsica seems, in any case, to have owed more to the general strategic weakness of their position (the fact that Sardinia had fallen to the Allies meant that the Germans risked being encircled) than to the strength of forces confronting them on the island.

The most important military discussions of 1944 excluded the French entirely. The British and Americans planned their landings in northern Europe without consulting de Gaulle, partly because experience had taught them that the Free French were bad at keeping secrets. De Gaulle was only allowed to return to Britain from Algeria shortly before the Normandy landings began. The Allies did not, initially, anticipate any Free French presence in their forces. They planned to send their own political representatives to establish civilian government, as they had in Italy. As D-Day approached, de Gaulle and Churchill had a succession of violent arguments. Finally, it was agreed that the British and Americans would not impose their own civilian government on liberated France, and that de Gaulle would permit a token Free French presence amongst the forces landing in Normandy.

As it turned out, the Free French participation in the D-Day landings was very token indeed. Of the 156,000 Allied soldiers who landed in Normandy on 6 June 1944, 177 were French marines of the Kieffer Commando. Nominally these men were part of the Free French forces, though they had been trained by, and integrated with, the British commandos, and were, in fact, already halfway across the Channel by the time de Gaulle finally authorized their presence amongst the Allied armies. The fate of the Kieffer Commando illustrated the animosities of the liberation. De Gaulle rejected the request of Thierry D'Argenlieu, the Free French admiral, that the members of the Commando be awarded the Order of the Liberation on the grounds that they were a 'British unit'; on the other hand, the post-war French navy (heavily marked by the Pétainism of most of its officers) was reluctant to grant much recognition to the Commando, which it saw as excessively close to de Gaulle.

De Gaulle arrived in Normandy soon after the Allied landings and, in defiance of the agreements he had made with the Allies, began to establish his own civilian representatives. His first encounters with the French population in 1944 were important. He had never been elected to office. He had been brought up amongst right-wing Catholics who regarded much of the French population with disdain. His only contact with ordinary Frenchmen was that of a rather aloof officer with conscript troops. His information about French public opinion came from the speculations of a few Resistance leaders, who were themselves an isolated minority. He had been shaken by newsreel footage of Pétain visiting Paris, and apparently being well received, in April 1944. If the crowds had booed de Gaulle in 1944, he would have been finished. The political capital that he had so painfully built up over the previous four years could have disappeared in a few days. As it turned out, de Gaulle was well received in Bayeux, the first town in mainland France to be liberated. A man who had awkward relations with individual French people discovered that he loved French crowds.

Most inhabitants of newly liberated territory did not, however, see de Gaulle or any other representative of the Free French. Most were passive, and frightened, spectators in a conflict between the Allies and the Germans. Allied troops were initially blocked in a pocket around their landing beaches in Normandy. They did not break out of this until mid-July, and only did so at the cost of hard fighting. The Norman countryside, full of hedgerows and ditches in which defenders could hide, made for a difficult advance. The Germans fought hard. There are almost 80,000 of them in the six German military cemeteries in Normandy, and the bodies of German soldiers were still being found in improvised graves as late as 2003.

The Allied advance became easier as they escaped from Normandy. On 15 August, a second Allied landing, Operation Anvil, was staged in Provence. The Allies now had two bridgeheads and important ports through which they could bring in reinforcements. By the end of August there were two million Allied troops in France. The Germans did not, however, give up. Most of them retreated eastwards towards Germany. They staged a counter-attack that almost retook Strasbourg at the beginning of 1945. Besieged German soldiers in Lorient, La Rochelle and Dunkirk did not surrender until Russian soldiers were in Berlin.

The liberation exposed, or at least coincided with, divisions amongst the Germans as well as the Allies. A group of German officers tried to kill Hitler on 20 July 1944. A number of Germans in France had been involved in the plot. One of these was the German commander, Karl-Heinrich von Stülpnagel. When it seemed that Hitler had been killed, von Stülpnagel ordered the arrest of SS officers and Nazi officials in Paris. When it became clear that the coup had failed, he ordered the release of those who had been arrested, apparently in a bid to spare his associates from reprisals. Stülpnagel had no illusions about his own fate. He was arrested and driven east. On the way, he asked his driver to stop in a village near Verdun, where he had fought in the First World War, and where, he said, he wanted to pay his respects to his fallen comrades. In fact, he tried to shoot himself. However, by now almost paralytically drunk, he did not succeed. He was revived and, blinded by his wound, taken to Berlin, where he was hanged two weeks later. Four years later, his cousin and predecessor as German commander in Paris, Otto von Stülpnagel, killed himself in French custody while awaiting trial for war crimes.

The effects of the bomb plot were also felt lower down the military hierarchy. Jacques-Alain de Sédouy recalled that the German officers billeted in his family's country house in Normandy discussed the plot in animated terms. Their discussions, fuelled by calvados and fear, finished with a shot being fired by the anti-Hitler colonel at the pro-Hitler major.[15]

The Allies softened up their targets in the places they intended to attack with bombing and artillery barrages. Some coastal towns had been all but wiped out as early as 1943. In Rennes, a third of all houses were destroyed. In Saint-Lô, a base for German submarines that was bombed eight times between 6 and 22 June, nine out of every ten houses were destroyed. Whole towns had to be rebuilt after the war: Le Havre's municipal council built a classic example of neo-Stalinist architecture; Saint-Malo's eighteenth-century buildings were so carefully rebuilt that only the most well-informed tourists know how badly the town was damaged in 1944. The experience of cities that were regarded as strategically important in Normandy, Brittany and the north was particularly grim, but, even in rural Normandy, Alain Corbin recalls that no one around him talked of liberation; they simply described the summer of 1944 as being the time of the 'bombardments'.[16]

Other parts of France got off more lightly. After the battles in Normandy in July, the Allied advance became quicker and, generally, less likely to cause civilian casualties. The liberation of Paris was in a category of its own. The city itself, as opposed to its industrial suburbs, had not been bombed much during the war, and de Gaulle's remarks on 25 August about Paris being 'broken and martyred' must have sounded rather hollow to the inhabitants of, say, Caen. However, many people expected that Paris would not survive the liberation. Indeed, night-time walks through the quiet blacked-out streets of the capital acquired a special charm in 1943 because everyone expected it to be destroyed by retreating German forces.[17] Paris was spared only because Dietrich von Choltitz, the commander who had replaced von Stülpnagel, broke explicit orders to blow up the city. The capital was a strange place during the last fortnight of German occupation. The metro stopped running on 15 August, thus reinforcing people's sense of being enclosed in their own particular *quartiers*. The Swedish consul negotiated a truce that spared both sides too many casualties.

Most Germans simply left the city and headed east. Ernst Jünger, in a characteristically self-conscious gesture, left a rose on the dressing table of the room that he occupied in the Hôtel Raphaël before saying goodbye to Paris. Christian de la Mazière, a young French collaborationist, spent a last night with one of his mistresses before driving his sports car amongst the lorries heading for Germany, where he joined a unit of the Waffen SS.[18]

The Allied landings in the south of France were very different from those in Normandy. The invading force was primarily French rather than British and American. French in this context, however, did not mean men from mainland France: more than half of all French troops in the summer of 1944 came from the colonies.[19] In the long term, the use of troops from the French Empire to liberate France produced conflict. Troops were drawn from both the Muslim and European parts of the Algerian population. Members of both groups had often not set foot on the mainland before and both groups now assumed that France owed them particular kinds of debts. The debts to Algeria's European population could only be repaid at the expense of Algeria's Muslims and vice versa. It is no accident that there was savage inter-racial violence in Algeria on 8 May 1945, the day the Second World War ended in Europe.

In the short term, however, the liberation proceeded more easily in the south of France than in the north. One day after the landings in Normandy, American troops were still trying to fight their way off Omaha beach; one day after the landings in Provence, General Patch installed his headquarters at the Hôtel Latitude 43 in Saint-Tropez.[20] Allied commanders were taken aback by their own success in southern France. They had assumed that it would take twenty days to capture Toulon, but they were in the city after barely a week.[21] The Germans put up less of a fight in the south – sometimes they simply melted away, surrendered or tried to cross the Spanish frontier – and the French Resistance was more visible and active there. Some towns, including Marseilles, were taken by the Resistance before the Allied armies arrived.

Even, and perhaps especially, when they were retreating from the Allies, German troops still posed a threat to French civilians. Indeed, in some ways the summer of 1944 was the most dangerous period of the occupation for many French people. For most of the previous four years, the German presence in France had been confined to certain areas. For more than half the occupation they had not penetrated into the southern zone at all. Furthermore, the German presence was heaviest in towns, on the coast and around railways and main roads. Suddenly, after June 1944 German troops were on the move again. Some retreated from Normandy whilst others moved up from the south to reinforce their embattled comrades. Germans were now keen to avoid main roads and railways, which presented easy targets for Allied bombing. The German presence increased in areas where they had been little seen before. In the Auvergne, the German population went from two hundred to more than a thousand; the town of Saint-Flour, which had been home to just a few soldiers, was suddenly the base for a major garrison.[22] German troop movements often disrupted relations that had been established over the previous four years. German soldiers found themselves in areas they did not know and where they had no contacts. Local commanders who believed themselves to have established a modus vivendi with the French population in a particular area were furious when the brutality of newly arrived troops destroyed such relations.

In Haute-Vienne, troops from SS Panzer Das Reich division, many of whom had spent the last three years on the Eastern Front, were heading north to join their comrades in Normandy. On 8 June they entered Tulle, which had recently been declared to be liberated by a group of *maquisards*, and hanged ninety-seven men. On 10 June a battalion of the division arrived at the village of Oradour-sur-Glane, a small market centre. Oradour had, until this stage, had a relatively benign experience of war and occupation. Food was plentiful and some inhabitants claimed that they had not seen a German uniform until the summer of 1944. There does not seem to have been much of the Resistance around Oradour, but the German battalion believed there to be a cache of arms there and demanded that guns be handed over to them. When no guns were produced, the SS placed the men of the village in various outbuildings and put the women and children in the church. The SS troops then shot the men and burned the buildings in which their bodies lay. On the altar of the church, the soldiers placed a box which exploded, setting the building on fire. A total of 642 people, of whom 393 people were normally resident, died at Oradour. Only a few people who had been in the village itself survived. Roger Godfrin, an eight-year-old refugee from the Lorraine, ran when the SS came to his school and managed to get away in spite of being shot at. The bulk of the survivors were those who had been out of the village on business: the Germans stopped a tram returning from Limoges in the evening and removed the twenty-two passengers from Oradour, who were held for two hours and then released to fend for themselves. Twelve men were absent in German prisoner of war camps or performing labour service in Germany. Children from the village and outlying hamlets were heavily represented amongst victims because they had been at school, and some mothers who came looking for their children when they did not return in the afternoon were also killed.[23]

Aspects of the Oradour massacre – particularly the killing of women and children in the church – had special resonance in post-war France as did the awkward fact that some of the men who carried out the massacre were Alsatians, forcibly incorporated into the German forces. Oradour, preserved in its ruined state, has become an official memorial. There were, however, quite large numbers of similar massacres in France in the summer of 1944. Sometimes the euphoria of liberation and the horror of killing were very close together. The single most important date in the French official memory of 1944 is probably 25 August (the day that Paris was liberated). This was also the day on which between seventy and a hundred German troops killed 130 people (ranging in age from four months to eighty-nine years) in the village of Maillé in Indre-et-Loire.

Frenchmen did not fight against the English or Americans; Pétain reminded them on 14 June 1944 that France was neutral in the war between Germany and the western Allies. French forces did, however, continue to fight against the Resistance in France itself. Darnand had become secretary general for the maintenance of order in the Vichy government in January 1944. The Milice that he had founded to support Vichy was increasingly involved in repression of the Resistance. The Germans had allowed the *francs gardes* of the Milice to be armed in November 1943. In the spring of 1944, *miliciens* helped wipe out Resistance forces on the Plateau des Glières. As the liberation approached, the Milice became increasingly radical and increasingly made up of ideological fanatics or young desperadoes. It was still nominally loyal to Vichy but in practice had begun to see the state as its subordinate rather than its master. *Miliciens* formed drumhead courts martial to try resisters and ordered firing squads made up of gendarmes to carry out their sentences. Pétain belatedly tried to distance himself from his government's creation in August 1944 (as we saw in Chapter 2). It is easy to dismiss *miliciens* as doomed psychopaths committed to the destruction of everything, including themselves, by the summer of 1944, but even at this stage they were not simply instruments of the Germans. The Milice had, in a terrible way, a degree of subtlety and flexibility that the Germans lacked and that made them particularly effective in anti-partisan warfare: the Germans used Frenchmen to fight against partisans in Italy and Poland as well as in France. The Milice were savage in their treatment of Jews and left-wingers as well as Resistance fighters, but they recognized that the indiscriminate violence of some German units was counterproductive. In June 1944 Darnand wrote to the SS commander in France, giving a detailed account of German violence, and saying that he supported harsh reprisals against 'bandits', but adding that German attacks on women and children were damaging relations between the French and the Germans.[24]

MEETING THE ALLIES

What were relations with the liberating Allies like when they got out of their tanks and lorries? It quickly became obvious to the French that the Allies were not all the same. The Americans were more numerous and better equipped than the British. American technological and construction skills seemed particularly impressive in a country that had improvised its way through four years of penury. The Americans built enormous camps in Normandy that they named after brands of cigarettes (which must have reinforced the equation that many French people made between Americans and prosperity). The Lucky Strike camp stretched over 600 hectares and contained 11,600 tents. It was inhabited by 58,000 Americans and 3,000 German prisoners of war, who acted as cooks and cleaners for their new masters.[25] French-speaking Canadians were, not surprisingly, the soldiers with whom French civilians established the easiest rapport.

For some time after the liberation, the French authorities continued the Vichy policy of opening private letters and tapping telephones as a means of finding out about public opinion, and particularly about attitudes to the Allies. They then communicated their reports to the Allies themselves. These investigations always focused on a small sample (because the well-to-do were more likely than the general population to have telephones or write letters and because only a minority within this minority expressed any opinion about the Allies). They produced, however, some striking results. Systematic surveys conducted in Normandy, Dijon, Rouen and Toulouse suggested that feelings ran highest in Normandy, where the Allied presence was highest and fighting had been most intense. Throughout France, opinion seemed to be unfavourable to the Americans and favourable to the British (though in practice British presence in some areas was so low that it was hard to know what this favour meant). In Normandy, in one week in February 1945, 98,699 letters (12.7 per cent of all letters sent) were intercepted. Of these 1,621 expressed an opinion of the Allies. A total of 734 writers expressed an opinion hostile to the Americans whilst 466 were favourable and 122 were equivocal; 199 expressed a favourable attitude to the British whilst 53 were unfavourable and 47 were equivocal.[26]

The Americans were blamed for the casualties caused by high altitude bombing (the British were believed to be more accurate and also, having been bombed themselves, to be more sympathetic to the plight of civilians),[27] and for having betrayed the French by pushing on to the east and leaving poorly equipped French troops ('barefoot or in clogs'[28]) to deal with the pockets of German resistance on the Atlantic coast: 'When it is a question of destroying French factories they come with their big Flying Fortresses, and now that it is necessary to destroy submarine bases into which a thousand German troops are crammed, you no longer see them.'[29] Americans were also reproached for the damage caused by troops, the harassment of Frenchwomen (of which more below), and being excessively generous to their

German prisoners, who were believed to have easier lives than French civilians.[30]

A few people expressed hostility to the Americans in terms that seemed to echo Pétainist or collaborationist themes: 'The Americans are rabid businessmen, certain of them even carry it to the point of Jewishness.'[31] Others compared liberation by the Allies with occupation by the Germans. In August 1944 the prefect of the Maine-et-Loire wrote that the local population prayed: 'Lord liberate us from our protectors and protect us from our liberators.'[32] Some letters intercepted by the French authorities argued that the Americans were 'more uncompromising and egotistical than the Germans'.[33] One man wrote: 'The Germans were well behaved . . . The Americans behaved like pigs. They invaded my cousin's estates, only stayed twelve hours but found time to break down two doors . . . they carried off some bibelots from the cabinet in the lower room.'[34]

Only a small minority of French people compared the Americans unfavourably to the Germans and this small minority was drawn from amongst the wealthiest people (hence the references to damage done to chateaux, bibelots and antiques) in the areas where American presence was highest. Likening the Americans to the Germans was unfair, particularly so in the light of what some German units were doing in parts of France in June and July 1944. The Allies did not, to take just two examples, seize young men for compulsory labour service (they paid good wages to civilians who worked for them), or threaten to shoot local notables if the population did not behave. The Allies probably brought more food to France than they took from it. Where the Germans had been systematically ruthless with the population, the Allies were confused and tactless. American generosity in the first days after their arrival sometimes raised unrealistic hopes, and American military authorities acted to suppress the black market operations that were conducted by their own troops. The French often felt humiliated by their very dependency. One Frenchman recognized ruefully: 'After acting like beggars, we can't hold it against the Americans for treating us as such.'[35] Clocks provide an interesting illustration of the various kinds of relations in play. In 1940 the Germans had decreed that occupied France would work on German time. The Allies did not impose their time zones on France, though the large American base at Cherbourg kept its clocks on what locals described as 'American time', an hour ahead of those of the town.[36]

Allied armies were overwhelmingly made up of young men. The French adult civilian population was predominantly female. The contact between Allied soldiers and French civilians in northern France usually meant a contact between adult men on one side and women or children on the other. One American soldier wrote: 'What a funny war it is with soldiers living side-by-side with eighty-year-olds, women and young children.'[37] Allied soldiers felt that they knew how to behave to women and children. They were meant to be generous and protective, to hurl sweets from their jeeps and to kiss pretty girls who gave them flowers (the public and chaste kisses of the liberation did not have the same significance as the more private, and less socially acceptable, embraces that came later). On the other hand, Allied soldiers were often ill at ease with adult Frenchmen when they encountered them. They believed that the French army had performed badly in 1940, and they often thought that the Resistance units they met had done no real fighting. Underlying much Anglo-American discussion in 1944 was the suspicion that the French were not 'real men'. An American publication told GIs: 'Don't be surprised if a Frenchman steps up to you and kisses you. That doesn't mean he's a queer. It just means he's an emotional Frenchman, and damn glad to see you.'[38]

Like their German predecessors, Allied commanders in France worried about sex. They worried, however, about different things. The Germans had taken a brutally functional attitude to French-women; their main concern had been to prevent the spread of venereal disease. The Americans, by contrast, refused to accept that their troops might frequent prostitutes. In Reims, the Germans had reserved three brothels for their troops. The Americans promptly put these places off limits to their soldiers.[39] The French, who had always sought to regulate prostitution rather than eliminate it, disliked this approach. They argued that it would increase unregulated prostitution, and that Frenchwomen were more likely to be harassed in the streets if American soldiers did not have a commercial outlet for their passions. A Frenchwoman wrote to a friend in October 1944: 'Fortunately the house of prostitution is getting back into working order, we will then have a much easier time.'[40]

In practice, American troops and Frenchwomen did get to know each other. The basic French lessons provided by an American army newspaper are revealing. GIs were taught to say: 'Are you married?', 'Would you like to go for a walk?' and 'I will miss you.' Alongside the numerous fleeting liaisons between Frenchwomen and American soldiers, some long-term relationships were born. In 1945 French GI brides went out to join demobilized fiancés in Kansas and Ohio. A few Americans installed themselves in France. Wayne Powers, a married army driver from Missouri, met Yvette Bleuse in a bar in Mont d'Origny in the Somme in November 1944. He deserted from his unit to join her. In January 1945 he was briefly arrested by French forces, but managed to escape. He spent the next thirteen years hiding in his lover's house and bringing up the five children that the two of them had together. French gendarmes finally found him in March 1958. Fortunately, the ardour of American military prosecutors had cooled by this time and Powers was soon released to rejoin his family.[41]

The American army contained a large number of black troops. Being mainly excluded from combat units, black soldiers were particularly likely to be behind the lines, concerned with transport and supply: there were, for example, 15,000 black American soldiers in the port of Cherbourg, which meant that there was one for every two French civilians in the town. Such roles gave black troops good opportunities to develop relations with French civilians. Often it was black troops who conducted the illicit dealings by which American petrol was traded for food and money.

Black soldiers were not automatically thrown out of bars or attacked for talking to white women, as they would have been in parts of the United States. However, France was not free of racism, and the places in which black American soldiers congregated after the liberation often had little previous experience of black men. One girl wrote to a friend: 'The Americans are here – we are very glad – I speak to them a little in English. They give us a bit of everything (cigarettes, chocolates, sweets, chewing gum) but unfortunately they are negroes and fool about with the women and the girls. So papa won't let me go out any more. It makes me laugh.'[42] Most people in

Normandy were less relaxed than this girl, and many intercepted letters reflect panic about sexual attacks that were attributed to black American soldiers. One writer said that milkmaids going to the fields needed armed escort and added, 'many miss German discipline';[43] another insisted that 'cows and ewes', as well as women and girls, were at risk of attack.[44]

When it came to alleged sexual delinquency of black soldiers, French complaints were sympathetically received by the American authorities, who were themselves obsessed by the need to prevent sexual contact between black men and white girls. The Americans punished 68 of their own soldiers for rape in France between June 1944 and June 1945; most of these men were black. The military authorities in France executed 21 men for rape; the first execution was carried out just eight days after D-Day. Fifteen of the executions were carried out in public, sometimes in the presence of children as young as fourteen. All but three of the executed men were black.[45]

RESISTANCE

British and Americans tended to judge the French Resistance as though it were a conventional military force, and their judgement was rarely favourable. Resisters were lightly armed and, for the most part, poorly trained. A large proportion of the young men who came down from the hills in 1944 were too young to have undergone military service; they were thin, short boys (stunted by wartime penury), who some-times did not even know how to use their own weapons. They did not impress British and American officers. The Resistance that the Allies valued was the collection of intelligence, usually carried out by a small elite of operatives, sometimes trained by, and operating under the orders of, British agents.

Attitudes to the sexual identity of the Resistance are interesting. In the immediate aftermath of the liberation, its spokesmen made much of its masculinity. Frenchwomen gained the vote for the first time in post-war elections, but this innovation owed little to male perceptions of women's role in the war. In any case, women were rarely rep-resented on those bodies that had, supposedly, emerged out of the

Resistance. In the Maine-et-Loire, the *Comité Départemental de la Libération* proposed 243 people to sit on juries charged with judging alleged collaborators. Only three of these were women, and one of them (Eugénie Poilane, who had been deported for her work in the Resistance) did not even know that she had been discussed as a potential juror until a historian told her in January 2000.[46] Members of the Resistance often presented themselves as saviours of French virility; hence the frequency with which they blamed women for the dishonour of France. The British, by contrast, reserved much of their admiration for female operatives, such as Violette Szabo, who had the characteristics – discretion, discipline, modesty – that the mass Resistance of 1944 seemed so conspicuously to lack.

De Gaulle's view of the Resistance was complicated. On the one hand, he was a highly political man by 1944 who understood that Resistance action could be justified in terms that went beyond simple military efficacity. He drew some of his legitimacy vis-à-vis the Allies from the claim that the Resistance inside France supported him. On the other hand, having earned his military rank on the battlefields of two world wars, he was contemptuous of movements that seemed to be made up of self-appointed colonels. There was a more complicated feature of de Gaulle's relation to the Resistance. Precisely because he drew his own prestige and power from the Resistance idea, de Gaulle was threatened by any individual who might claim to interpret or incarnate that idea.

In some ways, the attitude of the Resistance to de Gaulle mirrored that of de Gaulle to the Resistance. Just as the general approved of the Resistance as an idea whilst disapproving of many of its particular incarnations, so the Resistance approved of de Gaulle as an idea whilst often finding de Gaulle as a man to be awkward. During the occupation, relations between de Gaulle and the Resistance had been facilitated by the general's absence. Few French people knew anything about his pre-war career or his political opinions (those who did know about, and approve of, his pre-war attempts to reform the French army were generally supporters of Pétain). A Vichy report concluded that 'Gaullism seems to many people to be a sort of anti-German thought, more than a policy or a programme'.[47] Admiral Leahy, American ambassador at Vichy in 1942, believed that 'Gaullism' referred to the kingdom that had been invaded by Julius Caesar rather than the French general in London.

De Gaulle's relations were worst with that select group of Resistance leaders who were eminent enough to meet him before 1944. Jacques Lecompte-Boinet, founder of Ceux de la Résistance, met the general in Algiers in 1943. Lecompte-Boinet was keen to talk about the Resistance in France and, in particular, to stress the special character of Resistance in the northern zone, in which his own movement was based. As it turned out, he hardly had a chance to open his mouth. After dinner, de Gaulle talked at Lecompte-Boinet for three hours, referring to himself in the third person. At the end of this monologue, Lecompte-Boinet offered de Gaulle a packet of cigarettes that he had brought from France, where tobacco was a rare and valuable commodity. De Gaulle, a chain-smoker during the war, swept them aside saying: 'I only smoke American cigarettes.'

During and after the liberation of France, de Gaulle ceased to be a voice on the radio and became a real person for the French. Many resistants did not like the real person much. Though still, nominally, the head of a broad political coalition, de Gaulle behaved increasingly like a man of the right. Furthermore, he was notably cool towards Resistance leaders. He met Colonel Gaspar, leader of the Maquis in the Auvergne, briefly in July 1945 during an official visit with the Sultan of Morocco, but made no gesture to distinguish him from the other officials in a receiving line.[48]

The tension between de Gaulle and the internal Resistance was not the only one to become apparent at the liberation. There was also a division between Communists and their enemies. Sometimes this conflict involved Communist-dominated Resistance bodies attacking those they accused of Pétainism or collaboration, which explains the fact that some former Pétainists were willing to support de Gaulle as a defender of order. There was also, and perhaps more importantly, a division in the Resistance itself between Communists and non-Communists. Early leaders of the Resistance – Henri Frenay, Philippe Viannay, Jacques Lecompte-Boinet – had often been men of the right. Most had ceased to think of themselves as right-wingers by 1944, but they also often remained suspicious of the Communist Party. They reproached the party for its attitude in the aftermath of the Hitler–

Stalin pact, and often believed that the Communist Party had subsequently infiltrated and exploited the Resistance.

There was an important division in the Communist Party itself
between the leadership and much of its base. The leaders of the party
had all been prominent before 1939, and all had supported the Hitler–
Stalin pact. Maurice Thorez, the party leader, had deserted from the
French army in 1940 and subsequently spent the war in Moscow. At
local level, however, many Communists had been hostile to the Hitler–
Stalin pact and often entered into clandestine action against Vichy
and the Germans before the invasion of the Soviet Union. Membership
of the party, which had dropped sharply after the Hitler–Stalin pact,
was high again in 1944 and many had been brought into the party
through Resistance action. The new Communists of 1944 were often
drawn from outside the Communist Party's traditional base in the
industrial working class. Party membership increased in rural areas,
such as Haute-Savoie, where the Resistance had been strong. New
members were Communists of a particular sort. There was an important difference between someone who had turned to Communism as
a part of the anti-fascist struggle in 1943 and someone who had
lived through the period of 'class-against-class' strategy, by which the
Communist Party had pitted itself against democratic socialism, in
the late 1920s. The clandestine nature of the Resistance, which made
centralized discipline difficult to enforce, and the needs of the war,
which made the Communists subordinate ideological divisions to
short-term military effectiveness, had all helped to hide the splits
within Communism. With the liberation, they became visible again.
Communists who had been active in the Resistance were less disciplined than their party leaders and more prone to push for radical
social change, the punishment of collaborators or even revolution.
However, Stalin did not want revolution in western Europe and,
curiously, it was the very undemocratic Moscow loyalists in the French
Communist Party leadership who protected French democracy by
suppressing those Communists who were most keen to seize power in
France. By the early 1950s, most Resistance leaders had been purged
from the leadership of the Communist Party.

There was another more subtle and awkward division in the
Resistance. Early leaders, such as Emmanuel d'Astier de la Vigerie,

had been conscious, almost more than anything else, of their isolation. They saw themselves as being cut off from the rest of French society, especially from their own bourgeois milieu. The nature of the Resistance increased their sense of isolation. The movement valued secrecy and rigid separation between different units. There was always an element of bluff as Resistance leaders pretended, to each other and to potential recruits, that they had more support than they really did. As the Resistance grew, leaders had little contact with the new entrants into their movement. Sometimes early leaders were in London, Algeria or Buchenwald by the time that Resistance became a mass movement in 1943 and 1944. All of this contributed to a gulf between those who saw themselves as 'resistants of the first hour' and those they derided as 'resistants of the eleventh hour'. The Resistance of 1944 – large-scale, public, plebeian – seemed a world away from the secret meetings of 1940. Distaste for 'resistants of the eleventh hour' often intersected with anti-Communism or anti-working class feeling. The denunciation of 'resistants of the eleventh hour' was usually unfair. The Resistance only became a mass movement in 1944, partly because its leaders were only willing to allow it to assume such a role once they knew that Allied landings were imminent. Besides, derogatory remarks about people who joined the Resistance in the last few months of the occupation took no account of the fact that this was also the period when the Resistance was involved in the most bitter fighting.

At local level, all sorts of animosities against, and within, the Resistance came to the surface in the years following the liberation. In Dax, Léonce Dussarrat, who had led the local Maquis under the *nom de guerre* 'Léo des Landes', became a notable figure after the war. He founded a prosperous business, was active in the society of holders of the Légion d'honneur and, eventually, had a local school named after him. He also wrote frequent letters to the authorities complaining about expressions of hostility to him. Some of this hostility came, at least in Dussarrat's eyes, from former Pétainists.[49] Dussarrat's most bitter enemy, however, was François Dals. Born in 1887, Dals was a retired civil servant from the tax inspectorate. He had fought in the First World War and was widely regarded as a sober and respectable person. He had never married but, in 1924, he had had a son, André Anne, whom he had brought up. The son had joined the Maquis under Dussarrat's command and, with three other boys, been captured by the Germans. Dals had made Dussarrat promise to negotiate the boys' release but negotiations had failed and, on 12 June 1944, André Anne was shot.

After the war, Dals was obsessed by the memory of his son. He went to the trial in Toulouse of the German officer who had commanded the boy's execution and shot at the officer when he was acquitted (Dals was released after pleas from Resistance veterans). After this, he directed his hostility at Dussarrat whom he blamed for military incompetence, in particular for having posted the boys to an exposed position just outside Dax, and for having failed to negotiate the release. Dals attacked Dussarrat in the street, and every year, on the anniversary of his son's death, he wrote him an abusive letter.[50]

PURGES

With the liberation went purges. The Resistance had attacked a number of collaborators, and published lists of people to be punished at the liberation. Increasingly, people who knew they were vulnerable moved away from places where they were known or into places where the Germans would be able to provide protection; this usually meant moving into towns. The Resistance had assassinated around 2,500 people by June 1944.

Violence was concentrated immediately before and after the liberation: around 5,000 people were killed during this period, either in assassinations or fighting between Resistance and Milice or in summary executions immediately after the liberation. Attacks by both the Resistance and their opponents became more common and more violent immediately before the liberation and, in particular, in the period between the first Allied landings and their arrival in a particular area. The most famous Resistance assassination of a Frenchman (that of the Vichy progagandist Philippe Henriot) took place in Paris on 28 June.

Purges took several forms. First, there was the *épuration sauvage*: violent attacks by Resistance groups or angry crowds, that took place without any legal process. Such attacks involved assassinations, lynchings and the shaving of women's heads (of which more below). There were also summary executions carried out after brief courts martial.

The confusion of the times and the reticence of those who committed acts of violence during the liberation means that it has been hard for historians to establish exactly how many people were victims of the *épuration sauvage*. In the Maine-et-Loire, the Ministry of the Interior suggested in 1948 that only two people had been killed; the gendarmerie in 1959 reckoned that the figure should have been 29 whilst the local correspondent of the Institut d'Histoire du Temps Présent in 1982 believed that it should have been 46.[51] In the Haute-Loire, estimates of the number of summary executions carried out at the liberation varied from 42 (the estimate made by the gendarmerie in 1959) to 77 (the estimate made by the prefect in 1948).[52] A local historian argues that both of these figures are too low, and that the real figure should be 141 (117 men and 24 women). Most of those shot were relatively young (the largest single group was made up of men in their thirties). Many bodies were never identified.

Most of those killed during the *épuration sauvage* had been involved in violence against the Resistance (as members of the Milice or as denouncers of their compatriots). Many were captured in an area where memories of violence were fresh: sometimes the executions took place just after a period of fighting. However, this was also a period in which all sorts of scores, including some that did not relate directly to the political divisions of Vichy, could be settled. Black marketeers were sometimes punished, even when their behaviour had not benefited the Germans. The Communist Party took its revenge against dissidents and enemies; four Trotskyites were shot in the Haute-Loire.

Denouncers of the *épuration sauvage* portrayed it as a period in which the Resistance was at war with society: the trials of some Resistance activists during the late 1940s and early 1950s for crimes of pillage and violence are sometimes presented as a reaction against the *épuration sauvage*. In fact, however, the division between an *épuration sauvage* around the liberation and a restoration of legality several years later is false. The state often punished crimes committed during the liberation very quickly. In the Maine-et-Loire, three Resistance fighters, who had killed a suspected collaborator in September 1944, were sentenced to prison terms in August 1945.[53] Georges Dubosq had already been convicted of thirty-three offences by 1940. During the occupation he worked first for the Germans and then (calling himself 'Capitaine Lecoz') purported to be a Resistance leader, in which capacity he ruled over the town of Loches for several days. In October 1944 the regional prefect had him arrested. He was tried for eighteen murders and shot in May 1946.[54] Sometimes the extra-legal violence of the liberation was itself part of an attempt to impose discipline on the Resistance, or on those who claimed to act in its name. People were shot for pillaging farm houses. In the Haute-Loire, four resistants were shot, two of them for desertion.[55]

The victims of the *épuration sauvage* were mainly drawn from the most underprivileged parts of society. Such people were over-represented in the agencies that had been most associated with violent collaboration. They also lacked the resources to flee or hide in 1944. Race played a part in violence at the liberation. People of non-French origin had often worked for, or occasionally fought for, the Germans. Both under Vichy and at the liberation, many talked of a need to 'purify' France of un-French elements. Those who seemed foreign made inviting targets at a time when many were looking for someone to blame for France's humiliation. Often, they were particularly vulnerable to retribution because they were highly visible and because they had no one in France to protect them. Even before the liberation, North Africans associated with the Germans were in violent conflict with the rest of French society: on 9 June 1944 a North African, described as a corporal in the Luftwaffe, fired on two French policemen, killing one and wounding the other; he was then nearly lynched by the crowd before being rescued by Germans troops.[56] A Vietnamese laundress was lynched by a Paris mob who believed her to be a 'Japanese spy'.[57] In the Morbihan, at least fifteen North Africans were executed – an astonishing figure given that the total number of North Africans in the department was only sixty.[58] Racial attacks at the liberation fitted in with the desire to 'purify' France that was both a reaction against Vichy and a continuation of some aspects of Vichy rhetoric.

By contrast, the most privileged sections of society usually escaped relatively lightly. A certain proportion of Pétainists and collaborators retreated to Germany with the occupying army. Simply getting out of France until the passions of the liberation had cooled could save someone's life. Léon Gaultier was a Frenchman who had served as a lieutenant with the SS. When he returned to France in July 1945, a woman spat on him and said: 'If we had got you last August.' As it was, Gaultier faced a court not a lynch mob, was sentenced to ten years' hard labour and served three.[59] Some of those who had fled France subsequently took refuge in neutral countries. Jean Jardin, Laval's *chef de cabinet*, presided over a colony of former Pétainists around Lake Lausanne in Switzerland; it was from there that he established La Presse du Cheval Ailé, which did much to nurture the image of a horrific purge in France by publishing books such as Alfred Fabre-Luce's *Au nom des silencieux*. Many Pétainists did not return until their former political associates in France were being released from prison.

There was also a formal, legal purge after the liberation. Sometimes people were tried for offences – such as 'intelligence avec l'ennemi' – that had existed in law before 1940. Sometimes they were tried for offences, such as having held office under Vichy or voting full powers to Marshal Pétain, that had been defined retrospectively. Special kinds of courts were created at the liberation. 'High courts of justice', the courts that tried major figures such as Pétain, and courts of justice, which dealt with smaller fry, were much like ordinary criminal courts except that their juries were nominated from amongst those seen as having good patriotic credentials. Specially created *chambres civiques* passed sentences of *indignité nationale*, which meant that people were deprived of the right to vote or hold office for a certain period of time. Generally speaking, the higher the accused were in the social scale the more likely they were to receive a formal trial rather than rough justice from their neighbours. The trials of Pétain, whose death sentence was commuted to life imprisonment, and Laval, who was executed, produced few surprises (in any case, Pétain, by now almost ninety years old, said little at his trial).

Overall, about 310,000 cases, involving 350,000 people, were referred to courts. Six out of ten defendants, however, were released quickly for lack of evidence. Around 125,000 people were tried and 100,000 of these were convicted, though 49,723 were sentenced to *indignité nationale* without any additional prison sentence. Of those who were punished in some physical way, 25,901 went to prison and 13,339 were sentenced to *travaux forcés* (some joked that the initials TF stamped on their coats stood for 'toujours fidèle à Pétain'). In all, 7,055 were sentenced to death, but only 2,861 death sentences were passed in the presence of the accused; those sentenced *in absentia* had to be retried if and when they were caught.

The trials, executions and imprisonments that followed the liberation came to play a large part in the mythology of the right. The very fact that many victims of the legal purge were men from bourgeois backgrounds made their punishment seem all the more striking: the chaplain of Fresnes prison talked of the time when 'le tout Paris' was in the cells.[60] Pétainists made much of their status as victims. Pierre-Antoine Cousteau, a collaborationist and brother of the undersea explorer, began one of his books with the memorable words: 'On 23 November, a large, smooth man, wearing a splendid red robe, trimmed with white rabbit fur, told me rather coldly, that I was condemned to death.'[61] Cousteau's sentence was subsequently commuted. François Brigneau ends his memoirs with his recollections of 6 February 1945, the day of the execution of the collaborationist poet Robert Brasillach.[62] In 1957, the extreme-right journal *Rivarol* surveyed 3,607 of its readers: it found that 36 per cent of them had been imprisoned at the liberation and 3 per cent had, for a time, been under sentence of death.[63]

Many defendants were acquitted, many death sentences were commuted and most of those convicted were released within a few years (there were two large-scale amnesties in 1951 and 1953). Some men who had come very close to the firing squad served little time in prison. A thirty-nine-year-old member of the Milice, who had sat on an illegal court martial that condemned Resistance activists on 2 August 1944, was then himself sentenced to death. However, the sentence was overturned on a technicality (he had been prosecuted in both the civilian court and a court martial). A retrial in March 1945 reduced his sentence to twenty years. In 1951 he was released and in

1966 he was officially 'rehabilitated'.[64] Those who could afford good lawyers were particularly likely to survive. Defence lawyers became the new heroes of the right, which had often in the past been rather disdainful of the *pays légal*.

Two lawyers were particularly important. Jacques Isorni, who defended Pétain in 1945, led the Pétainist Union des Nationaux et Indépendants et Républicains into parliament in 1951. Jean-Louis Tixier-Vignancour, who had run Vichy radio for a time, was himself imprisoned for eighteen months after the liberation. He then became a key defence lawyer for the right. He saved a number of his clients from the firing squad – one of them was sentenced and spared four times. Tixier's enthusiasm took him outside the courtroom. In 1949 he fought a duel with Pierre Nordmann, a Resistance veteran and brother of a man who had been deported after denunciation by one of Tixier's clients.[65] In 1965 he fought a different kind of duel when he challenged de Gaulle in the presidential elections.

The relations between the various forms of formal and informal purges varied with time and place. Generally, the *épuration sauvage* was most extensive in the south of France. The south was, to a great extent, liberated by French forces, and sometimes by the Resistance, rather than by the Allies. It was also the area where the Maquis had been most extensive and where the Franco-French struggles that pitted Milice against Resistance had been most severe. More generally, the purge was most restrained in areas where conflict during the occupation had been lightest; it was most violent in areas with a history of massacre and reprisal. However, legal and extra-legal punishment did not function independently of each other. Often popular violence pressured the authorities into taking more vigorous action. Sometimes victims were dragged from prison by lynch mobs. Popular violence sometimes increased as it seemed that central government was becoming too lenient. Public anger flared in 1945, at the end of the war, when three different processes coincided. First, de Gaulle seemed ever more inclined to pardon collaborators or to commute death sentences. Secondly, internment camps were closed so that suspected collaborators who had been put in protective custody were released. Thirdly, concentration camp victims, including some Resistance activists who owed their imprisonment to denunciation by their compatriots, began to return to France. Attacks on suspected collaborators, often involving the placing of explosives near their houses, continued into at least 1946 and such illegal and clandestine attacks seem to have increased as the state was seen as less effective in punishing collaboration.

Most of all, it should be stressed that the heavy emphasis on simple forms of punishment that can be counted, particularly executions, blinds us to the full variety of forms of retribution taken at the liberation. Punishment did not always involve either violence or trials in court. Around 100,000 people were interned at some point in the months following the liberation; internment had no legal basis until October 1944 though, in practice, internees were often lucky to be removed from popular anger. Prefects sometimes declared people *interdit de séjour* (that is, forbidden from residing in departments where their presence might provoke disorder). Departmental liberation committees sometimes imposed the humiliations normally reserved for state-registered prostitutes (including compulsory medical inspection for venereal disease) on women who were believed to have been close to the Germans. Foreigners were simply expelled from the country. Sometimes a Comité d'Épuration Professionelle could sanction people. A central Comité d'Épuration Professionelle operating at national level examined a total of 1,538 cases and found 191 people guilty. Some people were forbidden from exercising authority in their companies and this created a curious situation in which men could be prevented from managing a company they owned. Civil servants were particularly vulnerable to dismissal – around 35,000 were sacked. Such sanctions were applied for a variety of reasons. Some were punished because of their excessive zeal in carrying out the wishes of the Vichy government or in helping the Germans, but some purges were used as a means to rid the state of incompetent workers. State agencies had taken on large numbers of temporary workers during the occupation in order to fill the posts left vacant by men who were prisoners of war in Germany. With the return of prisoners, it was often convenient to have a reason to dispose of temporary workers, especially women.[66]

Sometimes punishment did not involve formal process at all. People perceived as Pétainists or collaborators were discreetly told that their presence in a particular area, or their association with a particular company, would be damaging to them or their associates. Sometimes it was hard to know whether a punishment was official or not. The prefect of the Maine-et-Loire decided that the deputy to the mayor of Rochefort-sur-Loire was discredited by the support he had shown for his pro-German son during the occupation. However, the prefect also said that the dismissal was not to be published in the press, 'or even explicitly mentioned in the decree'. The prefect added that the victim of this sanction 'must be forgotten'.[67] People were shunned or boycotted; sometimes the houses of alleged collaborators were marked with an H for Hitler. In small towns especially, the violence and retribution of the occupation and then the liberation left almost impossibly painful legacies that made relations between neighbours very difficult.

An episode in the Landes shows how difficult it could be for communities to live together after 1945. A young woman, who had had a child by a German soldier in 1944, had been imprisoned at the liberation and subsequently declared *interdite de séjour* for ten years. She was believed to have denounced a local hotelier as a Communist and thus brought about his deportation to Germany. In 1947 the woman asked the prefect for permission to return to her home village. She wanted to look after her aged mother and hoped that her mother would help her with her child. The prefect took soundings in the village. The woman's victim said that he did not mind his denouncer returning but that he would not answer for his actions 'if faced with the slightest display of irony or arrogance on the part of Mademoiselle B.': lower-class women who had mixed with the Germans were often accused of having ideas above their station.[68] The prefect's private intelligence suggested that the hotelier was a good man but prone to lose control of himself when under the influence of drink. The woman did return to her village but she rarely dared go out.

FEMMES TONDUES

No image of the liberation has received more attention in recent years than that of women with shaved heads (*femmes tondues*). The most famous depiction of the public cutting of hair (*tontes*) is the photograph taken by Robert Capa in Chartres on 18 August 1944. It shows a woman with her head shaved being marched down the Rue du Cheval Blanc, near to the cathedral, by a jeering crowd. She carries a baby and is accompanied by an old man, presumably her father, who carries a bundle. Capa himself never described the circumstances in which he took this photograph; the journalist Charles Wertenbaker, who accompanied him in Chartres, did: 'The patriots were bringing in women collaborators, old ones who had helped the Germans or operated black markets and younger blowsy ones who had sold themselves to the Germans. They were lined up against a wall, some with their hair already clipped close to the skull, and in the centre of the courtyard was a pile of grey and blond hair. In the corner of the courtyard a woman and a boy were selling red wine by the glass.'[69]

The location of the scene photographed by Capa raises all sorts of questions. Chartres, an old town in a part of France that had been celebrated by the nationalist poet Péguy, was an important symbol. It seems doubly symbolic now (though few people can have realized this in 1944) because the préfecture, which can be seen in the background of Capa's photograph, had, in 1940, contained the office of the Resistance martyr Jean Moulin. The cathedral is about a hundred metres away from the Rue du Cheval Blanc. One assumes that the bells would have been ringing. Did priests try to intervene? Did any women think of seeking sanctuary in the cathedral?

We know almost nothing about the woman in the Capa photograph. The anthropologist Alain Brossat walked up and down the Rue du Cheval Blanc in the early 1990s asking passers-by if they could identify her.[70] People gave him two dozen mutually exclusive accounts of who she was. We can guess that the woman was accused of having slept with a German soldier and that her baby had a German father. More generally, it is likely that she was young and poor. She probably worked in one of those occupations (laundress or waitress) that brought Frenchwomen into contact with German soldiers. She may have hung around the Hôtel Jehan de Beauce, the slightly rough establishment by the station in Chartres, and she may have dabbled in prostitution.

The photograph of the woman in Chartres is, in some respects, unrepresentative. The presence of the baby, which gives the picture much of its effect, was rare, perhaps because vengeful crowds at the liberation were seldom so uncontrolled that they would have risked the safety of a child, or perhaps because most women who had children by German soldiers arranged for the children to be looked after by other people. The presence of her father would also be unusual. Many women who were reproached for their relations with German soldiers were the children of unmarried mothers or had poor relationships with their fathers. Some of them had been driven out of the family home by abuse. Men were sometimes strikingly unsympathetic to their female relatives: in the Ille-et-Vilaine, a man wrote to the authorities saying that he did not mind the fact that his niece had had her head shaved but that he did mind that her attackers trespassed in his house when they dragged her out.[71] Some men cut their own daughters' hair. More common than the presence of fathers during *tontes*, was the presence of mothers and sisters: often more than one female member of the same family had her hair cut at the same time. In fact, the woman photographed by Capa appears in less famous photographs with an older woman, apparently her mother, whose head has also been shaved.[72]

Chartres's experience of the occupation was distinctive. A departmental capital between Paris and the Atlantic coast, the town contained large numbers of Germans during the occupation. It was big enough to attract people from surrounding villages who sought work (big enough too, perhaps, to attract young women who wanted to get away from the immediate effects of local disapproval in small communities), but it was too small for affairs to go unnoticed, or for women to disappear at the liberation. Chartres is surrounded by a plain of rich agricultural land. This meant that the occupation was less harsh than it would have been elsewhere. Food was comparatively plentiful. It was also relatively easy for young men threatened by Service du Travail Obligatoire to find work and shelter on the farms around Chartres (this was good territory for *réfractaires*). On the other hand, it was bad territory for *maquisards*, because there are no hills or woods. In short, the area around Chartres contained a lot of young men who had been obliged to flee their homes during the occupation, but who had not taken up arms against the Germans.

One assumes that these men, veterans of an uncomfortable but unheroic war, carried out the *tontes* of 1944.

It is hard to go beyond such speculation because the liberation of Chartres, as of everywhere else, meant a suspension of normal authority and hence an interruption of documentary records. Occasionally, the archives of the Eure-et-Loir (kept, as it happens, close to the Rue du Cheval Blanc) give us a tantalizing glimpse of something that happened on the day that Chartres was liberated. In September 1945 the police investigated a man who had volunteered to work in Germany. Working for the Germans was one of the offences for which women sometimes had their hair cut. However, police concluded that Georges M.'s departure could be blamed on his wife. Georges M., already working for the Germans in France, had thrown his wife's German lover out of the family house in February 1942. He then claimed that he had gone to Germany to escape possible retribution. His wife subsequently had a child by a German. Georges M. had returned to France by August 1944 and had, apparently, 'conducted himself well' on the day that Chartres was liberated. This good conduct involved firing a gun (it seems that he did so in celebration rather than because he was shooting at anyone). His wife does not seem to have been subject to any police proceedings. It would be interesting to know whether her hair was cut on 18 August 1944 and whether her husband was one of the men who organized *tontes*.[73]

The *femmes tondues* were not just a subject of interest to photographers. They are also present in novels published after the war. Marguerite Duras's *Hiroshima mon amour* revolves around a woman whose head has been shaved at the liberation, as does Guy Croussy's *La Tondue*. Scenes of head-shaving are described in novels such as Louis Gilloux's *OK Joe* and Violette Leduc's *La Bâtarde*. The Resistance poet Paul Éluard published a poem, 'Comprenne qui voudra', in December 1944 about the *femmes tondues*, which was cited by Georges Pompidou in 1969 when he discussed the case of Gabrielle Russier, a schoolteacher who had committed suicide after an affair with one of her pupils.[74] Brassens composed a song, 'La Tondue', about the scenes he had seen in Paris in 1944.

The *faits divers* sections of French newspapers sometimes contain haunting details that hint at the long-term consequences of *tontes*. In

1983 gendarmes in Saint-Flour in the Auvergne broke down the door of a house, the inhabitants of which had begun to provoke complaints through their dirtiness and strange behaviour. Inside they found a fifty-three-year-old woman who had shut herself up after her head was shaved at the liberation. With her was her fifty-five-year-old brother and the body of her mother, who had died two years previously. Émile Louis, accused of a string of particularly brutal rapes and murders, recalled, as a ten-year-old boy entrusted to a foster family by the *Assistance Publique*, coming home to find that his sisters had been *tondues*.[75]

How and when did *tontes* occur? They did not begin with the liberation. Women suspected of being too close to the Germans were liable to attack as early as 1943. The frequency of *tontes* increased at the liberation. Their incidence declined during the winter of 1944–5, but then increased at the end of the European war. Women who had volunteered to work in Nazi Germany, often women who had had German lovers, were sometimes shaved on their return. So too were some of the women who remained with Germans in the Lorient pocket until May 1945. The hostility to people associated with the Germans may have been increased by the return of French deportees from concentration camps: some of these deportees believed that women had denounced them.[76] *Tontes* seem to have been most common in the northern and western part of France (that part occupied by the Germans since 1940). They happened most in areas where there had been large concentrations of Germans troops and were more common in towns than in the countryside (presumably because women associated with the Germans had usually moved into towns).

Strikingly absent from all the discussion of *femmes tondues* is any account by a woman who had her head shaved or, for that matter, any account by someone who did the shaving. All our information about *tontes* comes from people who watched rather than from participants. The most famous fictional accounts of the *filles tondues* tend to present them as 'petites bonniches'. They are seen as young, socially underprivileged, and overwhelmingly 'guilty' of sleeping with German soldiers. The significant minority of *femmes tondues* who were middle-aged, relatively wealthy and guilty of black marketeering or political collaboration tend to be ignored. Two novelists illustrate the process. Marguerite Duras wrote about the *tonte* of a seventeen-year-old petite bourgeoise from Nevers who had fallen in love with a German soldier, but her own personal knowledge of the event seems to have been drawn from her friend Betty Fernandez, a middle-aged Parisian who was shaved because she was the wife of a leading collaborationist. Similarly, Louis Guilloux's diaries describe two *tontes*. One involved a fifty-five-year-old lycée *professeur* who was accused of having displayed political sympathy for the Germans; the other involved a middle-aged fishmonger who was accused of having had an affair with a German soldier.[77] But when he came to write his autobiographical novel of the period, *OK Joe*, these two middle-aged and prosperous women were transmuted into a teenage *bonne d'auberge*.

More recent accounts based on archival evidence have paid more attention to the middle-aged and middle-class and argue that only about half of women whose hair was cut were accused of sleeping with Germans. Different versions are linked to different kinds of evidence. Novelists and poets looking for a striking story will tend to overstate the youth and 'innocence' of victims. Reliance on official records will tend to overstate the role of those most likely to make official complaints or to be subject to formal legal proceedings, who are also likely to be the oldest and most bourgeois victims. In any case, attempts to define victims in terms of age or the crimes with which they were reproached can be deceptive. Often *tontes* involved women of very different ages – sometimes daughters, mothers and even grandmothers. Furthermore, the various crimes of which women were accused were often seen to overlap. Women who slept with Germans often also worked for them and were often accused of leading generally debauched lives. Association with Germans was sometimes seen to go with black marketeering and, in particular, with that variety of black marketeering that was seen as socially unacceptable, and women who slept with Germans were often also accused of denouncing their compatriots, though these accusations rarely stood up to police scrutiny.

People who approved of *tontes* often justified them as a means by which the order of Vichy and the occupation were overthrown, but things could be more complicated. Individual German soldiers may have enjoyed their affairs with Frenchwomen, but the German military authorities did not approve of such relations. Similarly, the Vichy authorities disapproved of women who consorted with Germans. Vichy officialdom, the German military authorities and those who claimed to represent the Resistance at the liberation, all shared a desire to redraw clear lines between prostitutes and 'respectable' women, lines that seemed to have been blurred by the circumstances of war. A shaven head was a good means to distinguish and label the 'non-respectable'.

Sometimes *tontes* were accompanied by other forms of violence or humiliation: women might be stripped, tarred and feathered or, in the worst circumstances, executed. At other times, people who carried out *tontes* regarded themselves as acting with restraint and care. Some women had their hair cut in barbers' shops. Their persecutors often stressed that their aim was to humiliate rather than to hurt. People cutting hair clearly believed that they were acting in accordance with an established and accepted moral code. In Saint-Brieuc, people held up pictures of a woman with her German lover, as a warning to young girls in the crowd, but the Resistance fighters refused to parade the victim herself in public, because she suffered from a weak heart.[78]

Many observers claimed, at least in retrospect, to have disapproved of *tontes*. Robert Doisneau's attitude contrasted sharply with that of his fellow photographers travelling with Allied armies. He wrote later: 'The only thing that I refused to photograph was the ugliness of popular demonstrations, the women who'd been shaved, the women led around naked in the streets, I refused to do that. People said to me: "Go on, photograph that!" But it's a shame, terrible, the beastliness. A woman alone facing a band of sadists. The crowd is an awful thing.'[79] Two historians recalled their horror at the *tontes*. Georgette Elgey said that the sight of a woman having her head shaved in the square at Saint-Martin-en-Haut near Lyons 'spoilt my happiness for a time'.[80] Alfred Grosser was so horrified by the scenes in Marseilles that he locked himself in his room and listened to Beethoven's First Symphony.[81] The reactions of Grosser and Elgey were all the more striking because they were both Jews who had every reason to be overjoyed at the liberation. Some newspapers and Resistance organizations campaigned against the *tontes*, though direct intervention by French people to stop *tontes* was rare.

Denunciations of the *tontes* often went with moral elitism. Denouncers stressed the savage character of the crowd. Often such denunciations fitted in with the distinction between the 'real' Resistance – that of a small group of heroes who had fought since 1940 – and the false Resistance, the vengeful and cowardly acts of a mass movement that emerged at the liberation. It is significant that the two most famous literary evocations of *tontes*, Éluard's poem 'Comprenne qui voudra' and Marguerite Duras's *Hiroshima mon amour* were both written by people who thought of themselves as 'real' resistants. It is, in fact, almost impossible to know how the crowd reacted to *tontes*. We often see photographs of crowds gathered around women whose heads were being shaved. Often people in the crowds seem to be laughing or grinning (for that matter the women being shaved sometimes seem to be laughing), but it is impossible to know how many disapproved of what they saw or how many came to disapprove after the event. In the Var, three *institutrices* were shaved at the liberation, supposedly for having entertained German officers. They were denounced by a male teacher, who seems to have resented his relatively subordinate status, particularly with regard to the headmistress of the school, who was only twenty-two years old. The inspector of schools drew attention to the 'personal bitterness' that built up in a small village but he also remarked: 'At the start of the school year, a number of mothers expressed their sympathy [for the teachers] which is quite normal.'[82]

Where was the French state when women had their heads shaved? In part, the answer to this question is 'nowhere'. A headmistress who was trying to protect a teacher in her school in the south-west was told by the mayor of her town 'not to get too mixed up in this matter'.[83] The *tontes* often happened when Vichy's authority had melted away and before any alternative power had been established. Local authorities had no central power to appeal to or to back them up. The authority of policemen and gendarmes had, in any case, been undermined during the final stages of the occupation. They had often seemed passive and unheroic spectators to a conflict that pitted Resistance fighters against the Milice. Many may have been relieved that the crowds vented their anger on women rather than on themselves. Sometimes the state's participation in *tontes* was more direct. Jacques Bounin, the Commissaire de la République in Montpellier, claimed in his memoirs that he himself had authorized *tontes*.[84] Similar orders were sometimes given by local authorities. Agents of the state could be caught in an odd situation. They disapproved of illegal violence and disorder but they also disapproved of the women who had incurred the wrath of the community. In 1945, almost a year after the initial disorders of the liberation, a woman who had volunteered to work in Germany after having had numerous affairs with German soldiers (though not, apparently, having shown any political sympathy for Nazism), returned to her home village of Tosses and was shaved. A policeman described the incident thus: 'The same day [the day of her return] her head was shaved, to the great satisfaction of the Tossais, up to and including the authorities who, while recognizing and disapproving the illegality of the gesture, approved of its judicious character.'[85]

In northern France, at least, Allied soldiers were, almost by definition, present at the moment of the liberation and *tontes* often took place in front of them.[86] Many pictures of *tontes* were taken by photographers attached to Allied armies. Often the very women who associated with American and British troops were those who had previously been seen with Germans. One American recalled that he and his comrades sought out girls with shaven heads knowing them to be good 'for a little collaboration' (knowing too, perhaps, that the French authorities would not be sympathetic to a girl with a shaven head who complained of being harassed). On at least one occasion, a girl accused of *collaboration sentimentale* was attacked by her compatriots when in the company of British soldiers.

Allied troops did occasionally protect individual women, but soldiers were under orders not to intervene in disputes between the French. Sometimes the *tontes* seem to have fitted quite neatly into the generally contemptuous attitude that some Allied soldiers had to the French. The very existence of the *femmes tondues* seemed to suggest that the French were a race of collaborators. Equally, the treatment of *femmes tondues* suggested that a large part of the French male population felt guilty about their own behaviour during the occupation, or were so cowardly that they were only willing to attack defenceless women.

Peter Elstob was a radio operator in an armoured unit of the British army. In June 1944 his tank broke down in a village in the Normandy Bocage, thus trapping him and his comrades there for three days. He watched three women (a grandmother of sixty-five, her daughter in her late thirties and her granddaughter of sixteen) being punished for collaboration. The three women were said to have entertained German soldiers at their auberge. The daughter and granddaughter had slept with them (the latter was said to have been in love with a German officer, which made some villagers judge her less harshly). Condemnation, in this case, seemed linked to money as much as sex: 'The price of the mother's favours was variously estimated at 500 to 1,000 francs, and that made these thrifty housewives very angry – that and the fact that because of these women German officers had been well fed while the people were not.' The heads of the mother and daughter were shaved. Elstob, under orders not to meddle in French affairs,[87] prevented his own working-class Liverpudlian driver from stepping in. Elstob himself, however, intervened to protect the oldest woman. He told the leader of the local Maquis, 'a cruel brute' of about twenty: 'She is too old . . . war is for men . . . you are young and strong . . . the Boche is young and strong too . . . there are many Boches five kilometres south of here – go there.'[88]

Who shaved women's heads? Sometimes the *tondeurs* came from the same milieu as the *tondues*. In Brittany it was, apparently, regarded as quite rare for a woman not to know the men who shaved her head. On one occasion, a man who attacked a girl returning from working in Germany was the girl's cousin and had himself gone to Germany as a 'volunteer' worker after having stolen from the monks who employed him.[89] Members of the Forces Françaises de l'Intérieur tried to shave the head of a primary school teacher in the south-west. The victim (Mademoiselle D.) said that her would-be attackers were 'young men from Tarnos and are led by Pierrot L. [Pierrot is a name that suggests familiarity] who has something against me, I do not know why'. The attack ended when the teacher made it clear that she knew 'M.E.', a member of the *Comité Départemental de la Libération*.[90]

Some women made formal complaints about their treatment. Complaints tended to come from the older and more bourgeois victims; not surprisingly, they tended to be the ones with the resources and confidence to undertake formal proceedings. They also tended to come from women who were being pursued for political or economic crimes through other avenues. The women about whom most has been written – those who were young and poor and accused of purely sexual crimes – are the ones who are least likely to have left any written trace of their experience. Such women were not, however, entirely passive. They sometimes rebelled against their treatment. In Cap Breton (on the Atlantic coast) a list of 'women who were notorious for being close to the Germans' was pinned up. An eighteen-year-old hairdresser tore up the list, because she claimed that her own name should not have been included on it.[91] Most of all, women did one thing in order to avoid *tontes* or as a result of them: they fled. Women associated with the Germans often left their home towns. Often they were formally or informally encouraged to do so (though sometimes the obligation to report to police stations kept them at home until their case had been considered by the authorities). Paris, a city big enough to get away from one's own past, was by far the most common destination.[92]

DISAPPOINTMENT

The memory of the liberation, like that of the 1940 defeat, was often associated with the memory of summer weather. Allied landings in Normandy began shortly before midsummer. Warm weather made it easier for people to abandon their homes and flee into the countryside in order to avoid bombing. Young men had often delayed their departure for the Maquis until the warm weather began in the spring of 1944. The festive atmosphere of the liberation went with the summer. Some towns celebrated the Fourteenth of July soon after the departure of German soldiers. As in 1940, hostilities interrupted the baccalauréat examinations (candidates for the Latin paper in 1944 were asked to discuss a passage from Tacitus on the 'inconvenience of living in coastal areas in time of war').

The autumn of 1944 changed the atmosphere in important ways. As in 1940, the beginning of the academic year brought a certain resumption of normal routines. Conspicuously, however, things had not returned to normal. There was still fighting on French soil. Food and fuel were still in short supply, sometimes more so than during the occupation, and French people dreaded the beginning of winter. Christmas 1944 was celebrated around trees decorated with the tinfoil that Allied bombers had dropped to distort German radar. Many of those whose homes had been bombed in Caen or Saint-Lô were still homeless in 1945. The American journalist Janet Flanner wrote in her diary on 17 January 1945:

Liberated Paris is now occupied by snow. Parisians are colder than they have been any other winter of the war. They are hungrier than they have been during any other winter of the war. They are the hungriest they have been since the Prussian siege of Paris, when their grandparents ate mice. Because there is still a lack of coal to transport anything, even coal, the citizenry is still waiting, muffled to its ears, for its single sack per person due last August. Electricity has just been ordered turned off all over France from morning till evening, except for an hour at noon, perhaps for the women in the dark to see what little they are cooking. For fear that the plumbing will burst, the water is turned off in many Parisian apartment houses and office buildings except between noon and two o'clock, too late to do most people any good.[93]

ABSENCE

The winter of 1944–5 strengthened awareness of absences. In December 1944 a nine-year-old boy, the son of a prisoner of war, asked his mother: 'When did Papa last write?' The answer was 29 October. The boy was lucky. Some of his classmates had not heard from their fathers for four or five months.[94] Around two million French people were in Germany; their numbers had been increasing ever since 1942, and had increased sharply in 1943 (with the advent of Service du Travail Obligatoire). In 1944 fewer young men had left for Germany under the STO programme but fewer still had come back on leave or been given the chance to desert. During the liberation, the Germans sometimes snatched workers as they left. Vichy had outlawed dancing in 1940 because it considered such festivities to be indecent when so many Frenchmen were in prisoner of war camps. In the summer of 1944 French people had danced in public again, but in October de Gaulle's government, conscious of how many French people remained in Germany, resurrected the ban on public dancing.

The remaining members of the Vichy government were taken to Germany and installed in a castle in the spa town of Sigmaringen. Laval and Pétain now refused to exercise their offices. However, Pétain agreed that Fernand de Brinon, formerly Vichy's ambassador to occupied Paris, could lead a French governmental delegation, which was to protect the interests of French citizens in Germany. Jacques Doriot established a separate Committee for National Liberation, which fantasized about dropping agents into 'American-occupied' France, until Doriot was killed in an Allied air attack.

French officials already in Germany in June 1944, that is, those who dealt with prisoners of war and French workers in German factories, were disconcerted by the arrival of those Frenchmen who followed the German army in its retreat from France. The new arrivals, political 'refugees' as their compatriots sometimes described them, were keen to seize on any position that might give them importance in the eyes of their German patrons. Marcel Déat, who had been Vichy's last Minister of Labour, attempted to make himself the representative of French workers in Germany. Gaston Bruneton, the head of the official Commissariat for French workers in Germany, resisted Déat's initiatives. He himself had returned to Germany from Paris in June 1944, apparently driven by concern for French workers in Germany rather than by the desire to flee from reprisals in France.[95] Bruneton emphasized his continuing loyalty to Pétain, whom he met at Belfort during his journey from France and then again at Sigmaringen.[96] The German authorities were divided and had matters more pressing than internal squabbles amongst the French to attend to. Bruneton wanted to maintain working relations with French collaborationist leaders and their associates whilst keeping the 'apolitical' character of his own agency. In practice, his position was hard to maintain. Faced with a request for a 'European' policy, one of his subordinates said bluntly: 'We can no longer be European, because European implies collaboration.'[97]

The presence of collaborationist 'refugees' from France in Germany meant that life for Frenchmen there became more awkward. Until the summer of 1944, they had been able to talk more or less freely amongst themselves. They could assume that most of their compatriots were anti-German or, at least, not likely to denounce them for expressing anti-German sentiments. After September 1944, this changed. French workers, who enjoyed no protection under the Geneva Convention, were increasingly conscious that they might be denounced by their compatriots.[98] The civil war that had raged in France itself was brought to German factories. The divisions and mutual suspicions of the French population in Germany intertwined with increasing Gestapo surveillance in the aftermath of the failed attempt on Hitler's life and with a more general hostility to foreigners on the part of the German population.

Most problems faced by French people in Germany, however, were not directly linked to politics. Letters and parcels from France now had to be delivered via the Red Cross – they often took months to get through. Food became more scarce and work rates more intense as the Germans struggled to squeeze as much as possible out of their war economy. Worst of all, French workers suffered from the impact of bombing by American and British forces. This became a severe problem after the Allied landing in Italy gave the USAAF and the RAF new bases from which they could reach Germany. The suffering was felt by everyone in Germany, but French workers suffered particularly badly because they were concentrated in factories that were crucial to the war effort (that is, those that were most likely to be bombed), and were sometimes denied access to bomb shelters: in Essen, 13.8 per cent of foreign workers were killed by bombing compared to 7.7 per cent of the overall population.[99] Bombing contributed to the general disruption of French life in Germany. Workers lost their accommodation and often their personal possessions (the absence of adequate clothing was a particular problem in the winter of 1944–5).

The harshest experience of all for many French workers came at the very end with the breakdown of order that accompanied German defeat. For those in Austria and east Germany, liberation by Russian forces was often a more terrifying experience than imprisonment by German ones. The French missions to workers, influenced by Pétainist thinking, regarded the Russians with horror and went to great lengths to ensure that they were picked up by American troops. The attitude of ordinary French workers was more complicated. The advance guards who liberated camps were generally greeted warmly. The mass of troops who arrived later were described in less favourable terms. Several witnesses, perhaps echoing the Nazi propaganda to which they had been exposed,[100] wrote of 'mongol hordes'. Soviet troops often underwent terrifying mood swings, governed by the availability of drink and women.

Some Frenchmen saw rapes. One estimated that 30 per cent of Austrian women between the ages of fifteen and fifty were raped by Soviet soldiers.[101] Some victims were women with whom the French workers were themselves associated. In one camp, Soviet soldiers obliged Frenchmen to take them to the barracks of Polish women, who were then raped along with three Frenchwomen in the same camp.[102] Two French workers who hid in a German flat saw the owner and her daughter being raped by Soviet soldiers.[103] A group of French workers travelled with a Hungarian woman (who was pregnant by one of them) and with two Frenchwomen (who were accompanied by their Greek lovers). Their lives were overshadowed by the fear of rape. When Russian troops finally caught them, the Hungarian woman managed to free herself but the Frenchwomen were raped. The French-men were obliged to fight with the Greek men in order to prevent the latter from seizing weapons and launching a suicidal attack on the Russians.[104] Frenchmen who tried to protect women from Russian soldiers were sometimes killed.[105]

Many prisoners of war were also liberated by the Red Army. Inmates of camps had the easiest time in this respect. They were concentrated in large groups and their status was clear to Soviet troops. Members of small work Kommandos, previously the most fortunate prisoners, found liberation more difficult. They risked being mistaken for German civilians or deserting German soldiers. Many recalled the moment of liberation as one of supreme disillusionment. Communists who went to greet their victorious comrades had their watches stolen.[106] Henri Laloux wrote that he would prefer to have been able to say that the Russians were like the Americans, 'handsome, dirty and proud throwing sweets to the admiring children'. What he actually described was an encounter with drunken soldiers from Mongolia who stole from the prisoners and raped a girl of twelve. One of the Russians tried to take Laloux's cape, which would almost certainly have meant his death, given that the Prussian winter had not yet ended. Only the intervention of a colleague who spoke Russian saved Laloux.[107]

Around 300,000 Frenchmen, mostly prisoners of war, were repatriated from Germany or central Europe via the Soviet Union. Most were released from German captivity before their comrades were liberated by the Americans in the west, but then took longer to return home. Many spent time in transit camps in Poland or the Soviet Union. Some were taken on foot or by train to Odessa, where it was initially planned to repatriate them by sea. Eventually most went back across Germany by train (a few reached their homes over a year after liberation).

RETURN

From February 1945 until early 1946 (and especially in April and May 1945) French people who had been in Germany were returning home. The arrival of one group caused considerable shock. Most French people had very little idea of conditions in German concentration camps. Many assumed that Resistance fighters who had been deported by the Germans would be kept in conditions more or less akin to those of prisoners of war. One bourgeois Parisian, meeting his sister at the Gare de Lyon after her release from Ravensbrück, asked 'where is your luggage?'[108] Deportees themselves often felt out of place in the country to which they returned. Hélie de Saint Marc, who returned to a bourgeois family in the south-west after having spent most of his twentieth year in Buchenwald, felt that the only relative with whom he had anything in common was a cousin who had joined the Milice during the last stages of the occupation. Saint Marc ultimately found his home in the Foreign Legion.[109]

French attention in 1945 was focused on concentration camps, to which resistants had been sent, rather than extermination camps, to which Jews had been sent. The Jews who had been most vulnerable to deportation were those of foreign origin who had few relatives or associates to remember their plight in France, and only a tiny minority of Jews who had been deported returned to France.

The French authorities attempted to sort people returning from Germany. This meant, in particular, that they tried to track down anyone who had shown sympathy for Nazism or who had denounced their compatriots. More generally, they tried to separate those who had volunteered to work in Germany from those who had been compelled to do so. Volunteers were denied the material advantages (extra rations and small sums of money) given to labour deportees and were sometimes investigated by the police (though volunteering to work in Germany was not, in itself, a crime). Precisely because volunteer workers so often came from 'non-respectable' parts of society, investigation into their circumstances often had a strongly moralistic tone. Employers and mayors were interrogated about the general conduct of returning volunteers and often described them in terms of their overall morality rather than in terms of their relations with the occupying forces: people whose supposed crime involved working for the Germans were often accused of being work-shy.

Because women had not been formally obliged to go to Germany, they attracted special attention from post-war investigators. Though women seem to have constituted only a minority of those who volunteered to work in Germany, they usually made up more than half of those who were investigated by the police on their return. In the Eure-et-Loir, for example, 116 women (as against 95 men) were investigated by police and 56 women (as against 43 men) were prosecuted, though only 183 women (as against 983 men) had asked for passports to go to Germany as volunteer workers.[110] Official appraisal of women returning from Germany was particularly moralistic. Their sex lives in general (not just their sexual relations with German soldiers) were discussed and women who escaped punishment often did so by proving that they were 'respectable'. A police report on a hairdresser returning to Paris gave substantial grounds for supposing that she had not been any kind of collaborator (she seems to have been compelled to go to Germany and had been imprisoned there for refusing to work in a factory). However, the police decision not to proceed against her seems to have been linked to a more general moral judgement; her employer reported that 'her conduct was not criticized', that she was 'serious and honest' and that she had 'no associations apart from friends at work'.[111] A girl returning to Morbihan told her interrogators that she had met a French prisoner of war in Germany with whom she had had her 'first physical relations' and that she was now pregnant by him and engaged to him.[112] One girl returning to Brittany showed her interrogators a medical certificate attesting that she was a virgin.[113] In the Eure-et-Loir, the departmental purge commission seems to have been inclined to leniency with regard to one woman because she was a 'jeune fille sérieuse' who was to marry 'a prisoner met in exile'.[114] A number of women asserted their respectability with reference to their husbands or fiancés. In Brittany, a woman admitted that she had behaved badly but then said that her husband had pardoned her 'careless faults' and that a judgement against her would hurt him because he had performed 'his duty as a resistant'.[115]

Men returning from Germany sometimes found it difficult to fit back into French society. Sometimes there were political reasons for this. Returnees were often seen as having been passive during the war. They, especially the 300,000 who had returned via the Soviet Union, were often strongly anti-Communist at a time when a quarter of the French population voted Communist and a much larger proportion was pro-Soviet. Pierre Thomas, a former *déporté du travail*, wrote of being asked about the Soviet Union by workers in France on his return: 'Could I tell these workers, impregnated with Marxist-Leninist philosophy, that the Soviet paradise was still purgatory?'[116] Pierre Picard-Gilbertier, a labour deportee who had been liberated by the Red Army, also found that his views of the Soviet Union were unwelcome in post-war France.[117] One of his companions showed his scars on returning to France and reported that he had been shot by Soviet soldiers two days after the liberation; a French officer said: 'Even if it's true, shut your mouth, that's my advice.'[118]

Sometimes return was difficult at a more intimate level. Labour deportees had been away from France for a relatively short period (usually less than two and a half years) and, in most cases, were still quite young (often not much older than an ordinary Frenchman would have been at the moment of his return from military service). Most of them married, began their professional lives and appeared to return to 'normal' life. Only during the 1980s, when retired men tried to explain their lives to their grandchildren in brief self-published memoirs, did it become clear how far labour deportees had been affected by their experience.

Prisoners of war had more obvious difficulty. Most of them had been away from home for five years. About half had been separated from wives and children. One prisoner's wife recalled that her young son had slept in her bed ever since 1940, and was reluctant to cede his place to the strange, prematurely aged man who had returned from his Stalag. Women who greeted returning prisoners (especially women who appeared in 'masculine' guise by wearing uniform or smoking) were often abused. François Cavanna described an ugly scene in a reception centre for returning prisoners:

Young girls from excellent families passed amongst us with buckets and aluminum bottles. In the buckets was red wine. They plunged the bottles into the plonk and held them out with a big, open smile: 'A bit of red, old chap?' . . . Riot spread, there was rape in the air . . . Smart officers came to the rescue of the big-hearted girls who could have been their sisters or their fiancées.[119]

Some prisoners felt that their masculinity was threatened by the fact that they had led passive lives for the last five years and by the fact that women had assumed more active roles in their absence.[120]

Between the arrival of American troops in North Africa in November 1942 and the return of the last French prisoners and deportees from Germany via the Soviet Union (in 1946 or later), French people experienced many different kinds of liberation. Some Resistance veterans looked back on the liberation as a time of disappointment, a time when France ought to have undergone a social and political revolution but failed to do so. Many saw 'their' liberation as having been usurped by someone else. People who saw themselves as the 'real' Resistance were particularly hostile to the Communists and Gaullists who proved so adept at manipulating memories of Resistance and liberation –

though the Communists and Gaullists were both soon marginalized in the political system of the Fourth Republic.

The liberation was not a time of unqualified rejoicing. The arrival of Allied troops in mainland France often marked the beginning of the most violent period of the war for French people. Nazi persecution continued (the last train taking Jews from Paris left on 18 August 1944) but this was now mixed with the less systematic violence of massacres carried out by German troops operating in areas they did not know and with the damage inflicted in some areas by Allied bombardment. In all sorts of ways, the liberation could be a period of horrible suffering. Marie-José was born in Lillebonne in the south-west of France on 17 June 1944. Her mother, Thérèse, was an eighteen-year-old girl; her father was a German soldier. Amazingly, the father managed to get leave from his unit (already fighting in Normandy) to visit his lover and their child. He held Marie-José in his arms and said that she was a 'beautiful baby'. Then he returned to Normandy. Thérèse heard that her lover had been in a prisoner of war camp in England for a time but she never saw him again.[121]

Perhaps the most curious absence at the liberation was Vichy. Pétainism was not displaced by the first liberation (that of North Africa) because the Americans and their French allies had no particular interest in overthrowing it. De Gaulle and his associates subsequently drove most Pétainists out of the French administration in North Africa, but they did so mainly for reasons of realpolitik rather than principle. Events in the town of Vichy were an odd little sideshow in the summer of 1944. Pétain did not want to be seen to abandon his post voluntarily and the Germans did not want to leave him behind in France. A discreet deal was struck. On 20 August German soldiers broke down the doors of the Marshal's apartment at the Hôtel du Parc. Pétain's entourage protested but his bodyguards did not open fire. A crowd of around two hundred gathered outside in the Rue des États-Unis and sang the 'Marseillaise' as the Vichy government left its capital. Allied troops did not, however, arrive in Vichy, a place of no strategic importance. Once the Germans had gone, the town was liberated by a mixture of *maquisards* who had come down from the surrounding hills and policemen who were only too happy to find themselves once again on the right side.

Pétainism was not displaced by the liberation of mainland France because it had, to a large extent, ceased to exist by the summer of 1944. Jean Guéhenno wrote in Paris on 22 August 1944 (just before de Gaulle arrived) that Vichy had 'vanished like a puff of smoke'. In one sense, of course, Vichy did vanish. Few people expressed much loyalty to the regime after the beginning of 1943. By 1944, it simply had no authority. There is another sense, though, in which Vichy was invisible at the liberation, in that so many of its assumptions were taken for granted. All sorts of aspects of the liberation – its emphasis on 'Frenchness' and masculinity, and its desire to 'clean' France – would have fitted neatly into a Pétainist view of the world.

Merdecluse

VLADIMIR. – Mais tu as bien été dans le Vaucluse?

ESTRAGON. – Mais non, je n'ai jamais été dans le Vaucluse! J'ai coulé toute ma chaude-pisse d'existence ici, je te dis! Ici! Dans la Merdecluse!

VLADIMIR. – Pourtant nous avons été ensemble dans le Vaucluse, j'en mettrais ma main au feu. Nous avons fait les vendanges, tiens, chez un nommé Bonnelly, à Roussillon. (Samuel Beckett, *En attendant Godot*)

Bonnelly, a 'surly truculent man', was real. When Samuel Beckett had fled to Roussillon from Paris after a corrupt priest betrayed the Resistance network of which he was a member, he worked on Bonnelly's farm. What Beckett's own life in Roussillon was like is a matter of some debate. One biographer says that he worked on Bonnelly's farm because he was desperate for food; another suggests that, able to obtain money from his family in neutral Ireland, he was relatively well off and that he worked on the farm partly just to kill time. Beckett himself would almost certainly be contemptuous of attempts to root his play in some specific historical or biographical circumstance.

Whatever the reality of Beckett's experience, 'Merdecluse' is an appropriate title for the conclusion to a book on wartime France. The first and simplest conclusion of this book is that life for most French people between 1940 and 1944 was miserable. In recent years, discussion of the period has laid an ever heavier emphasis on those people who suffered most horribly: Jews who were deported and killed, Resistance fighters who were tortured to death, gypsies who were interned, women who were abused and humiliated at the liberation. Sometimes this focus gives the impression that life for the rest of the

French population was bearable or even pleasant. This is not true. Even those people who did not attract the animosity of Vichy or the Germans – even, indeed, some of those people on whom Vichy looked with favour – suffered from the lack of food, from the threat of German violence and from displacement as they sought to escape the fighting in 1940 or again in 1944. At one time or another, over two and a half million French people were held in Germany (either as workers or as prisoners of war). About one in five Frenchmen were in Germany for at least part of the war. This did not just affect *them*. It affected families who were missing their adult males (something that had economic as well as emotional consequences) and it affected young men who abandoned their normal lives in order to avoid coming to German attention.

Suffering was not evenly distributed amongst the French population. The rich could buy their way around rules in all sorts of ways, and often their actions – by forcing up black market prices, for example – made life worse for the poor. Inhabitants of the countryside (especially fertile areas in which more than one kind of crop was cultivated) were better off than inhabitants of the cities, not just because they had more food but also because their chances of avoiding contact with the Germans were higher. However, privilege was always relative. Young men who were sent to work in German factories may have resented their bourgeois contemporaries whose families had pulled strings to get them jobs in French coal mines (and hence exemption from compulsory labour service), but working in a coal mine (especially the over-worked, poorly maintained coal mines of 1943) was hardly attractive. Farmers rarely went hungry, but the profits they made during the occupation were often illusory: having several hundred thousand francs under the mattress was not necessarily useful at a time of high inflation when there was little to buy. Sometimes the short-term gains of 1940–44 went with land that was worked excessively or inappropriately in ways that produced long-term damage.

In the interview he gave for the film *The Sorrow and the Pity*, Pierre Mendès France gave a striking description of his escape from a French prison in 1941. Having climbed to the top of the prison wall, he noticed a young couple under a tree beneath him. The boy was trying to persuade the girl to come home with him. Mendès waited breathless until the girl yielded to the boy's entreaties, at which point he jumped down into the street. He suggested that the incident epitomized his feelings about 'love, freedom and escape'. Mendès always laid a heavy emphasis on freedom and choice: the most important word in his political lexicon was 'choisir'.

Perhaps the couple under the tree would have had a more complicated relationship to the notions of freedom and choice than the officer and politician perched above them. The couple were young and, presumably, working class. Their lives in ordinary times would have been more constrained than that of Mendès. They would have been subject to the authority of their parents and employers. The occupation would have made things worse. The young man would almost certainly have been called up for compulsory labour service in 1943. The girl's resistance to her suitor, which exasperated Mendès, may not just have been the result of moral reservations: a woman who became pregnant was suddenly subject to all sorts of new constraints, and a number of those women who were punished after the war for having 'volunteered' to work in Germany seem to have gone partly because they had been abandoned by the fathers of their children.

For Mendès, the divisions in his life during the occupation were relatively clear. For one thing, the defeat of 1940 marked a sharp break. Before this date, he was a privileged member of the social and political elite; after it he was condemned because of his left-wing political views and his Jewishness (though he maintained some powerful contacts). Equally, for Mendès, there was a clear division between freedom on one side of the wall and imprisonment on the other. For most French people, constraint was less obvious but also, in some respects, harder to escape from. Very few people were physically confined. The majority of French prisoners of war did not live behind barbed wire, and the majority of young men called up for compulsory labour service arrived at the station without guards. However, very few people felt they were making free choices. Often all courses of action open to them would have unpleasant consequences, and their only hope was to choose the course that would be least horrible. People obeyed Vichy or the Germans because they feared reprisals against themselves, or because they feared losing even the very limited advantages they sometimes enjoyed.

Matters were made more complicated by the fact that for many French people 1940 did not mark a sharp break between freedom and oppression but rather a stage in which constraints that had existed before the war were intensified. Foreigners had enjoyed only limited rights in Third Republic France; they did not have the vote and did not have the automatic right to stay in the country. Pressures on foreigners intensified after the summer of 1940, partly because they were particularly vulnerable during the wave of unemployment that followed the defeat, and partly because Vichy and the Germans sometimes simply press-ganged them into certain kinds of work. Prostitutes were subject to formal regulations, which meant that they had to endure regular medical inspections and were placed under the authority of brothel-keepers (who had official status) and of the *police des moeurs*. After 1940, pressures on prostitutes became more intense as Vichy enacted new laws (which increased the powers of brothel-keepers) and the Germans imposed their own regulation in areas frequented by their soldiers. The number of unregistered 'clandestine' prostitutes increased during the occupation, but these women were not free. They were harassed by the police, ordered around by pimps and often driven out of their own towns by the pressure of 'respectable' opinion. People with criminal convictions were another group with limited freedom. Even when they were released from prison, they could be forbidden to live in particular areas and could be subject to the continued attentions of the police. After 1940, the number of people convicted of crimes increased (partly because of simple hunger) whilst conditions in prison became much worse. The police force became more aggressive in their pursuit of deviance of all kinds. Legal minors were under the formal control of their parents. This had severe consequences for those children who did not have parents and who were entrusted to the *Assistance Publique* and thus to the authority of the state.

The complexity of 'freedom' in wartime France is illustrated by the fact that post-war authorities so often condemned those who had 'volunteered' to work or fight for the Germans. Yet those who 'volunteered' were often drawn from those groups who did not enjoy full freedom even in the purely legal sense of the word and whose 'real' freedom was even more limited by poverty, isolation or lack of information. Just as 1940 did not mark a sharp break in these people's lives, 1944 did not always bring liberation. This was not just because some of them had gone to Germany (or followed Germans into their last defensive strongholds in western France); it was also because the purge that accompanied the liberation created whole new swathes of people whose freedom was restricted in some way. People were forbidden to live in particular areas or forbidden to work in particular professions. Women who had associated with the Germans were declared to be registered prostitutes and subjected to medical inspections.

If freedom was complicated, so was authority. The Germans and the Vichy government both issued specific instructions that affected the lives of French people. Both the Germans and the Vichy leaderships, however, were divided in complicated ways, which meant that there were occasions on which Germans connived at the escape of French prisoners of war and occasions on which departmental prefects, loyal to Vichy, were in bitter conflict with the Milice, established by Vichy. Simply saying where the French state began and ended is complicated. Some agencies were specifically established by the new regime and staffed with people loyal to it. Even here, there could be divisions because some Vichy agencies (the Scapini Mission to prisoners of war or the Légion des Combattants) espoused a conservative and patriotic Pétainism that often brought them into conflict with more explicitly collaborationist agencies loyal to Laval. Besides, Vichy took over a whole state apparatus that had existed before it and that continued to exist after it. Sometimes this continuity of institutions went with discontinuity of personnel; thus Vichy made numerous appointments to the prefectural corps in 1940 and this corps was heavily purged at the liberation. There were, however, other institutions in which the same people remained in place through the period from, say, 1936 to 1946. Seeking specifically Pétainist elements in the French administration can, in any case, be deceptive because there were certain respects (especially with regard to those underprivileged groups described above) in which Vichy policy continued that of the Third Republic and was continued by the governments of the Fourth Republic.

It is not always clear where the divide between state and society lay in wartime France. Mayors of small villages and even the rural gendarmerie drew their nominal authority from the state but whatever real power they possessed often sprang from their informal relations with powerful local figures.

Sometimes the most pressing constraints in people's lives did not come directly from Vichy or the Germans at all but were mediated through French society. Young men who went to work in Germany in 1943 may, in formal terms, have been responding to an order that had been given by the Vichy government (itself under pressure from the Germans). However, the young men in question often perceived their decision as being made with reference to their own communities. They felt under pressure from local notables, or sometimes from their own fathers, to go in order to avoid reprisals against their communities or against their families. The power of the French family increased greatly during the occupation (for reasons that had little to do with Vichy's official policy of familialism). The best-off people in France were those who had wealthy and supportive families with links to the countryside. The worst-off were those who were persecuted within their own family: young girls who were abused by their stepfathers were particularly likely to 'volunteer' to work for the Germans.

Families were often a key aspect of the constraints that governed the lives of French people during the occupation. The most important thing that impelled Frenchmen who had been evacuated to England in the summer of 1940 to return home was the desire to be reunited with their families. Most of those who crawled through woods and swam across rivers to cross the various demarcation lines in 1940 were trying to rejoin relatives. It is interesting to speculate about how family circumstances influenced some very prominent people. Charles de Gaulle would probably not have let the fate of his relatives influence his actions, but the fact that his mother died in France shortly after he left for London in 1940 must have made his defiance of Vichy easier. Would Jean Moulin have been less willing to take risks if he had been the happily married father of four children (instead of being a womanizing divorcee with no strong attachments to anyone except his sister)? Would François Mitterrand have been less brave, and ultimately less willing to break with his own conservative background, if he had not been jilted by his fiancée when he was in a German prisoner of war camp?

Just as the constraints of the occupation were often mediated through the social structures of family and community, so they were also mediated through the cultural structures of people's understanding. In some ways, historians who 'demythologize' the period actually move us further away from understanding it because people's perceptions and actions were so heavily influenced by false information. False information affected political views. Historians may know, to take the most obvious example, that Laval did not force Pétain into collaboration with the Germans, but the fact that many people saw Pétain as somehow distinct from his own government goes a long way to explaining why loyalty to the Marshal was sometimes so durable. False information also explains many more small-scale decisions taken by people with regard to their daily lives. Prisoners did not make the most of the chance to escape before being taken to Germany in the summer of 1940 because they believed, wrongly, that they would soon be released. Similarly, many young men agreed to go to Germany when called up for Service du Travail Obligatoire in 1943 because they believed, again wrongly, that sanctions would be taken against their families if they did not do so.

Diaries and memoirs of the occupation are full of beliefs that we know, in retrospect, to be false, but diaries and memoirs are usually written by people who are relatively well informed and educated. Imagine how a thirty-nine-year-old illiterate woman from Chartres, who had taken two German lovers and then volunteered to work in Germany, can have understood her experience. Assuming that, like nine-tenths of women who worked for the Germans, she spoke no German, she can only have communicated with her lovers and employers in simple pidgin French. When her first lover was posted to the Russian front, she can have had no means of staying in touch with him. Did his comrades explain where he had gone? Did she try to get other people to write letters on her behalf? Did she hope to resume contact with one or other of her lovers by going to Germany? She would, presumably, have been unable to read the documents that she signed when she went to Germany, and she can have had few means of staying in touch with anyone she knew in France when she went there. By the time that she returned, she seems to have abandoned all attempt to explain or justify herself. She insisted to her interrogators that she had never denounced anyone, but beyond that her responses were autistically uncommunicative.[1]

What memory did the everyday constraints of wartime France leave after 1945? Some sorts of experience were more insistently recalled than others. The 'memory' of prisoners of war tended to focus on those relatively privileged prisoners in camps, especially officers' camps, and on those who were well enough connected to get repatriated early. Stalag IA, which housed *aspirants*, had only 3,000 inmates but generated an entire journal dedicated to its memory. By contrast, the 250,000 'transformed' prisoners – those, mainly underprivileged prisoners who agreed to accept the status of civilian workers – have no place in French collective memory. There is no association to represent them, they have no official status and there is, so far as I am aware, not a single retrospective account written by one of them.

Different memories of the occupation were sometimes mutually exclusive. Writers about prisoners of war or labour deportees often described themselves as working on 'forgotten' experiences, though in practice both categories of people were more recalled than those of, say, people who had volunteered to work for the Germans.

The memory of the First World War was a unifying one. A very substantial proportion of the French adult male population had undergone similar experiences and those experiences were increasingly seen as sources of pride. By contrast, there was no single unifying experience of the Second World War. Experience in the Loire, where food was relatively plentiful, was different from that in Marseilles, where food was very scarce. Experience in the Pas-de-Calais, where Germans were present in large numbers from 1940 until 1944, was very different from experience in a hill village in the Auvergne where the Germans barely appeared until the summer of 1944. Experience of liberation in Normandy (the scene of heavy fighting between Allied and German troops) was different from that of the south-west, which was largely liberated by the Maquis and which, consequently, often saw the violent settling of scores between French people.

Memories were divisive as well as divided. This was not simply because of explicit political divisions that pitted collaborators,

Pétainists and Resistance fighters against each other. It was also because of more small-scale and local animosities that involved communities and even families. The village of Roussillon in the Vaucluse in which Beckett spent the later part of the war was not badly off during the occupation. Food was not as plentiful as visitors might have hoped (Escoffier's widow ran the local hotel), and the Vaucluse was not in an area as fertile as, say, the Beauce, but it did support several different kinds of agriculture and the surrounding area was, at least, self-sufficient in food. When Laurence Wylie visited the village in 1950 he found that people did not get along as well as they had done before the war. Perhaps the locals discussed the reasons for this more frankly with an outsider than they would have done with each other. Wylie wrote:

The division between villagers and farmers ... became more acute. The villagers, who had to depend on the country people for food, complained that the farmers charged them black-market prices, that often the farmers refused to sell them anything, preferring to sell their goods on the black market in the city. The farmers complained that the villagers tried to buy produce at legal prices and then take it to the city to sell it at black-market prices. Each incident increased suspicion and jealousy. Whenever anyone received a special gasoline or clothing or food ration there were always *les autres* who started a rumour that it was obtained illegally. It seemed that no one could do anything without arousing the antagonism of someone else.[2]

Memory of day-to-day life under the occupation was influenced by something else. During the thirty years after the Second World War, the years that the French know as the 'trente glorieuses', the French economy grew fast. The division between countryside and city diminished. Distinctions of locality that had mattered so much during the occupation were blurred by transport, television and social mobility. People writing autobiographical accounts of their lives during the occupation, the kind that many men wrote for the benefit of their grandchildren during the 1980s, were aware that they were trying to evoke a world that would seem distant and inexplicable to many of their readers. This was not simply because the prospect of foreign invasion or highly repressive government became remote. The social conditions that had governed many people's lives during the occupation had completely disappeared. When the inhabitants of the village of Roussillon wanted to cash in on Beckett's wartime sojourn, they had to strip the house in which he had lived of all its modern amenities in order to 'recreate' the occupation.

Notes

Place of publication for English books is London, and for French books is Paris, unless otherwise indicated.

THE UNFREE FRENCH: INTRODUCTION

1. The phrase 'archival bedrock' is used in Robert Paxton, *Vichy France 1940–1944: Old Guard and New Order* (1972), p. 397.
2. Paxton and Michael Marrus, *Vichy France and the Jews* (1981).
3. For the view that Vichy's anti-Semitism was 'plagiarized' from the Germans, see Guy de Rothschild, *The Whims of Fortune* (1985).
4. Annie Kriegel, *Ce que j'ai cru comprendre* (1991), p. 123.
5. Dominique Veillon has published 'serious' history of occupied France under her own name and works aimed at a broader audience, and often treating more social themes, in collaboration with Dominique Missika. See, for example, Dominique Veillon, *Le Franc-tireur: Un journal clandestin, un mouvement de résistance* (1977) and Dominique Missika, *La Guerre sépare ceux que s'aiment, 1939–1945* (2001).
6. Henri Amouroux, *La Grande Histoire des Français sous l'occupation* (10 vols., 1976–93).
7. Fondation Nationale des Sciences Politiques, *Le Gouvernement de Vichy, 1940–1942* (1972), pp. 91–6.
8. René Limouzin, *Le Temps des J3* (1983) and *Le Temps des vérités* (1991).
9. Daniel Cordier, *Jean Moulin: L'inconnu du Panthéon* (3 vols., 1989–93).
10. Jacques Laurent, *Histoire égoïste* (1976), is a particularly striking example of a book that deliberately teases historians; see, for example, p. 335.

CHAPTER 1. SUMMER 1940

1. Raymond Aron, *Mémoires: 50 ans de réflexion politique* (1983), p. 231.
2. Paris, Archives de la Préfecture de Police (PP), BA 2105, report on events of 18/20 Dec. 1940.
3. Roger Langeron, *Paris, juin 40* (1946). In his diary, the prefect of Paris police Roger Langeron talks of the death of Martel and fifteen other suicides on 14 June 1940.
4. Simone de Beauvoir, *La Force de l'âge* (1960), p. 457.
5. Cl Carles, 'La Corniche de Montpellier de 1939 à 1942', *Revue d'histoire de la deuxième guerre mondiale*, 112 (1978), pp. 8–28.
6. Alexander Werth, *The Last Days of Paris* (1940), p. 209.
7. Ginette Guitard-Auviste, *Paul Morand, 1888–1976: Légende et vérités* (1994), p. 213.
8. Paul Jankowski, *Communism and Collaboration: Simon Sabiani and Politics in Marseille, 1919–1944* (New Haven, 1989), p. 74.
9. C. Denis Freeman and Douglas Cooper, *The Road to Bordeaux* (1940), p. 292.
10. Roger Tessier, *Carnets de guerre et de captivité d'un Rochefortais, 1939–1945* (Rochefort, 1998), p. 37.
11. Paris, Archives Nationales (AN), F 9 2242, commandant Élie Charnal to Scapini, 14 Oct. 1941.
12. AN, F 9 2242, prefect of the Vendée to Secretary of State for War, 24 May 1941, enclosing a letter (unsigned and undated), apparently from M. Allain who had commanded the guards.
13. Alfu (this is, apparently, the only name of author), *Léo Malet: Parcours d'une oeuvre* (Amiens, 1998).
14. Gustave Folcher, *Les Carnets de guerre de Gustave Folcher, paysan languedocien, 1939–1945* (2000), pp. 148 and 149.
15. Francis Ambrière, *Les Grandes Vacances* (1956, first published in 1946), p. 37.
16. Yves Durand, *La Vie quotidienne des prisonniers de guerre dans les Stalags, les Oflags et les Kommandos, 1939–1945* (1987), p. 35.
17. Ibid., p. 34.
18. Ibid., p. 36.
19. Joseph Raoux, *Pas si simple* (Privas, 1998), p. 101.
20. Sandrine Lallam, 'La Population de la Seine et les forces d'occupation allemandes, 14 juin 1940–25 août 1944', Mémoire de Maîtrise, Paris IV (2000), p. 36.

21. Ibid., p. 42.

22. Bernard Pierquin, *Journal d'un étudiant parisien sous l'occupation, 1939–1945* (1983), p. 35.

23. Étienne Dejonghe and Yves Le Maner, *Le Nord-Pas-de-Calais dans la main allemande, 1940–1944* (Lille, 2000), p. 222.

24. Nicole Dombrowski, 'Beyond the Battlefield: The French Civilian Exodus of 1940', Ph.D., New York University (1995), p. 204.

25. Micheline Bood, *Les Années doubles: Journal d'une lycéenne sous l'occupation* (1974), p. 25, entry for 18 June.

26. Lallam, 'La Population de la Seine et les forces d'occupation allemandes', p. 62.

27. Mireille Albrecht, *Vivre au lieu d'exister: La vie exceptionnelle de Berty Albrecht, compagnon de la libération* (Monaco, 2001), p. 175.

28. Lallam, 'La Population de la Seine et les forces d'occupation allemandes', p. 62.

29. Guy de Rothschild, *The Whims of Fortune* (1985).

30. Jacques Benoist-Méchin, *La Moisson de quarante: Journal d'un prisonnier de guerre* (1941), pp. 121–34.

31. Langeron, *Paris, juin 40*, p. 24.

32. José Gotovitch, 'Les Belges du repli: Entre pagaille et organisation', in Max Lagarrigue (ed.), *1940: La France du repli; L'Europe de la défaite* (2001), pp. 51–64, at p. 57.

33. Cited in Dombrowski, 'Beyond the Battlefield', p. 208.

34. Lallam, 'La Population de la Seine et les forces d'occupation allemandes', p. 36.

35. Ibid.

36. Langeron, *Paris, juin 40*.

37. Ephraïm Grenadou and Alain Prévost, *Grenadou, paysan français* (1978, first published 1966), p. 197. An army vet told Grenadou that he was mad to leave.

38. Yves Durand, 'Une adolescence paysanne et lycéenne sous l'occupation: Témoignage et réflexions', in Jean-William Dereymez (ed.), *Être jeune en France (1939–1945)* (2001), pp. 63–70.

39. Grenadou and Prévost, *Grenadou, paysan français*, pp. 195–200.

40. Freeman and Cooper, *The Road to Bordeaux*, pp. 195–6.

41. Edmond Dubois, *Paris sans lumière, 1939–1945: Témoignages* (Lausanne, 1946), p. 58.

42. Ibid., p. 60.

43. Sarah Fishman, *The Battle for Children: World War II, Youth Crime, and Juvenile Justice in Twentieth-Century France* (Cambridge, Mass., 2002), p. 48.

44. Barbara, *Il était un piano noir: Mémoires interrompus* (1998), p. 17.

45. Bood, *Les Années doubles*, p. 25.

46. Arthur Griffon, *Adolescence paysanne en Franche-Comté: Doubs, 1937–1941* (Besançon, 1990).

47. Gotovitch, 'Les Belges du repli', p. 57.

48. Pierquin, *Journal d'un étudiant parisien sous l'occupation*, pp. 13–27.

49. Zoltán Szabó, *L'Effondrement: Journal de Paris à Nice, 10 mai 1940–23 août 1940* (2002), p. 125.

50. Louis Noguères, *Vichy, juillet 40* (2000), p. 59.

51. Nick Atkins, *The Forgotten French: Exiles in the British Isles, 1940–1944* (Manchester, 2003), p. 39.

52. PP, BA 1804, report, 26 June 1940.

53. Andrew Lycett, *Ian Fleming: The Man Behind James Bond* (1995), p. 116.

54. Dubois, *Paris sans lumière*, p. 64.

55. Jean Vidalenc, *L'Exode de mai-juin 1940* (1957), p. 376.

56. Nicole Dombrowski, 'Surviving the German Invasion of France: Women's Stories of the Exodes of 1940', in Dombrowski (ed.), *Women and War in the Twentieth Century: Enlisted With or Without Consent* (1999), pp. 116–37, at p. 117.

57. Stanley Hoffmann, 'Témoignage', in Lagarrigue (ed.), *1940: La France du repli*, pp. 15–20.

58. Lisa Bésème-Pia, *Recettes de Vendée, Loire-Atlantique, Charente et Deux-Sèvres importées en Ardennes et ailleurs: Depuis l'exode de 1940* (Langres, 1992).

59. N. Loeffler, S. Moll, G. Platt, M. Shneider, E. Schultess and J. Werthlé, *Mémoire d'un exode: L'Évacuation de Saint-Louis 1939/1940* (Saint-Louis, 1989), p. 37.

60. Lynne Taylor, *Between Resistance and Collaboration: Popular Protest in Northern France, 1940–1945* (2000), p. 107.

61. Ibid., p. 108.

62. Sandrine Lallam values the impact of pillaged goods in the Seine during the first three months of occupation at 6,847,787 francs. See Lallam, 'La Population de la Seine et les forces d'occupation allemandes', p. 59.

63. For the behaviour of the Paris police in June 1940, see Langeron, *Paris, juin 40*.

64. Dombrowski, 'Beyond the Battlefield', p. 140.

65. Ibid., p. 166.

66. Taylor, *Between Resistance and Collaboration*, p. 107.

67. Henri Drouot, *Notes d'un Dijonnais pendant l'occupation allemande, 1940–1944* (Dijon, 1998), entry for 25 Aug.

68. Pierre Miquel, *L'Exode, 10 mai-20 juin 1940* (2003), p. 111.

69. Albert Castères, *Pour que ça se sache aussi* (2001), pp. 38–40.

70. Vladimir Lossky, *Sept jours sur les routes de France: Juin 1940* (1997).

71. Robert Paxton, *Vichy France: Old Guard and New Order* (1972), p. 15.

72. De Beauvoir, *La Force de l'âge*, p. 467.

73. Bood, *Les Années doubles*, p. 24.

74. Françoise Giroud, *Si je mens* (1972), p. 76.

75. De Beauvoir, *La Force de l'âge*, p. 451.

76. Charles Rist, *Une saison gâtée: Journal de la guerre et de l'occupation, 1939–1945*, ed. Jean-Noel Jeanneney (1983), p. 71.

CHAPTER 2. VICHY

1. Borough Guides, *Vichy* (Cheltenham, 1919), p. 10.

2. Michèle Cointet, *Vichy capitale, 1940–1944* (1993), p. 57.

3. Henri Du Moulin de Labarthète, *Le Temps des illusions* (Geneva, 1946), p. 16.

4. Ginette Guitard-Auviste, *Paul Morand, 1888–1976: Légende et vérités* (1994), p. 214.

5. Du Moulin de Labarthète, *Le Temps des illusions*, p. 171.

6. Lucien Rebatet, *Les Décombres* (1942), p. 480.

7. Alfred Fabre-Luce, *Vingt-cinq années de liberté: L'épreuve (1939–1946)* (1964), p. 55.

8. René Belin, *Du Secrétariat de la CGT au Gouvernement de Vichy* (1978), p. 127.

9. Olivier Wieviorka, *Les Orphelins de la République: Destinées des députés et sénateurs français (1940–1945)* (2001), p. 15. Thrivier did not, in fact, serve on the Conseil National for very long.

10. Louis Noguères, *Vichy, juillet 40* (2000), p. 57.

11. Ibid., pp. 148–9.

12. Wieviorka, *Les Orphelins de la République*, p. 15.

13. The Soviet representative in Vichy was upgraded to ambassadorial status in March 1941.

14. Elizabeth Wiskemann, *The Europe I Saw* (1968), p. 158.

15. Cointet, *Vichy capitale*, p. 137.

16. Pierre Taittinger, *Ce que le pays doit savoir* (1941), p. 84. Taittinger said that the navy was, of all the armed services, 'the least gangrened'.

17. Alexander Werth, *The Last Days of Paris* (1940), p. 195, entry for 14 June: 'Darlan had always been a good man, and very pro-British.'

18. George E. Melton, *Darlan: Admiral and Statesman of France, 1881–1942* (1998).

19. Jean-Claude Barbas (ed.), *Philippe Pétain, Maréchal de France, chef de l'état français: Discours aux Français, 17 juin 1940–20 août 1944* (1989), p. 33.

20. Cited in Pierre Servent, *Le Mythe Pétain: Verdun ou les tranchées de la mémoire* (1992), p. 210.

21. Bénédicte Vergez-Chaignon, *Le Docteur Ménétrel: Éminence grise et confident du Maréchal Pétain* (2002).

22. Joseph Barthélemy, *Mémoires: Ministre de la Justice, Vichy, 1943–1945* (1989), p. 67.

23. Michèle Cointet, *Pétain et les Français* (2002), pp. 144–9.

24. Simon Kitson, 'The Marseilles Police in Their Context: From the Popular Front to the Liberation', D.Phil., University of Sussex (1995), p. 69.

25. Editor's note in Barbas (ed.), *Philippe Pétain: Discours aux Francais, 17 juin 1940–20 août 1944*, p. 85. The redrafting of the speech in Pétainist style was not, in this case, very successful. Supporters of Bergery recognized the speech instantly as being the work of their leader: Philippe Burrin, *La Dérive fasciste: Doriot, Déat, Bergery* (1986), p. 362.

26. Bruno Goyet, *Henri d'Orléans, Comte de Paris (1908–1999): Le prince impossible* (2001), p. 269.

27. In 1991 Jean Guitton wrote that Pétain's insistence on remaining at his post had ruined his reputation but saved the lives of prisoners. He added: 'Is it not the definition of love to sacrifice oneself to save others?' Letter to General Le Groignac, cited in Xavier Walter, *Un roi pour la France: Henri Comte de Paris, 1908–1999. Essai de biographie intellectuelle et politique pour servir à la réflexion d'un prince du XXIe siècle* (2002), p. 287.

28. Jean Guitton, *Pages brûlées: Journal de captivité, 1942–1943* (1984, first published in 1943), p. 170, entry for 28 Dec. 1942.

29. Marc Bergère, *Une société en épuration: Épuration vécue et perçue en Maine-et-Loire. De la libération au début des années 50* (Rennes, 2003), p. 87.

30. Cited in 'De Gaulle mon père', interview between Michel Tauriac and Philippe de Gaulle in *Le Point*, 17 Oct. 2003.

31. Antoine Prost, 'Verdun', in Pierre Nora (ed.), *Les Lieux de mémoire* (1997), pp. 1755–80, at p. 1761.

32. D. J. Taylor, *Orwell: The Life* (2003), p. 97.

33. Receiving journalists on 18 Nov. 1940, Pétain said: 'I am often accused of being the enemy of journalists . . . I have not seen journalists much because they scare me. During the other war I did not see members of parliament.'

34. Du Moulin de Labarthète, *Le Temps des illusions*, p. 21.

35. In February 1941, René Benjamin, Pétain's biographer, dined with the Marshal seven times: François Darlan, nominally the second most important person in the government, did not do so once. Cointet, *Pétain et les Français*, p. 141.

36. Thierry Bouclier, *Tixier-Vignancour: Une biographie* (2003), p. 66.

37. Jacques Le Roy Ladurie, *Mémoires, 1902–1945* (1997), p. 204.

38. Jean-Paul Cointet, *La Légion Française des Combattants, 1940–1944: La tentation du fascisme* (1995), p. 71.

39. David Gautier, 'Jean Borotra, 1898–1994: Au service de ses engagements', Mémoire de Maîtrise, Paris I (2001).

40. Georges Belmont (Pelorson), *Souvenirs d'outre-monde: Histoire d'une naissance* (2001).

41. Guitard-Auviste, *Paul Morand*, p. 218.

42. Xavier Vallat, *Le Nez de Cléopâtre: Souvenirs d'un homme de droite, 1919–1944* (1957), p. 203.

43. Ibid., p. 193.

44. Ibid., p. 189. Vallat suggested that Laval's arguments served no purpose for the right (which was already prone to support Pétain) and repelled part of the left.

45. Dominique Paoli, *Maxime, ou le secret Weygand* (Brussels, 2003) discusses rumours about Weygand's paternity.

46. Cointet, *La Légion Française des Combattants*, pp. 210, 212 and 401.

47. PP, BA 1793, unsigned note, 6 Dec. 1943, quoting circular by Raymond Brassié, an associate and friend of Gervais, a *directeur adjoint* of the Légion.

48. Darnand's relationship with Catholicism was idiosyncratic. The ceremonies of the Milice were saturated with religious reference – though Darnand himself seems to have broken with the Church after the Vatican's condemnation of Action Française in 1926. Charbonneau described him as practising 'un anticléricalisme vieille France'. Henry Charbonneau, *Les Mémoires de Porthos* (1981), p. 422.

49. Cited in Philippe Buton, *La Joie douloureuse: La libération de la France* (2004), p. 83.

50. René Benjamin, *Le Grand Homme seul* (1943), p. 39.

51. Miranda Pollard, *Reign of Virtue: Mobilising Gender in Vichy France* (Chicago, 1998), p. 35.

52. For a description of life in the American embassy at Vichy, see Adam Nossiter, *The Algeria Hotel: France, Memory and the Second World War* (2001).

53. Irwin Wall, *The United States and the Making of Post-war France,*

1945–1954 (Cambridge, 1991), p. 20. For writing on America and Vichy France generally, see William D. Leahy, *I Was There* (New York, 1950); Robert Murphy, *Diplomat Among Warriors* (New York, 1964); William Langer, *Our Vichy Gamble* (New York, 1947); Joel Hurstfield, *America and the French Nation, 1939–1945* (Chapel Hill, NC, 1986).

54. Émile Laure, *Pétain* (1941), pp. 416–20.

55. Benjamin, *Le Grand Homme seul*, p. 39.

56. Du Moulin de Labarthète said that he had heard the phrase at a rally in Paris in 1934. *Le Temps des illusions*, p. 157.

57. Philippe Ariès, *Un historien du dimanche* (1980), p. 81.

58. Gilles Martinez, 'Comment les libéraux sont arrivés à Vichy: Étude d'un parcours paradoxal', *Revue d'histoire moderne et contemporaine*, 4/63 (1999), pp. 571–90.

59. Du Moulin de Labarthète, *Le Temps des illusions*, p. 157.

60. Cointet, *La Légion Française des Combattants*, p. 207.

61. René Benjamin, *Le Maréchal et son peuple* (1941), p. 6.

62. Ibid., p. 5.

63. Laure, *Pétain*, p. 421.

64. Alfred Fabre-Luce, cited by Pierre Assouline in *Le Nouvel observateur*, 21–7 Sept. 1989.

65. Maurice Martin du Gard, *La Chronique de Vichy, 1940–1944* (1975), p. 146, entry for July 1941.

66. Cointet, *Pétain et les Français*, p. 209.

67. Cited in Pierre Laborie, *Les Français des années troubles* (2001), p. 30.

68. Jean-Marie Flonneau, 'L'Évolution de l'opinion publique de 1940 à 1944', in Jean-Pierre Azéma and François Bédarida (eds.), *Vichy et les Français* (1990), pp. 506–22.

69. Bernard Lecornu, *Un préfet sous l'occupation allemande* (1984), pp. 135–7.

70. Ibid.

71. On the circumstances in which François Lehideux took the oath to Petain, see Michèle Cointet, *Pétain et les Français*, p. 208.

72. Cointet, *La Légion Française des Combattants*, p. 406. In fact, the original oath of loyalty taken by members of the Légion contained no direct reference to Pétain.

73. Ibid., p. 191.

74. AN, F 9 2193, 'Rapport de M. Herbert délégué permanent de Scapini, sur la prêtestation de serment aux prisonniers rapatriés', 27 April 1942.

75. Charles Rist, *Une saison gâtée: Journal de la guerre et de l'occupation, 1939–1945*, ed. Jean-Noel Jeanneney (1983), editor's introduction, p. 21.

76. Edmond Duméril, *Journal d'un honnête homme pendant l'occupation allemande (juin 1940–août 1944)*, ed. J. Bourgeon (Thonon-les-Bains, 1990), p. 72, entry for 26 Oct. 1940.

77. Louis Guilloux, *Carnets, 1921–1944* (1978), p. 280, entry for 26 Feb. 1943.

78. PP, BA 1784.

79. PP, BA 1784, report, 30 April 1941.

80. See, for example, Duméril, *Journal d'un honnête homme pendant l'occupation allemande*, p. 72, entry for 26–7 Oct. 1940.

81. Liliane Schroeder, *Journal d'occupation, Paris 1940–1944: Chronique au jour le jour d'une époque oubliée* (2000), p. 64.

82. Henri Drouot, *Notes d'un Dijonnais pendant l'occupation allemande, 1940–1944* (Dijon, 1998), p. 8, entry for 2 Oct. 1940.

83. Ibid., p. 10, entry for 11 Oct. 1940.

84. Ibid., p. 49, entry for 14 Dec. 1940.

85. Ibid., entry for 28 Feb. 1940. Presumably, although Drouot did not allude to it, it was Flandin's replacement by Darlan that provoked his loss of faith in Pétain.

86. AN, F 9 3003, Fleury to Heuclin, 28 May 1943. A footnote has been added to the text of this letter. Fleury was the representative in Switzerland of the Légion Française des Combattants. Heuclin tried to have Fleury dismissed but Admiral Bard refused to allow this, saying that there was no one to replace Fleury. I have not been able to find any more information about the operation of the Légion in Switzerland (Cointet's book on the Légion does not mention Fleury or any presence of the Légion in Switzerland). I assume, given that this letter is to be found in an archive concerned with prisoners of war, that the Légion in Switzerland was concerned with those prisoners, more than 30,250 of them, who had been interned in Switzerland.

87. Werth, *The Last Days of Paris*, p. 137.

88. In 1940 French people in the occupied zone were allowed to communicate with their relatives in the unoccupied zone by means of pre-written cards allowing certain kinds of information to be relayed. It was, for example, possible to write 'X is without news of Y', 'A is ill' or 'B is well'. On 6 October 1940 someone signing himself Dupont-Durand filled in such a card with news that included the statements 'British aviation is well'; 'German aviation is gravely ill' and 'the British admiralty is without news of the Italian fleet'.

89. Burrin, *La Dérive fasciste*, p. 361.

90. Quoted in Jacques Cantier, *L'Algérie sous le régime de Vichy* (2002), p. 40.

91. Rémy Handourtzel, *Vichy et l'école, 1940–1944* (1997), p. 39.

92. Drouot, *Notes d'un Dijonnais*, p. 7, entry for 26 Sept. 1940.

93. Schroeder, *Journal*, p. 50, 23 Aug. 1940.

94. Marie Bonaparte, *Mythes de guerre* (1945), pp. 119–23.

95. Raoul Girardet, a young man from a royalist background, described himself as 'drunk with joy' when he heard of Hitler's invasion of the Soviet Union because he knew that the 'boches were screwed'. Pierre Assouline and Raoul Girardet, *Singulièrement libre: Entretiens avec Pierre Assouline* (1990), p. 68.

96. Quoted in Cointet, *Pétain et les Français*, p. 233.

97. Vallat, *Le Nez de Cléopâtre*, p. 199.

98. Cited in Handourtzel, *Vichy et l'école*, p. 216. The authors of this report seem to have inferred the opinions of primary school teachers from their pre-war affiliations.

99. Jacqueline Sainclivier, 'Étude départementale: Les notables en Ille-et-Vilaine', in Azéma and Bédarida (eds.), *Vichy et les Français*, pp. 382–8, at pp. 384–5.

100. Michèle Cointet, *Le Conseil National de Vichy, 1940–1944* (1989), p. 17.

101. Bergère, *Une société en épuration*, pp. 199–202.

102. AN, F 9 3678, Direction des Services de l'Armistice to Secrétaire Général des Anciens Combattants, 9 Aug. 1941.

103. Cointet, *La Légion Française des Combattants*, p. 226.

104. Cointet, *Le Conseil National de Vichy*, p. 14.

105. Mont-de-Marsan, Archives Départementales des Landes (ADL), 81 W 1, 'Un groupe de révolutionnaires nationaux' to de Brinon, 8 May 1941, and a second letter from the same 'group' to sub-prefect at Dax, 6 June 1941.

106. There is a large file of correspondence on this matter in ADL, 81 W 1. See in particular from sub-prefect of Dax to mayor of Meilhan, 4 Nov. 1937.

107. Quoted in Pierre Laborie, *L'Opinion publique sous Vichy* (1990), p. 247.

108. Cointet, *Le Conseil National de Vichy*, p. 16.

109. Laborie, *L'Opinion publique sous Vichy*, p. 257.

110. Eric Jennings, *Vichy in the Colonies: Pétain's National Revolution in Madagascar, Guadeloupe and Indochina. 1940–1944* (Stanford, Calif., 2001), p. 37.

111. Ibid., p. 200.

112. Cantier, *L'Algérie sous le régime de Vichy*, p. 377.

113. Jill Matcham, 'Maréchal Nous Voilà! Quebec and Pétain: *Le Devoir*, 1939–1942' (undergraduate long essay, King's College, London, 2000).

114. Drouot, *Notes d'un Dijonnais*, p. 253, 15 Aug. 1941.

115. Martin du Gard, *La Chronique de Vichy*, p. 173.

116. Erwan Saladin, 'La Nuit à Rennes sous l'occupation, 18 juin 1940-4 août 1944', Mémoire de Maîtrise, Université de Rennes II (2001), p. 120.

117. Schroeder, *Journal*, p. 68, entry for 13 Feb. 1941.

118. Sandrine Lallam, 'La Population de la Seine et les forces d'occupation allemandes, 14 juin 1940–25 août 1944', Mémoire de Maîtrise, Paris IV (2000), p. 70.

119. Ibid.

120. Jacques Bénoist-Méchin, *La Moisson de quarante: Journal d'un prisonnier de guerre* (1941), p. 336.

121. Abel Bonnard, *Inédits politiques*, ed. Olivier Mathieu (1987), p. 188.

122. Quoted in Pierre Assouline, *Hergé* (1996), p. 243.

123. Pascal Ory, *Le Petit Nazi illustré: Vie et survie du Téméraire (1943–1944)* (1979, 2002), p. 20.

124. Benjamin, *Le Grand Homme seul*, p. 11.

125. Jacques le Goff, *Entretiens avec Marc Heurgon: Une vie pour l'histoire* (1996), pp. 29–31.

126. Drouot, *Notes d'un Dijonnais*, p. 10, entry for 11 Oct. 1940.

127. Ibid., entry for 14 Nov. 1940.

128. Duméril, *Journal d'un honnête homme pendant l'occupation allemande*, p. 72, entry for 25–6 Oct. 1940.

129. Rémi Dalisson, 'La Propagande festive de Vichy: Mythes fondateurs, relecture nationaliste et contestation en France de 1940 à 1944', *Guerre mondiale et conflits contemporains: Revue d'histoire*, 207 (2002), pp. 5–35.

130. Natalie Dompnier, *Vichy à travers les chants: Pour une analyse politique du sens et de l'usage des hymnes sous Vichy* (1996), p. 56.

131. Benjamin, *Le Grand Homme seul*, p. 37.

132. Edgar Faure, *Avoir toujours raison . . . c'est un grand tort* (1984), p. 160.

133. PP, BA 1793, 'Défilé de la Légion des Volontaires Français', 19 June 1943.

134. AN, F 60 1447, Fourst to le Commissaire Général [of the Chantiers de la Jeunesse], 20 March 1943. Report by Marsaud, 29 May 1943.

135. AN, F 60 1448, 'Rapport à M. le Chef de la Mission de la Jeunesse auprès du Chef du Gouvernement sur les départs à Pont de Claix des jeunes des Chantiers de la Jeunesse au titre du service obligatoire du travail', 1 June 1943. Report by coach driver, 29 May 1943.

CHAPTER 3. LIVING WITH THE ENEMY

1. Ephraïm Grenadou and Alain Prévost, *Grenadou, paysan français* (1978), p. 203.

2. Maurice Rajsfus, *Paris, 1942: Chroniques d'un survivant* (2002), pp. 29–30.

3. Louis Guilloux, *Carnets, 1921–1944* (1978), pp. 284–5, entry for 21 March 1943.

4. Eric Alary, *Le Canton de Bléré sous l'occupation: Une position unique en France* (1994), p. 96.

5. Jean-Claude Catherine, *La Ligne de démarcation en Berry-Tourraine, 1940–1944* (Châteauroux, 1999), p. 121.

6. Philippe Souleau, *La Ligne de démarcation en Gironde: Occupation, résistance et société* (Périgueux, 1998), p. 23.

7. Ibid. About a third of all requests to cross the line involved dealing with death or illness in the family; half concerned the exploitation of land or professions.

8. On Jews interned for attempting to cross the demarcation line see, for example, PP, BA 1839, note, 4 March 1942, on the Grinwald family.

9. Catherine, *La Ligne de démarcation en Berry-Tourraine*, p. 67.

10. Ibid., p. 62.

11. Ibid., p. 68.

12. Eric Alary, *La Ligne de démarcation* (2002), p. 64.

13. Marguerite Poiré, *Mes années volées: Journal d'exil d'une jeune Lorraine dans les Sudètes, 1943–1945* (2001).

14. Pierre Billard, *Louis Malle: Le rebelle solitaire* (2003), p. 40.

15. In 1898, Prince Louis, serving in Algeria, had had a daughter, Charlotte-Louise-Juliette, apparently by a washerwoman. During the Second World War, the prince fell in love with an actress whom he eventually married.

16. Pierre Abramovici, *Un rocher bien occupé: Monaco pendant la guerre, 1939–1945* (2001).

17. PP, BA 1784, note, 29 July 1940.

18. Ernst Jünger, *Premier journal parisien*, II: *1941–1943* (1980), p. 62, entry for 13 Nov. 1941.

19. Ibid., p. 67, entry for 13 Feb. 1942.

20. Philippe Burrin, *La France à l'heure allemande, 1940–1944* (1995), p. 95.

21. Jacques Le Roy Ladurie, *Mémoires, 1902–1945* (1997), p. 219.

22. Robert Gildea, *Marianne in Chains: In Search of the German Occupation* (2002), p. 70.

23. Edmond Duméril, *Journal d'un honnête homme pendant l'occupation*

allemande (juin 1940-août 1944), ed. J. Bourgeon (Thonon-les-Bains, 1990), pp. 99–104.

24. Sandrine Lallam, 'La Population de la Seine et les forces d'occupation allemandes, 14 juin 1940–25 août 1944', Mémoire de Maîtrise, Paris IV (2000), p. 47.

25. The statue was pulled down shortly afterwards, and Mangin's son-in-law, Jacques Lecompte Boinet, became one of the first leaders of the French Resistance.

26. Sacha Guitry, *Quatre ans d'occupations* (1947), p. 356.

27. Roger Peyrefitte, *La Fin des ambassades* (1953), pp. 306–8.

28. PP, BA 1792, report by gendarmes from Pantin, 23 Nov. 1940.

29. Lallam, 'La Population de la Seine et les forces d'occupation allemandes', p. 106.

30. See, for example, PP, BA 1794, Commissaire de la Voie Publique, 4ème arrondissement, to Directeur Général de la Police Municipale, 27 Oct. 1943. A drunken German soldier, rebuffed by a *fille publique* in a bar, had fired shots.

31. Lallam, 'La Population de la Seine et les forces d'occupation allemandes', p. 55.

32. Liliane Schroeder, *Journal d'occupation, Paris 1940–1944: Chronique au jour le jour d'une époque oubliée* (2000), p. 59, entry for 6 Dec.

33. PP, BA 1792, report by Albert L., 17 Nov. 1943.

34. Erwan Saladin, 'La Nuit à Rennes sous l'occupation, 18 juin 1940–4 août 1944', Mémoire de Maîtrise, Université de Rennes II (2001), p. 188.

35. Solène Gouedard, 'Les Relations franco-allemandes: Un cas particulier. Les réquisitions de logements à Rennes à partir de 1940', Mémoire de Maîtrise, Rennes II (2001).

36. Henri Drouot, *Notes d'un Dijonnais pendant l'occupation allemande, 1940–1944* (Dijon, 1998), wrote frequent entries about this subject during the first year of the occupation. In August 1941 (p. 264) Drouot wrote that he had given up recording traffic accidents caused by the Germans, presumably because they were so numerous.

37. James Knowlson, *Damned to Fame: The Life of Samuel Beckett* (1997), p. 319.

38. Schroeder, *Journal*, pp. 28–9, entry for 10 July 1940.

39. Ibid., p. 48, entry for 23 Aug. 1940.

40. Lynne Taylor, *Between Resistance and Collaboration: Popular Protest in Northern France, 1940–1945* (2000), p. 29.

41. PP, BA 1784, letter from Oscar de Ferenzy, 14 June 1940.

42. Duméril, *Journal d'un honnête homme pendant l'occupation allemande*, p. 5, entry for 26–9 Aug. 1940.

43. Ibid., p. 22, entry for 28 Jan. 1941.

44. Ibid., p. 160, entry for 12 Sept. 1941.

45. Ibid., p. 236, entry for 21 Oct. 1942. For relations between Hotz and Duméril, see also Robert Gildea, *Marianne in Chains*.

46. Duméril, *Journal d'un honnête homme pendant l'occupation allemande*, p. 219, entry for 9 March 1941.

47. Catherine Offredic, 'Travailler volontairement au service des Allemands pendant la seconde guerre mondiale: L'exemple des femmes des Côtes-du-Nord et du Finistère, à travers les dossiers des procédures judiciaires des chambres civiques, 1940–1946', Mémoire de Maîtrise, Rennes II (2000), p. 76. On the comparative scarcity of women working for the Germans who spoke German, see ibid., p. 45.

48. Caroline Robert, 'Les Femmes travailleuses volontaires avec les Allemands durant la seconde guerre mondiale, dans le Morbihan, à travers les archives de la chambre civique', Mémoire de Maîtrise, Rennes II (2000), p. 46.

49. Paul Sanders, *Histoire du marché noir, 1940–1946* (2001), p. 35.

50. ADL, 81 W 1, C. to prefect, 15 April 1944. Duverger to sub-prefect of Dax, 23 March 1944.

51. Christian Bougeard, 'Les Chantiers allemands du Mur de l'Atlantique', in Bernard Garnier and Jean Quellien (eds.), *La Main d'oeuvre française exploitée par le IIIe Reich* (Caen, 2003), pp. 185–204.

52. Patrice Arnaud and H. Bories-Sawala, 'Les Volontaires . . . dimensions statistiques, images, mythes et réalités', ibid., pp. 107–26, at pp. 111–12.

53. AN, F 9 2191, 'Rapport établi pour le consul général Noël Henry', unsigned, 1 April 1942.

54. AN, F 60 1452, police report, 1 Sept. 1943.

55. AN, 83 AJ 17, report from Sudetenland, undated.

56. PP, BA 1790, cabinet of prefect, report about Yvonne C., 15 Sept. 1945.

57. PP, BA 1790, note about Marcel C., 22 June 1945.

58. Julie Chassin, 'Les Travailleurs volontaires ont-ils été indignes? L'exemple des travailleurs volontaires du Calvados', in Garnier and Quellien (eds.), *La Main d'oeuvre française*, pp. 544–62, at p. 560.

59. AN, F 9 2191, 'Rapport établi pour le consul général Noël Henry', unsigned, 1 April 1942.

60. Jean-Pierre Harbulot, *Le Service du Travail Obligatoire: La région de Nancy face aux exigences allemandes* (Nancy, 2003), p. 114.

61. PP, BA 1790, response to letter from police in Orléans, 27 Nov. 1942.

62. Harbulot, *Le Service du Travail Obligatoire*, p. 220.

63. PP, BA 1790, report by Commissaire de Police de Belleville to Directeur de la Police Judiciaire about Robert Maurice V., 11 June 1945.

64. Juliette Goublet, *Oder Neisse 1943: Les cahiers de soeur Gertrude, volontaire pour la relève* (Aurillac, 1971), pp. 16–17.

65. Chartres, Archives Départementales de l'Eure-et-Loir (ADEL), 1 W 78, report of Commission d'Épuration of Comité Départemental de la Libération, 25 June 1945, Madeleine P., who left France in February 1944, had been persuaded by a friend to join the PPF. Suzie C., who incited P. to join the PPF, also persuaded Micheline J. This would mean that a sample of over two hundred volunteers contained three members of collaborationist parties.

66. ADEL, 14 W 62, prefect to prefect of Paris police, 9 July 1943; attached letter from sub-prefect of Châteaudun to prefect, 5 July 1943.

67. ADEL, 14 W 62, prefect to prefect of police, 15 Feb. 1944.

68. ADEL, 20 W 304, prefect to Commissaire de Police, 25 Jan. 1943: 'Son attitude envers la politique du Maréchal est loyale.'

69. ADEL, 14 W 62, Commissaire de Police to prefect, 30 May 1943.

70. PP, BA 1788, prefect of police of Paris to prefect of Orléans, 8 Jan. 1943. A French common criminal, having escaped from prison in 1940, was arrested for another offence and then joined with political prisoners in singing revolutionary songs.

71. ADEL, 14 W 62, prefect to prefect of police, 7 Feb. 1944.

72. ADEL, 20 W 304, Inspecteur des Services de l'Assistance to prefect of Eure-et-Loir, 21 Sept. 1943.

73. Taylor, *Between Resistance and Collaboration*, p. 28.

74. Harbulot, *Le Service du Travail Obligatoire*, p. 114.

75. See, for example, PP, BA 1790, report on volunteers returning to Belleville, 4 June 1945; four out of six volunteers cited unemployment as their reason for going.

76. ADEL, 1 W 78, police report on Roger E., 10 Oct. 1945.

77. ADEL, 1 W 78, various reports.

78. ADEL, 1 W 78, Commission d'Épuration, report about René P., 10 Aug. 1945.

79. ADEL, 1 W 78, Commission d'Épuration, report on Raymond S., 27 Aug. 1945.

80. Bernd Zielinski, 'L'Exploitation de la main d'oeuvre française par l'Allemagne et la politique de collaboration (1940–1944)', in Garnier and Quellien (eds.), *La Main d'oeuvre française*, pp. 47–65, at pp. 50–52. Patrice Arnaud suggests that 40,000 volunteers out of 72,000 who left France by 23 August 1941 were French; Arnaud and Bories-Sawala, 'Les Volontaires . . . dimensions statistiques', ibid., p. 111.

81. PP, BA 1790, Commissaire Principal du 16ème arrondissement to Directeur Général de la Police Municipale, 23 June 1945. A group of three

returning volunteers contained two Yugoslavs and one Russian. At least one man who volunteered to work in Germany was a German national. BA 1788, response to enquiry from Orléans by prefect of police about twenty-nine volunteers, 8 Jan. 1943.

82. Annie-Paule Dimeglio, 'Le Service du Travail Obligatoire dans le département du Var', Mémoire de Maîtrise, Nice (1972), p. 161.

83. PP, BA 1790, report from Belleville on Boris C., of Bulgarian nationality, 14 June 1945.

84. ADEL, 1 W 78, Commissaire de Police to Commissaire du Gouvernement, 12 July 1945.

85. ADEL, 20 W 304, prefect to prefect of police, 13 Sept. 1943, enclosing letter from father of Castello A. about his son, born 5 Dec. 1922: 'My son went to Germany without anyone asking my opinion. Consequently, I do not think that it is useful for me to give my authorization now.' See also ADEL, 14 W 62, prefect to prefect of police, 13 Aug. 1943, about Marcel G., whose mother had refused authorization.

86. ADEL, 14 W 62, prefect to prefect of police, 14 Aug. 1943, about André D., born 1924, whose parents had not been traced.

87. ADEL, 1 W 78, interrogation of Colette G., 18 June 1945.

88. Arnaud and Bories-Sawala, 'Les Volontaires . . . dimensions statistiques, images, mythes et réalités', in Garnier and Quellien (eds.), La Main d'oeuvre française, pp. 107–26, at p. 120.

89. Ibid., p. 121.

90. AN, F 22 2024, Secrétaire Général à la Main d'Oeuvre to Secrétaire Général du Maintien de l'Ordre, 6 May 1944.

91. Guy Pedron, La Prison sous Vichy (1993), pp. 53 and 58.

92. AN, F 9 2191, 'Rapport établi pour le consul général Noël Henry', unsigned, 1 April 1942.

93. ADL, Rs 77, prefect of Gironde to prefect of Landes, 7 Aug. 1942.

94. ADL, Rs 77, letter from prefect of Landes (not clear to whom), 18 July 1942.

95. André Laurens, Une police politique sous l'occupation: La Milice française en Ariège, 1942–1944 (Foix, 1982), pp. 128–31.

96. Paul Jankowski, Communism and Collaboration: Simon Sabiani and Politics in Marseille, 1919–1944 (New Haven, 1989), pp. 90 and 91.

97. PP, BA 1793, report, unsigned, 15 June 1943. The man convicted of murder in September 1940 had not been considered responsible for his actions and had been placed in a place of éducation surveillée until reaching his majority.

98. PP, BA 1793, report, 1 Feb. 1943.

99. PP, BA 1793, report signed Baylot, 14 June 1943.

100. PP, BA 1793, report, unsigned, 22 Aug. 1943.

101. Philip French, *Malle on Malle* (1993), p. 100.

102. Jean-Marc Berlière, *Les Policiers français sous l'occupation: D'après les archives inédites de l'épuration* (2001), pp. 116–18.

103. PP, BA 1794, report from 19th arrondissement, 6 Oct. 1943.

104. PP, BA 1794, report 'Au sujet d'un incident à la Gare Saint-Lazare', 26 March 1943.

105. PP, BA 1793, 'Liste nominative des gradés et gardiens blessés dans la soirée du 27 août 1943 (2e anniversaire de la LVF)'.

106. PP, BA 1793, report, unsigned, 14 June 1943.

107. PP, BA 1793, report, signed Marcel Jalliot, 29 Aug. 1943.

108. PP, BA 1800, 8 Sept. 1943, 'Armement des fonctionnaires des services actifs de la Préfecture de Police'. The police asked for 462 sub-machine guns and 24,397 automatic pistols.

109. PP, BA 1793, Commissaire Principal of 8th arrondissement to Directeur Général de la Police Municipale, 29 March 1944.

110. PP, BA 1792, letter from Directeur Général to prefect of police, 7 Nov. 1943.

111. PP, BA 1850, Brunel to Directeur de la Police Judiciaire, 23 July 1941.

112. ADL, Rs 1076, Marmillod to Commissaire Principal du Service des Renseignements Généraux, 11 Feb. 1944.

113. Offredic, 'Travailler volontairement au service des Allemands', p. 78.

CHAPTER 4. JEWS, GERMANS AND FRENCH

1. AN, F 22 2024, Departmental Delegate of Commissariat Général à la Main d'Oeuvre to Regional Commissioner, 31 Jan. 1944. I assume this is the Sigismund Moszkowski who arrived at Auschwitz on convoy number 68 from Drancy in February 1944.

2. Antoine Sabbagh (ed.), *Lettres de Drancy* (2002), p. 59.

3. Andrew Shennan, *Rethinking France: Plans for Renewal 1940–1946* (Oxford, 1989), p. 44.

4. Pierre Assouline and Raoul Girardet, *Singulièrement libre: Entretiens avec Pierre Assouline* (1990), p. 34.

5. Maurice Martin du Gard, *La Chronique de Vichy, 1940–1944* (1975), p. 89, entry for 7 Dec. 1940.

6. Quoted in Rémy Handourtzel, *Vichy et l'école, 1940–1944* (1997), pp. 243–4.

7. For details of this case, see Ingrid Galster, *Sartre, Vichy et les intellectuels* (2001).

8. Deirdre Bair, *Samuel Beckett: A Biography* (1978).

9. Maurice Rajsfus, *Paris, 1942: Chroniques d'un survivant* (2002), p. 46.

10. Micheline Bood, *Les Années doubles: Journal d'une lycéenne sous l'occupation* (1974), p. 142, entry for 1 June 1942.

11. Emmanuelle Rioux, 'Les Zazous: Un phénomène socio-culturel pendant l'occupation', Mémoire de Maîtrise, Paris X (1987).

12. Cédric Gruat and Cécile Leblanc, *Amis des juifs: Les résistants aux étoiles* (2005), p. 22.

13. PP, BA 1839, 20 June 1942, 'Liste des aryennes internées au camp des Tourelles pour avoir manifesté leur sympathie pour les juifs, et soumises au port de l'Étoile de David et de l'inscription "amie des juifs".'

14. Gruat and Leblanc, *Amis des juifs*, pp. 31–5.

15. Léon Poliakov, *L'Auberge des musiciens: Mémoires* (1981), p. 125.

16. Marie Reille's story emerged at the trial of Maurice Papon, though she was herself dead by this time. After the liberation, she complained about the role that the French authorities had played in her deportation but was told that these matters were covered by 'prefectoral immunity'.

17. Jack Adler, *The Jews of Paris and the Final Solution* (Oxford, 1987), p. 10.

18. David Diamant, *Le Billet vert: La vie et la Résistance à Pithiviers et Beaune-la-Rolande* (1977), p. 122.

19. André Kaspi, *Les Juifs pendant l'occupation* (1997), p. 148.

20. On the difficulty of getting out of France for Jews, see Vicki Caron, *Uneasy Asylum: France and the Jewish Refugee Crisis, 1933–1942* (Stanford, Calif., 1999).

21. Claude Lévi-Strauss, *Tristes Tropiques* (1955), p. 19.

22. Carole Fink, *Marc Bloch: A Life in History* (Cambridge, 1991), p. 265.

23. Even people whose experiences ought to have been similar often disagree about the attitudes of French schools to Jews. On 7 December 1997, Simone Dreyfus-Gamelon wrote to *Le Monde* to say how badly treated she had been at her lycée during the occupation. Many Jewish women wrote in response insisting that they had been well treated.

24. Pierre Billard, *Louis Malle: Le rebelle solitaire* (2003), p. 462.

25. Guy de Rothschild, *The Whims of Fortune* (1985).

26. Adrian Nossiter, *The Algeria Hotel: France, Memory and the Second World War* (2001), p. 194.

27. Georgette Elgey, *The Open Window* (1974, first published in France in 1973), p. 20.

28. Ibid., p. 35.

29. Ibid., p. 32.

30. Annie Kriegel, *Ce que j'ai cru comprendre* (1991), p. 137.

31. Ibid., pp. 128–9.

32. Maurice Rajsfus, *1953: Un 14 juillet sanglant* (2003); *La Police et la peine de mort, 1977–2001: 196 morts* (2002).

33. Adler, *The Jews of Paris*, p. x.

34. Annette Wieviorka and Floriane Azoulay, *Le Pillage des appartements et son indemnisation* (2000). See also Brigitte Vital-Durand, *Domaine privé* (1996).

35. Georges Gheldman, *16 juillet 1942* (2005). Gheldman tells his story, and reproduces many documents, on his website. Gheldman's parents were on convoy number 7 from Drancy to Auschwitz. Of the 999 people on this convoy, 17 survived.

36. Yair Auron, *Les Juifs d'extrême gauche en mai 68: Une génération révolutionnaire marquée par la Shoah* (1998).

37. Pierre Goldman, *Souvenirs obscurs d'un juif polonais né en France* (2005); Michaël Prazan, *Pierre Goldman: Le frère de l'ombre* (2005).

38. Alfred Brauner, *Ces enfants ont vécu la guerre* (1946), p. 211.

CHAPTER 5. FRENCHWOMEN AND THE GERMANS

1. ADL, 81 W 1, C. to prefect of Landes, 15 April 1944.

2. ADEL, 1 W 78, interrogation of Gaston P., 15 June 1945.

3. Charles Rist, *Une saison gâtée: Journal de la guerre et de l'occupation, 1935–1945*, ed. Jean-Noel Jeanneney (1983), p. 110.

4. Maurice Rocqueil cited in J. Daures, *Nos vingt ans volés: L'histoire des 2,700 Aveyronnais victimes des camps nazis du travail forcé* (Rodez, 1993), p. 255.

5. AN, F 9 2183, *directeur du cabinet* to *homme de confiance* Stalag VIA, 10 July 1942.

6. Robert Zaretsky, *Nîmes at War: Religion, Politics and Public Opinion in the Gard, 1938–1944* (University Park, Pa., 1995), p. 144.

7. Marc Bergère, *Une société en épuration: Épuration vécue et perçue en Maine-et-Loire. De la libération aux début des années 50* (Rennes, 2003), p. 309.

8. Philippe Burrin, *La France à l'heure allemande, 1940–1944* (1995), p. 213.

9. Jean-Paul Picaper and Ludwig Norz, *Enfants maudits* (2004).

10. Marc Hillel and Clarissa Henry, *Au nom de la race* (1975).

11. Burrin, *La France à l'heure allemande*, p. 213.

12. Picaper and Norz, *Enfants maudits*, p. 109.

13. Ibid., p. 142.

14. Ibid., p. 321.

15. Caroline Robert, 'Les Femmes travailleuses volontaires avec les Allemands durant la seconde guerre mondiale, dans le Morbihan, à travers les archives de la chambre civique', Mémoire de Maîtrise, Rennes II (2000), p. 32.

16. ADEL, 1 W 78, report by Paul Prades, 28 Aug. 1945. M. said that he had ejected a German from his wife's kitchen in February 1942, and then left because he feared reprisals. See also 1 W 78, Commission d'Épuration, 22 June 1945. André L., who left in August 1942, feared that his wife, who frequented Germans, would denounce him for sabotage.

17. Catherine Offredic, 'Travailler volontairement au service des Allemands pendant la seconde guerre mondiale: L'exemple des femmes des Côtes-du-Nord et du Finistère, à travers les dossiers des procédures judiciaires des chambres civiques, 1940–1946', Mémoire de Maîtrise, Rennes II (2000), p. 119.

18. ADEL, 1 W 78, report by Paul Prades, about Hélène B., 17 July 1945.

19. Bergère, *Une société en épuration*, p. 154.

20. François Rouquet, *L'Épuration dans l'administration française: Agents de l'état et collaboration ordinaire* (1993), p. 131.

21. Quoted in Rémy Handourtzel, *Vichy et l'école, 1940–1944* (1997), p. 227.

22. Marc Bergère, 'Épuration vécue et perçue à travers le cas du Maine-et-Loire: De la libération au début des années 50', Thèse de Doctorat, Rennes II (2001), p. 660.

23. Robert, 'Les Femmes travailleuses', p. 37. Women brought before the Chambres Civiques were not an entirely representative sample: they were mainly people who were seen to have aggravated their case in some way.

24. Patrice Arnaud and Helga Bories-Sawala, 'Les Volontaires . . . dimensions statistiques, images, mythes et réalités', in Bernard Garnier and Jean Quellien (eds.), *La Main d'oeuvre française exploitée par le IIIe Reich* (2002), pp. 107–26, at p. 111. Note that Jean-Pierre Azéma, in the introduction to the same book, gives the figure of 40,000 women volunteers in Germany.

25. PP, BA 1790, report, unsigned, 16 Aug. 1945, about Simone B., born 8 Aug. 1926.

26. Offredic, 'Travailler volontairement au service des Allemands', p. 116.

27. ADEL, 1 W 78 contains a number of accounts of women who were taken to Germany under false pretences. See, for example, report by Paul Prades about A., 11 Nov. 1945.

28. Offredic, 'Travailler volontairement au service des Allemands', p. 69.

29. Pierre Thomas, *STO à Berlin: Et les sirènes rugissaient* (Signy-le-Petit, 1991), p. 73.

30. ADEL, 1 W 78, Commission d'Épuration, 24 Aug. 1945. When the woman returned she had a new lover and a baby and, according to her interrogators, was no longer interested in her first four children.

31. ADEL, 1 W 78, Commissaire de Police to Commissaire du Gouvernement, 31 July 1945, about Marcelle D. Note that the Commissaire de Police states that she was fifteen at time of departure; interrogation of the woman herself (30 July 1945) suggests that she was sixteen. See also Commission d'Épuration, 20 July 1945, report on Marcelle G., who left in 1942 at the age of seventeen.

32. ADEL, 1 W 78, Commission d'Épuration, 9 July 1945, report on Marcelle, Jean and Raymonde F.

33. ADEL, 1 W 78, Commission d'Épuration, 29 June 1945, report on Léone N.

34. ADEL, 1 W 78, Commission d'Épuration, 27 Aug. 1945, report on Martinette G. who went to Germany in January 1945; ibid., report, undated, signed Lefèbre and Gossare, about Marie B. She claimed that the father of her child was a 'soi-disant réfractaire'. She broke with him before the child was born, went to Germany, and returned to Paris in time for the child's birth. Her child died aged six weeks.

35. ADEL, 1 W 78, Commission d'Épuration, 13 Aug. 1945.

36. AN, 83 AJ 28, Dr Fevrier to Bruneton, 16 Dec. 1944.

37. AN, 83 AJ 28, 'Liste des femmes enceintes', 5 Jan. 1945.

38. ADEL, 1 W 78, interrogation of Madeleine L., 25 June 1945; see also the second quotation at the beginning of this chapter.

39. Odette Chambroux, *L'Exilée* (Les Monédières, 1990).

40. ADL, Rs 77, Commissaire de Police to mayor of Dax, 22 April 1941.

41. AN, F 9 2193, report by Herbert, délégué à Châlons-sur-Marne, 7 June (no year given but seems to be 1941).

42. Offredic, 'Travailler volontairement au service des Allemands', p. 84.

43. Micheline Bood, *Les Années doubles: Journal d'une lycéenne sous l'occupation* (1974), p. 180, entry for 16 Dec. 1942.

44. Ibid., p. 184, entry for 4 Feb. 1943.

45. Ibid., p. 101, entry for 15 April 1941.

46. Ibid., p. 140, entry for 30 May 1941.

47. Ibid., p. 186, entry for 4 Feb. 1943.

48. Ibid., p. 175, entry for 13 Dec. 1942.

49. Ernst Jünger, *Premier journal parisien*, II: 1941–1943 (1980), p. 15, entry for 6 April 1941.

50. Ibid., p. 29, entry for 26 May 1941.

51. Ibid., p. 30, entry for 30 May 1941.

52. Ibid., p. 26, entry for 20–21 May 1941.

53. ADL, Rs 77, prefect of Landes to regional prefect in Bordeaux, 6 Nov. 1942.

54. This rule was often disregarded; the archives of the Eure-et-Loir contain numerous instances of minors who went to Germany without parental authorization. In Brittany, Madame R., who encouraged girls to go to Germany, told them that she could circumvent the problem of parental authorization. Offredic, 'Travailler volontairement au service des Allemands', p. 116.

55. ADEL, 81 W 1, police report, 2 Aug. 1945, sent to Directeur des Renseignements Généraux à Paris.

56. In the Landes, the Germans particularly trusted Dr B. because of his collaboration with them in medical examinations of prostitutes. See ADL, Rs 1076, prefect of Landes to sub-prefect of Dax, 4 Nov. 1942.

57. Bergère, *Une société en épuration*, p. 161.

58. Letter from doctor of Feldkommandantur 518 to the head of the Police des Moeurs in Nantes, 27 April 1944, cited in Edmond Duméril, *Journal d'un honnête homme pendant l'occupation allemande (juin 1940–août 1944)*, ed. J. Bourgeon (Thonon-les-Bains, 1990), p. 397.

59. Paul Sanders, *Histoire du marché noir, 1940–1946* (2001), p. 144.

60. Erwan Saladin, 'La Nuit à Rennes sous l'occupation, 18 juin 1940–4 août 1944', Mémoire de Maîtrise, Université de Rennes II (2001), p. 91.

61. Ibid., p. 99.

62. ADEL, 1 W 78, Commissaire de la Police to Commissaire de la République about Olga B., 14 June 1945.

63. ADEL, 1 W 78, interrogation of Eugénie A., 13 June 1945.

64. ADEL, 1 W 78, report, 26 July 1945, by Lavasserie and Falconnet.

65. Saladin, 'La Nuit à Rennes sous l'occupation', p. 103.

66. Robert Gildea, *Marianne in Chains: In Search of the German Occupation* (2002), p. 77.

67. ADL, Rs 77, prefect of Landes to prefect of Gironde, 26 Aug. 1942. The Germans wished to remove the A. family, and particularly Charlotte A. (born 1921) who had already been interned twice 'for having contaminated German soldiers'.

68. Lucien Andréani wrote of meeting women of loose morality from Marseilles; cited in Daures, *Nos vingts ans volés*, p. 103. A French industrialist visiting his workers in Germany in December 1942 (that is, slightly before the destruction of the *vieux port*) was told that 'the inhabitants of all the brothels in Marseilles had been sent to Germany': Stanford University,

Hoover Institution, Monod archives, report on visit to Berlin, 1–22 Dec. 1942. On the destruction of the *Vieux Port*, see Ahlrich Meyer, *L'Occupation allemande en France, 1940–1944* (2002).

69. Ulrich Herbert, *Hitler's Foreign Workers: Enforced Foreign Labour in Germany under the Third Reich* (Cambridge, 1997), p. 220.

70. Gildea, *Marianne in Chains*, p. 266.

71. PP, BA 1840, 'État nominatif des internées du camp de Brens aptes pour aller travailler en Allemagne'.

72. AN, F 9 2191, 'Rapport établi pour le consul général Noël Henry', unsigned, 1 April 1942.

73. AN, F 60 1451, 'Note sur le service de la main d'oeuvre française en Allemagne', signed Laporte, 17 Sept. 1943.

74. Christian Bougeard, 'L'Intérêt stratégique de la Bretagne pendant la 2ème guerre mondiale et les répercussions économiques et humaines: Les prélèvements de main d'oeuvre' (no publisher, no date; in library of Institut d'Histoire du Temps Présent).

75. PP, BA 1788, response by Renseignements Généraux to police in Orléans, 27 Nov. 1942.

76. Thomas, *STO à Berlin*, pp. 71–3.

77. Luc Capdevilla, *Les Bretons au lendemain de l'occupation: Imaginaire et comportement d'une sortie de guerre, 1944–1945* (Rennes, 1999), p. 51.

78. Antoinette (twenty years old), quoted in Robert, 'Les Femmes travailleuses', p. 76.

79. AN, F 9 2193, Châlons-sur-Marne, 9 June 1941, report by Herbert: the major had written directly to the commandant of Stalag VIIA who had advised him to write to the German authorities in France.

80. Gildea, *Marianne in Chains*, p. 78.

81. PP, BA 1794, report, unsigned, 19 Jan. 1943, and Commissaire de la Voie Publique du IVe arrondissement to M. le Directeur Général de la Police Municipale, 28 March 1944.

82. Quoted in Alex Kershaw, *Blood and Champagne: The Life and Times of Robert Capa* (2002), p. 216.

83. Picaper and Norz, *Enfants maudits*, p. 85.

84. Several examples of such relations can be found in ADEL, 1 W 78.

85. Bood, *Les Années doubles*, p. 162, entry for 2 Oct. 1942.

86. Robert, 'Les Femmes travailleuses', p. 80, suggests that only 3.5 per cent of women who worked for the Germans were members of collaborationist parties.

87. ADEL, 14 W 62, Commissaire de Police to prefect, about Henriette D., 8 Feb. 1944.

88. Bergère, *Une société en épuration*, p. 336.

89. Offredic, 'Travailler volontairement au service des Allemands', p. 83.

90. ADEL, 1 W 78, Commissaire de Police to prefect, 5 Jan. 1946: 'It must moreover be noted that Lina M., who had prolonged relations with German soldiers, does not seem to have denounced French people to them.' Ibid., Commissaire de Police to Commissaire du Gouvernement about A., 12 Nov. 1945: 'To our knowledge, no complaint has been made against the woman A. for denunciation.' Ibid., M. K., Communist mayor of Tillay-le-Péneux, who said, of a woman who had volunteered to work in Germany, that he did not recall her denouncing anyone; declaration recorded by gendarmes Voinchet and Riguet, 2 Oct. 1945. Police reports of 28 Sept. and 2 Oct. 1945.

91. Bergère, *Une société en épuration*, p. 336. See also Robert, 'Les Femmes travailleuses', p. 102.

92. ADEL, 1 W 78, report of Commissaire Spécial in Chartres to prefect, about Marcelle C., 28 Aug. 1945.

93. ADEL, 1 W 78, Commissaire de Police to Commissaire du Gouvernement, about Yvette B, 9 June 1945.

94. ADEL, 1 W 78, interrogation of Mme D. (landlady), 14 June 1945.

95. ADEL, 1 W 78, interrogation of Paul L. (landlord), 13 June 1945.

96. Bergère, 'Épuration vécue et perçue', p. 299.

97. Picaper and Norz, *Enfants maudits*, p. 199.

98. ADEL, 1 W 78, Commission d'Épuration, 21 Aug. 1945.

99. Saladin, 'La Nuit à Rennes sous l'occupation', p. 97.

100. On rape by German soldiers in 1940, see Chapter 1. On rape of French-women in German employment, see Robert, 'Les Femmes travailleuses', pp. 105–6.

101. AN, F 7 14898, 'Incidents dûs aux troupes de l'occupation', sent with a letter from Darnand to Oberg, 16 March 1944; the girl's name was Rosina Povese and she was killed on 26 Feb. 1944.

102. Offredic, 'Travailler volontairement au service des Allemands', p. 27.

103. Robert, 'Les Femmes travailleuses', p. 98.

104. ADEL, 1 W 78, report by Commissaire Spécial in Chartres, 28 Aug. 1945, about Marcelle C., a maid born in 1924 who had followed her lover back to Germany. It was accepted that she had denounced no one, but the population of the village of Orgères protested that no penalty had been imposed on her because she showed herself 'arrogant and provocative'.

CHAPTER 6. CAPTIVITY: FRENCH PRISONERS OF WAR, 1940–1942

1. Jean Guitton, *Un siècle, une vie* (1988), p. 30.

2. François Cavanna, *Les Russkoffs* (1981), pp. 25–6.

3. Edgar Morin, *Autocritique* (1970, first published 1959), p. 51.

4. Henri Du Moulin de Labarthète, *Le Temps des illusions* (Geneva, 1946), p. 186.

5. André Joliot, *Regards en arrière* (1990), p. 136.

6. On the atmosphere in Koenigstein, see Pierre Arnal, 'Remarques éparses et verbales sur mon expérience comme délégué de la Mission Scapini', in Georges Baud, Louis Devaux and Jean Poigny (eds.), *Mémoire complémentaire sur quelques aspects des activités du Service Diplomatique des Prisonniers de Guerre: SDPG-DFB-Mission Scapini, 1940–1945* (1984), pp. 17–48, at p. 43.

7. Yves Durand, *La Vie quotidienne des prisonniers de guerre dans les Stalags, les Oflags et les Kommandos, 1939–1945* (1987), p. 54.

8. Jean Guitton, *Pages brûlées: Journal de captivité, 1942–1943* (1984, first published in 1943), p. 127, entry for Oct. 1942.

9. Francis Ambrière, *Les Grandes Vacances* (1956, first published in 1946), p. 112.

10. Maurice Duverne, *Mémoires de guerre: 1940–1945* (Mercurey, 1996), no pagination.

11. AN, F 60 1450, 'Libération des prisonniers de guerre coloniaux', no date or signature (though one of the reports in an annexe IV is dated 12 Oct. 1943 and the list of prisoners in annexe V is dated 31 Jan. 1944). The list in annexe V suggested that there were 31,234 prisoners in Frontstalags on 31 Jan. 1944. A total of 4,600 colonial prisoners were guarded by Frenchmen. The author of this report believed that setting French troops to guard colonial prisoners had been a mistake because it encouraged the prisoners to look on the French as their jailers rather than their comrades. He also suggested, astonishingly, that African troops considered themselves better treated by the Germans than by the French.

12. Martin Thomas, 'The Vichy Government and French Colonial Prisoners of War, 1940–1944', *French Historical Studies*, 25/4 (2002), pp. 657–92, at p. 657.

13. Roger Tessier, *Carnets de guerre et de captivité d'un Rochefortais, 1939–1945* (Rochefort, 1998).

14. Jean-Joseph Brustier, *Mes années de captivité dans le Reich hitlérien*

(1997), p. 31. Germain Lagier, *Un instituteur dans les Basses Alpes* (Digne-les-Bains, 1983), p. 127.

15. Gustave Folcher, *Les Carnets de guerre de Gustave Folcher, paysan languedocien, 1939–1945* (2000), p. 188.

16. Yves Bourges, *Témoignage, 1939–1945* (Montfort-sur-Meu, 1997), p. 81.

17. Lagier, *Un instituteur dans les Basses Alpes*, p. 130.

18. François Mitterrand, cited in Pierre Péan, *Une jeunesse française: François Mitterrand, 1934–1947* (1994), p. 125.

19. Durand, *La Vie quotidienne des prisonniers de guerre*, p. 159.

20. For prosecutions for cruelty to animals, see AN, F 9 2742, hearing in Neustettin, 29 Sept. 1944.

21. Alain Le Ray, *Première à Colditz* (Grenoble, 2004, first edition 1976). Henry Chancellor, *Colditz: The Definitive History* (1998), pp. 38–9.

22. PP, BA 2096, report by Commissaire de Police du quartier de Clignancourt to Directeur de la Police Judiciaire, 25 Dec. 1941.

23. AN, F 9 2742, report, 12 Oct., no year, on case of Jacques G., who had acquired a stolen bicycle from a Pole as part of an escape attempt.

24. AN, F 9 2742, Stalag IA, service juridique, 'Affaire Recco'.

25. Ambrière, *Les Grandes Vacances*, p. 91.

26. Richard Vinen, *The Politics of French Business, 1936–1945* (Cambridge, 1991), p. 126.

27. AN, F 9 2193, report by Herbert, delegate at Châlons-sur-Marne, 5 Aug. 1941.

28. AN, F 9 2193, report by Caignard, delegate at Compiègne, on repatriations from 4 to 17 Dec. 1941.

29. Jean Legros, *Stalag IA* (1945), p. 131.

30. Jean Moret-Bailly, 'Les Kommandos du Stalag XVIIB', *Revue d'histoire de la deuxième guerre mondiale*, 37 (1960), pp. 31–52.

31. Bordeaux, Archives Départementales de la Gironde, 34 W 281, 'Note de renseignements', 8 Oct. 1946.

32. Jean Guéhenno, *Journal des années noires (1940–1944)* (2002, first published in 1947), p. 147, entry for 6 June 1941. *Notre avant guerre* (1941) is an account of Brasillach's youth, education and right-wing opinions.

33. AN, F 9 2193, report by Herbert, 5 Aug. 1941. See also report by Herbert, 12 July 1941, on Le B.'s activities in Stalag XIV where he was the *homme de confiance* and ran the 'bureau national Breton'.

34. Duc de Brissac, *La Suite des temps, 1938–1958* (1974), p. 39.

35. L'Amicale du Camp des Aspirants, *Le Camp des aspirants pendant la deuxième guerre mondiale, 1939–1945* (1991), p. 164.

36. Sacha Guitry, *Quatre ans d'occupations* (1947), pp. 363–79. See also Maurice Martin du Gard, *La Chronique de Vichy, 1940–1944* (1975), p. 153, which suggests that Guitry's prisoners were not just a retrospective invention.

37. Charles Rist, *Une saison gâtée: Journal de la guerre et de l'occupation, 1939–1945*, ed. Jean-Noel Jeanneney (1983), p. 190.

38. Étienne Dejonghe and Yves Le Maner, *Le Nord-Pas-de-Calais dans la main allemande, 1940–1944* (Lille, 2000), p. 224.

39. Henry Charbonneau, *Les Mémoires de Porthos* (1981), p. 329.

40. AN, F 9 2192, Scapini Mission to the Paris delegate of the Secretary of State for War, 2 Nov. 1942.

41. AN, F 9 2191, Scapini Mission to M. le Contrôleur de l'Armée Sous-Directeur du Service de PG, 21 Dec. 1942.

42. AN, F 9 2191, Bonnafous to Scapini, 3 Nov. 1942.

43. AN, F 9 2193, information from prisoners arrived at Compiègne, 11 Aug. 1942.

44. AN, F 9 2191, 'Note pour M. Schuman', from *bureau d'études*, unsigned and undated.

45. AN, F 9 2193, information from prisoners arrived at Compiègne, 11 Aug. 1942.

46. AN, F 9 2191, 'Note pour les Services Diplomatiques des Prisonniers de Guerre', from Berlin service about the requirements of Établissements Louvril-Montbad-Aulnoye, 1 Feb. 1943.

47. AN, F 9 2193, information from prisoners arrived at Compiègne in June 1943, 20 July 1943, Stalag VIIB; see also ibid., report on Stalag XIA where the *homme de confiance* had been liberated 'parce qu'il leur en imposait trop', and report on Stalag XB and Stalag XIIID, where the *homme de confiance*, 'perfect in every way', had been repatriated.

48. AN, F 9 2193, report on prisoners arrived at Compiègne in June 1943, 20 July 1943.

49. AN, F 9 2193, report on repatriated prisoners arrived at Compiègne, June 1943.

50. AN, F 9 2191, Gabriel Vignes, *homme de confiance* Stalag IIC, 30 Aug. 1943.

51. AN, F 9 2191, extracts from letters received by the Service Diplomatique des Prisonniers de Guerre; this quotation from letter of 13 Aug. 1942.

52. Folcher, *Les Carnets de guerre*, p. 201.

53. AN, F 9 2191, note for the delegation in Berlin, signed Guion, 3 Nov. 1943.

54. AN, F 9 2191, Roussanne, to editor of *L'Oeuvre*, undated, responding to an article that had appeared on 8 Feb. 1943.

55. AN, F 9 2191, Commission de la Relève, 8 Sept. 1942.

56. AN, F 9 2191, aide-memoire, unsigned, Aug. 1943.

57. Pierre Bugeaud, *Militant: Prisonnier de guerre. Une bataille pour l'histoire* (1990), p. 16.

58. Durand, *La Vie quotidienne des prisonniers*, p. 105. Several hundred NCOs were sent to Poland from Stalag XVIIA alone.

59. René Dufour, *Captivité et évasion au pays des Sudètes* (1982), p. 37.

60. Durand, *La Vie quotidienne des prisonniers*, pp. 80–90.

61. Brustier, *Mes Années de captivité*.

62. Tessier, *Carnets de guerre et de captivité*, p. 51.

63. Legros, *Stalag IA*, p. 40.

64. Dufour, *Captivité*, p. 40 and *passim*.

65. Arnal, 'Remarques éparses et verbales', in Baud, Devaux and Poigny (eds.), *Mémoire complémentaire*, p. 39. Arnal talks of a system of semi-liberty with prisoners promising not to escape, but stresses that conditions varied greatly.

66. Duverne, *Mémoires de guerre*.

67. Dufour, *Captivité*, p. 39.

68. French records about prosecutions of French prisoners of war often allude to poaching. In Stalag IA in a single unspecified year there were nine prosecutions for poaching as opposed to only six for all other thefts. See handwritten ledger in AN, F 9 2727.

69. Folcher, *Les Carnets de guerre*, p. 213.

70. AN, F 9 2742, *conseilleur juridique*, Stalag IA, to head of delegation of Service Diplomatique des Prisonniers de Guerre, 12 Oct., no year given.

71. Joseph Raoux, *Pas si simple* (Privas, 1998), p. 110: 'Quant à moi, je suis fils de cultivateur. Je sais tenir un outil et conduire un cheval.'

72. Charbonneau, *Les Mémoires de Porthos*, p. 297.

73. Claude Delaunay, *Drôle de guerre et tourisme en Bavière, 1939–1945* (La Roche-sur-Yon, 2003), p. 64.

74. Raoux, *Pas si simple*, p. 148.

75. AN, F 9 2193, Herbert to Scapini on prisoners arrived at Compiègne on 1 Nov. 1943, 8 Nov. 1943.

76. AN, F 9 2193, report on prisoners arrived at Compiègne in June 1943, 20 July 1943.

77. Jean Moret-Bailly, 'Le Camp de base du Stalag XVIIB', *Revue d'histoire de la deuxième guerre mondiale*, 25 (1957), pp. 7–45, at p. 26.

78. Ibid.

79. AN, F 9 2193, report on prisoners repatriated via Compiègne 26 Feb. to 15 March.

80. Louis Althusser, *Journal de captivité* (1992), entries for 22 Dec. 1941, 26 Aug. 1942 and 11 April 1944.

81. Giulia Gemelli, *Fernand Braudel* (1995), p. 76. A more detailed account of Braudel's captivity is given in Pierre Daix, *Braudel* (1995).

82. Péan, *Une jeunesse française*, p. 140.

83. Marius Perrin, *Avec Sartre au Stalag 12 D* (1980).

84. Ibid., pp. 129 and 57.

85. Péan, *Une jeunesse française*, pp. 127 and 130.

86. Louis Althusser, *L'Avenir dure longtemps; suivi de, Les Faits: Autobiographies* (1992), p. 100.

87. AN, F 9 2193, information from prisoners arrived at Compiègne, 23–31 Dec. 1943; in work Kommando 246 of Stalag XIIA, only 5 out of 20 men were members of the *cercle Pétain*.

88. AN, F 9 2193, report from delegate at Compiègne, 15 March (no year given but seems to be 1942).

89. Charbonneau, *Les Mémoires de Porthos*, p. 342.

90. AN, F 9 2193, information from prisoners arrived at Compiègne in June 1943, 20 July 1943.

91. Ibid.

92. AN, F 9 2193, information from prisoners arrived at Compiègne, 11 Aug. 1942.

93. AN, F 9 2193, report by Herbert, 2 Aug. 1941.

94. AN, F 9 2193, information from prisoners arrived at Compiègne in June 1943, 20 July 1943: 'Some French prisoners of war, of foreign origin and often undeclared Jews, are with the Germans and they give them all the gossip in the Stalag, denouncing the opinions of some without regard for the consequences.'

95. AN, F 9 2193, report by Caignard at Compiègne on information from repatriated prisoners, 27 Jan.–25 Feb. 1942.

96. See Henri Giraud, *Mes évasions* (1946).

97. Martin du Gard, *La Chronique de Vichy*, p. 194, entry for 3 May 1942.

98. Stanford University, Hoover Institution, Henri Honoré Giraud, 'Report to Pétain on the cause of the defeat', 26 July 1940. The copy of the report is in English.

99. AN, F 9 2193, report on prisoners arrived at Compiègne in June 1943.

100. AN, F 9 2193, information from prisoners arrived at Compiègne in June 1943, 20 July 1943.

101. Ibid.

102. AN, F 9 2193, report on prisoners arrived at Compiègne in June 1943, 20 July 1943. In Stalag XXB morale 'reached its highest point at the end

of December 1942 on account of events in North Africa. Now it is falling because prisoners of war fear another winter which will be all the worse because all materials, coal and so on are becoming rarer and rarer.'

103. Guitton, *Un siècle, une vie*, p. 259.

104. AN, F 9 2193, report by Herbert to Scapini, 27 April 1943.

105. AN, F 60 1450, undated report, attached to note by Chef du Gouvernement, Secrétariat Général, 29 Feb. 1944. The report describes two visits by Martin Sonnery and Commissaire Marsaud made in July and September 1943, and a further visit made by Sonnery in January 1944. The views cited are those of Colonel Loureau, also spelt Oureux in same report.

106. PP, BA 2096, report, 24 March 1943.

CHAPTER 7. SURVIVAL

1. PP, BA 1808, L'Administrateur en Chef du Service Départemental de Contrôle Économique de la Seine to Secretary of State for Agriculture, 30 Oct. 1942.

2. Robert Zaretsky, *Nîmes at War: Religion, Politics and Public Opinion in the Gard, 1938–1944* (University Park, Pa., 1995), p. 175.

3. Jean-Louis Panicacci, 'Les Alpes-Maritimes', in Dominique Veillon and Jean-Marie Flonneau (eds.), *Le Temps des restrictions en France (1939–1949)* (1996), pp. 195–212, at p. 209.

4. Zaretsky, *Nîmes at War*, p. 178.

5. Charles Rist, *Une saison gâtée: Journal de la guerre et de l'occupation, 1939–1945*, ed. Jean-Noel Jeanneney (1983), p. 413, entry for 3 July 1944.

6. Ibid., p. 408, entry for 9 June.

7. Panicacci, 'Les Alpes-Maritimes', p. 201.

8. Paul Sanders, *Histoire du marché noir, 1940–1946* (2001), p. 138.

9. Ernst Jünger, *Premier journal parisien*, II: *1941–1943* (1980), p. 148, entry for 4 July 1941.

10. Liliane Schroeder, *Journal d'occupation, Paris 1940–1944: Chronique au jour le jour d'une époque oubliée* (2000), p. 60, entry for 13 Dec. 1940.

11. Zaretsky, *Nîmes at War*, p. 175.

12. Robert Brasillach, *Journal d'un homme occupé* (1955), p. 163.

13. Dominique Veillon, *Vivre et survivre en France, 1939–1947* (1995), p. 128.

14. Catherine Offredic, 'Travailler volontairement au service des Allemands pendant la seconde guerre mondiale: L'exemple des femmes des Côtes-du-Nord et du Finistère, à travers les dossiers des procédures judiciaires des chambres civiques, 1940–1946', Mémoire de Maîtrise, Rennes II (2000), p. 75.

15. Fabrice Virgili, *La France virile: Des femmes tondues à la libération* (2000), p. 37.

16. PP, BA 2093, report dated 22 Dec. 1940.

17. Sandrine Lallam, 'La Population de la Seine et les forces d'occupation allemandes, 14 juin 1940–25 août 1944', Mémoire de Maîtrise, Paris IV (2000), p. 106.

18. Paula Schwartz, 'La Répression des femmes communistes (1940–1944)', in François Rouquet et Danielle Voldman (eds.), *Les Cahiers de l'Institut d'Histoire du Temps Présent*, 31: *Identités féminines et violences politiques (1936–1946)* (1995), pp. 25–37, at p. 30.

19. Henri Drouot, *Notes d'un Dijonnais pendant l'occupation allemande, 1940–1944* (Dijon, 1998), p. 283, entry for 18 Sept. 1941.

20. Erwan Saladin, 'La Nuit à Rennes sous l'occupation: 18 juin 1940–4 août 1944', Mémoire de Maîtrise, Université de Rennes II (2001), p. 73.

21. John Sweets, *Choices in Vichy France: The French Under Nazi Occupation* (Oxford, 1986), p. 20.

22. PP, BA 2093, report undated (obviously 1941), 'Le ravitaillement de Paris'.

23. Lynne Taylor, *Between Resistance and Collaboration: Popular Protest in Northern France, 1940–1945* (2000), p. 47.

24. Rémi Foucault and Jacques Renard, 'La Mayenne', in Veillon and Flonneau (eds.), *Le Temps des restrictions en France*, pp. 79–100, at p. 80.

25. Jacques-Alain de Sédouy, *Une enfance bien-pensante sous l'occupation, 1940–1945* (1998), p. 19.

26. PP, BA 1810, Préfecture de Police, Service de Répression des Fraudes et de Contrôle des Prix, report on week of 19–26 March, 26 March 1943.

27. Michel Cépède, *Agriculture et alimentation en France durant la IIème guerre mondiale* (1961), p. 283.

28. Veillon, *Vivre et survivre en France*, p. 137.

29. Jean Guéhenno, *Journal des années noires (1940–1944)* (2002, first published in 1947), p. 233.

30. Georgette Elgey, *The Open Window* (1974, first published in France in 1973), p. 83.

31. Cépède, *Agriculture et alimentation en France durant la IIème guerre mondiale*, p. 415.

32. Sanders, *Histoire du marché noir*, p. 74.

33. Veillon, *Vivre et survivre en France*, p. 169.

34. René Limouzin, *Le Temps des vérités* (1991), p. 50. Rist, *Une saison gâtée*, p. 209.

35. On fathers taking children's rations, see Rémy Cazals, *Les Écoliers de*

Tournissan, 1939–1945 (Toulouse, 1978), p. 119. Dominique Jamet, *Un petit Parisien, 1941–1945* (2001), p. 10. Schroeder, *Journal*, p. 76, entry for 21 April 1941.

36. Cépède, *Agriculture et alimentation en France durant la IIème guerre mondiale*, pp. 366–7.

37. AN, F 22 1775, Bichelonne to inspecteurs du travail, 31 Dec. 1941.

38. Rist, *Une saison gâtée*, pp. 414–15.

39. PP, BA 2258, list of 42 judgements, 21 Aug. 1942.

40. Monique Luirard, *La Région stéphanoise dans la guerre et dans la paix (1936–1951)* (Saint-Étienne, 1980), p. 626.

41. Sanders, *Histoire du marché noir*, pp. 28–30.

42. Ephraïm Grenadou and Alain Prévost, *Grenadou, paysan français* (1978), p. 204.

43. PP, BA 2258, anonymous letter, 10 Nov. 1943.

44. Robert Gildea, *Marianne in Chains: In Search of the German Occupation* (2002), p. 28.

45. Veillon, *Vivre et survivre en France*, p. 180.

46. Sanders, *Histoire du marché noir*, p. 55.

47. PP, BA 2258, 21 Jan. 1943, Directeur du Service Départemental de Contrôle Économique to l'Administrateur en Chef du Service Départemental de Contrôle Économique de la Seine.

48. Sanders, *Histoire du marché noir*, p. 49.

49. Ibid., p. 57.

50. Limouzin, *Le Temps des vérités*, p. 93.

51. Taylor, *Between Resistance and Collaboration*, p. 128.

52. Guy Pedron, *La Prison sous Vichy* (1993), p. 53. It is true that the population of Riom prison would have increased greatly during this period (the overall population tripled during the occupation), but this increase was nowhere near as great as the increase in the death rate and, in any case, most of the new arrivals would have been young men.

53. Max Lafont, *L'Extermination douce: La cause des fous* (2000). Lafont's interpretations, first published in 1987, are attacked in Henry Rousso and Eric Conan, *Vichy: Un passé qui ne passe pas* (1994). More recently, see J. L. T. Birley, 'Famine: The Distant Shadow over French Psychiatry', *Journal of Psychiatry* (2002), pp. 298–9 and the report in *Le Monde* (on 17 Oct. 2003) on recent research by Isabelle von Bueltzingsloewen and her colleagues.

54. Paul Abrahams, 'Haute-Savoie at War, 1939–1945', Ph.D., University of Cambridge (1992).

55. Grenadou and Prévost, *Grenadou, paysan français*, p. 205.

56. Cited in Dominique Veillon and Jean-Marie Flonneau, 'Introduction', in

Veillon and Flonneau (eds.), *Le Temps des restrictions en France*, pp. 7–24, at p. 19.

57. Sanders, *Histoire du marché noir*, p. 158.

58. Foucault and Renard, 'La Mayenne', in Veillon and Flonneau (eds.), *Le Temps des restrictions en France*, p. 98.

59. Cépède, *Agriculture et alimentation en France durant la IIème guerre mondiale*, p. 214.

60. Sweets, *Choices in Vichy France*, p. 78.

61. Cazals, *Les Écoliers de Tournissan*, p. 106.

62. Ibid., p. 85.

63. Laurence Wylie, *Village in the Vaucluse* (Cambridge, Mass., 1974), p. 33.

64. André de Cambiaire, *L'Autoconsommation agricole en France* (1952), p. 26.

65. *La Fille du puisatier* finishes with a group of peasants listening to Pétain's first speech as head of state.

66. Gildea, *Marianne in Chains*, p. 117.

67. Jean Hugo, *Le Regard de la mémoire* (1984), p. 473.

68. Taylor, *Between Resistance and Collaboration*, p. 140.

69. Edmond Dubois, *Paris sans lumière, 1939–1945: Témoignages* (Lausanne, 1946), p. 130.

70. Christian Bougeard, 'Les Côtes du Nord', in Veillon and Flonneau (eds.), *Le Temps des restrictions en France*, pp. 343–64, at p. 349.

71. Cépède, *Agriculture et alimentation en France durant la IIème guerre mondiale*, p. 392.

72. Foucault and Renard, 'La Mayenne', in Veillon and Flonneau (eds.), *Le Temps des restrictions en France*, p. 84.

73. Jamet, *Un petit Parisien*, p. 58.

74. Duc de Brissac, *La Suite des temps, 1938–1958* (1974), p. 101.

75. PP, BA 2258, Directeur du Service Départemental de Contrôle Économique à Versailles to l'Administrateur en Chef du Service Départemental de Contrôle Économique de la Seine, 21 Jan. 1944.

76. Bordeaux, Archives Départementales de la Gironde, 34 W 44, prefect of Tarn-et-Garonne to Secretary of State for the Interior, 9 May 1944. Apparently the minister had asked for 8,000 children to be accommodated; the regional prefect of the Gironde hoped to send 5,000 children.

77. Ibid., Directeur Départemental des Réquisitions Françaises et Allemandes, des Réfugiés et Sinistrés to regional prefect, 18 Sept. 1943.

78. Yves Durand, 'Une adolescence paysanne et lycéenne sous l'occupation', in Jean-William Dereymez (ed.), *Être jeune en France (1939–1945)* (2001), pp. 63–70.

79. Limouzin, *Le Temps des vérités*, p. 46.

80. Edgar Morin, *Commune en France: La métamorphose de Plodémet* (1967).

81. Christian Font, 'Une enquête orale menée en Aveyron', in Veillon and Flonneau (eds.), *Le Temps des restrictions en France*, pp. 503–26, at p. 512.

82. Eugène Martres, 'Le Cantal', ibid., pp. 119–33, at p. 121.

83. Foucault and Renard, 'La Mayenne', ibid., p. 94.

84. Grenadou and Prévost, *Grenadou, paysan français*, p. 211.

85. Marc Bergère, 'Épuration vécue et perçue à travers le cas du Maine-et-Loire: De la libération au début des années 50', Thèse de Doctorat, Rennes II (2001), p. 547.

86. H. R. Kedward, *In Search of the Maquis: Rural Resistance in Southern France, 1942–1944* (Oxford, 1993), p. 200.

87. Grenadou and Prévost, *Grenadou, paysan français*, p. 204.

88. Grenadou's relations with his former teacher have already been discussed. Note also the case of Claude Jamet. As a lycée teacher and socialist activist in Poitiers, Jamet had earned the admiration of two *instituteurs*: the Brouchons, in a village 8 kilometres from Poitiers. Throughout the occupation the Brouchons provided Jamet and his family with food.

89. Marc Ferro, *Pétain* (1987), p. 468.

90. Michèle Cointet, *Le Conseil National de Vichy, 1940–1944* (1989), p. 14.

91. On complicity between officials and black marketeers, see Gildea, *Marianne in Chains*, p. 132.

92. Saladin, 'La Nuit à Rennes sous l'occupation', p. 50.

93. Limouzin, *Le Temps des vérités*, p. 51.

94. Ibid., p. 48.

95. Cépède, *Agriculture et alimentation en France durant la IIème guerre mondiale*, p. 124.

96. Richard Vinen, *The Politics of French Business, 1936–1945* (Cambridge, 1991).

97. PP, BA 2093, report, signed André Cougole, 7 March 1941.

98. Lallam, 'La Population de la Seine et les forces d'occupation allemandes', p. 106.

99. ADL, 81 W 1, report, signed Duverger, 2 Feb. 1942.

100. ADL, 81 W 2, prefect of Landes to sub-prefect of Dax, 26 Nov. 1946.

101. Marc Bergère, *Une société en épuration: Épuration vécue et perçue en Maine-et-Loire: De la libération au début des années 50* (2003), p. 154.

102. Saladin, 'La Nuit à Rennes sous l'occupation', p. 45.

103. On *faux policiers*, see Grégory Auda, *Les Belles Années du 'milieu'*,

1940–1944: Le grand banditisme dans la machine répressive allemande en France (2002). See also François Marcantoni, *Un homme d'honneur: De la Résistance au milieu* (2002).

104. PP, BA 2115, Georges Veber to Directeur Général de la Police Judiciaire, 14 March 1943, about case of A., a German army deserter born in February 1908; report in file on incidents 1 June–20 Aug. 1942 on German national born 1901; report in file on incidents after 21 April 1944 on deserter from German army born 1911; report in file on incidents 1 Oct. 1941–31 May 1942 on German national born 1901.

105. PP, BA 1793, report by Fromont, 29 Aug. 1943.

106. PP, BA 1793, report by Neuges and Lemaire, 7 Jan. 1943.

107. PP, BA 2115, 21 April 1944.

108. PP, BA 1793, report, signed Lignon, 1 March 1944.

109. PP, BA 2115, case 191 in file on events 1 June–20 Aug. 1942.

110. PP, BA 2115, case 316 in file on events 25 Dec. 1942–6 May 1943.

111. PP, BA 2115, case 689 in file on events 1 Jan.–15 March 1944.

112. PP, BA 1793, Commissaire de la Circonscription de Montreuil to Directeur Général de la Police Municipale, 7 Jan. 1944.

113. Alfred Brauner, *Ces enfants ont vécu la guerre* (1946), p. 208.

114. Jean-Louis Bory, *Mon village à l'heure allemande* (1945), p. 84.

115. Jamet, *Un petit Parisien*, p. 64.

116. Lallam, 'La Population de la Seine et les forces d'occupation allemandes', p. 148.

117. Limouzin, *Le Temps des vérités*, p. 45.

118. Yves Laurent, *Aventures d'un réfractaire face à l'occupant* (Narbonne, 1989), p. 86.

119. Bergère, *Une société en épuration*, p. 154.

120. Jean-Pierre Levert, Thomas Gomart and Alexis Merville, *Un lycée dans la tourmente: Jean-Baptiste Say, 1934–1944* (1994).

121. Dominique Veillon, *La Mode sous l'occupation* (1990), p. 105.

122. Jamet, *Un petit Parisien*, p. 96.

CHAPTER 8. STOLEN YOUTH: SERVICE DU TRAVAIL OBLIGATOIRE

1. Rosine Vergnes, 'La Main d'oeuvre française au service de l'occupant allemand dans le département d'Eure-et-Loir (1940–1944)', Mémoire de Maîtrise, Université d'Angers (2 vols., 1999), vol. i, p. 35.

2. Jean Quellien, 'Les Travailleurs forcés en Allemagne: Essai d'approche

statistique', in Bernard Garnier and Jean Quellien (eds.), *La Main d'oeuvre française exploitée par le IIIe Reich* (2003), pp. 67–84, at p. 75.

3. More than 80 per cent of those sent to Germany before 1943 were workers and more than a third were metallurgists; ibid., p. 80.

4. Yves Durand, 'Une adolescence paysanne et lycéenne sous l'occupation', in Jean-William Dereymez (ed.), *Être jeune en France (1939–1945)* (2001), pp. 63–70, at p. 67.

5. Vergnes, 'La Main d'oeuvre française au service de l'occupant allemand', vol. i, p. 10: 'This term is a name that is stuck to all men who went to work in Germany.'

6. Dany Lejeune, 'Le STO en Seine Inférieure', Mémoire de Maîtrise, Rouen (1977).

7. Vergnes, 'La Main d'oeuvre française au service de l'occupant allemand', vol. i, p. 155, suggests that *insoumis* referred to those who were never documented, that *défaillants* referred to those who were called up but failed to appear and *réfractaire* referred to those who were actively sought by the authorities.

8. J. P. Azéma, 'Introduction générale', in Garnier and Quellien (eds.), *La Main d'oeuvre française*, pp. 9–14, at p. 11.

9. Jean-Pierre Harbulot, *Le Service du Travail Obligatoire: La région de Nancy face aux exigences allemandes* (Nancy, 2003), p. 537.

10. See Arnaud Schlippi, 'La Fédération Nationale des Rescapés et Victimes des Camps Nazis du Travail Forcé: Histoire et combats', in Garnier and Quellien (eds.), *La Main d'oeuvre française*, pp. 603–16, and Annette Wieviorka, 'La Bataille du statut', ibid., pp. 617–24.

11. Jean Guibal, *Un Gardois réfractaire au STO en Allemagne: Au hasard des chemins* (Nîmes, 1989), pp. 9–11.

12. Ibid., p. 15.

13. Ibid., pp. 18–19.

14. Ibid., p. 55.

15. Ibid., p. 59.

16. Ibid., p. 61.

17. PP, BA 1790, report of visit of M. Bidault to centres proposed for 'guarded lodging', 25 Feb. 1943.

18. PP, BA 1790, 'Note de service', 28 Feb. 1943.

19. PP, BA 1790, report by Walter, 3 Aug. 1943.

20. Michel Grattier de Saint-Louis, 'Relève forcée et STO dans le Rhône (1942–1944): Partir ou ne pas partir', in Garnier and Quellien (eds.), *La Main d'oeuvre française*, pp. 247–67, at p. 253.

21. Quellien, 'Les Travailleurs forcés en Allemagne', in Garnier and Quellien (eds.), *La Main d'oeuvre française*, p. 79.

22. Grattier de Saint-Louis, 'Relève forcée et STO dans le Rhône', in Garnier and Quellien (eds.), *La Main d'oeuvre française*, p. 266.

23. AN, F 60 1451, 'Note sur le service de la main d'oeuvre française en Allemagne', 17 Sept. 1943.

24. On changing perceptions of STO, see Raymond Ruffin, *Journal d'un J3* (1979), p. 218. Ruffin knew a woman whose husband was killed in Essen while performing STO.

25. Harbulot, *Le Service du Travail Obligatoire*, p. 512.

26. J. P. Harbulot, 'Les Jeunes et le STO: Mythes et réalités', in Dereymez (ed.), *Être jeune en France*, pp. 183–9, at p. 188.

27. AN, F 60 1447, Pirel to le Commissaire Général des Chantiers de la Jeunesse, 18 Oct. 1943.

28. AN, F 22 2024, Directeur Régional MOP to Secrétaire Général à la Main d'Oeuvre, 3 Feb. 1941 (presumably, in reality, 1944).

29. Jacques Le Roy Ladurie, *Mémoires, 1902–1945* (1997), p. 399.

30. Bernd Zielinski, 'L'Exploitation de la main d'oeuvre française par l'Allemagne et la politique de collaboration', in Garnier and Quellien (eds.), *La Main d'oeuvre française*, pp. 47–65, at p. 59.

31. AN, F 7 14886, account, dated 19 April, of Franco-German conference on 17 April. Déat and Bichelonne were particularly worried by the extent to which rural artisans were affected by STO.

32. ADEL, 116 W 181, account of meeting at Feldkommandantur 55 on 15 Feb. 1944. The French representatives suggested that Spanish and Italian workers who currently worked in protected factories in France might be sent to Germany and replaced by 'French workers of greater interest'. The Germans refused this request.

33. André Gabs-Mallut, *Entre vivre ou mourir* (2000), p. 20.

34. André Delapierre, *Ceux du DAF: Souvenirs d'un travailleur forcé en Allemagne* (Livry-Gargan, 1973).

35. Marie Thérèse Liange-Patural, *Sauvain se souvient: 80 ans de vie militaire à Sauvain de 1914 à 1994* (Sauvain, 1995), p. 91. Two young men from the town hid in a cave over the winter.

36. Pierre Lagarde, *Ils ont subi des chemins de traverse: Témoignage, juin 1943-mai 1945* (Besançon, 1989), p. 16.

37. Zielinski, 'L'Exploitation de la main d'oeuvre française', in Garnier and Quellien (eds.), *La Main d'oeuve française*, p. 57.

38. Delapierre, *Ceux du DAF*, p. 11.

39. On STO as a rite of passage, see Jean-Louis Bory, *Mon village à l'heure allemande* (1945), p. 105.

40. François Cavanna, *Les Russkoffs* (1981), p. 18.

41. Pierre Picard-Gilbertier, *Armée rouge et Danube bleu* (Dijon, 1993), p. 31.

42. Marcel Ayot, *Comment on joue sous la botte nazie, ou la Trilogie antagonique au STO: Histoires vécues et poèmes* (Clermont l'Hérault, 1985), p. 9.

43. Victor Savary, *Journal de Victor Savary: Service du Travail Obligatoire, STO, Berlin 1943–1944. Les tribulations d'un Chanzéen dans le grand Reich* (Nantes, 1998).

44. Yves Laurent, *Aventures d'un réfractaire face à l'occupant* (Narbonne, 1989).

45. Roger Micard, *Pour l'honneur: Contribution à l'historique des prélèvements de main d'oeuvre parmi les jeunes français par l'Allemagne nazie* (Libourne, 1987), pp. 44 and 51.

46. AN, F 60 1448, 'Note sur la situation des chantiers de la Jeunesse au regard du Service du Travail Obligatoire', undated.

47. AN, F 60 1447, Pierre Dunard to Chef du Gouvernement, 2 Aug. 1943.

48. AN, F 60 1447, General de la Porte du Theil to Chef du Gouvernement, 2 Oct. 1943.

49. Pierre Martin, *La Mission des Chantiers de Jeunesse en Allemagne 1943–1945* (1992), pp. 25–9.

50. Sarah Fishman, *The Battle for Children: World War II, Youth Crime, and Juvenile Justice in Twentieth-Century France* (Cambridge, Mass., 2002), p. 192.

51. AN, F 22 2023, Secrétaire Général à la Main d'Oeuvre to directeurs de l'administration centrale, 1 Feb. 1944.

52. AN, F 22 2024, 'Mutation de Charles de F.', 6 March 1944.

53. ADL, Rs 77, Feldkommandantur 541 to prefect of Landes, 26 Jan. 1943.

54. On the hunt for bourgeois false farmers, see AN, F 60 1452, 'Rapport 52', 17 June 1943. See also ADL, Rs 94, note by Crauste for sub-prefect of Dax, 27 July 1943, about F., a law student from Bordeaux who had, apparently, bought a farm with the specific aim of avoiding STO. See also the letter from a prefect (unidentified) to a father of a young man who had 'passed himself off as a farmer', dated 9 April 1943 and reproduced in Louis Guilloux, *Carnets, 1921–1944* (1978), p. 287.

55. ADL, Rs 77, M. Claverie, inspecteur du travail, to prefect of Landes, 7 April 1943.

56. Paris, Institut d'Histoire du Temps Présent, ARC 105. 'Témoignage de M. Georges Morel, Ingénieur des Mines. Les mines des Cévennes pendant la guerre 1939–1945'.

57. Philippe Ariès, *Un historien du dimanche* (1980), p. 90.

58. Bernard Pierquin, *Journal d'un étudiant parisien sous l'occupation, 1939–1945* (1983), p. 101, entry for 30 June 1943.

59. R. Bourderon, 'Mouvement de la main d'oeuvre et STO dans les mines du Gard', *Revue d'histoire de la deuxième guerre mondiale*, 112 (1978), pp. 47–66.

60. AN, F 60 1451, unsigned note to or from de la Porte du Theil, 11 June 1943.

61. AN, F 60 1452, note for the Minister (i.e. of Labour) from *cabinet* of Ministry of Education, 9 Oct., unsigned. This estimate about numbers going to Germany apparently came from the father of a student.

62. AN, F 60 1452, Émile Bernon to Chef du Gouvernement, 'Mission sur les engagements des mineurs de fond', 23 June 1943.

63. AN, F 7 14886, account, dated 19 April, of Franco-German conference on 17 April.

64. AN, F 60 1450, telegram from Chef du Gouvernement to prefects, 5 July 1943.

65. Jean-Louis Quereillahc, *Mémoires de la déportation du travail en Allemagne nazie, 1943–1945* (Linas, 1990), p. 20.

66. AN, F 60 1452, Émile Bernon to Chef du Gouvernement, 'Mission sur les engagements des mineurs de fond', 23 June 1943.

67. Jean Raibaud and Henri Henric (eds.), *Témoins de la fin du IIIe Reich: Des polytechniciens racontent* (2004).

68. AN, F 60 1452, note for the Minister (i.e. of Labour), from *cabinet* of Ministry of Education, 9 Oct. 1943, unsigned. The note alleged that *grandes écoles* were circumventing STO and added: 'In the colonies [that is, in the Ministry of Colonies], young men are nominated directly as sergeants in colonial units with 4,000 francs per month to guard coloured prisoners in Sologne.'

69. Harbulot, *Le Service du Travail Obligatoire*, p. 529.

70. Annie-Paule Dimeglio, 'Le Service du Travail Obligatoire dans le département du Var', Mémoire de Maîtrise, Nice (1972), p. 106.

71. AN, F 1 A 3775, 'Prélèvement de main d'oeuvre dans la région de Marseille', received 13 March 1944, circulated 7 April 1944. This document is taken from Free French intelligence, derived from its agents in the Vichy administration.

72. ADL, Rs 1076, Commissaire de Police of Dax to sub-prefect of Dax, 28 April 1943.

73. ADL, Rs 94, police report, signed Juristi, 1 May 1943.

74. ADL, Rs 94, police report, signed Cruaste, 7 April 1943.

75. PP, BA 1790, Mirabaud to Moyer, 25 Feb. 1944.

76. Michel Gratier de Saint-Louis, 'Les Réquisitions de main d'oeuvre pour

l'Allemagne dans le Rhône, 26 octobre 1942–10 août 1944', Mémoire de Maîtrise, Lyon II (1980).

77. Jean Edmond, *De Quarré les Tombes à Berlin, 1943–1945* (1995).

78. AN, F 60 1447, Bichot to de la Porte du Theil, 'Affaire Jolivot', 13 July 1943.

79. AN, F 60 1448, report by Loubert Bie, 4 June 1943.

80. AN, F 60 1452, 'Rapport 52', 17 June 1943.

81. AN, F 60 1447, Commissaire Bour to Commisssaire Régional d'Auvergne, 6 Aug. 1943.

82. AN, F 60 1448, on the inefficacity of roving special sections, see General Martin of gendarmerie nationale to Chef du Gouvernement, 23 Dec. 1943.

83. AN, F 60 1451, Procureur Général près de la Cour d'Appel de Limoges to Garde des Sceaux, 9 Sept. 1943.

84. AN, F 7 14898, 'Incidents dûs aux troupes de l'occupation', file sent with letter from Darnand to Oberg, 16 March 1944.

85. AN, F 60 1447, report of Commissaire Régional de la Province des Pyrénées-Gascogne about the 'Tenue morale et matérielle des groupements 28 et 38' (covering letter dated 19 Nov. 1943).

86. AN, F 60 1454, Dr Igler to prefect of Vaucluse, 1 March 1944: 'I regret that several times people have objected to me that these are mayors who only fulfil their functions in an honorary capacity and because of this cannot be exposed to personal attacks.' See also ADL, Rs 1076, sub-prefect of Dax to prefect of Landes, 25 Jan. 1944, suggesting that mayors would resign if sanctioned for failing to help with STO.

87. AN, F 60 1452, sub-prefect of Dole to regional prefect in Dijon, 8 Sept. 1943.

88. AN, F 7 14886, account, dated 19 April, of Franco-German conference on 17 April, Glatzel speaking.

89. Octave Fort, *'Tu es encore davantage mon fils', ou l'Histoire d'un requis en Allemagne: 1943–1945* (Le Château d'Olonne, 1994), p. 33. See also Alexandre Billaud, *Alexandre ou les Malheurs de Centio* (1986), p. 270.

90. ADEL, 14 W 93, prefect of Loire to regional prefect, 3 Aug. 1943.

91. André Pioger, *La Relève et le Service du Travail Obligatoire dans la Sarthe (1942–1944)* (1971), p. 23. See also ADEL, 116 W 22, circular from Inspection de la Santé, dated 29 Oct. 1942.

92. J. Daures, *Nos vingt ans volés: L'histoire des 2,700 Aveyronnais victimes des camps nazis du travail forcé* (Rodez, 1993).

93. ADL, Rs 1076, prefect of Landes to sub-prefect of Dax, 4 Nov. 1942. See also ibid., health inspector to Dr Prater (the German military doctor), 5 Nov. 1942.

94. ADL, Rs 94, prefect of Landes to Mme R., 13 Dec. 1944.

95. Vergnes, 'La Main d'oeuvre française au service de l'occupant allemand', vol. i, p. 72.

96. AN, F 60 1447, note for Laval, 5 June 1943.

97. AN, F 60 1448, Commissaire Général des Chantiers de la Jeunesse to Secrétaire Général auprès du Chef du Gouvernement, 29 May 1943. Bernon to Minister of the Interior, 4 June 1943. In June 1943, Dr P., a *conseiller départemental*, mayor of the village of Bozel and former president of the Légion Française des Combattants in Bozel, turned up at a camp of the Chantiers de la Jeunesse and removed four men in his car. When challenged, he explained that he was doing a favour for the father of one of the men. He was arrested but it was noted that he was 'a very influential person in the area'.

98. AN, F 7 14886, 19 April 1944, account of conference of 17 April. Déat admitted that French doctors charged with conducting medical inspections were treating their regular clients differently from other young men.

99. AN, F 60 1447, report of Commissaire Régional de la Province des Pyrénées-Gascogne, 19 Nov. 1943.

100. Maurice Georges, *Le Temps des armes sans arme: Une tranche d'histoire à Berlin* (Beaugency, 1990), p. 47.

101. Pierre Bohin, *Il y a cinquante ans* (Gournay-en-Bray, 1996), pp. 8 and 9. See also Michel Caignard, *Les Sacrifiés, Récit d'un ancien STO* (Périgueux, 1985), p. 26.

102. AN, 83 AJ 28, report signed Jacques Robert and Louis Gilbert. The first page of the report is missing.

103. AN, F 60 1451, report by prefect of the Nièvre, 30 June 1943.

104. Daures, *Nos vingt ans volés*, p. 88.

105. M. Boivin, 'Les Réfractaires au travail obligatoire: Essai d'approche globale et statistique', in Garnier and Quellien (eds.), *La Main d'oeuvre française*, pp. 493–515, at p. 501.

106. Yves Durand, 'Une adolescence paysanne et lycéenne sous l'occupation', in Dereymez (ed.), *Être jeune en France*, p. 67.

107. AN, F 60 1452, sub-prefect of Dole to regional prefect of Dijon, 8 Sept. 1943.

108. AN, F 60 1450, de la Porte du Theil to Chef du Gouvernement, 3 July 1943, about the mayor of Chuzelle in the Isère who had, apparently, incited his son to desert from the Chantiers de la Jeunesse in order to avoid STO.

109. AN, F 60 1448, de la Porte du Theil to prefect of Hérault, 28 Aug. 1943.

110. Julia Quellien, *Les Réfractaires au travail obligatoire dans le Calvados* (Caen, 2003), p. 65.

111. Ibid., p. 52.

112. Pierre Faraud, *Ni traître, ni héros: Du Vercors à Marseille via Montélimar, Avignon, et le Thor, 1943–1945. Chantiers de la Jeunesse, clandestinité, armée* (Le Thor, 1994), p. 7.

113. Ibid., pp. 9 and 29.

114. Ibid., p. 62.

115. René Limouzin, *Le Temps des vérités* (1991), pp. 127–37.

116. André Larue, *Brassens: Une vie* (1982).

117. Quellien, *Les Réfractaires au Travail Obligatoire dans le Calvados*, p. 115.

118. Ibid., p. 114.

119. Gabs-Mallut, *Entre vivre ou mourir*, p. 20.

120. Edmond, *De Quarré les Tombes à Berlin, 1943–1945*.

121. Quereillahc, *Mémoires de la déportation du travail en Allemagne nazie*, p. 22. Quereillahc and his father feared that his younger brother Henri would be deported.

122. Robert Belot, *Aux frontières de la liberté* (1998).

123. Paul Fourtier-Berger, *Nuits bavaroises ou les désarrois d'un STO: Chroniques, 1943–1945* (Romilly-sur-Seine, 1999), p. 32.

124. Picard-Gilbertier, *Armée rouge et Danube bleu*, p. 35.

125. ADEL, 116 W 181, account of meeting at Feldkommandantur 55 on 15 Feb. 1944. A German representative at this meeting insisted that fathers and brothers of men who had not turned up for STO could be taken in their place.

126. Faraud, *Ni traître, ni héros*, p. 61.

127. Pierre Rigoulet, *Les Enfants de l'épuration* (1993), pp. 127–65.

128. Paris, Institut d'Histoire du Temps Présent, ARC 086. André Noisette, 'Chronique de deux années de STO en Allemagne: 27 août 1943–juin 1945', p. 22.

129. Laurent, *Aventures d'un réfractaire face à l'occupant*, p. 1.

130. Pierre Abramovici, *Un rocher bien occupé: Monaco pendant la guerre, 1939–1945* (2001), p. 197.

131. Quellien, *Les Réfractaires au travail obligatoire dans le Calvados*, p. 104.

132. Monique Luirard, *La Région stéphanoise dans la guerre et dans la paix (1936–1951)* (Saint-Étienne, 1980), p. 465.

133. PP, BA 1788, account of meeting organized by Commissariat Général à la Main d'Oeuvre Française en Allemagne, 30 Nov. 1943.

134. AN, F 60 1447, report of gendarmes enclosed with letter from Bichot to Commissaire Général, 20 July 1943.

135. ADEL, 116 W 199, prefect of Eure-et-Loir to Procureur d'État Français

at Châteaudun requesting list of people currently in prison born between 1919 and 1922, 28 June 1943. See also correspondence in ADEL, 116 W 18.

CHAPTER 9. THE FRENCH IN GERMANY, 1943–1945

1. AN, 83 AJ 17, report by commandant Pommès-Barrère, 15 Jan. 1944, headed 'Compte rendu du commandant Pommès-Barrère'. The visit to Germany took place from 29 Nov. to 22 Dec. 1943.

2. AN, F 60 1452, contrôle postal, 1 Sept. 1943.

3. Albert Castères, *Pour que ça se sache aussi* (2001), p. 14. Castères, a civilian worker sent to Germany, was in a camp in East Prussia that contained 150 or so prisoners of war and 50 civilian workers. He believed that there was little difference between the prisoners of war and the civilians, and seems himself to have been unclear about the difference between those deported under the STO programme and those deported under the *relève* programme.

4. Jean-Louis Quereillahc, *Mémoires de la déportation du travail en Allemagne nazie, 1943–1945* (Linas, 1990), p. 26.

5. Ibid., p. 298.

6. Jean Pierre Ganter, *Une jeunesse heureuse assassinée* (1994), p. 45.

7. Michel Caignard, *Les Sacrifiés: Récit d'un ancien STO* (Périgueux, 1985).

8. André Michel, *En liberté dans cette cage, en cage dans ces libertés: Journal d'un étudiant contraint au STO en Allemagne, 4 août 1943–2 juin 1945* (Gentilly, 1995).

9. AN, F 7 14889, Bruneton to Darnand, 18 Jan. 1944.

10. Michel Crozier, *Ma belle époque* (2002), pp. 20–21.

11. Pierre Destenay, *Babel germanique* (1948), p. 50.

12. Ganter, *Une jeunesse heureuse assassinée*, p. 18.

13. Georges Caussé, *Mémoires d'un Tarnais STO en Allemagne, 1943–1945* (Toulouse, 1997), p. 26.

14. Ibid., p. 17.

15. On the political dispute between *requis* and prisoners of war, see François Cavanna, *Les Russkoffs* (1981), p. 27. Cavanna claims to have received the following lecture from a prisoner: 'Don't talk ill of Pétain. Pétain is Verdun. My father was there . . . Pétain, he is busy screwing them all over, the boches. And then, for a start, don't get things mixed up: us, we are prisoners of war, we are soldiers. You cannot say just anything.' For a less lurid account, see Lucien Andréani, cited in J. Daures, *Nos vingt ans volés: L'histoire des 2,700 Aveyronnais victimes des camps nazis du travail forcé* (Rodez, 1993), p. 171: 'We who were twenty, we found a great deal of serenity and wisdom from

the contact with prisoners'; but Andréani adds that *requis* sometimes shocked prisoners by their anti-Vichy views: 'The Pétain myth was deeply implanted amongst these exiles.'

16. Daures, *Nos vingt ans volés*, p. 167: 'We were suspicious of volunteers and did not frequent them . . . amongst them one found numerous . . . dubious individuals who had signed up to avoid prison.'

17. Victor Savary, *Journal de Victor Savary: Service du Travail Obligatoire, STO, Berlin 1943–1944. Les tribulations d'un Chanzéen dans le grand Reich* (Nantes, 1998), p. 4. Savary and his friends, who regarded Arras as the south, seem to have regarded volunteers, criminals and southerners as almost the same thing: later he found a 'Corsican, come to Germany to avoid prison', stealing from him; ibid., p. 17.

18. Stanford University, Hoover Institution, Monod archives, report on visit to Berlin, 1–22 Dec. 1942.

19. Caignard, *Les Sacrifiés*, p. 64.

20. Charles-Henri-Guy Bazin, *Déporté du travail à la BMW-Eisenach* (Cubnezais, 1986), p. 57.

21. Destenay, *Babel germanique*, p. 23.

22. Cavanna, *Les Russkoffs*, p. 186.

23. AN, F 60 1450, undated report, attached to note by Chef du Gouvernement, Secrétariat Général, 29 Feb. 1944. The report describes two visits by Martin Sonnery and Commissaire Marsaud made in July and September 1943, and a further visit made by Sonnery in January 1944.

24. Jean Charles, *La Vie des Français en Allemagne: Ceux du tac* (1945), p. 73.

25. Patrice Arnaud, 'La Délégation officielle française auprès de la deutsche Arbeitsfront (1943–1945)', Mémoire de Maîtrise, Paris I (1995).

26. Georges Moullet-Echarlod, *La Faim au ventre: Service du Travail Obligatoire* (1978), pp. 350–51.

27. Pierre Lagarde, *Ils ont subi des chemins de traverse: Témoignage, juin 1943-mai 1945* (Besançon, 1989), p. 45.

28. Arnaud, 'La Délégation officielle', p. 122.

29. 'Les Amis du colonel Furioux', *Le Colonel* (Saint-Étienne, 1987).

30. Ibid., p. 171.

31. Account of Pierre Chanteret, in Pierre Martin, *La Mission des Chantiers de Jeunesse en Allemagne 1943–1945* (1992), p. 201.

32. Georges Toupet, ibid., p. 216.

33. Pierre Lamoureux, ibid., p. 188.

34. Pierre Dillard, *Suprêmes témoignages* (1945).

35. On the presence of French and Belgian nuns in Germany, see Joseph

Gelin, *Nuremberg, 1943–1945: L'expérience d'un prêtre ouvrier* (Petit Clamart, 1946), pp. 18 and 58.

36. Ibid., p. 6: 'There were six French priests who were free workers in Nuremberg: three prisoners who had become civilians [i.e. 'transformed' prisoners], two young priests conscripted by STO and one (say the word) volunteer.'

37. Ibid., p. 14.

38. Paul Beschet, *Mission en Thuringe au temps du nazisme* (Saint-Armand, 1989), p. 40.

39. Michel Gerbeaux, *20 ans après: Un déporté se souvient* (Dreux, 1965), p. 32.

40. Michèle Cointet, *L'Église sous Vichy, 1940–1945: La repentance en question* (1998), p. 294.

41. Gelin, *Nuremberg, 1943–1945*, p. 44.

42. Beschet, *Mission en Thuringe*.

43. Ibid. Beschet believed that 'the transformed prisoners ran things' in the Montagna camp attached to the tank factory.

44. AN, 83 AJ 17, report by commandant Pommès-Barrère, 15 Jan. 1944. The visit to Germany took place from 29 Nov. to 22 Dec. 1943. On the transformation of French prisoners, see also Georges Scapini, *Mission sans gloire* (1960).

45. On pressure applied to prisoners, see Gustave Folcher, *Les Carnets de guerre de Gustave Folcher, paysan languedocien, 1939–1945* (2000), p. 200. See also Maurice Duverne, *Mémoires de guerre: 1940–1945* (Mercurey, 1996).

46. Caussé, *Mémoires d'un Tarnais*, p. 26: '8 August, an important day for us. This morning, the prisoners [150 of them in the factory] were transformed into [civilian] workers.'

47. AN, 83 AJ 17, report by commandant Pommès-Barrère, 15 Jan. 1944. The author believed that no reprisals were taken against men who refused transformation, though such men were put on Abwehr files so that further improvements in their status were ruled out. A 'Compte rendu pour le Service Diplomatique des Prisonniers de Guerre', 7 March 1944, illegible signature in 83 AJ 17, said that Pommès-Barrère was wrong, and that reprisals had been taken against prisoners who refused transformation.

48. AN, F 9 2193, report on prisoners repatriated via Compiègne in June, 20 July 1943.

49. Ibid., section on Stalag IIA.

50. Ibid.

51. AN, 83 AJ 17, report by Pommès-Barrère; he believed that in some areas

almost all transformed prisoners lived in towns and worked in industry, though his own statistics suggested that 1,200 of 3,200 transformed prisoners in Stalag IB and 2,000 of the 12,000 transformed prisoners in Saxony worked in agriculture. An undated, unsigned report in 83 AJ 17 said that between 60,000 and 70,000 *transformés* worked in agriculture.

52. AN, 83 AJ 17, report by Pommès-Barrère, 15 Jan. 1944.

53. Ibid.

54. AN, F 9 2193, report on prisoners repatriated via Compiègne in June, 20 July 1943.

55. AN, F 9 2193, report, Herbert to Scapini, 8 Nov. 1943, on prisoners arrived at Compiègne on 1 Nov. 1943.

56. AN, 83 AJ 17, note for Commissaire Bounaix, illegible signature, 12 Nov. 1944.

57. AN, 83 AJ 17, see numerous reports on this subject.

58. AN, 83 AJ 17, 'Rapport mensuel du mois de mai 1944', Westfalen Nord Münster.

59. AN, 83 AJ 1, Raymond D. to Parlange, 19 Dec. 1943.

60. AN, 83 AJ 1, letter to Roger D., 2 March 1944.

61. AN, 83 AJ 17, 'Rapport mensuel du mois de mai 1944', Westfalen Nord Münster.

62. AN, 83 AJ 28, Mademoiselle Beyer to regional delegate, 19 Dec. 1944.

63. AN, 83 AJ 1, letter to Parlange, illegible signature, 5 Nov. 1943.

64. AN, 83 AJ 2, letter from Pierre M., 5 Dec. 1943. See also remarks written on the back of the letter.

65. Vincennes, Service Historique de l'Armée de Terre, Papiers Desdouits, 'Solitude' by prisoner in Stalag XIIA.

66. AN, F 9 2183, report from Stalag VIIIC, Bureau de Renseignements, Service Juridique, signed by Daniel-Lamazière, 3 Nov. 1941, transmitted by *homme de confiance* to Scapini. There had been sixty requests for divorce since August and two-thirds of these came from the 4,000 men living in the camp (normally, residents of the camp would account for no more than 10 per cent of all prisoners in a Stalag).

67. Laurence Wylie, *Village in the Vaucluse* (Cambridge, Mass., 1974), p. 117.

68. PP, BA 2096, Scapini to prefect of Paris police, 13 Oct. 1942: 'The prisoner has much affection for his wife and is not opposed to a reconciliation.'

69. PP, BA 2096, 11 July 1944, prefect of police to Président du Comité d'Assistance aux Prisonniers de Guerre about the case of M.R.

70. A number of reports, prepared in response to prisoners' enquiries about the conduct of their wives, can be found in PP, BA 2096. See, for example,

letter of 10 October 1942 from Scapini to the prefect of police about the wife of André C. who 'wants above all to know how his child is looked after'.

71. AN, 83 AJ 1, letter from secretary of Stalag XII to *homme de confiance* of Stalag XII, 17 April 1944.

72. See AN, F 9 2183, note for the delegation in Berlin, signed Pierre Guion, 7 Dec. 1943.

73. AN, F 9 2183, Desbons to *homme de confiance* of Stalag IIID, 3 Dec. 1941. See also attached report from procureur de la république of Saint-Omer, 5 Nov. 1941.

74. AN, F 9 2183, prefect of Loire-Inférieure to Scapini, 22 Feb. 1943.

75. AN, F 9 2183, letter from *bureau d'études* to *homme de confiance* of Stalag IIID about Albert M., signed Roussanne, 30 March 1943.

76. PP, BA 2096, letter from prefect of police to Scapini about M.L., 26 Nov. 1942.

77. AN, F 9 2183, Scapini to Dupuis, 1 Sept. 1942.

78. AN, F 9 2183, *bureau d'études* to *homme de confiance* of Stalag VIIC, 23 June 1943.

79. AN, F 9 2183, Minister of Defence to Minister of Justice, on repression of adultery by prisoners' wives, 19 March 1942.

80. AN, F 9 2183, Commissariat Général aux Prisonniers de Guerre Rapatriés et aux Familles de Prisonniers de Guerre (signed *chef de cabinet*), 15 March 1943, to Scapini. Quoted in note for the delegation in Berlin, 5 April 1943.

81. See, for example, AN, F 9 2183, *bureau d'études* to *homme de confiance* of Stalag VB, 14 Sept. 1943.

82. AN, F 9 2183, note for the delegation in Berlin from *bureau d'études*, signed Roussanne, 6 April 1943.

83. AN, F 9 2183, *bureau d'études* to *homme de confiance* of Stalag XIIID, signed Desbons, 3 Aug. 1942.

84. AN, F 9 2183, letter from mayor of Le Mans, 25 Aug. 1942, enclosed with letter from prefect of Sarthe sent to Scapini Mission, 27 Aug. 1942.

85. Fernande Dailly, *La Femme du prisonnier* (1997).

86. ADEL, 1 W 78, report by Lavasserie and Falconnet, 26 July 1945.

87. PP, BA 1790, letter from secrétariat of Stalag IIIB to Commissaire de Police of quartier de Javel, 24 May 1945, about Lilly C.

88. AN, F 9 2183, letter from maison du prisonnier of Nancy, 15 May 1943.

89. AN, F 9 2183, Roussanne to *homme de confiance* of Stalag VA, 20 May 1943.

90. Caroline Robert, 'Les Femmes travailleuses volontaires avec les Allemands durant la seconde guerre mondiale dans le Morbihan, à travers les archives de la chambre civique', Mémoire de Maîtrise, Rennes II (2000), p. 78.

91. Jean-Paul Picaper, *Le Crime d'aimer: Les enfants du STO* (2005) is about liaisons between Frenchmen and German women during the Second World War.

92. Joseph Raoux, *Pas si simple* (Privas, 1998), p. 120. Jean-Joseph Brustier, *Mes années de captivité dans le Reich hitlérien* (1997), p. 53.

93. S. Delattre, 'La Défense des prisonniers devant les tribunaux allemands', in Georges Baud, Louis Devaux and Jean Poigny (eds.), *Mémoire complémentaire sur quelques aspects des activités du Service Diplomatique des Prisonniers de Guerre: SDPG-DFP-Mission Scapini, 1940–1945* (1984), pp. 161–8.

94. AN, F 9 2727, a ledger containing handwritten tables describing prosecutions against French prisoners in various camps month by month. The year is not specified.

95. AN, F 9 2742, Gabriel Vignes to Scapini Mission, 30 Nov. 1943.

96. AN, F 9 2744, hearing in Munich, 9 Feb. 1945.

97. AN, F 9 2744, Marcel Caron, *conseilleur juridique* of Stalag VIIIA, to Scapini, 31 Aug. 1943.

98. AN, F 9 2744, hearing in Munich, 17 March 1944. A French prisoner denied caressing a girl but admitted hitting her. He was sentenced to four months, a light sentence.

99. AN, F 9 2747, report from Stalag IIA, signed Le Culloch and Cuni, 20 Sept. 1944.

100. AN, F 9 2743, hearing in Münster, 14 March 1944.

101. AN, F 9 2744, hearing in Munich, 12 Oct. 1944.

102. AN, F 9 2743, hearing in Chemnitz, undated.

103. AN, F 9 2746, Colonel de Pinsun to Le Cholone.

104. AN, F 9 2742, Stalag IID, hearing in Stettin, 15 June 1944.

105. AN, F 9 2742, report of *conseilleur juridique* of Stalag IA on cases heard on 14 Oct. 1943.

106. AN, F 9 2742, hearing in Neustettin, 29 Sept. 1944.

107. AN, F 9 2742, hearing in Neustettin, 28 Feb. 1944.

108. Raoux, *Pas si simple*, p. 140.

109. René Dufour, *Captivité et évasion au pays des Sudètes* (1982), p. 61.

110. Roger Tessier, *Carnets de guerre et de captivité d'un Rochefortais, 1939–1945* (Rochefort, 1998), p. 67.

111. Duverne, *Mémoires de guerre*.

112. Brustier, *Mes années de captivité*, p. 202.

113. AN, F 9 2183. The original letter had been sent by Mme B. (an 'irreproachable woman with a young daughter') to the maison du prisonnier of the Vosges; it was then sent to the Scapini Mission who forwarded it to the

homme de confiance of Stalag XVIII on 18 June 1943. On 18 November 1943 the *homme de confiance* wrote to say that the man appeared to be back on good terms with his wife.

114. AN, F 9 2183, note for delegation in Berlin, about Gustave D. (number 4588 in XIIF of Kommando 200B), signed F. Roussanne, 16 Dec. 1943.

115. Georges Simenon, *Maigret et les braves gens* (1962).

116. Georges Musnik, *Par-dessus mon épaule* (1996), p. 33.

117. AN, F 9 2743, hearing in Chemnitz, 20 Oct. 1943.

118. AN, F 9 2743, Delattre to head of delegation of Service Diplomatique des Prisonniers de Guerre, 6 Sept. 1943.

119. Henry Charbonneau, *Les Mémoires de Porthos* (1981), p. 325.

120. Yves Durand, *La Vie quotidienne des prisonniers de guerre dans les Stalags, les Oflags et les Kommandos, 1939–1945* (1987), p. 80.

121. Caussé, *Mémoires d'un tarnais*, p. 7. See also Jean Edmond, *De Quarré les Tombes à Berlin, 1943–1945* (1995), and Bazin, *Déporté du travail*, p. 80.

122. Pierre Bohin, *Il y a cinquante ans* (Gournay-en-Bray, 1996), p. 40.

123. Octave Fort, *'Tu es encore davantage mon fils', ou l'Histoire d'un requis en Allemagne: 1943–1945* (Le Château d'Olonne, 1994). See also Pierre Picard-Gilbertier, *Armée rouge et Danube bleu* (Dijon, 1993), p. 42.

124. AN, F 1 A 3777, April 1944, 'Misère physique des déportés'. This was a Free French report on the administration inside France.

125. AN, 83 AJ 2, letters from M., 18 Aug. 1944 and 9 July 1944; replies 1 and 3 Sept. 1944. Sometimes the French authorities seem to have been more sympathetic to requests by French prisoners to marry east European women. See correspondence on this matter in AN, F 9 2724 and AN, F 9 2726.

126. Quereillahc, *Mémoires de la déportation du travail en Allemagne nazie*, p. 84.

127. Ganter, *Une jeunesse heureuse assassinée*, pp. 21, 26 and 32.

128. Pierre Thomas, *STO à Berlin: Et les sirènes rugissaient* (Signy-le-Petit, 1991), p. 61.

129. Cavanna, *Les Russkoffs*, pp. 188 and 364.

130. ADL, 283 W 108, letter, 15 June 1945, from sub-prefect of Dax to prefect of Landes.

131. ADL, 283 W 108, report on case of Roger D. and Olga M., 8 June 1945.

132. ADL, 283 W 108, police report, 22 Oct. 1945.

133. ADL, 283 W 108, report by Commissaire des Renseignements Généraux of Mont-de-Marsan, about Robert D. and Sophia M., 10 Oct. 1945.

134. ADL, 283 W 108, report from Ministry of the Interior, 26 Nov. 1945

135. PP, BA 2096, note for Directeur de la Police Judiciaire, dated 3 Feb. 1947, and attached report sent by Ministry of Foreign Affairs, Direction

des Unions Internationales (27 Jan. 1947). See also report by Captain Massonnet in Warsaw, 15 Jan. 1947.

136. ADL, 293 W 108, account of meeting of this commission on 20 Sept. 1945 in préfecture of Landes.

137. Musnik, *Par-dessus mon épaule*, p. 28.

138. AN, F 9 2245, note from the delegation in Berlin, 14 July 1944.

139. PP, BA 2096, prefect of police to Scapini about prisoner of war P., 18 Dec. 1942, and attached report, 8 Dec. 1942.

140. AN, F 9 2191, 'Rapport sur la dernière relève, Stalag III', signed Louis Jobard, *homme de confiance*, 27 Nov. 1943. The report revealed that all prisoners who were fathers of four children other than 'nos trois camarades israélites' had been released.

141. AN, F 9 2245, Commissariat Général aux Prisonniers de Guerre Rapatriés to Chef des Services Diplomatiques des Prisonniers de Guerre, 13 July 1944, about the case of Maurice K. who had been repatriated from Stalag XIID after an accident at work but was subsequently arrested by the German authorities.

142. L'Amicale du Camp des Aspirants, *Le Camp des aspirants pendant la deuxième guerre mondiale* (1991), pp. 143–4.

143. AN, F 9 2744, hearing in Marburg, 2 June 1944.

144. Jean Moret-Bailly, 'Le Camp de base du Stalag XVIIB', *Revue d'histoire de la deuxième guerre mondiale*, 25 (1957), pp. 7–45, at p. 30.

145. Arnaud, 'La Délégation officielle', p. 181.

146. Stanford University, Hoover Institution, Monod archives (just one carton), report on visit to Berlin, 12–28 June 1943.

147. André Gabs-Mallut, *Entre vivre ou mourir* (2000), p. 30.

148. Henri Rousso, *Pétain et la fin de la collaboration: Sigmaringen, 1944–1945* (Brussels, 1984), p. 339.

149. Arnaud, 'La Délégation officielle', p. 226.

150. The report by Sonnery and Martin of July 1943 (AN, F 60 1450, cited above) alluded to the 'Camp d'Auschwytz' as a place 40 kilometres from Katowice where 350 men from the Chantiers occupied four huts in the middle of an immense camp of Belgian and French workers. The report, written before Toupet's intervention, alluded to the 'painful presence of political prisoners on the same work sites'.

CHAPTER 10. SUNSET OF BLOOD: THE LIBERATION

1. André Héléna, *Les Clients du Central Hôtel* (1959).
2. Alan Moorehead, *Eclipse* (1945).
3. Cited in Peter Novick, *The Resistance versus Vichy* (1968), p. 14.
4. Quoted in *Le Monde*, 7 May 2004.
5. London, National Archives (NA), WO 219/4600, record number 2297, letter of 10 Nov. 1944.
6. Franz-Olivier Giesbert, *L'Américain* (2004), p. 69.
7. François Nourissier, *À défaut de génie* (2000), p. 111.
8. Henri Giraud, *Un seul but, la victoire: Alger, 1942–1944* (1949).
9. Novick, *The Resistance versus Vichy*, p. 46.
10. François Kersaudy, *De Gaulle et Churchill* (1981), p. 213. Eric Roussel is sceptical about the story, pointing out that Roosevelt's son believed his father to be fatalistic about his personal security; Eric Roussel, *Charles de Gaulle* (2003), p. 345.
11. AN, F 60 1450, Louis Tartarin to Directeur Général des Chantiers de la Jeunesse, 21 Jan. 1944.
12. François Picard, *L'Épopée de Renault* (1976), p. 228.
13. Marc Bergère, *Une société en épuration: Épuration vécue et perçue en Maine-et-Loire. De la libération au début des années 50* (Rennes, 2003), p. 307.
14. Philippe Buton, *La Joie douloureuse: La libération de la France* (2004), p. 23.
15. Jacques-Alain de Sédouy, *Une enfance bien-pensante sous l'occupation, 1940–1945* (1998), p. 124. The colonel was arrested but later, having been taken prisoner by the Americans, escaped.
16. Alain Corbin, *Historien du sensible: Entretiens avec Gilles Heuré* (2000), p. 11.
17. Maurice Duverger, *L'Autre côté des choses* (1977).
18. Christian de la Mazière, *Le Rêveur casqué* (1972).
19. Buton, *La Joie douloureuse*, p. 19.
20. Hilary Footitt, *War and Liberation in France: Living with the Liberators* (2004), p. 97.
21. Buton, *La Joie douloureuse*, p. 82.
22. Megan Koreman, *The Expectation of Justice: France, 1944–1946* (Durham, NC, 1999).
23. Sarah Farmer, *Martyred Village: Commemorating the 1944 Massacre at Oradour-sur-Glane* (Berkeley, 1999).

24. AN, F 7 14898, Darnand to Oberg, 16 June 1944.

25. Élizabeth Coquart, *La France des GIs: Histoire d'un amour déçu* (2003), pp. 142 and 155.

26. NA, WO 229/3, week of 12–18 Feb. 1945.

27. NA, WO 219/1792B, record 1576, extract from letter, 13 Oct. 1944, from Chambéry: '[If they had been bombed] they would understand as the English understand.'

28. NA, WO 219/1792B, record 1970, letter from Saint Brieuc, 6 Oct. 1944.

29. NA, WO 219/1792B, record 1497, extract from letter from Maine-et-Loire, 16 Oct. 1944.

30. NA, WO 219/1792B, record 1636, 29 Oct. 1944.

31. NA, WO 219/1792B, record 1575, letter from Toulon, 8 Oct. 1944.

32. Bergère, *Une société en épuration*, p. 31.

33. NA, WO 219/1792B, record 1980, 27 Oct. 1944.

34. NA, WO 219/1792B, record 1626, 23 Oct. 1944.

35. NA, WO 219/1792B, record 1749, letter from Le Mans, 28 Oct. 1944.

36. Hilary Footitt, *War and Liberation in France*, p. 87.

37. Ibid., p. 6.

38. Ibid., p. 31.

39. Ibid., p. 165,

40. NA, WO 219/1792B, record 1634, 25 Oct. 1944.

41. For Powers' story, see Coquart, *La France des GIs*, pp. 103–11 and pp. 223–47.

42. NA, WO 219/1792B, record 1006, 5 Aug. 1944.

43. NA, WO 219/1792B, record 1512, 18 Oct. 1944.

44. NA, WO 219/1792B, record 1635, 7 Oct. 1944.

45. J. Robert Lilly, *La Face cachée des GIs: Les viols commis par des soldats américains en France, en Angleterre et en Allemagne pendant la seconde guerre mondiale (1942–1945)* (2003), pp. 154–84.

46. Bergère, *Une société en épuration*, p. 167.

47. John Sweets, 'L'Auvergne', in Jean-Pierre Azéma et François Bédarida (eds.), *Vichy et les français* (1990), pp. 523–33, at p. 530.

48. Henry Rousso, *Le Syndrome de Vichy 1944–198-* (1987), p. 87.

49. ADL, 81 W 2, Dussarrat to prefect, 26 Nov. 1946. Ibid., Dussarrat to Minister of the Interior, 4 Nov. 1955.

50. ADL, 81 W 2, Renseignements Généraux des Landes, report, 17 Nov. 1955.

51. Bergère, *Une société en épuration*, p. 35. Bergère believes that the first, and lowest, figure is closest to the truth.

52. Pascal Gibert, 'Conflit, pouvoirs et société dans un département au lende-

main de l'occupation: L'épuration en Haute Loire, 1944–7', Mémoire de DEA, Université de Clermont II (2000), p. 39.

53. Marc Bergère, 'Épuration vécue et perçue à travers le cas du Maine-et-Loire: De la libération au début des années 50', Thèse de Doctorat, Rennes II (2001), p. 554.

54. Bergère, *Une société en épuration*, pp. 133–4.

55. Gibert, 'Conflit, pouvoirs et société', p. 54.

56. PP, BA 1793, 'Incidents avec la LVF, 3–10 juin'.

57. S. Marshall, *Bringing up the Rear*, quoted in Alain Brossat, *Libération, fête folle, 6 juin 44–8 mai 45: Mythes et rites ou le grand théâtre des passions populaires* (1994), p. 83.

58. Luc Capdevilla, *Les Bretons au lendemain de l'occupation: Imaginaire et comportements d'une sortie de guerre, 1944–1945* (Rennes, 1999), p. 133.

59. Buton, *La Joie douloureuse*, p. 131.

60. Jean Popot, *J'étais aumônier à Fresnes* (1962).

61. Pierre-Antoine Cousteau, *Après le deluge* (1959), p. 7.

62. François Brigneau, *Mon après guerre* (1985), p. 363.

63. Joseph Algazy, *La Tentation néo-fasciste en France, 1944–1965* (1984), p. 132.

64. Bergère, *Une société en épuration*, p. 131.

65. Thierry Bouclier, *Tixier-Vignancour: Une biographie* (2003), p. 80.

66. François Rouquet, *L'Épuration dans l'administration française: Agents de l'état et collaboration ordinaire* (1993).

67. Bergère, *Une société en épuration*, p. 188.

68. ADL, 81 W 2, report of Sûreté Nationale, 4 March 1947. Letter from Mlle B. to prefect, 29 May 1947, and report of Renseignements Généraux des Landes, 28 April 1948.

69. Charles Wertenbaker, *Invasion*, quoted in Alex Kershaw, *Blood and Champagne: The Life and Times of Robert Capa* (2002), p. 142. The edition of Wertenbaker's *Invasion* that I have found does not seem to contain this quotation, or indeed any reference to Capa's arrival in Chartres.

70. Alain Brossat, *Les Tondues: Un carnaval moche* (1994).

71. Capdevilla, *Les Bretons au lendemain de l'occupation*, p. 161.

72. The photograph is reproduced in Corran Laurens, 'La Femme au turban: Les femmes tondues', in H. R. Kedward and Nancy Wood (eds.), *The Liberation of France: Image and Event* (1995), pp. 155–80, at p. 169. The photograph here is captioned: 'A girl collaborator sits with her mother and her German-fathered child.'

73. ADEL, 1 W 78, Commissaire de Police to Commissaire du Gouvernement près de la Cour de Justice de Chartres, 1 Sept. 1945.

74. Raymond Jean and Mavis Gallant, *The Affair of Gabrielle Russier* (1973). Note that Russier was an educated and mature woman having an affair with a younger man, whilst many of the *tondues* of 1944–5 were very young women of almost no education. Note too that one of the ways in which Russier had shocked local society was by cutting her hair short.

75. Corinne Herrmann and Philippe Jeanne, *Les Disparues d'Auxerre* (2001), p. 215.

76. Bergère, *Une société en épuration*, p. 312. In La Pommeraye on 13 July 1945, three returned deportees attacked a woman whom they believed to have denounced them.

77. Louis Guilloux, *Carnets, 1921–1944* (1978), pp. 410 and 413.

78. Ibid., p. 413.

79. Peter Hamilton, *Robert Doisneau: A Photographer's Life* (1995), p. 108.

80. Georgette Elgey, *The Open Window* (1974, first published in France in 1973).

81. Alfred Grosser, *La Passion de comprendre: Noël Copin interroge Alfred Grosser* (1977), p. 34.

82. Rouquet, *L'Épuration dans l'administration française*, p. 131.

83. Ibid., p. 138.

84. Jacques Bounin, *Beaucoup d'imprudence* (1974).

85. ADL, 81 W 1, report, 2 Aug. 1945, unsigned, sent to Directeur des Renseignements Généraux à Paris.

86. Footitt suggests that *tontes* were the form of French activity most frequently mentioned in Allied accounts (presumably she is talking simply about Normandy): *War and Liberation in France*, p. 53.

87. NA, WO 229/27. A note signed Colonel Boehnke, dated 15 July 1944, headed 'Demonstrations by civilians against collaborators', stressed that it was 'eminently desirable' that Allied forces should not intervene in such circumstances.

88. 'Amateur Liberators', article by Peter Elstob published in the *New Statesman* on 9 Sept. 1944 and republished in *Lines of Dissent: Writing from The New Statesman 1913 to 1988* (1988), pp. 115–19.

89. Fabrice Virgili, *La France virile: Des femmes tondues à la libération* (2000), p. 209.

90. François Rouquet, *L'Épuration dans l'administration française*, p. 137.

91. ADL, 81 W 1, report by gendarmes, 1 Dec. 1944.

92. On women who went, or asked permission to go, to Paris, see ADEL, 1 W 78, Commissaire de Police to prefect, 28 Aug. 1945, about Yvette B. who wanted to leave Mainvilliers and go to Paris because she was shunned in her locality and unable to obtain work; ibid., gendarmerie nationale report by

Rozière, 4 July 1945, on Jacqueline D., a twenty-three-year-old who wished to leave her village and go to Paris because she was unable to obtain work.

93. Janet Flanner, *Paris Journal, 1944–1965*, ed. William Shawn (1966), p. 12.

94. Rémy Cazals, *Les Écoliers de Tournissan, 1939–1945* (Toulouse, 1978), p. 140.

95. Bruneton was not seen as having acted in a particularly reprehensible way and was not very severely punished when he finally returned to France in 1945.

96. AN, 83 AJ 3, report on journey to Berlin, unsigned, 14 Sept. 1944.

97. Ibid.

98. AN, 83 AJ 17, report, unsigned, 31 Dec. 1944, délégation régionale Mainfranken to direction générale: 'Denunciations made wrongly and at random by the refugees sometimes stir things up (witness the arrest of my assistant M. Laruelle). I hope that with time this excess of zeal on the part of our compatriots will calm down and that they will discredit themselves with the local authorities. I need hardly say that I myself am constantly a target for their action.'

99. Ulrich Herbert, *Hitler's Foreign Workers: Enforced Labour in Germany under the Third Reich* (Cambridge, 1997), p. 317.

100. Maurice Georges, *Le Temps des armes sans arme: Une tranche d'histoire à Berlin* (Beaugency, 1990), p. 249.

101. Louis Gèze, quoted in Pierre Martin, *La Mission des Chantiers de la Jeunesse en Allemagne 1943–1945* (1992), p. 310.

102. Jacques de Mauvaisin, ibid., p. 308.

103. Jean-Louis Quereillahc, *Mémoires de la déportation du travail en Allemagne nazie* (Linas, 1990), p. 234.

104. Pierre Picard-Gilbertier, *Armée rouge et Danube bleu* (Dijon, 1993), pp. 27, 28, 63.

105. Martin, *La Mission des Chantiers*, p. 307.

106. Maurice Duverne, *Mémoires de guerre: 1940–1945* (Mercurey, 1996), no pagination.

107. Henri Laloux, *Avril 1945: Libéré par l'Armée rouge. L'incroyable odyssée d'un prisonnier de guerre français* (1997).

108. Flanner, *Paris Journal*, p. 25.

109. Hélie de Saint Marc, *Mémoires: Les champs de braises* (1995).

110. Rosine Vergnes, 'La Main d'oeuvre française au service de l'occupant allemand dans le département d'Eure-et-Loir (1940–1944)', Mémoire de Maîtrise, Université d'Angers (2 vols., 1999), vol. ii, p. 61.

111. PP, BA 1790, Le Mans, report by Louvigne, to head of Sûreté, 16 June

1945. This woman was described as 'conscripted by the Germans to work in a factory in Germany'.

112. Caroline Robert, 'Les Femmes travailleuses volontaires avec les Allemands durant la seconde guerre mondiale, dans le Morbihan, à travers les archives de la chambre civique', Mémoire de Maîtrise, Rennes II (2000), p. 65.

113. Capdevilla, *Les Bretons au lendemain de l'occupation*, p. 210.

114. ADEL, 1 W 78, Commission d'Épuration, 10 Aug. 1945.

115. Catherine Offredic, 'Travailler volontairement au service des Allemands pendant la seconde guerre mondiale: L'exemple des femmes des Côtes-du-Nord et du Finistère, à travers les dossiers desprocédures judiciaires des chambres civiques, 1940–1946', Mémoire de Maîtrise, Rennes II (2000), p. 43.

116. Pierre Thomas, *STO à Berlin: Et les sirènes rugissaient* (Signy-le-Petit, 1991), p. 96.

117. Picard-Gilbertier, *Armée rouge et Danube bleu*, p. 112.

118. Ibid., p. 235.

119. Cavanna, *Les Russkoffs*, p. 406.

120. François Cochet, *Les Exclus de la victoire: Histoire des prisonniers de guerre, déportés et STO* (1992); Christophe Lewin, *Le Retour des prisonniers de guerre français: Naissance et développement de la FNPG 1944–1952* (1986); Sarah Fishman, *We Will Wait: Wives of French Prisoners of War, 1940–1945* (New Haven and London, 1991).

121. Jean-Paul Picaper and Ludwig Norz, *Enfants maudits* (2004), p. 86.

MERDECLUSE

1. ADEL, 1 W 78, interrogation of A., 11 Nov. 1945.

2. Laurence Wylie, *Village in the Vaucluse* (Cambridge, Mass., 1974), pp. 28–9. James Knowlson still found traces of animosity in the village thirty years later; James Knowlson, *Damned to Fame: The Life of Samuel Beckett* (1997), p. 323.

Bibliography

BOOKS AND ARTICLES

Place of publication for English books is London, and for French books is Paris, unless otherwise indicated.

Abramovici, Pierre, *Un rocher bien occupé: Monaco pendant la guerre, 1939–1945* (2001).

Adler, Jack, *The Jews of Paris and the Final Solution* (Oxford, 1987).

Alary, Eric, *Le Canton de Bléré sous l'occupation: Une position unique en France* (1944).

—— *La Ligne de démarcation* (2002).

Albrecht, Mireille, *Vivre au lieu d'exister: La vie exceptionnelle de Berty Albrecht, compagnon de la libération* (Monaco, 2001).

Alfu, *Léo Malet: Parcours d'une oeuvre* (Amiens, 1998).

Algazy, Joseph, *La Tentation néo-fasciste en France, 1944–1965* (1984).

Althusser, Louis, *Journal de captivité* (1992).

—— *L'Avenir dure longtemps; suivi de, Les Faits: Autobiographies* (1992).

Ambrière, Francis, *Les Grandes Vacances* (1956, first published in 1946).

L'Amicale du Camp des Aspirants, *Le Camp des aspirants pendant la deuxième guerre mondiale, 1939–1945* (1991).

'Les Amis du colonel Furioux', *Le Colonel* (Saint-Étienne, 1987).

Amouroux, Henri, *La Grande Histoire des Français sous l'occupation* (10 vols., 1976–93).

Ariès, Philippe, *Un historien du dimanche* (1980).

Aron, Raymond, *Mémoires: 50 ans de réflexion politique* (1983).

Assouline, Pierre, *Hergé* (1996).

—— and Girardet, Raoul, *Singulièrement libre: Entretiens avec Pierre Assouline* (1990).

433

Atkins, Nick, *The Forgotten French: Exiles in the British Isles, 1940–1944* (Manchester, 2003).

Auda, Grégory, *Les Belles Années du 'milieu', 1940–1944: Le grand banditisme dans la machine répressive allemande en France* (2002).

Auron, Yair, *Les Juifs d'extrême gauche en mai 68: Une génération révolutionnaire marquée par la Shoah* (1998).

Aymé, Marcel, *Le Passe-Muraille* (1943); contains 'En Attendant'.

—— *Le Vin de Paris* (1947); contains 'La Traversée de Paris' and 'Le Faux Policier'.

Ayot, Marcel, *Comment on joue sous la botte nazie, ou la Trilogie antagonique au STO: Histoires vécues et poèmes* (Clermont l'Hérault, 1985).

Azéma, Jean-Pierre, and Bédarida, François (eds.), *Vichy et les français* (1990).

Bair, Deirdre, *Samuel Beckett: A Biography* (1978).

Barbara, *Il était un piano noir: Mémoires interrompus* (1998).

Barbas, Jean-Claude (ed.), *Philippe Pétain, Maréchal de France, chef de l'état français: Discours aux Français, 17 juin 1940–20 août 1944* (1989).

Barthélemy, Joseph, *Mémoires: Ministre de la Justice, Vichy, 1943–1945* (1989).

Baud, Georges, Devaux, Louis, and Poigny, Jean (eds.), *Mémoire complémentaire sur quelques aspects des activités du Service Diplomatique des Prisonniers de Guerre: SDPG-DFB-Mission Scapini, 1940–1945* (1984).

Bazin, Charles-Henri-Guy, *Déporté du travail à la BMW-Eisenach* (Cubnezais, 1986).

Beauvoir, Simone de, *La Force de l'âge* (1960).

Belin, René, *Du Secrétariat de la CGT au Gouvernement de Vichy* (1978).

Belmont (Pelorson), Georges, *Souvenirs d'outre-monde: Histoire d'une naissance* (2001)

Belot, Robert, *Aux frontières de la liberté* (1998).

Benjamin, René, *Le Maréchal et son peuple* (1941).

—— *Le Grand Homme seul* (1943).

Bénoist-Méchin, Jacques, *La Moisson de quarante: Journal d'un prisonnier de guerre* (1941).

Bergère, Marc, *Une société en épuration: Épuration vécue et perçue en Maine-et-Loire. De la libération au début des années 50* (Rennes, 2003).

Berlière, Jean-Marc, *Les Policiers français sous l'occupation: D'après les archives inédites de l'épuration* (2001).

Beschet, Paul, *Mission en Thuringe au temps du nazisme* (Saint-Armand, 1989).

Bésème-Pia, Lisa, *Recettes de Vendée, Loire-Atlantique, Charente et Deux-Sèvres importées en Ardennes et ailleurs: Depuis l'exode de 1940* (Langres, 1992).

Billard, Pierre, *Louis Malle: Le rebelle solitaire* (2003).

Billaud, Alexandre, *Alexandre ou les Malheurs de Centio* (1986).

Birley, J. L. T., 'Famine: The Distant Shadow over French Psychiatry', *Journal of Psychiatry* (2002), pp. 298–9.

Bohin, Pierre, *Il y a cinquante ans* (Gournay-en-Bray, 1996).

Bonaparte, Marie, *Mythes de guerre* (1945).

Bonnard, Abel, *Inédits politiques*, ed. Olivier Mathieu (1987).

Bood, Micheline, *Les Années doubles: Journal d'une lycéenne sous l'occupation* (1974).

Borough Guides, *Vichy* (Cheltenham, 1919).

Bory, Jean-Louis, *Mon village à l'heure allemande* (1945).

Bouclier, Thierry, *Tixier-Vignancour: Une biographie* (2003).

Bougeard, Christian, 'L'Intérêt stratégique de la Bretagne pendant la 2e guerre mondiale et les répercussions économiques et humaines: Les prélèvements de main d'oeuvre' (no publisher, no date; in library of Institut d'Histoire du Temps Présent).

Bounin, Jacques, *Beaucoup d'imprudence* (1974).

Bourderon, R., 'Mouvement de la main d'oeuvre et STO dans les mines du Gard', *Revue d'histoire de la deuxième guerre mondiale*, 112 (1978), pp. 47–66.

Bourges, Yves, *Témoignage, 1939–1945* (Montfort-sur-Meu, 1997).

Brasillach, Robert, *Notre avant guerre* (1941).

—— *Journal d'un homme occupé* (1955).

Brauner, Alfred, *Ces enfants ont vécu la guerre* (1946).

Brigneau, François, *Mon après guerre* (1985).

Brissac, Duc de, *La Suite des temps, 1938–1958* (1974).

Brossat, Alain, *Libération, fête folle, 6 juin 44–8 mai 45: Mythes et rites ou le grand théâtre des passions populaires* (1994).

—— *Les Tondues: Un carnaval moche* (1994).

Brustier, Jean-Joseph, *Mes années de captivité dans le Reich hitlérien* (1997).

Bugeaud, Pierre, *Militant: Prisonnier de guerre. Une bataille pour l'histoire* (1990).

Burrin, Philippe, *La Dérive fasciste: Doriot, Déat, Bergery* (1986).

—— *La France à l'heure allemande, 1940–1944* (1995).

Buton, Philippe, *La Joie douloureuse: La libération de la France* (2004).

Caignard, Michel, *Les Sacrifiés: Récit d'un ancien STO* (Périgueux, 1985).

Cambiaire, André de, *L'Autoconsommation agricole en France* (1952).

Cantier, Jacques, *L'Algérie sous le régime de Vichy* (2002).

Capdevilla, Luc, *Les Bretons au lendemain de l'occupation: Imaginaire et comportement d'une sortie de guerre, 1944–1945* (Rennes, 1999).

Carles, Cl, 'La Corniche de Montpellier de 1939 à 1942', *Revue d'histoire de la deuxième guerre mondiale*, 112 (1978), pp. 8–28.

Caron, Vicki, *Uneasy Asylum: France and the Jewish Refugee Crisis, 1933–1942* (Stanford, Calif., 1999).

Castères, Albert, *Pour que ça se sache aussi* (2001).

Catherine, Jean-Claude, *La Ligne de démarcation en Berry-Tourraine, 1940–1944* (Châteauroux, 1999).

Caussé, Georges, *Mémoires d'un Tarnais STO en Allemagne, 1943–1945* (Toulouse, 1997).

Cavanna, François, *Les Russkoffs* (1981).

Cazals, Rémy, *Les Écoliers de Tournissan, 1939–1945* (Toulouse, 1978).

Cépède, Michel, *Agriculture et alimentation en France durant la IIème guerre mondiale* (1961).

Chambroux, Odette, *L'Exilée* (Les Monédières, 1990).

Chancellor, Henry, *Colditz: The Definitive History* (1998).

Charbonneau, Henry, *Les Mémoires de Porthos* (1981).

Charles, Jean, *La Vie des Français en Allemagne: Ceux du tac* (1945).

Cochet, François, *Les Exclus de la victoire: Histoire des prisonniers de guerres, déportés et STO* (1992).

Cointet, Jean-Paul, *La Légion Française des Combattants, 1940–1944: La tentation du fascisme* (1995).

Cointet, Michèle, *Le Conseil National de Vichy, 1940–1944* (1989).

—— *Vichy capitale, 1940–1944* (1993).

—— *L'Église sous Vichy, 1940–1945: La repentance en question* (1998).

—— *Pétain et les Français* (2002).

Coquart, Élizabeth, *La France des GIs: Histoire d'un amour déçu* (2003).

Corbin, Alain, *Historien du sensible: Entretiens avec Gilles Heuré* (2000).

Cordier, Daniel, *Jean Moulin: L'inconnu du Panthéon* (3 vols., 1989–93).

Cousteau, Pierre-Antoine, *Après le deluge* (1959).

Crossy, Guy, *La Tondue* (1980).

Crozier, Michel, *Ma belle époque* (2002).

Dailly, Fernande, *La Femme du prisonnier* (1997).

Daix, Pierre, *Braudel* (1995).

Dalisson, Rémi, 'La Propagande festive de Vichy: Mythes fondateurs, relecture nationaliste et contestation en France de 1940 à 1944', *Guerre mondiale et conflits contemporains: Revue d'histoire*, 207 (2002), pp. 5–35.

Daures, J., *Nos vingt ans volés: L'histoire des 2,700 Aveyronnais victimes des camps nazis du travail forcé* (Rodez, 1993).

Deforges, Régine, *La Bicyclette bleue* (1983).

Dejonghe, Étienne, and Le Maner, Yves, *Le Nord-Pas-de-Calais dans la main allemande, 1940–1944* (Lille, 2000).

Delapierre, André, *Ceux du DAF: Souvenirs d'un travailleur forcé en Allemagne* (Livry-Gargan, 1973).

Delaunay, Claude, *Drôle de guerre et tourisme en Bavière, 1939–1945* (La Roche-sur-Yon, 2003).

Dereymez, Jean-William (ed.), *Être jeune en France (1939–1945)* (2001).

Destenay, Pierre, *Babel germanique* (1948).

Diamant, David, *Le Billet vert: La vie et la Résistance à Pithiviers et Beaune-la-Rolande* (1977).

Dillard, Pierre, *Suprêmes témoignages* (1945).

Dombrowski, Nicole, 'Surviving the German Invasion of France: Women's Stories of the Exodes of 1940', in Dombrowski (ed.), *Women and War in the Twentieth Century: Enlisted With or Without Consent* (1999), pp. 116–37.

Dompnier, Natalie, *Vichy à travers les chants: Pour une analyse politique du sens et de l'usage des hymnes sous Vichy* (1996).

Drouot, Henri, *Notes d'un Dijonnais pendant l'occupation allemande, 1940–1944* (Dijon, 1998).

Du Moulin de Labarthète, Henri, *Le Temps des illusions* (Geneva, 1946).

Dubois, Edmond, *Paris sans lumière, 1939–1945: Témoignages* (Lausanne, 1946).

Dufour, René, *Captivité et évasion au pays des Sudètes* (1982).

Duméril, Edmond, *Journal d'un honnête homme pendant l'occupation allemande (juin 1940–août 1944)*, ed. J. Bourgeon (Thonon-les-Bains, 1990).

Durand, Yves, *La Vie quotidienne des prisonniers de guerre dans les Stalags, les Oflags et les Kommandos, 1939–1945* (1987).

Duras, Marguerite, *Hiroshima mon amour* (1959).

Dutourd, Jean, *Au Bon Beurre ou dix ans de la vie d'un crémier* (1966).

Duverger, Maurice, *L'Autre côté des choses* (1977).

Duverne, Maurice, *Mémoires de guerre: 1940–1945* (Mercurey, 1996).

Edmond, Jean, *De Quarré les Tombes à Berlin, 1943–1945* (1995).

Elgey, Georgette, *The Open Window* (1974, first published in France in 1973)

Elstob, Peter, 'Amateur Liberators', *New Statesman*, 9 September 1944, republished in *Lines of Dissent: Writing from The New Statesman 1913 to 1988* (1988), pp. 115–19.

Fabre-Luce, Alfred, *Vingt-cinq années de liberté: L'épreuve (1939–1946)* (1964).

Faraud, Pierre, *Ni traître, ni héros: Du Vercors à Marseille via Montélimar, Avignon, et le Thor, 1943–1945. Chantiers de la jeunesse, clandestinité, armée* (Le Thor, 1994).

Farmer, Sarah, *Martyred Village: Commemorating the 1944 Massacre at Oradour-sur-Glane* (Berkeley, 1999).

Faure, Edgar, *Avoir toujours raison . . . c'est un grand tort* (1984).

Ferro, Marc, *Pétain* (1987).

Fink, Carole, *Marc Bloch: A Life in History* (Cambridge, 1991).

Fishman, Sarah, *We Will Wait: Wives of French Prisoners of War, 1940–1945* (New Haven and London, 1991).

—— *The Battle for Children: World War II, Youth Crime, and Juvenile Justice in Twentieth-Century France* (Cambridge, Mass., 2002).

Flanner, Janet, *Paris Journal, 1944–1965*, ed. William Shawn (1966).

Folcher, Gustave, *Les Carnets de guerre de Gustave Folcher, paysan langue-docien, 1939–1945* (2000).

Fondation Nationale des Sciences Politiques, *Le Gouvernement de Vichy, 1940–1942* (1972).

Footitt, Hilary, *War and Liberation in France: Living with the Liberators* (2004).

Fort, Octave, *'Tu est encore davantage mon fils', ou l'Histoire d'un requis en Allemagne: 1943–1945* (Le Château d'Olonne, 1994).

Fourtier-Berger, Paul, *Nuits bavaroises ou les désarrois d'un STO: Chroniques, 1943–1945* (Romilly-sur-Seine, 1999).

Freeman, C. Denis, and Cooper, Douglas, *The Road to Bordeaux* (1940).

French, Philip, *Malle on Malle* (1993).

Gabs-Mallut, André, *Entre vivre ou mourir* (2000).

Galster, Ingrid, *Sartre, Vichy et les intellectuels* (2001).

Ganter, Jean-Pierre, *Une jeunesse heureuse assassinée* (1994).

Garnier, Bernard, and Quellien, Jean (eds.), *La Main d'oeuvre française exploitée par le IIIe Reich* (Caen, 2003).

Gelin, Joseph, *Nuremberg, 1943–1945: L'expérience d'un prêtre ouvrier* (Petit Clamart, 1946).

Gemelli, Giulia, *Fernand Braudel* (1995).

Georges, Maurice, *Le Temps des armes sans arme: Une tranche d'histoire à Berlin* (Beaugency, 1990).

Gerbeaux, Michel, *20 ans après: Un déporté se souvient* (Dreux, 1965).

Gheldman, Georges, *16 juillet 1942* (2005).

Giesbert, Franz-Olivier, *L'Américain* (2004).

Gildea, Robert, *Marianne in Chains: In Search of the German Occupation* (2002).

Giraud, Henri, *Mes évasions* (1946).

—— *Un seul but, la victoire: Alger, 1942–1944* (1949).

Giroud, Françoise, *Si je mens* (1972).

Goldman, Pierre, *Souvenirs obscurs d'un juif polonais né en France* (2005).

Goublet, Juliette, *Oder Neisse 1943: Les cahiers de soeur Gertrude, volontaire pour la relève* (Aurillac, 1971).

Goyet, Bruno, *Henri d'Orléans, Comte de Paris (1908–1999): Le prince impossible* (2001).

Grenadou, Ephraïm, and Prévost, Alain, *Grenadou, paysan français* (1978).

Griffon, Arthur, *Adolescence paysanne en Franche-Comté: Doubs, 1937–1941* (Besançon, 1990).

Grosser, Alfred, *La Passion de comprendre: Noël Copin interroge Alfred Grosser* (1977).

Gruat, Cédric, and Leblanc, Cécile, *Amis des juifs: Les résistants aux étoiles* (2005).

Guéhenno, Jean, *Journal des années noires (1940–1944)* (2002, first published in 1947).

Guibal, Jean, *Un Gardois réfractaire au STO en Allemagne: Au hasard des chemins* (Nîmes, 1989).

Guilloux, Louis, *OK Joe* (1976).

—— *Carnets, 1921–1944* (1978).

Guitard-Auviste, Ginette, *Paul Morand, 1888–1976: Légende et vérités* (1994).

Guitry, Sacha, *Quatre ans d'occupations* (1947).

Guitton, Jean, *Pages brûlées: Journal de captivité, 1942–1943* (1984, first published in 1943).

—— *Un siècle, une vie* (1988).

Hamilton, Peter, *Robert Doisneau: A Photographer's Life* (1995).

Handourtzel, Rémy, *Vichy et l'école, 1940–1944* (1997).

Harbulot, Jean-Pierre, *Le Service du Travail Obligatoire: La région de Nancy face aux exigences allemandes* (Nancy, 2003).

Harris, Ruth, 'The Child of the Barbarian: Rape, Race and Nationalism in France during the First World War', *Past and Present*, 141 (1993), pp. 170–206.

Héléna, André, *Les Clients du Central Hôtel* (1959).

Herbert, Ulrich, *Hitler's Foreign Workers: Enforced Foreign Labour in Germany under the Third Reich* (Cambridge, 1997).

Herrmann, Corinne, and Jeanne, Philippe, *Les Disparues d'Auxerre* (2001).

Hillel, Marc, and Henry, Clarissa, *Au nom de la race* (1975).

Hugo, Jean, *Le Regard de la mémoire* (1984).

Hurstfield, Joel, *America and the French Nation, 1939–1945* (Chapel Hill, NC, 1986).

Jackson, Julian, *France: The Dark Years, 1940–1944* (Oxford, 2001).

Jamet, Dominique, *Un petit Parisien, 1941–1945* (2001).

Jankowski, Paul, *Communism and Collaboration: Simon Sabiani and Politics in Marseille, 1919–1944* (New Haven, 1989).

Jean, Raymond, and Gallant, Mavis, *The Affair of Gabrielle Russier* (1973).

Jennings, Eric, *Vichy in the Colonies: Pétain's National Revolution in Madagascar, Guadeloupe and Indochina* (Stanford, Calif., 2001).

Joliot, André, *Regards en arrière* (1990).

Jünger, Ernst, *Premier journal parisien*, II: *1941–1943* (1980).

—— *Second journal parisien*, III: *1943–1945* (1980).

Kaspi, André, *Les Juifs pendant l'occupation* (1997).

Kedward, H. R., *In Search of the Maquis: Rural Resistance in Southern France, 1942–1944* (Oxford, 1993).

—— and Wood, Nancy (eds.), *The Liberation of France: Image and Event* (1995).

Kersaudy, François, *De Gaulle et Churchill* (1981).

Kershaw, Alex, *Blood and Champagne: The Life and Times of Robert Capa* (2002).

Knowlson, James, *Damned to Fame: The Life of Samuel Beckett* (1997).

Koreman, Megan, *The Expectation of Justice: France, 1944–1946* (Durham, NC, 1999).

Kriegel, Annie, *Ce que j'ai cru comprendre* (1991).

La Mazière, Christian de, *Le Rêveur casqué* (1972).

Laborie, Pierre, *L'Opinion publique sous Vichy* (1990).

—— *Les Français des années troubles* (2001).

Lafont, Max, *L'Extermination douce: La cause des fous* (2000).

Lagarde, Pierre, *Ils ont subi des chemins de traverse: Témoignage, juin 1943-mai 1945* (Besançon, 1989).

Lagarrigue, Max (ed.), *1940: La France du repli; L'Europe de la défaite* (2001).

Lagier, Germain, *Un instituteur dans les Basses Alpes* (Digne-les-Bains, 1983).

Laloux, Henri, *Avril 1945: Libéré par l'armée rouge. L'incroyable odyssée d'un prisonnier de guerre français* (1997).

Langer, William, *Our Vichy Gamble* (New York, 1947).

Langeron, Roger, *Paris, juin 40* (1946).

Larue, André, *Brassens: Une vie* (1982).

Laure, Émile, *Pétain* (1941).

Laurens, André, *Une police politique sous l'occupation: La Milice française en Ariège, 1942–1944* (Foix, 1982).

Laurent, Jacques, *Histoire égoïste* (1976).

Laurent, Yves, *Aventures d'un réfractaire face à l'occupant* (Narbonne, 1989).

Le Goff, Jacques, *Entretiens avec Marc Heurgon: Une vie pour l'histoire* (1996).

Le Ray, Alain, *Première à Colditz* (Grenoble, 2004, first edition 1976).

Le Roy Ladurie, Jacques, *Mémoires, 1902–1945* (1997).

Leahy, William, *I Was There* (New York, 1950).

Lecornu, Bernard, *Un préfet sous l'occupation allemande* (1984).

Leduc, Violette, *La Bâtarde* (1965).

Legros, Jean, *Stalag IA* (1945).

Levert, Jean-Pierre, Gomart, Thomas, and Merville, Alexis, *Un lycée dans la tourmente: Jean-Baptiste Say, 1934–1944* (1994).

Lévi-Strauss, Claude, *Tristes Tropiques* (1955).

Lewin, Christophe, *Le Retour des prisonniers de guerre français: Naissance et développement de la FNPG, 1944–1952* (1986).

Liange-Patural, Marie-Thérèse, *Sauvain se souvient: 80 ans de vie militaire à Sauvain de 1914 à 1994* (Sauvain, 1995).

Lilly, J. Robert, *La Face cachée des GIs: Les viols commis par des soldats américains en France, en Angleterre et en Allemagne pendant la seconde guerre mondiale (1942–1945)* (2003).

Limouzin, René, *Le Temps des vérités* (1991).

Loeffler, N., Moll, S., Platt, G., Shneider, M., Schultess, E., and Werthlé, J., *Mémoire d'un exode: L'Évacuation de Saint-Louis 1939/1940* (Saint-Louis, 1989).

Lossky, Vladimir, *Sept jours sur les routes de France: Juin 1940* (1997).

Luirard, Monique, *La Région stéphanoise dans la guerre et dans la paix (1936–1951)* (Saint-Étienne, 1980).

Lycett, Andrew, *Ian Fleming: The Man Behind James Bond* (1995).

Marcantoni, François, *Un homme d'honneur: De la Résistance au milieu* (2002).

Martin, Pierre, *La Mission des Chantiers de Jeunesse en Allemagne 1943–1945* (1992).

Martin du Gard, Maurice, *La Chronique de Vichy, 1940–1944* (1975).

Martinez, Gilles, 'Comment les libéraux sont arrivés à Vichy: Étude d'un parcours paradoxal', *Revue d'histoire moderne et contemporaine*, 4/63 (1999), pp. 571–90.

Melton, George E., *Darlan: Admiral and Statesman of France, 1881–1942* (1998).

Meyer, Ahlrich, *L'Occupation allemande en France, 1940–1944* (2002).

Micard, Roger, *Pour l'honneur: Contribution à l'historique des prélèvements de main d'oeuvre parmi les jeunes français par l'Allemagne nazie* (Libourne, 1987).

Michel, André, *En liberté dans cette cage, en cage dans ces libertés: Journal d'un étudiant contraint au STO en Allemagne, 4 août 1943–2 juin 1945* (Gentilly, 1995).

Miquel, Pierre, *L'Exode, 10 mai-20 juin 1940* (2003).

Missika, Dominique, *La Guerre sépare ceux que s'aiment, 1939–1945* (2001).

Moorehead, Alan, *Eclipse* (1945).

Moret-Bailly, Jean, 'Le Camp de base du Stalag XVIIB', *Revue d'histoire de la deuxième guerre mondiale*, 25 (1957), pp. 7–45.

—— 'Les Kommandos du Stalag XVIIB', *Revue d'histoire de la deuxième guerre mondiale*, 37 (1960), pp. 31–52.

Morin, Edgar, *Commune en France: La métamorphose de Plodémet* (1967).

—— *Autocritique* (1970, first published 1959).

Moullet-Echarlod, Georges, *La Faim au ventre: Service du Travail Obligatoire* (1978).

Murphy, Robert, *Diplomat Among Warriors* (New York, 1964).

Musnik, Georges, *Par-dessus mon épaule* (1996).

Noguères, Louis, *Vichy: juillet 40* (2000).

Noiriel, Gérard, *Les Origines républicaines de Vichy* (1999).

Nossiter, Adam, *The Algeria Hotel: France, Memory and the Second World War* (2001).

Nourissier, François, *À défaut de génie* (2000).

Novick, Peter, *The Resistance versus Vichy* (1968).

Ory, Pascal, *Le Petit Nazi illustré: Vie et survie du Téméraire (1943–1944)* (1979, 2002).

Paoli, Dominique, *Maxime, ou le secret Weygand* (Brussels, 2003).

Paxton, Robert, *Vichy France 1940–1944: Old Guard and New Order* (1972).

—— and Marrus, Michael, *Vichy France and the Jews* (1981).

Péan, Pierre, *Une jeunesse française: François Mitterrand, 1934–1947* (1994).

Pedron, Guy, *La Prison sous Vichy* (1993).

Perrin, Marius, *Avec Sartre au Stalag 12 D* (1980).

Peyrefitte, Roger, *La Fin des ambassades* (1953).

Picaper, Jean-Paul, *Le Crime d'aimer: Les enfants du STO* (2005).

—— and Norz, Ludwig, *Enfants maudits* (2004).

Picard, François, *L'Épopée de Renault* (1976).

Picard-Gilbertier, Pierre, *Armée rouge et Danube bleu* (Dijon, 1993).

Pierquin, Bernard, *Journal d'un étudiant parisien sous l'occupation, 1939–1945* (1983).

Pioger, André, *La Relève et le Service du Travail Obligatoire dans la Sarthe (1942–1944)* (1971).

Poiré, Marguerite, *Mes années volées: Journal d'exil d'une jeune Lorraine dans les Sudètes, 1943–1945* (2001).

Poliakov, Léon, *L'Auberge des musiciens: Mémoires* (1981).

Pollard, Miranda, *Reign of Virtue: Mobilising Gender in Vichy France* (Chicago, 1998).

Popot, Jean, *J'étais aumônier à Fresnes* (1962).

Prazan, Michaël, *Pierre Goldman: Le frère de l'ombre* (2005).

Prost, Antoine, 'Verdun', in Pierre Nora (ed.), *Les Lieux de mémoire* (1997), pp. 1755–80.

Quellien, Julia, *Les Réfractaires au travail obligatoire dans le Calvados* (Caen, 2003).

Quereillahc, Jean-Louis, *Mémoires de la déportation du travail en Allemagne nazie, 1943–1945* (Linas, 1990).

Raibaud, Jean, and Henric, Henri, *Témoins de la fin du IIIe Reich: Des polytechniciens racontent* (2004).

Rajsfus, Maurice, *Paris, 1942: Chroniques d'un survivant* (2002).

—— *La Police et la peine de mort, 1977–2001: 196 morts* (2002).

—— *1953: Un 14 juillet sanglant* (2003).

Raoux, Joseph, *Pas si simple* (Privas, 1998).

Rebatet, Lucien, *Les Décombres* (1942).

Rigoulet, Pierre, *Les Enfants de l'épuration* (1993).

Rist, Charles, *Une saison gâtée: Journal de la guerre et de l'occupation, 1939–1945*, ed. Jean-Noel Jeanneney (1983).

Rothschild, Guy de, *The Whims of Fortune* (1985).

Rouquet, François, *L'Épuration dans l'administration française: Agents de l'état et collaboration ordinaire* (1993).

—— and Voldman, Danielle (eds.), *Les Cahiers de l'Institut d'Histoire du Temps Présent*, 31: *Identités féminines et violences politiques (1936–1946)* (1995).

Roussel, Eric, *Charles de Gaulle* (2003).

Rousso, Henri, *Pétain et la fin de la collaboration: Sigmaringen, 1944–1945* (Brussels, 1984).

—— *Le Syndrome de Vichy 1944–198-* (1987).

—— and Conan, Eric, *Vichy: Un passé qui ne passe pas* (1994).

Ruffin, Raymond, *Journal d'un J3* (1979).

Sabbagh, Antoine (ed.), *Lettres de Drancy* (2000).

Saint Marc, Hélie de, *Mémoires: Les Champs de Braises* (1995).

Sanders, Paul, *Histoire du marché noir, 1940–1946* (2001).

Savary, Victor, *Journal de Victor Savary: Service du Travail Obligatoire, STO, Berlin 1943–1944. Les tribulations d'un Chanzéen dans le Grand Reich* (Nantes, 1998).

Scapini, Georges, *Mission sans gloire* (1960).

Schroeder, Liliane, *Journal d'occupation, Paris 1940–1944: Chronique au jour le jour d'une époque oubliée* (2000).

Sédouy, Jacques-Alain de, *Une enfance bien-pensante sous l'occupation, 1940–1945* (1998).

Servent, Pierre, *Le Mythe Pétain: Verdun ou les tranchées de la mémoire* (1992).

Shennan, Andrew, *Rethinking France: Plans for Renewal 1940–1946* (Oxford, 1989).

Shute, Nevil, *The Pied Piper* (1941).

Simenon, Georges, *Le Clan des Ostendais* (1947).

—— *Le Train* (1961).

—— *Maigret et les braves gens* (1962).

Souleau, Philippe, *La Ligne de démarcation en Gironde: Occupation, résistance et société* (Périgueux, 1998).

Sweets, John, *Choices in Vichy France: The French Under Nazi Occupation* (Oxford, 1986).

Szabó, Zoltán, *L'Effondrement: Journal de Paris à Nice, 10 mai 1940–23 août 1940* (2002).

Taittinger, Pierre, *Ce que le pays doit savoir* (1941).

Taylor, D. J. *Orwell: The Life* (2003).

Taylor, Lynne, *Between Resistance and Collaboration: Popular Protest in Northern France, 1940–1945* (2000).

Tessier, Roger, *Carnets de guerre et de captivité d'un Rochefortais, 1939–1945* (Rochefort, 1998).

Thomas, Martin, 'The Vichy Government and French Colonial Prisoners of War, 1940–1944', *French Historical Studies*, 25/4 (2002), pp. 657–92.

Thomas, Pierre, *STO à Berlin: Et les sirènes rugissaient* (Signy-le-Petit, 1991).

Vallat, Xavier, *Le Nez de Cléopâtre: Souvenirs d'un homme de droite, 1919–1944* (1957).

Veillon, Dominique, *Le Franc-tireur: Un journal clandestin, un mouvement de résistance* (1977).

—— *La Mode sous l'occupation* (1990).

—— *Vivre et survivre en France, 1939–1947* (1995).

—— and Flonneau, Jean-Marie (eds.), *Le Temps des restrictions en France (1939–1949)* (1996).

Vergez-Chaignon, Bénédicte, *Le Docteur Ménétrel: Éminence grise et confident du Maréchal Pétain* (2002).

Vidalenc, Jean, *L'Exode de mai-juin 1940* (1957).

Vinen, Richard, *The Politics of French Business, 1936–1945* (Cambridge, 1991).

Virgili, Fabrice, *La France virile: Des femmes tondues à la libération* (2000).

Vital-Durand, Brigitte, *Domaine privé* (1996).

Wall, Irwin, *The United States and the Making of Post-war France, 1945–1954* (Cambridge, 1991).

Walter, Xavier, *Un roi pour la France: Henri Comte de Paris, 1908–1999. Essai de biographie intellectuelle et politique pour servir à la réflexion d'un prince du XXIe siècle* (2002).

Werth, Alexander, *The Last Days of Paris* (1940).

Wieviorka, Annette, and Azoulay, Floriane, *Le Pillage des appartements et son indemnisation* (2000).

Wieviorka, Olivier, *Les Orphelins de la République: Destinées des députés et sénateurs français (1940–1945)* (2001).

Wiskemann, Elizabeth, *The Europe I Saw* (1968).

Wylie, Laurence, *Village in the Vaucluse* (Cambridge, Mass., 1974).

Zaretsky, Robert, *Nîmes at War: Religion, Politics and Public Opinion in the Gard, 1938–1944* (University Park, Pa., 1995).

UNPUBLISHED DISSERTATIONS

Abrahams, Paul, 'Haute-Savoie at War, 1939–1945', Ph.D., University of Cambridge (1992).

Arnaud, Patrice, 'La Délégation officielle française auprès de la deutsche Arbeitsfront (1943–1945)', Mémoire de Maîtrise, Paris I (1995).

Bergère, Marc, 'Épuration vécue et perçue à travers le cas du Maine-et-Loire: De la libération au début des années 50', Thèse de Doctorat, Rennes II (2001).

Dimeglio, Annie-Paule, 'Le Service du Travail Obligatoire dans le département du Var', Mémoire de Maîtrise, Nice (1972).

Dombrowski, Nicole, 'Beyond the Battlefield: The French Civilian Exodus of 1940', Ph.D., New York University (1995).

Gautier, David, 'Jean Borotra, 1898–1994: Au service de ses engagements', Mémoire de Maîtrise, Paris I (2001).

Gibert, Pascal, 'Conflit, pouvoirs et société dans un département au lendemain de l'occupation: L'épuration en Haute Loire, 1944–7', Mémoire de DEA, Université de Clermont II (2000).

Gouedard, Solène, 'Les Relations franco-allemandes: Un cas particulier. Les réquisitions de logements à Rennes à partir de 1940', Mémoire de Maîtrise, Rennes II (2001).

Gratier de Saint-Louis, Michel, 'Les Réquisitions de main d'oeuvre pour l'Allemagne dans le Rhône, 26 octobre 1942–10 août 1944', Mémoire de Maîtrise, Lyon II (1980).

Kitson, Simon, 'The Marseilles Police in Their Context: From the Popular Front to the Liberation', D.Phil., University of Sussex (1995).

Lallam, Sandrine, 'La Population de la Seine et les forces d'occupation allemandes, 14 juin 1940–25 août 1944', Mémoire de Maîtrise, Paris IV (2000).

Lejeune, Dany, 'Le STO en Seine Inférieure', Mémoire de Maîtrise, Rouen (1977).

Matcham, Jill, 'Maréchal Nous Voilà! Quebec and Pétain: Le Devoir, 1939–1942' (undergraduate long essay, King's College, London, 2000).

Offredic, Catherine, 'Travailler volontairement au service des Allemands pendant la seconde guerre mondiale: L'exemple des femmes des Côtes-du-Nord et du Finistère, à travers les dossiers des procédures judiciaires des chambres civiques, 1940–1946', Mémoire de Maîtrise, Rennes II (2000).

Rioux, Emmanuelle, 'Les Zazous: Un phénomène socio-culturel pendant l'occupation', Mémoire de Maîtrise, Paris X (1987).

Robert, Caroline, 'Les Femmes travailleuses volontaires avec les Allemands durant la seconde guerre mondiale, dans le Morbihan, à travers les archives de la chambre civique', Mémoire de Maîtrise, Rennes II (2000).

Saladin, Erwan, 'La Nuit à Rennes sous l'occupation, 18 juin 1940–4 août 1944', Mémoire de Maîtrise, Université de Rennes II (2001).

Vergnes, Rosine, 'La Main d'oeuvre française au service de l'occupant allemand dans le département d'Eure-et-Loir (1940–1944)', Mémoire de Maîtrise, Université d'Angers (2 vols., 1999).

ARCHIVES
Paris, Institut d'Histoire du Temps Présent

ARC 086. André Noisette, 'Chronique de deux années de STO en Allemagne: 27 août 1943–4 juin 1945'.

ARC 105. 'Témoignage de M. Georges Morel, Ingénieur des Mines. Les mines des Cévennes pendant la guerre 1939–1945.'

Vincennes, Service Historique de l'Armée de Terre

Papiers Desdouits.

Paris, Archives Nationales (AN)

83 AJ 1
83 AJ 2
83 AJ 17
83 AJ 28
F 1 A 3775
F 1 A 3777
F 22 1775
F 22 2023
F 22 2024
F 60 1447
F 60 1448
F 60 1450
F 60 1451
F 60 1452
F 60 1454
F 7 14886
F 7 14889
F 7 14898
F 9 2183
F 9 2191
F 9 2192
F 9 2193
F 9 2241
F 9 2242
F 9 2245
F 9 2246
F 9 2724
F 9 2726
F 9 2727
F 9 2742
F 9 2743
F 9 2744

F 9 2746
F 9 2747
F 9 3003
F 9 3678

Paris, Archives de la Préfecture de Police (PP)

BA 1784
BA 1788
BA 1790
BA 1792
BA 1793
BA 1794
BA 1800
BA 1804
BA 1808
BA 1810
BA 1839
BA 1840
BA 1850
BA 2093
BA 2096
BA 2097
BA 2105
BA 2115
BA 2258

Mont-de-Marsan, Archives Départementales des Landes (ADL)

81 W 1
81 W 2
283 W 108
Rs 77
Rs 94
Rs 1076

Chartres, Archives Départementales de l'Eure-et-Loir (ADEL)

Some archives in the Eure-et-Loir have recently been reclassified.
1 W 78
14 W 62
14 W 93
20 W 304
81 W 1
116 W 18
116 W 22
116 W 181
116 W 199

Bordeaux, Archives Départementales de la Gironde

34 W 44
34 W 281

London, National Archives (NA)

WO 219/1792B
WO 219/4600
WO 229/3
WO 229/27

Stanford University, Hoover Institution

Giraud, Henri Honoré, 'Report to Pétain on the cause of the defeat', 26 July 1940 (in English).
Monod archives, report on visit to Berlin, 1–22 Dec. 1942; report on visit to Berlin, 12–28 June 1943.

Index

Figures in italics indicate illustrations